BEYOND COURAGE

BEYOND COURAGE

One Regiment Against Japan
1941-1945

by

Dorothy Cave

I have seen men die, and, dying, say,
"Tell them how it was."

— Corporal Jack H. Aldrich —

Yucca Tree Press

Printed in the United States of America.

First Printing, 1992

Cave, Dorothy
Beyond Courage: One Regiment Against Japan, 1941-1945.

1. World War, 1939-1945 - Prisoners and prisons, Japanese. 2. Cave, Dorothy. 3. World War, 1939-1945 - Personal narratives, American. 4. World War, 1939-1945 - Concentration Camps - Philippines. 5. Prisoners of war - United States - Biography. 6. Prisoners of War - Philippines - Biography.
I. Title.

Library of Congress Catalog Card Number 91-068402
ISBN 0-9622940-7-1

Cover Design by John Cole/Cole Graphics
Maps by Ralph C. Izard

DEDICATION

In memory of my father

Harold Sergius Cave

who paid his dues in two World Wars

and

to all the valiant men

of the

200th and 515th Coast Artilleries (AA)

who were

"First in Spite of Hell"

Permission to use the following material has been received for:

Cover photograph - Nicholas Chintis

Quotations from the following:

Evans, William R., *Kora!* (Atwood Publishing Co., Rogue River, OR, 1968).

Gurulé, Bill F., *Fleeting Shadows and Faint Echoes of Las Huertas* (Carlton Press, New York, 1987).

Morton, Louis., *The Fall of the Philippines* (Office of the Chief of Military History, Department of the Army, Washington, D.C., 1953).

Peck, Harry M., Brig. Gen., NMNG 1908-1948, Entries in personal journal maintained as POW and reported in *Albuquerque Journal* 30 October 45 through 8 June 46. Permission granted by Lou D. Hoffman, grandson of Harry M, Peck.

Wainwright, General Jonathan M., Robert Considine, ed., *General Wainwright's Story* (Doubleday & Co., NY, 1946).

Wright, Jr., John M., *Captured on Corregidor: Diary of an American P.O.W. in World War II* (McFarland & Company, Inc. Publishers, Jefferson, NC 28640, 1988).

The 200th and 515th Coast Artillery insignia use is granted by the Adjutant General, New Mexico National Guard.

TABLE OF CONTENTS

LIST OF MAPS

LIST OF ILLUSTRATIONS

ACKNOWLEDGMENTS

First and most important, I wish to thank the survivors of Bataan and Corregidor who have helped me so enthusiastically with this book. They have given me interviews, diaries, testimonies, theses, correspondence, memoirs — and friendship. This is, in a very real sense, their book. I am also grateful to the many wives who have given me welcome and helped jog the memories of their husbands, and most especially to Jeanne Chintis for her friendship and understanding.

Families and friends of men who served have generously furnished me material and given me permission to use it, especially Wilma Malovich, Lora Cummins, Jessie Barnett, Lois Ream, Lou Hoffman, Trudy Tafoya, Goldie Buckner, Betty Huxtable, Jane Baclawski, and Helen and Merrill Longwill. Thanks to Arthur Bressi, Andrew Miller, Betty Jarrell, Benson Guyton, and Colonel Gerald Schurtz for valuable material, and to Charles Kaelen for his memories of the Cabanatuan Players. Mary McMinn, widow of Major James McMinn, gave me his testimony before the War Crimes Tribunal in Tokyo. When Lindalie Lein Halama discovered the previously unsuspected testimony of her grandfather, Colonel Memory Cain, she generously shared it with me.

For granting me access to files and records in the New Mexico National Guard headquarters in Santa Fe, I must thank Lieutenant Colonel Joseph L. Black, Programs Director in the Office of Militiary Affairs, and Major General Edward D. Baca, Adjutant General. Both Betty Sena at the State Library and Teresa McLean, Luna County Clerk, were generous in their efforts to help me locate material. And to my good friend Manuel Armijo, Past Commander of the New Mexico Bataan Veterans' Organization, my gratitude for the valuable records he procured for me, and for his haste in rushing them to me when time was precious.

I am particularly indebted to John Cole and Ralph Izard for their patience and professionalism in preparing the cover art and maps for this volume.

To Roger B. Farquhar I owe a special thanks for sending me the portion of John Gamble's diary in his possession, and his story of how he found it at Cabanatuan Prison Camp two days after its liberation by the Sixth Army Rangers. Farquhar, commander of the medical detachment to which the rescued men were brought, took three men back, at their request, to recover some diaries they had buried in a glass jar. "I picked up a large box full of personal papers of one kind or another in the camp while waiting . . . , then we left in a hurry when we heard shots nearby. I knew that under army regulations I had to turn over all the diaries and papers to G-2, but before doing so I copied this much of Gamble's diary because his was so moving and so well written." Time prevented his copying the rest, and he has since been unable to locate the remainder in the National Archives, where it supposedly resides. Nor have I.

A special thanks also to Cheryl Kindley, for weary hours transcribing tapes of interviews; and to my typist, Virginia Rood, who has deciphered my many illegibilities, cured my typos, endured my many changes, shaped the manuscript into readable form – and remained my friend.

I should like especially to thank three men from the Regiment for help "above and beyond the call," and for their faith and friendship. Neal Harrington, who worked until his retirement in the Pentagon, has ferreted military and archival material and saved me several trips to Washington. Jack Aldrich canvassed a large portion of New Mexico, unearthed papers and documents, transcribed many taped interviews, and performed other services too numerous to list. Nick Chintis has never been too busy to fill me in on technical details and on life in the field and the prison camps. Finally, all three have read the manuscript, corrected my many mistakes, and offered valuable suggestions. Any remaining errors are strictly mine.

Finally, I must thank my family for putting up with me these past six years, and most especially my mother, who drove with me many miles to gather material and conduct interviews, and has in many other ways made this book possible.

In editing diaries, letters, reports, theses, testimonies, and interviews, I have, for brevity and clarity, deleted unnecessary verbiage. For ease in reading, I have, in most cases, eschewed the use of ellipses; but in no instance have I changed the context.

My greatest regret is, for want of space, I have had to omit an enormous amount of fine material. No book, nor any lifetime, can possibly encompass the scope of any man or any regiment in the terrible four war years they endured. I hope I have captured some small trace of their spirit.

FOREWORD

i.

This is the story of a Regiment – a small, undermanned regiment, that, split into two smaller units, performed a job so large they became, toward the end, a brigade, and finally a legend.

They were a mixed bag of National Guardsmen from New Mexico – cowboys, ranchers, football players (some still in high school who lied about their ages), miners, college kids, professional men.[1] Their Commander was a journalist, their supply officer a postman, their chief medical officer an obstetrician.

Outsiders called them Mexicans, Anglos, and Indians. They called themselves brothers and *compadres*, long before integration became a national byword. Boiling amicably together in their regimental melting pot, they were likely the most narrowly provincial and the most widely American unit in the United States Army.

They were an independent, anti-military, go-to-hell outfit – and so disciplined that officers from other branches requested them for details.

They were the oldest continuous militia in the nation – cavalry until Washington dragged them kicking and screaming from their horses. They then became the youngest antiaircraft artillery regiment, carried the old western cavalry tradition to training at Fort Bliss, Texas, and vowed they'd be 'First in spite of Hell.' When cited as the best antiaircraft unit, "regular or otherwise" in the armed forces, it was said the regulars growled, "If those bastards are so damned good, let's send 'em to the Philippines where they can prove it."

---

[1] A number of Selective Service inductees from New Mexico and other states also joined the unit at Ft. Bliss to bring the 200th CA (AA) to Regimental strength.

They scorned the spit-and-polish boys, but they lived the "Duty, honor, country" motto as seriously as any West Point pro. They were the first unit in the Philippines to fire at the enemy. Then, too few in numbers and guns to guard Clark Field, they were ordered to split and guard Manila, too. On the retreat to Bataan, they protected the bridges and other key points as other units filed through. On the beleaguered peninsula, though officially antiaircraft, they fought in any capacity where they were needed. MacArthur called them his "New Mexico horse thieves," and wrote, "I knew them well and loved them." When the end came on Bataan, they were the only unit left intact. They fought then as infantry, and they held the last thin lines against the final, massive onslaught, and they stood alone. They were the last unit to surrender, and they did so protesting, and only when ordered by the high command.

Through native toughness and regimental brotherhood, their death rate was lower than average for Japanese prison camps; but because they went *in toto*, New Mexico lost more men per capita than any other state.

When cheered as heroes on their return from the long ordeal, they denied it; yet it is believed no fighting group in World War II won more unit citations than they.

"The highest calls a man can have," Corporal Luther Ragsdale once said, "are to serve his God and to serve his country." Their small Regiment that became two served both, proudly.

They were the 200th and 515th Coast Artilleries. This is their story.

ii.

In June 1989, Santana Romero of Taos Pueblo became Commander of the New Mexico Ex-POWs. Moved, the aging Indian warrior said he could best accept the honor in his own Tiwa tongue. A year later, when he turned the command over to his successor, he prayed, again in Tiwan. Few of his brothers understood the words, but all knew his meaning. Brotherhood needs not words.

I have seen this bond of brotherhood again and again in the six years I have worked on this book. I have attended their conventions, their parties, and their services, and I have seen among these men, as they came together, the greetings, the *abrazos*, the laughs, the tears. Max Villaloboz said it: "We stuck together then, we stick together now. We went through hell to get to heaven."

These are the men of 'Old Two Hon'erd' today, and I can humbly call them friends who have let me tell their story, so long untold. The years have passed, the memories have softened, and, though they know others can never really understand, they want their story told. They have granted me interviews, and talked long and freely; and they have shared with me their crumbling diaries (kept secretly in prison camps, and at great peril), their letters and records and testimonies. They reopened old memories and relived old scenes. They shared their souls, and paid their last debts to brothers who did not return, to "tell it like it was."

Individualists all, they share some traits in common. They are a stubborn bunch – had they not been, they would not have returned. Their humor is round, robust, and sometimes raucous. Though few are without the scars from war, from the years of filth, starvation, and brutality in Japanese prison camps, they laugh off their infirmities. "I've got no problem," Russell Hutchison insists, "as long as my ass is still tied on!"

They walk with pride – in self, in country, in the Regiment. Jack Boyer remembered how officers from other units bragged on their men in Zentsuji prison camp. "But they always added that when they needed men for a job, they asked for ours, from the 200th and 515th. We didn't have to brag on our men. The other officers did it for us."

Shortly before his death in March 1991, Cash Skarda said to me, "Old as I am, I'd go again if they needed me. And if I did, I'd want the men of the old 200th with me. Those guys know how to fight!"

Santana Romero, honored warrior of Bataan and Governor of Taos Pueblo, in his robes and symbol of office, with sacred Taos Mountain in the background. (Courtesy: Santana Romero.)

TAPS FOR THE 200th
9 April 1942

Crouched on a ridge overlooking the little airstrip they euphemistically called Cabcaben Airfield, an exhausted band of New Mexicans awaited dawn and death. Alone, with only a few rounds of antiquated ammunition for their 1903 Springfield rifles, they were the last unit still intact between the fleeing Fil-American troops and the massed Japanese army on a peninsula called Bataan.

They were the ragged remnants of the old 200th CA (AA), a New Mexico National Guard regiment sent to the Philippines just weeks ahead of war. Though nominally antiaircraft artillery, 'Old Two Hon'erd' had served in many capacities during the desperate four months on Bataan. Now, at the end, they fought as infantry. The Philippine 1st Constabulary and the 26th Cavalry were supposed to reinforce them, but they never arrived. The 200th stood alone.

The Japanese had opened up on 3 April – Good Friday – with a final massive air and artillery barrage. By evening streams of Filipino soldiers began pouring south past Captain Marvin Lucas on the only road, "barefoot, their rifles gone, no helmets. Behind them a lieutenant in a sedan shouted to the MPs to stop them and regroup, and then he roared off again. There was no way to stop that rout."

By evening of the fifth the Japanese had taken vital Mount Samat, and on the sixth they crushed the last attempt to counterattack. Under the continual barrage, the American lines crumbled, and all day on the seventh the men of the 200th watched detached clots of infantry stream to the rear, like debris breaking loose in the spring-flooded *acequias* back home in New Mexico. (It was, in fact, the effective firing of the 200th that made their escape possible, a retreating major told Lieutenant John Gamble.)

By the afternoon of the eighth the battle-numbed, deep-eyed infantrymen of the 31st were behind them, and the 200th received orders to destroy all artillery equipment not useful to infantry, proceed up the ridge, and hold the field as long as possible while the other troops crossed to Corregidor.

They spiked the 3-inch guns, smashed the range- and height-finders with picks and sledge hammers, and pounded the cables to junk. Tears grooved their dirt-caked faces as they buried the remains like dead buddies. Flying shrapnel dug into their flesh. Medics carried B Battery's Captain Frank Turner to the rear with serious wounds.

As night began to thicken, they started up the ridge. Filipinos clogged the road, so they followed the ditches. In the moonless night, with no betraying flashlights, they moved silently, except for the slap of their rifles and BARs (Browning Automatic Rifles), the scrape of shoes in the nearly knee-deep sand, and a few muttered 'damns' because they couldn't see; and some wondered if death, when it came with day, would be any blacker.

Half a mile separated the end of the airstrip from the bay. To the north the Japanese artillery flashed and roared like a monstrous Oriental dragon. South, toward Mariveles, the flames of burning ammunition lit the sky. From time to time another dump blew, shrapnel tore through the air, and explosions shook the ground. On the ridge the closer sounds of moving men were more tangible.

By midnight they were deployed, and they started digging in. They had few infantry weapons – only Springfields, pistols, and BARs. On the back side of the ridge they emplaced a few 37-mm. guns, but without armor-piercing shells they were useless against the tanks massed for the dawn assault. Their most powerful weapons were .30-caliber machine guns – "paper against steel," Gamble called them.

In the hours before the dawn they got what sleep they could. It wasn't much. In the jungle beyond the clearing, Japanese fires burned and shrill Japanese laughter rose. Sometime after midnight the earth began to heave, "like a mammoth monster sluggishly moving in his sleep," Gamble said, and added that the writhing trees seemed to prophesy catastrophe.

It didn't take an earthquake to predict the end for the gaunt Americans who, for four starving, malaria-beset months had waited for the promised reinforcements. Since December they had listened to assurances and pleas from Washington, to hold on a few more days. Hundreds of ships were on the way, they were told, and thousands of planes.

A few still believed it, or tried to, though privately they knew better. There was no help. They were the Battling Bastards of Bataan, no Mama, no Papa, no Uncle Sam. Just this last thin ragged line above an airstrip there were no planes left to land on, and at its end a cliff, and Manila Bay eighty feet below. The enemy massed on the other side with only Corregidor between, toward which the rest were headed. On Bataan, only the 200th still stood.

One later day the world would know their story. MacArthur would call Bataan "one of the decisive battles of the world," and history would confirm the judgment. Already, as the end approached, Bataan had become a symbol and inspired a nation, although the men who had made it so neither knew, nor, at that moment, particularly cared.

One later day the key role of the 200th in that decisive battle would be told. It was they who, as the other units filed onto the peninsula to make their historic stand, guarded the vital bridges at Calumpit and Layac Junction and other key points, and thereby insured the success of the retreat. The first unit in the Philippines to fire at the enemy, they were the last left fighting. Later, they would receive three Distinguished Unit Citations and the Philippine Presidential Citation. It is believed no unit in World War II received more.[1]

One later day in prison camp, Lieutenant James McCahon heard a 'regular' comment snidely about National Guardsmen. General Edward P. King remembered the staunch 200th, still intact at the end. "Had it not been for a National Guard unit," he answered tersely, "I would not have had a line to carry that white flag through."

As that last line waited for the dawn, few believed they would see another. Hungry and exhausted, men with no future, they remembered the past.

They remembered the prewar days at Fort Bliss, when they vowed they'd be 'First in Spite of Hell,' and then made good on it. They were newly converted from cavalry, and Congress hadn't voted money for ammunition, so their antiaircraft training was minimal. They fired a few paltry rounds on the 3-inch guns, and they mounted machine guns on fake 37-mms., dummies simulated from boxes and boards. Even so, they outgunned all the others, to be named "the best anti-aircraft unit, regular or otherwise," then available in the United States Armed Forces. They carried their pride like a guidon.

Sergeant Albert Senter remembered how 'Old Two Hon'erd' became a regimental nickname. When the draftees began to arrive, the New Mexicans among them vied to get into the 200th. Some, from Spanish-speaking mountain or border communities, spoke little English. This presented no problem within the regiment, half of whom were Hispanic, but encounters with other units were a different matter. Fearing the disgrace of dismissal from the service, the inductees memorized stock answers to prove linguistic competence.

---

[1] The United States Army has avoided officially ranking units as to number or value of decorations. It is, however, highly unusual for a single Regiment to receive two Presidential Unit Citations from the United States and one from another country, especially when earned within a four-month period. It is, so far as the author can ascertain, unique.

"What outfit you with?" the MPs barked.

"Two Hon'erd!" the newly made soldiers parroted proudly.

Private Vicente Ojinaga remembered the day he told his family goodbye. "Go with God," his father said, "and don't ever dishonor your flag." He hadn't.

As the first gray shaft of day stabbed the night like a bayonet, and the thick black began to drain into the edges of the jungle, the men of 'Old Two Hon'erd' looked around, and the dark shapes became men with eyes that knew more than young men's eyes should know.

They fixed bayonets.

Then it began. Sergeant Woodrow Hutchison "heard the rumble of tanks like distant thunder. And we had no ammunition that would penetrate armor. It was almost lights out."

Some had rifles. Sergeant Angelo Sakelares had a pistol and one grenade. They waited to open fire.

"Keep down," Major Paul Schurtz ordered. "We can't fight tanks with pistols."

Ramón Garcia was crying, and he looked at Sakelares. "We were taught to fight and die for our country."

Sak's voice was flat. "Well, all you got to do is stand up."

Gamble, his red hair blazing like a sacrificial flame in the first light, watched the tanks begin to roll forward, "and then we knew our time of life was very short."

Sergeant 'Ike' Garrett steeled for the assault. "Everybody else had run to the end of Bataan. We'd played a pretty good game, I thought, and we'd still fight. To the last man . . . . "

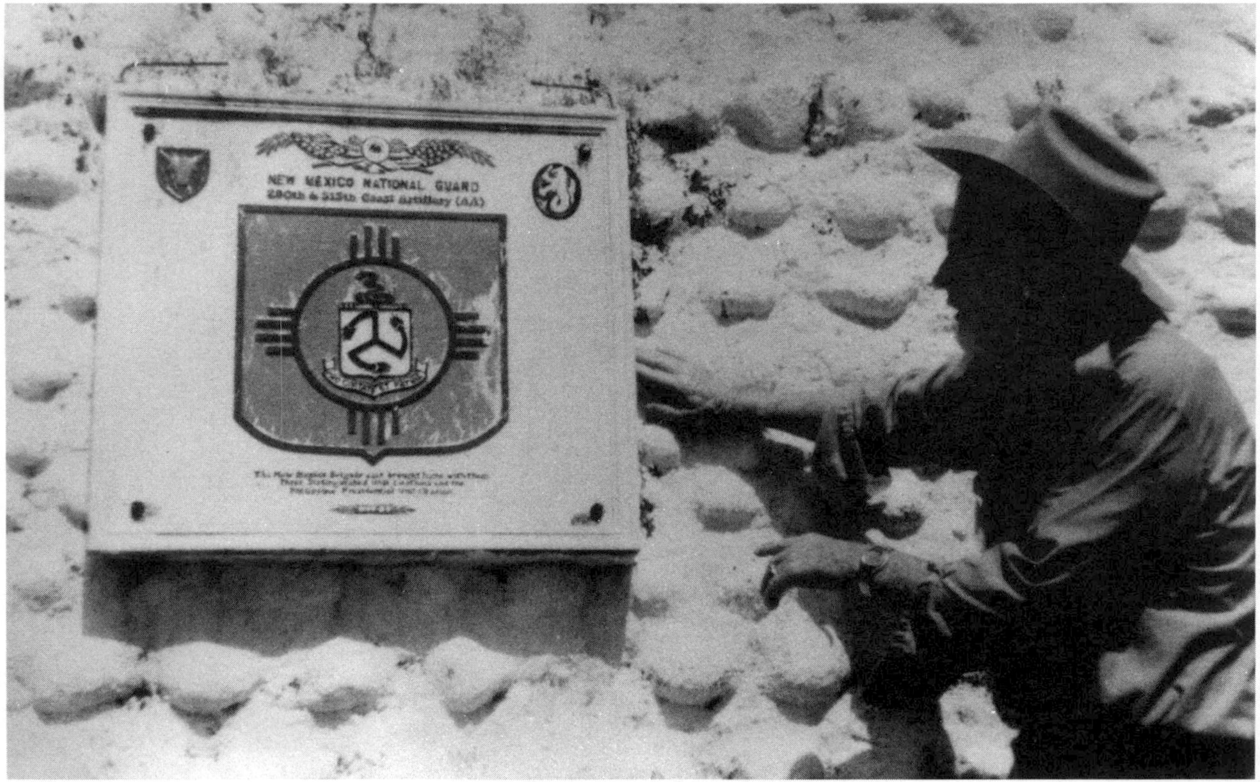

Dow Bond at the National Monument on Mount Samat, Bataan, inspects the bronze Brigade insignia plaque, dedicated to the 200th and 515th. (Courtesy: Dow Bond.)

BOOK I

'FIRST IN SPITE OF HELL'

"The 200th is hereby named the best anti-aircraft Regiment (regular or otherwise), now available to the United States armed forces for use in an area of critical military importance."

Official citation,
United States Army,
17 August 1941.

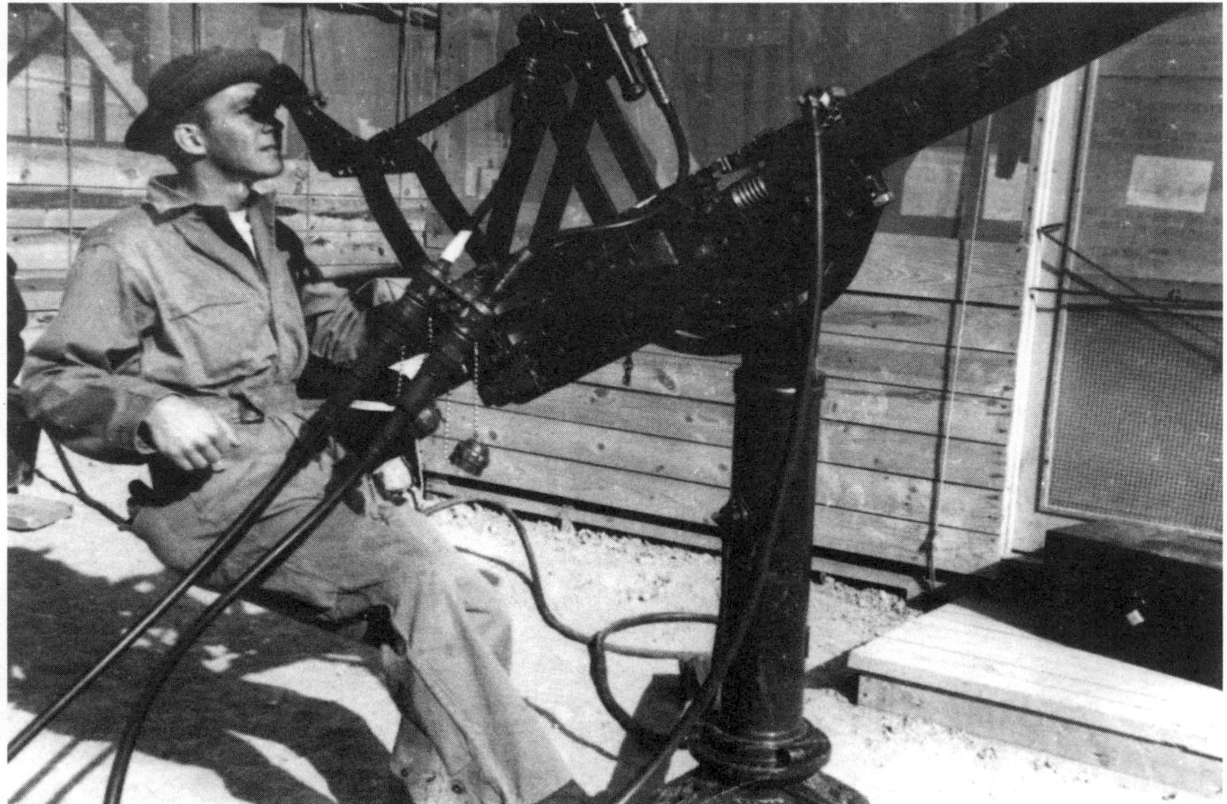

Dick Malone trains on a water-cooled .50-caliber machine gun at Fort Bliss. (Courtesy: Wallace Phillips.)

– 1 –

THE OLD GUARD

"In high school we automatically joined the Guard.
It was the custom. We were like a football team."
– Sergeant Angelo Sakelares –

They started out as the 111th Cavalry, and they remained horse soldiers at heart. They joined for many reasons – for a little extra money during the Depression; for adventure; because everyone else did. They joined for fun mostly, and for something else., too, something that had to do with soldiering, something a strong land breeds in men who love it.

The horses and sabers drew Angelo Sakelares. He was fourteen and played fullback for the Deming Wildcats. He was also something of a problem, and whenever any devilment occurred, the principal automatically sent for Sakelares. The Guard was a good outlet for Angel's creative energies.

Gregorio Villaseñor saw a movie one day – *Beau Gest* – and was enamored with the bugle's clean tones. Unable to read music, he bought a record of army bugle calls, paid four dollars for a used instrument, and began to practice. Working in a CCC camp, Greg thrilled when the Guard troop from Deming galloped by on night maneuvers. He wondered if they could use a bugler. They could.

Marvin Lucas was only fourteen, but he changed his birth date and no one questioned him too closely. Lucas recruited Russell Hutchison, and later, when they were students at the University of New Mexico, Hutch recruited Al Senter. The Guard needed ham radio operators, and Al fit the bill. He in turn enlisted Neal Harrington, who, pulled by the Old West cavalry tradition, headed for the armory, to be promptly rejected because of his eyesight. Undeterred, Harrington hung around, memorized the chart, returned sans glasses, and was in.

Playing football at the State Teachers College[1] Nicholas Chintis heard that Guard members could take their dates horseback riding on Sundays – without charge. He passed the word to his teammates. Steve Alex, Walter Gentry, and Al Wheeler cut English class and headed for the stables. "Sure, guys," drawled Sergeant Pryor Thwaits, "just sign here."

None had any idea what the Guard was, but it sounded good. Within months, however, they were in the Philippines dodging Japanese strafers. "Never," swore Alex as a Zero dived straight at him, "will I ever cut another English class!"

The pay lured some. In 1938 a buck private earned $15 a month and $1 a night for weekly drills. A corporal drew $22, a buck sergeant $30. A second lieutenant lived high on a magnificent $75.

Winston Shillito "hadn't the remotest idea what I had joined. When I got promoted to PFC, I took my shirt home and my mother asked whether the stripes pointed up or down. I didn't know, and I guessed wrong. And that was the beginning of my education."

The highlight of each year was the August encampment in the high country at Camp Maximiliano Luna, when the entire Regiment came together. Troops from Taos and Santa Fe

[1] Now Western New Mexico University in Silver City.

saddled up and rode overland. Others loaded horses, guns, and equipment onto trains, and at Las Vegas they unloaded and proceeded in horse-drawn wagon trains to the camp on its high mesa.

They rode the hills and canyons all day and at night they slept in pup tents. Shillito and the rest in Silver City's F Troop bivouacked next to the Carlsbad unit. "We had quite a rivalry, and fisticuffs weren't unusual. It wasn't animosity – we were just young and it was something to do. The real fun was to go into Las Vegas and carouse."

Each troop had its own personality. If the Carlsbad boys prided themselves on being the toughest, the Santa Fe group was famous for stealing whatever could be pried loose. Those from Clovis cherished their reputation as the Regimental rascals. On one occasion, detailed to furnish firewood for the kitchen, they cut all the fence posts in the entire area.

Life in the field was fun, but it was tough fun. The troops brought their own horses, but only half enough. The rest they leased from local ranchers, and many were unbroken or long unridden. Jim Huxtable described one summer's first formation as a "mass rodeo. Horses were bucking all over, equipment flew, and men with broken bones filled the dispensary. Some of those horses never were found."

The eastern boys furnished fun for the rest. Though drawn by the horses, Nick Chintis (to Shillito's amusement) had never ridden. "Nick was from Indiana, and didn't know what a horse looked like when he came to Silver City. He'd just learned to hang on when they took us to qualify for mounted firing. We put the horses in a lope and fired forty-fives at targets on both sides of a round track, back and forth across the horse's head. Well, Nick not only couldn't ride – he couldn't shoot either! Nobody knows how the horse – or Nick – survived."

Neither did Nick. "I told the captain I wasn't quite ready to fire off a horse, and he said, 'Oh, you can ride, Chintis.' I fired the first seven targets pretty good. Then I reached for my clip, and it had slipped down in my boot. I finally got it, but by then I was past the targets. I was firing everywhere – between the horse's ears – and everybody was running for cover.

"I fell off the horse right at the captain's feet. I looked up those shiny boots and into his face, and he said, 'Chintis, I agree. You need a little more practice!'"

Western by birth or choice, they quickly became cavalrymen. Few were strangers to life in the open, and what they didn't know about living off the land they learned. Competing against regular cavalry at Fort Bliss when they were mere boys, they learned to survive – and thanked God later.

They were known for their top-ranking polo team, and for the superb horse shows in their rock-built amphitheater; and they furnished the state university its equestrian instructor, Lieutenant Jim Sadler.

Their spectacular horsemanship attracted Paramount Pictures, and, in 1939 the 111th furnished the cavalry for *The Light That Failed*, filmed near Buckman (now Los Alamos). Russell Hutchison was an enthusiastic cast member. "We had two camps, the British camp on the Nile, and up the hill behind it, ours where we slept. The Fuzzy Wuzzies were Blacks from Los Angeles, and their feet got blistered from running barefoot in the sand."

Don Harris was more impressed with war games than movie making. "One night our goal was to slip into camp and get the colonel's boots out of his tent while he was in it. It was a wild night – raining – and we climbed the mesa and got the boots, and then charged whooping. We had a fine time."

They maneuvered, camped, and cooked, often above timberline – once, Hutch remembered, in eight inches of hail. "And the band always greeted us as we rode in, troop after troop. The bandmaster was mean and tough as old Sousa. He gave that band hell from dawn to dark."

In 1938 they trained and competed with regular cavalry units at Fort Bliss, Texas, and participated in an historic maneuver. Men and horses spread by thousands through the flats, camped among cactus and mesquite where White Sands Missile Range now guards the desert.

Their rations, Hutchison noted, "were stamped 'Horse Meat' and dated in the 1920s. The Army always unloaded all their old rations on the National Guard units."

Shillito started on the great maneuver as on a lark. "They issued us a jelly sandwich and we mounted up and headed into the desert. In the afternoon we watered our horses, and I lay down. When I woke up about dusk and got to the chow truck, there wasn't a bite left." (The meal, Hutch could have told him, consisted of spaghetti and sand.)

Shillito rode, sans supper, all night and all day. "In the afternoon we put up our shelter halves and the chow trucks were just setting up when the bugles blew, and it was off to battle. I got to the wagon and ate while the rest of the guys were fighting the imaginary foe.

"After four days of heat and dehydration, men started falling out, and so did horses. We had no chance to fill our canteens. At one lake, apparently contaminated, they set up artillery to keep us and the horses out. There was almost a stampede.

"Ambulances were hauling men out. Only a couple of our boys had to be picked up, but a lot had bleeding bottoms. Later they told us that was the roughest maneuver the Army ever held, and that we had stood up better than most of the regulars."

Those who, like Hutchison, became officers, worked up through the ranks. "All of us had been KPs, we'd all been on the picket line. And we always respected each other. When Howard Hazelwood made captain, his brothers were scared stiff of him! We had a strange discipline, like father-son. You respected your superior, even if you were a blood relation."

Called during crises, they fought forest fires, grasshoppers, and floods. When a coal-miners' strike in Gallup got violent, the Guard was called in. Hutch was just fifteen. "Those damn coal miners were all giants, and we were little old skinny high school kids!"

That didn't deter them. They knew they were good. "We didn't know how good until we visited the Guard armories in Amarillo. Those Texans were a sloppy outfit!" Because of its excellence, the New Mexico National Guard was among the earliest to enjoy federal recognition.

* * *

The unusual *esprit de corps* that characterized the New Mexicans derived in part from a proud lineage. The oldest continuous militia in the United States, the New Mexico National Guard dates back to 1598, when Spanish colonists mobilized against hostile Indians. As Spain began to withdraw military protection from its vast northern reaches, Indian raids increased and the importance of the militia grew, and continued to grow under the Mexican rule effected in 1821.

During the Mexican War, General Stephen Watts Kearney organized the first American militia in the territory, which distinguished itself in the battles of Santa Cruz and Embudo during the Taos Rebellion of 1847.

Under the command of Colonel Christopher 'Kit' Carson, the First New Mexico Cavalry, direct ancestor to the 111th, fought Confederate troops at Valverde, Albuquerque, Santa Fe, and Glorieta Pass; they fought Indians in the battle at Adobe Walls, and they continued fighting southwestern tribes until Geromino's final defeat in 1886.

The Territorial Milita was again mustered into federal service in 1898 as the Second Squadron of the First United States Volunteer Cavalry, better known as Roosevelt's Rough Riders. Embarking from Cuba on the transport *Yucatán*, they were dismayed when some of their troops and most of their horses were left behind.

Undeterred, the New Mexicans blazoned an outstanding record as infantry (a role they would be called on to play again half a century later in a place called Bataan). Ordered to seize Kettle Hill in support of the main thrust on nearby San Juan Hill, with New Mexico's E and G Troops in the vanguard, the Rough Riders secured the top against murderous fire and invested the heights above Santiago. Two weeks later the Spaniards surrendered.

Distinguishing himself in that action was the Captain of F Troop, Maximiliano Luna, for whom Camp Luna would be named. Luna later lost his life fighting guerrillas, the first New Mexican to be killed in war in the Philippines.[2]

---

2 At the conclusion of the Spanish-American War, Emilio Aguinaldo led Philippine guerrillas against the Americans who had freed his island. He had previously rebelled against Spanish rule.

The next action was on the Mexican border.

At 4:00 am, 9 March 1916, the flamboyant *bandito* Francisco 'Pancho' Villa, after having massacred eighteen Americans at Santa Ysabel, crossed the border into New Mexico, gutted the little town of Columbus, and killed another seventeen. Seeing smoke, thirty men from Deming's I Troop raced to Columbus to support the single squadron of regulars garrisoned there. Three days later reinforcements arrived from the Roswell Guard unit and joined Pershing to chase Villa into Mexico.

In 1917 and 1918, New Mexico National Guard units sailed for France. Notable was Roswell's Battery A, commanded by Captain Charles de Bremmond, which served in the 66th Field Artillery Brigade, engaged in four major battles, and was instrumental in destroying the vital bridge at Chateau-Thierry.

The past inspires; the future dares.

Since becoming a territory, New Mexico had provided major combat units in every war. Now another glared like a swollen monster from beyond once-protective oceans.

Across the Atlantic, Hitler occupied the Rhineland, Austria, and the Sudentenland. In March 1939 he swallowed the rest of Czechoslovakia and began to eye Poland.

Beyond the Pacific, the fire-breathing Japanese dragon conquered Manchuria in 1931, bellowed into China the next year, and answered world protestations by withdrawing from the League of Nations. In 1936 Tokyo signed an Anti-Comintern Pack with Germany, responded to President Roosevelt's 'quarantine speech' of 5 October 1937 by bombing the American gunboat *Panay* on the Yangtze in December, and shrugged a breezy, "so sorry."

The fateful year 1939 dawned menacingly. As Japanese bombs fell on American missions in China, the United States fleet moved into the Pacific; but Congress, afraid of antagonizing Japan, refused to fortify Guam.

Americans still focused on a more pleasant world. They laughed when Joe Louis k-o'd the swaggering Tony Galento; and in July, when the United States terminated its longtime trade treaty with Japan, a headline expressed the consensus that "UNITED STATES HAS JAPAN HOGTIED."[3] Of more concern was pug-jawed, bush-browed John L. Lewis who, in a voice like a freight train, demanded for labor "twenty-five lousy cents an hour."

That summer the boys of the 111th danced to Glenn Miller records; they sang "Beer Barrel Polka" and "South of the Border," and held hands with their girls in the movies, laughed at the Marx Brothers and Andy Hardy, thrilled to love and war in *Gone With the Wind*, and groaned when the girls gasped at close-ups of Gable. They tuned their radios to Jack Benny and Charlie McCarthy. And they listened lump-throated with the rest of America as Kate Smith belted out "God Bless America." They didn't know then it would become 'their' song.

Encampment at Luna that summer of 1939 was still fun, and still cavalry, but not for long: The War Department announced they should convert to another branch. A new intensity marked their maneuvers, a new awareness of change. It would not be the same again.

At summer's end the younger cavalrymen returned to textbooks and football, and Angelo Sakelares was elected president of the Junior Class at Deming High; but school wasn't the same that year either.

On 1 September Hitler invaded Poland. Two days later Britain and France declared war, and Churchill made the first of those speeches that would steady a nation beset, ending with a quietly emotional, "May God bless you all."

World War II had begun.

---

3 *Graphic* (Deming, NM) 8 February 1940 (at which date the abrogation went into effect).

– 2 –

THE CHANGING OF THE GUARD

"We are as good as any and better than most."
– Colonel Charles Gurdon Sage –

Don Harris never forgot that last cavalry parade. It was the summer of 1940, and the 111th passed in review with the regular regiments at Fort Bliss in the hard glare of desert sun and stark fact: They were losing their horses.

"A cavalry parade's really something. As you pass the reviewing stand, you grab your rifle from your scabbard, plant it by your thigh, and do an 'Eyes right.' You can hear those rifles all down the line . . . . Then they took away our horses."

Horses were going out of style, they were told; there'd be no horses in the next war. They didn't like it, but with customary pride they vowed to be 'First in Spite of Hell,' and, given a choice between field artillery and antiaircraft, chose the latter.

The War Department approved, provided the State would enlarge the armories to accommodate the additional personnel and equipment – no federal funds were available. As soon as Governor John E. Miles made the requisition, Colonel Charles Gurdon Sage relieved retiring Colonel Clyde Ely of command and began to reorganize. Cavalry troops became antiaircraft batteries. New building additions, new uniforms, and special field-training camps at the local armories betokened energetic change.

On 26 April 1940 the 111th Cavalry became officially, though briefly, the 207th Coast Artillery. New York objected – they wanted to retain the numeral from the New York unit of World War I fame. All right, agreed the New Mexicans, they could have the number if they'd pay for the new insignia. The pact was struck and the 200th was christened.

In June, ten days of instruction by 'regulars' at the School of Mines in Socorro gave Guard officers and noncoms training on AA equipment convoyed from Fort MacArthur, California. That summer's encampment – their last at Luna – was extended to three weeks. A few 3-inch guns arrived, but only for demonstration, for by 1940 weapons and ammunition were already going to European allies.

Soon thereafter, officers and a number of enlisted men began three-month courses at Coast Artillery School at Fortress Monroe, Virginia, a group at a time. There Sage, during his stay, wrote plaintively to Acting Commander Harry Peck: He hungered for New Mexico. Could Peck please ship him a crate of chile and tamales?

While the 200th trained for war, *blitzkrieg* rolled through Europe. The bulldog British plied the Channel and wrote Dunkirk into the annals of courage, awaited invasion, and steadied under continual bombing as Churchill pledged, "We shall not flag or fail . . . ."

The fall of France and the Netherlands orphaned their rubber- and oil-rich colonies and strategic bases, which Japan eyed greedily. Not to worry, the Japanese ambassador in Washington assured an edgy Secretary of State; Japan's intentions were honorable. Cordell Hull was skeptical.

When Chief of Staff George Marshall reported in May that the American Army could only combat-equip 75,000 men, America asked why. Where had the $71 million voted since 1933 gone?[1] The President hedged (it was an election year) and pledged ("Your boys are not going to be sent to any foreign wars"), Congress voted another $18 million for defense, and in Deming, New Mexico, Guard members at the Junior-Senior banquet sang "Auld Lang Syne" by candlelight, and wondered.

In August Petain gave in to Japanese demands for bases in northern Indo-China. In September Tokyo announced to a stunned world that Japan had joined the Axis. America replied to repeated aggression with increasing economic sanctions against Japan and large loans to China.

Marshall pled for matériel and for legislation to call Na-tional Guard units to active duty. In September the long-debated draft bill became law, and in October young Americans thronged to city halls across the land to register.

Three days after his reelection, the President pledged half of all war matériel produced in America to Britain. In December he announced the Lend-Lease program, which became law in March.

Shortly before Christmas the word came down. The 200th was being federalized. A few resigned. The rest prepared enthusiastically to leave in January.

Former members rejoined to be with old buddies. New men volunteered to be with friends who already belonged. University students took frantic early exams. Incumbent members set their affairs in order. Gurdon Sage turned over the Deming *Headlight* to his wife. Paul Schurtz resigned from the post office to head Regimental Supply, and George Colvard closed his obstetrical practice to become Senior Medical Officer. Neither Schurtz nor Colvard would return.

Tom Foy, fresh from Notre Dame with a law degree, asked the senior member of the firm if he'd still have a job when his year was up. The older lawyer nodded. "But you won't be back in a year, Tommie. You're going to have to fight a war first."

---

1 *Time*, 27 May 1940.

Regimental doctors gave physicals. A few underage were rejected. Tommy Santistevan, a buck sergeant with four years' service, was not yet eighteen, but after a birthday in January he reenlisted in Battery H, and Lieutenant Jack Boyer made sure Tommy got back his stripes.

Andrés Montoya, underweight but frantic to stay in the regiment, also turned to Boyer, who stuffed him with bananas until 'Doc' Richard Riley passed him – after which Montoya promptly, but happily, threw up.

They couldn't help Pete Perez. Pete was a champion bugler who, Lieutenant Dow Bond swore, "could raise up the blankets when he played reveille." But Pete failed his physical, and, with trembling lips, played his last Taps – for himself.

Those remaining weeks were hectic with preparations and inspections. Then, at armories across the state, the men of the 200th were sworn in. As of one minute past midnight, 6 January 1941, the Guardsmen were in Uncle Sam's Army.

On the fifteenth, parents, wives, and sweethearts gathered across New Mexico to see the boys off. Hundreds lined the tracks in Albuquerque, and Clovis, and Carlsbad, and Silver City as their men formed ranks, marched down the long brick walkways, and boarded the trains. On the sixteenth the truck convoys followed. Along the highways and at the depots townspeople waved them through, and the Guardsmen, in high spirits – or seeming so – leaned out the windows, yelled, waved back. Some clutched dogs in their arms; shrill yelps and wagging tails added their own excitement.

On to Fort Bliss!

"Each tent has a wooden floor and sidewalls," reported the 10 January *Headlight*, "electric lights and gas heat. Excellent mess halls and bath houses . . . . " It read like an ad for a posh camp.

It didn't quite tell all, as Fred Almeraz, arriving at night to find "no tops on the tents, the wind blowing, and us cold and hungry," could have amended.

Although Bliss was an old post, it had not yet expanded to accommodate the incoming Guard units or the masses of draftees that would soon swell their ranks. Dynamite blasts rocked the ground and trucks roared by with caliche for new streets. Guardsmen dug rocks to clear a parade field by day, shoveled sand from their cots at night, and tried to keep their tents intact during wind storms. They didn't always manage.

Bandmaster Jim McCahon saw life at Bliss as "one big party. We played for concerts, church services, retreat parades, and guard mounts. And always reveille. That was toughest – a reveille march on those cold windy days."

The 200th comprised a headquarters and two battalions, each with its own headquarters battery. First Battalion contained Battery A, with 60-inch Sperry searchlights, and B, C, and D with 3-inch guns – old models, with a maximum vertical range of 27,000 feet. America wasn't armed, and the 'regulars' got first pick. Second Battalion included Battery E, with .50-caliber machine guns, and F, G, and H with 37-mm. guns.

Because of the camaraderie between officers and men, Sage rotated officers to other batteries. It meant stricter discipline – and there could be a war. "It would be difficult," Boyer agreed, "to give your best friend an order that might jeopardize his life."

A few noncoms were assigned special duties, took correspondence courses at night, and received their commissions. It meant double duty and grueling training, but it made good officers.

Some did double duty without the commissions. From a tent, Al Senter operated the radio equipment, first for the Regiment, then for the whole Brigade, on top of his regular duties. He also served as instructor for the Brigade Radio School until a tonsillitis attack knocked out his voice, whereupon the school folded.

From the first, the 'regulars' looked down their hierarchical noses at the Guard units and assigned a regular NCO to advise each battery. Unhappy with this cavalier attitude, Sage (himself under the gun of Brigade command) goaded, guided, and galvanized his Regiment until, at the end of the initial thirteen-week training period he announced with assurance, "We are as good as any and better than most!"

From their original 750 men and officers they began to expand to a war-strength complement of 1,800. New Mexican volunteers flooding into Fort Bliss requested assignment to the 200th. They joined to beat the draft, to be with their friends, and to belong to the best.

Draftees began to arrive, and the New Mexicans among them, after a few days at the reception center, found themselves assigned to the 200th. Harry Steen, originally slated for Fort Dix, wasn't sure just how it happened, but, after being told to pack his gear and move across the road, found himself with old friends in the regiment. Pepe Baldonado was reassigned in the same group. That was fine with him – his brother Juan was already there. The Marines had rejected Robert Williams because his teeth were crooked. The 200th welcomed him – he was a New Mexican, wasn't he? Myrrl McBride, arriving with Indian friends from Acoma, was siphoned likewise. "Just a coincidence," he shrugged.

Lieutenant Gerald Greeman could have told him better. Acting as regimental personnel officer, Greeman got a list each week of draftees. He took the personnel officer at the reception center to a few parties, "got in good with the old boy, and said, 'I'll lay off the others, but let me have the New Mexicans.'" Greeman believed a homogeneous unit would be a strong one; everyone knew someone from his hometown battery. This homogeneity was one reason for the 200th's noted *esprit de corps*.

Each battery picked men for its specific needs. Sergeant Calvin Graef went through records for Battery G with Tom Foy. "If one had worked for Ma Bell, we'd grab him for communications. We got cooks for our kitchen and mechanics for our motor pool. And we ended up with the best personnel."

A few draftees lacked initial enthusiasm for the 200th, especially the ranch-reared, accustomed, like Charley Ross, to original thought, personal sovereignty, and open space. "They told me what I was going to do, and what I was not going to do, and I didn't like it!"

Cone Munsey found "no such thing as privacy. The latrines consisted of rows of stools and shower heads, and no partitions. The food was an experience also. Everything was boiled to a gob, fried to a crisp, or otherwise mutilated. We marched in midday heat and hiked ten miles wearing gas masks. Periodically we stripped, put on rubber rain coats, and stood in line to be inspected for venereal disease. Perspiration ran off in puddles."

America tried frantically to rearm with too little, too late. Weapons were few and obsolescent. Congress dragged its defense feet, strikes crippled production, and the President, proclaiming America "an arsenal of democracy," pledged to supply Britain with "planes and ships and guns and shells."

The 37-mm. batteries did with what they had. Foy's battery "simulated guns from boxes and broomsticks." Dow Bond's unit "fired rocks for ammunition and shouted 'bang.'" Santana Romero's battery had a gun but no ammunition. "I fed .50-caliber ammo from the First World War to that 37-mm. gun. Didn't work." Not one man ever fired a 37-mm. shell until the day the war began.

Those on the 3-inch guns fared a little better, and shot several times at plane-towed targets. When Willie Burrola's crew "nearly hit the plane one day, the pilot dropped the target and took off."

They cut fuzes, they loaded, they pulled lanyards. Battery A tracked planes with their searchlights, learned how to operate the generator, controls, and light- and sound-locators. Mostly, they trained with rifles – bolt-action 1903 Springfields, and never enough of them. Paul Roessler trained draftees "with wooden rifles and World War I helmets. Few knew how to use a 2-6-8."[2]

The only discrimination in the Regiment was a small snobbishness of 'originals' over 'draftees,' but it faded as the new men drew quickly into the spirit of fierce competition with other units, in sport or soldiery.

On the football field, baseball diamond, boxing ring, or firing range, the 200th was always in the championship, and

---

2 An early form of radar.

Luther Ragsdale felt "something between us the other regiments didn't have – maybe because we were from the same state. And it carried through the war. We always stuck together."

In more serious competition, communications units vied in laying wire, mess crews in handling food, truck crews in transporting men and equipment. Graef's battery, assembling heavy .50-caliber units, "broke all records. They had eleven minutes and we dropped it to four. We broke book rules and took shortcuts. We had oomph, and pride in our regiment. We were a wild bunch, but we had spirit."

They coalesced into a tight hard unit. "We were a cross-section of New Mexico," which, Ragsdale believed, was part of their strength. "Professors, students, miners, lumberjacks, cowboys, rodeo performers, sheepherders, farmers, bus drivers. We had Navajos, Pueblos, Apaches, Zunis. And everyone performed a hundred and twenty percent." Those who couldn't were weeded out.

An initial tendency to clot together in ethnic groups didn't last long, and Ragsdale soon noted a tempering that would become blue steel on Bataan. "We had no Mexicans, no Indians, no Anglos in the 200th. Just Americans."

When an outbreak of meningitis confined several batteries to quarters, the Indians in the Taos battery showed group loyalty in their own way. Each evening during the quarantine, to exorcise the scourge, they danced in full regalia, for the stricken, and for the whole regiment.

They danced again for relief for their fair-skinned brothers who suffered during long hikes in the 120° drouth. The deluge came. Water poured down arroyos, it cut through drill fields, it washed out tents. Regimental headquarters issued immediate orders: The Indians would henceforth perform no more rain dances.

Whatever their origin, they felt more 'one' than 'other,' and their bond to the land carried to that land's regiment. "From the first," asserted Manuel Armijo, "we were *amigos*."

* * *

When meningitis struck at Fort Bliss, Taos Indians danced to cure the stricken and protect the Regiment. A subsequent rain dance brought such torrents that Colonel Sage forbade further dancing. Left to right: José 'Mike' Romero, 'Big Jim' Lujan, Henry Lujan, Santana Romero, and Jimmy-K Lujan. (Courtesy: Santana Romero.)

The 200th had its characters. Irving Gulbas had escaped Hitler's Germany just ahead of the Jewish purges, and settled in El Paso, in time for the draft. He didn't want to be drafted, but he liked the 200th, so he refused a commission in another unit to stay with his friends, and managed to amuse himself with mild misconduct a considerable part of the time.

Battery C got Monday-morning laughs watching First Sergeant John Gamble, a former Santa Fe attorney, as he tried to do calisthenics after a hard night in Juarez. They never forgot the day when Gamble, returning from a weekend pass barely in time for reveille, found his shoes nailed to the floor and his coveralls nailed to the wall. A string of oaths as red as his hair rolled forth. "I'll prosecute the sonofabitch," he yelled. But no one ratted on 'Wild Bill' Haggedorn.

Military regulations were a joke to some – tough little cowboy Mack Nunn, who broke his arm when a bronc threw him in a rodeo forbidden to GIs; Elmer 'Fat Boy' Worthen, who disposed of his gas mask and kept his carrier filled with candy; and one Private Murphy, who always stood morning formation in his overcoat, even in August, because it was all he took time to grab at reveille.

Santana Romero (who would one day become Governor of Taos Pueblo) once decided to go home, was denied a pass, and, in the direct and uncomplicated way of his people, went anyhow. It cost him his corporal's stripes, an inconvenience he found minor. San had joined the 200th originally by the same straight logic – because he wanted to – though he had already been inducted into the Marine Corps. On leave in Taos before reporting to duty, he decided to go to Fort Bliss with his buddies, and joined the 200th. Presumably officers in Battery H squared it with the Marines.

A number of retreads from World War I reenlisted. Sergeants Jim Hamilton and Jesse Finley had served in France; so had Oliver Hartford, a tough old piece of cavalry leather who had chased Pancho Villa before that. Colonel Memory Cain, a Marine pilot before his cavalry days, had been shot down over France in 1918, captured, and made a German POW.

* * *

On a Friday afternoon in May, Angel Sakelares, Lawrence 'Buddy' Byrne, and Jim Huxtable, not daring to let their officers know how young they really were, waited until they were off duty and sped to Deming for their high-school graduation. En route they wrecked Buddy's car. A parent drove to get them and school authorities delayed the ceremony until the boys dashed in, still in their khakis and minus caps and gowns.

It didn't matter: They wore a uniform they were proud of.

If America entered the war, the United States pledged in a British-American agreement of 27 March 1941, she would give top priority to the defeat of Germany, and employ only defensive strategy in the Far East, even should Japan attack first.[3] So was born the 'Get Hitler First' strategy.

In April Japan signed a neutrality pact with the Soviet Union. In May the Germans torpedoed the *Robin Moor* and the President proclaimed unlimited emergency. In June Hitler attacked Russia.

Rumors of possible extension in the draft law, and of removing the ban on overseas duty, encouraged romance. A number of 200th sweethearts became 200th brides, and moved to Bliss. Lieutenant Dan Jopling met an army nurse, pert, blue-eyed Lucy Wilson. Neither knew they'd meet again in the Philippines.

The 200th played as hard as it worked. Juarez, just across the bridge, was a favorite hangout, where a few dollars went a long way for food, fun, or a good fight. Those confined to camp, as Ross and friends in C Battery found themselves one payday, sent buddies across the river to get "the mostest for the leastest." It led to a spectacular intramural battle.

Battery F, nourishing its reputation as the regimental 'tough guys,' didn't need the stimulus of Mexican gin. The cook

---

[3] United States. Cong. Joint Committee on the Investigation of the Pearl Harbor Attack. *Hearings*. 79th Cong., 15:1491. Washington: U.S. Govt. Printing Office; 1946 (hereafter cited as *Pearl Harbor Hearings*); and *Joint Army and Navy Basic War Plan "Rainbow 5,"* 32:70 (hereafter cited as *Rainbow 5*.) See also, Samuel Eliot Morison, *The Rising Sun in the Pacific, 1931-April 1942*, Vol. III of the series: *History of United States Naval Operations in World War II*. Boston: Little Brown & Co., 1948, pp. 51-52.

regularly chased men from the mess hall with a meat cleaver, and Charlie James once watched amused while "one guy got another down and tried to chew his ear off."

On one occasion a half-dozen Guardsmen banded together to visit a Juarez bawdy house. Gathering their collective nerve, they disappeared one by one through the courtyard and up the peripheral balconies, to return later with sheepish but pleased grins. When, after a considerable interval, two were still missing, the battery bugler mounted the band stand, borrowed a trumpet, and loudly blew 'Pay Call.'

Out rushed the missing Guardsmen – but not alone. From all directions, stuffing shirt tails, stampeded a herd – a great cross section of Fort Bliss soldiery.

Hank Lovato was in a bar in Ruidoso one night after maneuvers in that area when "somebody said something about Mexicans, and that started it. The Santa Fe guys had pistols – they were on MP duty – and started pistol-whipping the others. It spilled into the street – there must've been two hundred guys – until the state police broke it up. It wasn't dislike – we were all buddies – just an excuse to fight, and you needed some way to choose sides."

Life wasn't all brawls. Gonzo Drake and Pepe Baldonado, deciding to enrich the lives of Battery A with culture, unplugged a juke box in a local dive, told the bartender they were the repairmen the boss had sent for, and loaded it onto a battery truck. But when music issued from their tent with morning, their sergeant, unappreciative of their selfless contribution, roared to "get that thing back on the double!" Music had not soothed this savage breast, they sighed. Returning the treasure, they pronounced it fixed, and magnanimously told the startled owner there was "No charge."

Drastic changes in the Japanese military high command resulted in complete government control over finance and industry. A new conscription called for an additional one to two million men, and Japanese merchant ships were recalled from the Atlantic. Freed by the Russo-Japanese neutrality pact from danger of attack from behind, Japanese armies flooded into southern Indo-China, cutting off all avenues into China except the Burma Road, and almost entirely surrounding the Philippines. To keep the former open, American planes augmented the China Air Force. To defend the latter, the Philippine Army became part of the U.S. military force, USAFFE[4] was created, and retired General Douglas MacArthur, Military Adviser to the Philippine Commonwealth, was recalled to active duty and named commander. The US Asiatic Fleet, now based in Manila, would aid in Philippine defense.

The Far Eastern pot was about to boil over, and one fact glared like the red Rising Sun: The Philippines must be reinforced.

Another drama built in Washington as the vote neared for extending the draft to lengthen the conscription period to eighteen months. A bill to remove the ban on overseas service had already been scuttled. Should this one be defeated, draftees and Guardsmen would soon be going home, and the laborious army buildup would return to square one.

On 12 August, to packed galleries, the roll call began. "Alabama . . . ." A last-minute switch from "aye" to "nay" attempted to start a tide. No one responded. Speaker Rayburn banged his gavel. The ayes had it – 202 to 201.

Off the Newfoundland shore, Roosevelt and Churchill monitored the Washington drama while writing in the greatest secrecy one of their own. On the day the draft bill went to the White House for signature, came the announcement of the historic document they had finished just hours earlier. They called it the Atlantic Charter.

The sweeping ideals of nations rise from its individuals, and an army's strength from its regiments.

In the 200th, regimental pride was enormous. A monument, they decided, should mark their passage. They debated and discussed. Some submitted sketches, all critiqued, and at last they poured the concrete. In bright regimental colors, a circle enclosed one artillery shell. Four others pointed to the four

---

4 United States Armed Forces, Far East.

directions – reminiscent of the New Mexico Zia symbol – and between them, '200 – CA – AA – HQ.' Those proud letters said it all.

The 200th also decided to publish a regimental newspaper, and, sponsored by Colonel Peck and Chaplain Frederick Howden, the *Zia Post* went to press 5 May 1941. A brief history of the New Mexico militia outlined its proud record in America's wars. Then followed the regiment's "solemn promise that the 200th CA (AA) shall be again in the van of Famous New Mexico Military Organizations." It would prove both pledge and prophecy.

Across an ocean most of the New Mexicans had never seen, a message reached MacArthur's headquarters in Manila on 16 August. In response to his pleas for reinforcements, certain units would sail immediately for the Philippines.

Among those listed – though they didn't know it – was the 200th Coast Artillery.

– 3 –

"TO THE OCEANS WHITE WITH FOAM"

"Nobody but the Japs knew where we were going. But the trucks all had 'Manila' on the windshields."

– Sergeant Ike Garrett –

Just before they left, Battery A threw the best picnic Gonzo Drake could remember. Loading the piano from the chapel onto a dump truck – the battery never had a party without Gonzo on the keys, Pepe Baldonado on sax, and Carl Whittaker on drums – they jolted up McKelligan Canyon. It was nearly daylight when they rumbled down again and from the truck bed the combo lustily serenaded the otherwise silent streets of El Paso.

They didn't know they were shipping out until a few days before they left. First they toured New Mexico to field test the Regiment. On 8 August they set out, pulling their guns and searchlights in a 268-vehicle convoy that stretched several miles.

The 200th tours New Mexico in convoy preparatory to leaving for "an overseas assignment of great importance." (Courtesy: Wallace Philips.)

Rumors of an overseas mission rose behind them like trail dust, and many guessed this was a farewell tour.

They roared into Deming the first morning, pitched camp at the race track, performed tactical exercises, and thrilled the town with a parade and retreat, for which all the stores in Deming closed.

That night they moved out without headlights, to simulate a wartime movement, through Hot Springs, Socorro, and Belen. As they rolled into Albuquerque the next afternoon, city officials escorted them down Central Avenue, and thousands lined the curbs to cheer their boys. That night the city hosted a banquet and dance, and after a Sunday formal review, Governor Miles addressed them on behalf of a proud New Mexico. Bandmaster McCahon conducted a concert, and that night the searchlight battery tracked planes from Kirtland Field for their townsmen.

Tuesday they headed south to Roswell, repeated their demonstrations, and encamped in drenching rain. Through Artesia they passed, on to Carlsbad, and back to Bliss on the fifteenth.

There had been a few kinks. One driver flashed his headlights during the blacked-out run. Another, when a plane dived at the convoy in a simulated bombing, drove into a bar ditch. Sage blistered both. A short field maneuver on their return corrected a few tactical problems, and the regiment drew praise. They had performed well.

On Sunday morning, 17 August, two days after their return, Colonel Harry Peck received a summons. How would he like a trip to the tropics? asked General Oliver Spiller. It was the moment Peck had long expected.

"We're ready," he replied, and immediately phoned Sage, in Deming. Sage returned within the hour.[1]

The troops assembled. Army officials, they were told, after touring the nation to rate every antiaircraft unit in the country,

---

[1] Peck, Harry M., Brig. Gen., NMNG 1908-1948: Entries in personal journal maintained as POW and reported in *Albuquerque Journal* 30 October 1945 through 8 June 1946. This and all other quotations from Peck by permission of Lou D. Hoffman, grandson.

A soldier's farewell: Departing Fort Bliss for the Philippines, Nick Chintis kisses his bride. (Courtesy: Nick Chintis)

had officially named the 200th "the best anti-aircraft regiment, (regular or otherwise), now available to the United States Armed Forces"; therefore, they had been selected for "an overseas assignment of great importance."[2]

Some heard they were slated for Alaska. Others heard Samoa. Some suspected the Philippines and, like Charlie James, "had to look on the map to find it." Not even Sage and Peck were sure of their destination.

Enthusiastically the 200th prepared to leave. Wherever it might take them, an overseas mission promised fun and adventure. Those on temporary duty at other camps got hasty orders to rejoin the regiment. To escape Texas's three-day wait, several couples raced to Las Cruces for hasty weddings. The citizens of Deming bought cartons of cigarettes for the boys, which grew to a pyramid in the window of the Golden Eagle Drug Store.

McCahon, hospitalized with an infected ear and scared he might miss out, appealed to Sage, who secured his release just in time. Boyer, in charge of transportation, supervised while his men loaded equipment on a siding for two days and nights. The mess sergeant of Battery G, reputedly the meanest in the regiment, served steaks the night before they entrained.

They went in two echelons. On the 22nd – only five days after they'd received their orders – First Battalion marched aboard cars chalked with 'V for Victory,' and the Regimental Band caused chins to lift and chests to puff, and a few throat-clogging lumps to swell, as it played "O Fair New Mexico."

Second Battalion followed on the thirty-first. Paul Schurtz's wife and small son saw him off in El Paso, then raced the train to say goodbye again in Deming, where the gathered citizenry passed six hundred pounds of magazines through train windows to the boys.

Through the shimmering desert sun they rolled. Deming . . . Lordsburg . . . then New Mexico lay behind. Steel rails stretched glinting back to home. Through the Arizona sands they clattered, and black soot floated behind. California lay ahead, and the surging Pacific, and the big adventure.

---

[2] John Pershing Jolly, *History, National Guard of New Mexico*, n.p., 1964, 158.

* * *

At Angel Island in San Francisco Bay, clearing center and point of embarkation for the Far East, the 200th stood in lines for inoculations and medical exams, enjoyed a few good fights, and gave band concerts before they sailed – such good ones that the commanding general asked that the band be reassigned to Angel Island.

"Where I go my band goes," snapped Sage, and that ended that.

The center was manned by a regular army cadre who found amusement in taunting the Guardsmen. The New Mexicans stood it for a few days before they decided to retaliate.

Bond was officer in charge of the Guard when it happened. "I warned the Angel Island OD his men better quit calling us 'that Mexican outfit,' but he just sniggered. And that night they really got into it. The OD wanted me to go down and stop it – said my men were in trouble. I said, 'No, your men are, and they asked for it.' The 200th really mopped up that night."

While the 200th awaited sailing orders, America and Japan steered a collision course. Since 1940, United States embargoes and commercial blockage of licensing had drawn the economic noose increasingly tighter; and the warlords, desperate for oil, rubber, and metal, knew they must either seize these resources by force or abandon all plans for the 'New Order.'

A deadly struggle was waged within Japan itself, between the moderates who wished to avert war, and the militarists who wanted to strike at once, either at Siberia or at the oil-rich Dutch East Indies. Either move, they knew, would risk a war with the United States; but they believed Hitler's invasion of Russia, launched in June, would finish off the Soviets by August. Britain seemed doomed, and a surprise attack on the Philippines and on the American fleet in the Pacific, they reasoned, could bring a quick victory. On 2 July, at an Imperial Conference, the decision was made. The high command began to draft plans for simultaneous attacks on Malaya, Hong Kong, Guam, Wake, Pearl Harbor, and the Philippines.

On 24 July Japanese troops landed in southern Indo-China. The following day the United States froze all Japanese assets. Great Britain and the Netherlands followed suit.

Meanwhile, a deeply worried Prince Fumimaro Konoye, the moderate Premier, strove desperately for peace. On 16 July he forced the resignation of Foreign Minister Yosuki Matsuoka who, more than any other man, had steered Japan on her deadly course. Early in the year, unofficial envoys had brought moderate feelers to Washington and drawn up a Draft Understanding that offered unprecedented concessions, to be used as a basis for negotiations between Secretary of State Hull and the newly appointed Ambassador Kichisaburo Nomura. But the anti-American fulminations of the enraged Matsuoka had caused Hull to draw back, and to insert, instead, a new and rigid set of demands he knew Tokyo would reject.

Rid of Matsuoka, a desperate Konoye then sought to meet with Roosevelt personally, somewhere in the Pacific. Time was of the essence, he instructed Nomura. "We have reached a point," he stressed, "where we will pin our last hopes on an interview between the Premier and the President."[3]

From Tokyo, Ambassador Joseph C. Grew vigorously urged the meeting. Formulas would not solve the problem, he averred; but he believed the proposed meeting with Konoye, a man of honorable intent, could.[4]

It was the last chance to avert a tragic war.

On 30 August, two days after Nomura handed the proposal for the Konoye meeting to the President, the First Battalion of the 200th boarded the USS *President Pierce*. She was a converted passenger ship, her old lounges now filled with double-deck army cots.

Sweating longshoremen heaved boxes and yelled to one another in varied tongues. Davits creaked and swung heavy loads aboard. From below came muffled slams, and the decks vibrated. Along the quay, freighters from far niches of the

---

[3] *Pearl Harbor Hearings*, 12:20.

[4] Joseph C. Grew, *Turbulent Era: A Diplomatic Record of Forty Years, 1904-1945* (Boston: Houghton Mifflin, 1952). Vol. II. 1343.

world gorged or disgorged cargo, and their flags flapped their registry. Fish smells rode the air, and frog-throated tugs coursed the harbor on their own business.

The desert-bred New Mexicans were intrigued.

Sergeant Neal Harrington found life aboard "routine and dull. We watched the flying fish, schools of porpoises, and the reflections of moonlight on the ocean. We zigged and zagged as a precaution against phantom submarines. As we approached Hawaii, orders were issued that no shore leave would be granted until we looked spic and span. Some of the guys dragged their uniforms in the ocean tied to a line."

Once past Honolulu they were told their destination: The Philippines. Now their trip took on a slightly eerie cast as they sailed blacked out and escorted by a cruiser. The *Pierce* was the first American troopship to be convoyed in peacetime in Far Eastern waters.

Several days out of Honolulu the seas began to swell and a high wind blew. Many grew seasick. "It's all in your minds," swore Captain Fred Sherman. Then he, too, headed for the rail.

Steen thought a storm would be fun, until "those waves started coming in, fifty or sixty feet high, up over the ship, and that dang thing rocked back and forth. We couldn't get any sleep, and guys were sick all over the place."

The typhoon lasted thirty-six hours. Ninety-mile winds blew them off course. Lucas felt as if "we were on a match stick. The propellers would come out of the water, going like mad. They'd throw it in reverse. We could feel them throbbing in the air, and then they'd go down in the water again. The captain radioed the cruiser he was going to turn the ship and ride it out. We nearly rammed the cruiser in the night."

The ships, to show their positions, broke blackout orders, and in the sudden light men gasped as the cruiser loomed from the dark, dead ahead, first on one side, then the other.

Lieutenant Jack Bradley watched appalled as "Jeeps, 3-inch guns, and other equipment lashed to the deck broke chain moorings and washed overboard."

Through it all, Steen braved it out in the stern – he had drawn guard duty.

* * *

Ten days behind the *Pierce*, on 9 September, Second Battalion boarded the USS *President Coolidge*. Rumors still generated like fruit flies. They were going to Pago Pago, to Hawaii, to South America. Then on the dock they saw their guns and trucks, and stamped in large white letters they read, 'Manila, P.I.' Even so, many weren't sure – that could be ordinary military SNAFU, and the orders were sealed – but when a sailor forecast somberly, "There's a lot of you boys going to have a one-way ticket," Lee Roach knew they headed toward trouble.

Late in the afternoon the vibrations of the engines subtly changed rhythm, and the great ship slid from the pier, out toward the foaming Pacific. Men clustered at the rails and watched the bay widen between themselves and home. A light rain began to fall.

As they passed beneath the Golden Gate, Al Suttman turned to Shillito, and his voice was quiet. "Some of us," he said, "won't see that bridge again."

The *Coolidge* was far more luxurious than her sister ship. She had carried Ambassador Grew and his family to Japan nine years before, and the MacArthurs had honeymooned on her. This was her first trip as a troop transport, and her accommodations proclaimed her the aristocrat she was, with thickly carpeted salons, a swimming pool, and two theaters. Her old crew still served fine food, and a five-piece dance band played concerts alternately with the 200th's band.

The one thing missing was a bar, a deficiency Graef and Foy soon rectified. Graef "had charge of the military patrol, and Foy the cleanup, so we had the run of the ship. We got up when we felt like it, ate with the ship's crew, and had the connections to get liquid refreshment sent to our stateroom. And we had most of the officers of the 200th down in our room most of the time!"

Out of Honolulu a longboat brought orders aboard, and they went on war alert; the Japanese were already patrolling the Pacific. An escort joined them, and they sailed blacked out. A reconnaissance plane scouted periodically from the cruiser. The men knew then that a war was in the offing.

On they pushed. They watched the heavy bulk of diving whales and the quick grace of flying fish by day. But the other side of day is night, and they wandered the decks and scanned the lonely sea where eerie phosphorescence danced like glowing ghosts on the black water.

"I have decided there is more water in the world than there is land," Schmitz wrote home. "When we get to Manila we'll just lack a little of being halfway around the world . . . . They don't turn the lights on at night and nobody can smoke. This is Japanese territory."

Gulbas liked to play poker, and shared a stateroom with others of like persuasion. Thus constructively occupied into the nights, they failed to appear for morning calisthenics several days running, which earned them assignment to mop-up duty in the dining room. Soon friends began to razz them. ("You guys joined the Navy?" . . . "Look at them gobs swab!")

It wasn't long before Buster Wilkerson let swing with a mop, and a startled artilleryman hurtled through the air. It worked into a first-class free-for-all until baleful luck caused the ship's skipper to happen through the glass-enclosed walkway above.

Gulbas found himself in "a room with one porthole. They gave us some baskets and said we were going to peel spuds – for the rest of our journey. We began to shoot targets through the porthole – a miss cost you a dime and a hit won you a quarter. It was a good game until a guy from the galley crew came in and told us to get the hell out. So we went back to our room and started playing poker again. The officers thought we were peeling potatoes, and we sent out for food and cigarettes, and nobody bothered us the whole trip."

Into the Philippine Sea they pushed, and misty islands began to float ahead. One night they smelled land, dank and ripe and musty, and by morning green islands loomed. Through the archipelago they twined, past Mindoro, and as the Luzon shore crawled past, they crowded the railings. Never had these desert dwellers seen such green.

Manila Bay teemed with ponderous ships and little boats – rusty tugs, tiny native dugouts, fishing boats, interisland steamers, and darting pleasure craft. To their left loomed Corregidor – a sailor said it was once a Chinese pirate base, and later a penal colony – and beyond it rose a duskier green the informative sailor called Bataan. An old Spanish lighthouse guarded the bay from 'the Rock.'

Corporals Jack Aldrich and Ted Lockard missed Corregidor. They were too busy 'borrowing' Colonel John Luikhart's binoculars to watch the native outrigger *bancas*, and, as they neared the dock, the girls.

Gulls circled and swooped and cried, and Manila rose white and gleaming past tall palms and pale beaches and docks teeming with Oriental longshoremen. They had logged over six thousand miles from San Francisco.

As they filed down the gangplank, the Filipinos called out greetings. "Hi-Ho Silver!" hollered the children, and "Hello, Joe!"

But a few yelled, "Hey, Suckers!"

– 4 –

INNOCENTS ABROAD

"We knew the situation was serious – we could feel it in the air. There was trouble coming."
– Captain Marvin Lucas –

"Private Baldonado, forward!" Wondering which of them was in trouble, Pepe and Juan both reported, to find their old friend and priest from back home in Tularosa, New Mexico, happy-eyed Father Albert Braun, large of size and soul, now wearing a uniform and a chaplain's cross.

He waved aside an overnight-quarantine rule, said he was taking the boys to dinner, and promised the captain he'd have them back by midnight.

But how, wondered the captain, had he known when and where the *Pierce* would arrive?

Easy, boomed Father Braun. The boys' mother wrote him when they sailed. Simple logic and the newspapers told the rest. So much for top-secret information.

As the men debarked the next morning, a band greeted them, and, hearing as much Spanish as English among the Regiment, the musicians burst into "South of the Border" and asked what Mexico was doing in this war.

Jack Bradley, in charge of unloading the cargo holds of the *Pierce*, found "incredible SNAFUS in the 2-6-8 radar trucks. The connecting cables and M-4 directors were missing. We never were able to use the radar in combat, and had to rely on the old, not-too-reliable range-finders."

Hutchison, off the *Coolidge*, suspected sabotage when he found "our searchlights had the covers pierced, and the barrels and breaches of our guns had different threads on them and were useless. And everything was damaged from the bulk oil that leaked into the holds. It dripped out of everything."

Lucas, who had turned in the old searchlights at Fort Bliss for new ones, discovered the same old rejects being unloaded on Pier 7.

SNAFU? Or sabotage? *¿Quién sabe?*

They convoyed in trucks to Fort Stotsenberg. One group got lost and spent most of the night twisting back, towing the 3-inch guns behind the massive prime movers and huge searchlight trucks through the narrow little roads.

Sergeant Wayne Niemon had just reached his barracks when an alert sounded. "Our guns were packed in Cosmoline, and it took us all night to clean them. We never did learn what the alert was about."

As Huxtable's group rolled up, men from the advance detail greeted them with a sixteen-foot python they'd just caught under the barracks. James, dusty and sweaty, raced for the shower, to be jolted awake by icy water from mountain springs. Their barracks lacked certain amenities.

Fort Stotsenberg abutted Clark Field, which the 200th was assigned to guard. An old cavalry post, it now housed the 200th in a satellite cantonment area still under construction. *Sawali* barracks stood raised from the ground on pilasters, the windows shuttered against typhoon rains which, Harrington found, "deluged us for days and days, and we wondered why they didn't issue us web feet."

From the first they sensed something. Chintis "felt it coming. Tokyo Rose, or somebody like her, kept reminding us why we were here." Manuel Armijo – 'Army Joe' – heard "rumors there might be a war." Bob Mitchell didn't think so, "but the Filipinos did. They had blackout curtains in Manila, and sandbagged some of the buildings."

When Steen drove through the barrios, "the little kids ran out and asked, 'Japan boom-boom?' They knew the warlords had begun their powwows. When we got to camp they issued us live ammunition, and we knew something was in the wind."

Lorenzo Banegas had a premonition. "I see a dark cloud," he wrote his brother, "and you're behind it. Something is going to happen."

They all sensed it, though they gave it small thought – they were having too good a time – and when Secretary of the Navy Frank Knox warned on 11 November of "grim possibilities in the Pacific," they shrugged and called it scare tactics. What raised their adrenalin was the remark attributed to MacArthur: "The General," reported the regulars gleefully, "said he wanted soldiers, not Boy Scouts!"

War clouds thickened over Tokyo as the long struggle between the moderates and the militarists narrowed to a showdown between Konoye and his War Minister Hideki Tojo. On 6 September, while the *Pierce* wallowed in typhoon-tossed seas and the *Coolidge* prepared to sail, the Supreme War Council set a deadline. Konoye must break the diplomatic deadlock by 10 October. After that, they resolved, they would prepare immediately for war.[1]

Ambassador Grew continued to urge the President to meet with Konoye. Sir Robert Craigie, British Ambassador to Japan, believed such a meeting would be "a superb opportunity" to avert war.[2] So did Major General Charles Willoughby, Chief of Intelligence in the Far East.[3] Chief of Staff George C.

---

[1] *Pearl Harbor Hearings*, 20:4022. Morison 69.

[2] *Pearl Harbor Hearings*, 12:51.

[3] United States. Cong. Senate. Committee on the Judiciary, Internal Security Subcommittee, *Institute of Pacific Relations Hearings*. 82nd Cong., Washington: U.S. Govt. Printing Office: 1951, 2:382.

Marshall and Chief of Naval Operations Harold R. Stark believed a meeting could at least buy the four months they needed to arm the Philippines. In Washington, Nomura pressed urgently for the meeting.

Roosevelt and Hull remained intransigent.

The deadline passed with no reply from Washington. Konoye had failed. On 16 October his government fell, and with it the chance for peace. Within hours the new Premier was chosen, and on the eighteenth the thunder burst:

Tojo now led the nation.

The men of the 200th, exploring the island, were intrigued by tribes of pygmy aborigines who lived in the surrounding jungle. "Not much to see," Schmitz wrote home, "except the nasty villages and Igorots. They run around half dressed and live like hogs. Some have pants and some don't. When night comes, they just go to sleep where they are."

John Johnson thought, like most, "the Negritos didn't know anything. We had a cigarette lighter, and we said, 'Make fire! Magic!' The pygmy went into his hut and came out with a whole handful of lighters."

These small, barefoot natives, armed with bows and arrows, darted about the post at will. Attempts to bar them would have been futile, for they moved so quietly they could sneak past any guard. Their leader, known among the Americans as 'King Tut,' nattily dressed in top hat and loincloth, and carrying a cane, often sat in the reviewing stand with the commanding general to watch formal retreats.

A popular venture was to climb nearby Mount Pinatuba and sign one's name in a notebook in a rock cairn at the top. Go armed, they were told – the natives had but recently eschewed the gentle practice of headhunting. Accordingly, Aldrich and three buddies drew pistols, commandeered a Jeep, and set out. As they left the vehicle about halfway up, Negritos in loincloths surrounded them. One of the quartet grabbed his camera, started after a well-developed female, and tried to persuade her to remove her g-string for a nude photograph.

Before Aldrich knew it, "the situation deteriorated, and she was chasing my buddy, Jessie Adkins, around the clearing, swinging a machete at his heels. She was yelling at the top of her lungs – and so was he, screaming for us to start the Jeep and pull him in. We never did climb Mount Pinatuba."

Dan Jopling had other pursuits in mind. He remembered the attractive nurse from Fort Bliss. When twelve nurses arrived in October, he heard one mention her name, and he inquired further. Yes, Lucy Wilson was with them. Dan sped to Fort McKinley.

On 24 January 1941, Admiral James O. Richardson, Commander of the US Fleet in the Pacific, warned the President of a possible surprise attack on Pearl Harbor.[4] Three days later Ambassador Grew cabled a similar warning.[5] Washington, engrossed with the Lend-Lease bill for aid in the Atlantic, preferred to ignore the mounting crisis in the Pacific.

The Japanese continued to plan the attack. In August Tojo ordered details to be completed by November and opined that "war with the US would best begin in December or February." Military intelligence in Washington had this information by 3 November.[6]

Unaware, the 200th listened avidly to Don Bell's "News of the Day" over KMZH from Manila. "Alarmist, big mouthed, and brash," Harrington called Bell, "a real jingoist who kept daring the Japs to attack us."

So did the men listening. "Tojo," they sneered, "pee or get off the pot!"

They wore their new life like the latest fashion. For a few *pesos* a month, native houseboys made their beds, shined their shoes, gathered their dirty clothes, and returned them washed and starched – though, Ross found, "they smelled like carabao,

---

4 Mark Skinner Watson, *Prewar Plans and Preparations, United States Army in World War II,* Office of the Chief of Staff: Washington: U.S. Govt. Printing Office: 1950, 470.

5 United States. Dept. of State. *Peace and War: United States Foreign Policy 1931-1941*, Vol. II (Document No. 196), 618-19, Washington: U.S. Govt. Printing Office: 1943 (hereafter cited as *Peace and War*). And also, *Papers Relating to the Foreign Relations of the United States: Japan 1931-1941*, Vol. II, 133, Washington: U.S. Government Printing Office: 1943 (hereafter cited as *Foreign Relations*).

6 Watson 503.

because they washed in creeks, and we got that same smell, just like the Filipinos."

The officers really lived well. Hutchison's monthly mess bill of $7.50 "included every fancy dessert you could name, and Scotch and soda noon and night. Our laundry was $2.50, and included four sets of khakis a day, a set of whites, pajamas, and underwear six times a day."

Most of the families had left before the 200th arrived, sent homeward with elaborate *despedidas*, brave farewells that some knew might be final. A resulting order directed, "No shaving until further notice." It was a comic-opera gesture of men suddenly without women, a bit of bravado to make light of loneliness. It was rumor-making, though: Alfred Poe heard they were growing beards to go to Siberia.

Hutchison was bidden to attend a reception following the departure of the last dependents. "'Oh, for God's sake,' we grumbled, 'there's no women left and we're going to have a formal la-de-dah!' General King and his staff, all with beards, greeted us, stiff and formal, a damned saber and everything. We were politely sipping Scotch and soda, and no one wanted to be there.

"And all at once, 'TUMP, TUMP, TUMP,' went the drum, and General King said, 'Gentlemen, I have word that the tug pilot has just left the *Coolidge* and all the wives are at sea!' And the band broke out and here comes – you've never seen such a striptease! I was a young lieutenant – I saw more that night than I'd ever seen in my life!"

It was another stout-hearted gesture of frivolity.

For the most part, Lieutenant Ed Lingo found the post a bit stuffy. "We were required to change uniforms twice a day, and to change into shorts for golf and tennis. We had to wear whites at the Club, even on informal 'Wimpy Burger nights' when Chaplain Howden and I went to play cribbage."

Lucas seldom went to the Club because "the regulars looked down on us. We were new and National Guard, and we were tearing up their little playhouse."

The NCO Club was less formal, but here, too, the 200th drew glassy glances. The Hispanics and Indians felt it doubly. The felony of being Guardsmen, compounded by race, drew snide insinuation or outright rudeness. They didn't stand for it long. After several brawls, Sage declared it off limits to his men, and added that "we'd build our own club." Time would run out before they could.

Meanwhile they frequented the dance halls and honky-tonks in Angeles or the nearby *barrio* they called 'Sloppy Bottom,' where, tilting their heads to guzzle the popular San Miguel beer, their startled glances often espied the pythons that slithered along the chicken wire beneath the thatched ceilings.

Off duty, rank meant little to the New Mexicans. When Captain Otho Shamblin, easygoing until pushed, got crosswise with another officer, he told him to go to hell and moved in with the enlisted men, where, he said, he'd rather be anyway.

Clayton Irish, newly commissioned a second lieutenant, took his buddy Harrington to the stuffily exclusive Army-Navy Club in Manila. "We had just started on our first drinks when a regular officer came to our table and made it clear to Irish that officers didn't fraternize with enlisted men. Irish icily said he knew the protocol, and ordered another round." A friend was a friend in the 200th.

Hutchison was delighted when officers of the 26th Cavalry offered the use of their horses. "All us old cavalry types wrote our wives to send saddles, send bridles, send boots, and riding breeches, and polo mallets. That's where we had our fun on weekends."

McCahon "worked from seven until noon and took off. We went weekends to Manila, or to Baguio, or to the small submarine base at Subic Bay, or back into the hills. We were loose, we had more money than we could spend, and we had a ball until December."

It was fairly easy to get passes to Manila, and the boys were drawn to the teeming port, where modern buildings rose above the palm-lined boulevards and contrasted oddly with the old Spanish churches in the Intramuros. The streets pulsed with Filipina girls in bright native dresses, old ladies with betel-reddened teeth, turbaned Moros, and costumed Orientals. Vendors hawked their wares in a dozen jargons. Red-and-yellow Pambusco buses, which burned alcohol made from sugar cane and emitted funny-smelling exhaust fumes, honked wildly at heavy carabao-drawn carts, and pastel-painted Jeeps raced in and out of the heavy traffic.

They absorbed the sights and sounds and odors. The whole country smelled like a carabao wallow to Lieutenant James Walter Donaldson. They watched the great, clumsy carabao that lay in muddy pools with only nose, eyes, and horns visible until, with a lumbering upheaval and the sound of sucking mud, they erupted and took off. The boys rode the two-wheeled, pony-pulled *calesas* or boarded the narrow-gauge railway for the dense back country, and they wrote home enthusiastically of their adventures.

"Dear Folks," penned Schmitz innocently. "Sunday we went to Subic Bay and went swimming in the China Sea. They have gun emplacements over there that fold back into a hill and you can't see them. They are large, and plenty of them. This island is really protected."

They lay peaceful and quiet, those seven thousand pearls cast by a careless goddess into the Philippine Sea; but they were luxuries Washington was willing to forfeit. There would be no naval reinforcement of the Philippines, the President told a staff meeting in January 1941.[7]

Although by summer belated plans for Philippine defense had begun, they would not, Marshall announced, "jeopardize . . . major efforts made in the theater of the Atlantic."[8] Not until September did the Joint Board agree that reinforcing the islands might deter the Japanese from a Pacific war, and start planning to accomplish that defense by March 1942.

Early in November Japanese invasion forces began to sail toward their assigned launching points. General Homma established his command post in Formosa and awaited final orders.

* * *

7 Watson 124-25.

8 Louis Morton, *The War in the Pacific: Strategy and Command: The First Two Years,* Office of the Chief of Military History, Dept. of the Army, Washington: U.S. Govt. Printing Office: 1962, 98.

The central necessity of WPO-3 was the defense of Manila Bay, the only harbor west of Hawaii capable of serving the US fleet. If the Japanese landed on Luzon, delaying tactics would slow their advance while American forces entrenched on Bataan Peninsula, whence, with Corregidor, they could defend the bay for six months. By that time the Navy would arrive with ground forces. Naval Intelligence analysts, however, estimated a minimum of two years to fight across seven thousand miles of open sea lanes.

The strategy also assumed a single enemy. Yet the current war plan, 'Rainbow 5,' predicated a global conflict with Germany the prime target, implied the loss of Guam, Wake, and the Philippines, and planned no reinforcement. MacArthur objected, and on 1 October outlined a plan to defend the entire archipelago. Not until 21 November did the Joint Board approve. MacArthur went into action, reorganized the Philippine forces, and on 3 December named Lieutenant General Jonathan Wainwright Commander of the North Luzon Force.[9]

Even then the President planned to cut Pacific strength to make available more matériel to Britain.[10] Meanwhile, production was slow and transportation inadequate; training a late-called citizens' army was ponderous; and British and Russian needs still took priority over America's own.

The 192nd and 194th Tank Battalions arrived soon after the 200th. Additional guns and planes trickled in a few at a time, small drops in an ocean-sized bucket. MacArthur repeatedly requested more; Major General 'Hap' Arnold pushed for more air defense; and at length Marshall detailed for MacArthur plans for immediate reinforcements. The letter was never sent: It was dated 5 December.[11]

Antiaircraft artillery in the Philippines comprised the 60th on Corregidor and the 200th on Luzon. Plans for additional units never materialized. Skimpy but scrappy, with a fifth of the men

---

9 Foregoing WPO-3 and MacArthur's plans, cf. Louis Morton, *The War in the Pacific: The Fall of the Philippines,* Office of the Chief of Military History, Dept. of the Army, Washington: U.S. Govt. Printing Office: 1953, 61-69.

10 Watson 363-365.

11 Morton 48 & n.

and guns needed, the 77 officers and 1,732 enlisted men of the 200th set up to defend Clark Field and its thirty-five B-17s with their one battery of .50-caliber machine guns, the twenty-two 37-mm. guns (seven of which were found defective and sent to Manila for repair), and twelve 3-inch guns (of which one had to be sent to Corregidor with a faulty director).

Further complicating the chore was the difficulty of setting up gun emplacements. Peck recorded that "sites which in war we would have to use to protect Clark Field . . . were closed to us. They were private land and only the military reservation was open to us." (Even after the war began, Harrington remembered, "Captain Sherman was detailed to Manila to request legal authority to emplace 200th guns on Philippine territory.")

The same ammunition shortage that had plagued them at Bliss dogged them at Clark. Lingo's platoon "was told definitely, 'DO NOT BREAK THE SEAL on the ammunition box'. So prior to the day of the war, we had never seen a live round."

They set up the 2-6-8. The lack of ammunition prevented their discovering, until the actual attack, that the short cables connecting the 2-6-8 to the searchlights ran too close to the guns: The first blast knocked out the radar. Meanwhile, Steen, on the searchlight crew, "had fun trying to beat the 2-6-8 to be on target. When we did, we got a case of beer."

The Indians were especially adept at spotting planes. At a certain sound on their earphones they signaled their crew to turn on the searchlights. There, in the beam, would appear the plane. They seldom missed.

"The sands are running fast," Ambassador Grew wired Hull on 3 November; war could result "with dangerous and dramatic suddenness.[12] It was another warning ignored. Japan must be given an ultimatum, Hull snapped. Not yet, pled Marshall and Stark; give them four months to reinforce the Philippines.

---

[12] *Peace and War*, (Document No. 245), 772-75.

*   *   *

Japan also sought a reprieve. On 4 November the moderates pushed through two alternate proposals to submit to Hull, and that day Saburo Kurusu, unaware that detailed plans for war had that day been completed, slipped quietly out of Tokyo for Washington to aid Nomura in a last attempt to reach a *modus vivendi* before the deadline.

"It is absolutely necessary," Foreign Minister Togo wired Nomura, "this agreement be completed by the 25th of this month."[13] The intercept was in Hull's hands on the seventh. It meant, he knew, agreement or war.

The desperate Nomura sought an audience with the President.

McCahon felt a thickening of intensity at Fort Stotsenberg. "We had blackouts and drills, and we wore gas masks. We knew they were coming, but being young and naive, we thought we were well prepared."

Villaseñor watched the guns traverse and elevate, and he voiced the common opinion: "Those Japs won't stand a chance!"

Kurusu arrived in Washington on 15 November. Nomura met with the President three days later, and on the twentieth presented the final proposal and pled for a quick decision. The offer contained unprecedented concessions, and Kurusu opened the diplomatic door for abrogation of the Tripartite Pack. The President was evasive. Stark and Marshall added their pleas: The Fourth Marines were being evacuated from Shanghai, troops were en route to Manila, and another 21,000 would sail on 8 December. On the twenty-second a frantic Tokyo extended the deadline to the twenty-ninth.[14] Hull read the intercept and noted the date. "After that," he said, "war." [15]

---

[13] Morison 71. *Pearl Harbor Hearings,* 14:1055.

[14] *Pearl Harbor Hearings,* 12:165. Bruce R. Bartlett, *Cover-Up: The Politics of Pearl Harbor, 1941-1946*, (New Rochelle, NY: Arlington House, 1978), 47.

[15] Cordell Hull, *Memoirs of Cordell Hull* (New York: Macmillan, 1948) 1074.

In Deming, New Mexico, the citizens packed an enormous Christmas box for the boys of the 200th.

Older men were sent home. Draftees over thirty-five had already gone. Those over twenty-eight who wished to go would sail on 10 December. Armijo applied – he had a new baby girl at home. Gulbas applied also and, pressured by his captain, relinquished his sergeant's stripes to another in line; he wouldn't be needing them.

"Boys," he said gleefully, "I have had a wonderful vacation!"

"ALL MILITARY PERSONNEL REPORT TO YOUR UNITS IMMEDIATELY!"

Sergeant Orville Padilla heard the loudspeaker in a nightclub in Baguio. Foy and Graef heard it in a movie house in Manila. They returned to find the 200th on full alert and setting up in the field. It was 23 November.

They built dummy gun emplacements of bamboo to mask their paucity of guns. They stocked shells in underground shelters. After a week in the field, Sergeant Earl Harris knew there was "no question that war was coming, and where it would start. We were under complete blackout every night. After dark, one platoon at a time came in to shower, and went back out."

American reconnaissance planes flew daily over Formosa to observe the gigantic Japanese buildup. A Japanese task force steamed down the China coast.

Lucas took the searchlight battery out on night missions to pick up anything that flew over. "The first time out we picked up planes, but they'd turn immediately and fly away." He reported this to startled authorities at Clark. There'd been no American planes in that sector, they advised, and there would not be any that night. Try again. "We went back, set up, and picked up the same thing – more planes – and they'd turn and fly away."

Maynard Meuli felt a sudden unfriendliness on the part of some Filipinos. Talk of going home stopped. When Corporal Richard Trask went to the chaplain about an unreasonable captain, Howden advised him to do nothing. "We are on the verge of war," he said.

"Somebody," said Sergeant Jack Finley, "knows a lot more than we do."

At a tense White House meeting on 25 November the President said an attack was likely, perhaps by the following Monday, Stimson recorded. "The question was how we should maneuver them into the position of firing the first shot without allowing too much danger to ourselves."[16]

On that same day Army Intelligence notified Stimson that a large Japanese fleet carrying five divisions had been sighted off Formosa.[17]

Steen counted patrol planes that took off in the pre-dawn darkness. "They always told us how many were going out. A couple of mornings there was one extra plane. We reported it – they may have just thought we were nuts. Later we thought maybe they were Japs off a carrier."

Shillito observed a string of fires in the field each night in a straight line, and wondered what their significance might be. He would remember that path of fire later.

Admiral Stark and Brigadier General Leonard T. Gerow (standing in for Marshall) drafted a memo designed to avert, or at least postpone, war until the Philippines could be defended.[18] They were not told the President had already made his decision.

On the afternoon of 26 November Hull handed the ultimatum to the horrified diplomats: America had rejected the *modus vivendi*. Nomura paled and sat abruptly.

Marshall and Stark were equally horrified. They could now expect attack at any moment, they radioed MacArthur, Admiral

---

16 Stimson Diary, 25 November 1941, *Pearl Harbor Hearings*, 11:5433. See also Stimson's testimony, *Pearl Harbor Hearings*, 11:5421-22.

17 Morison 76.

18 Dated 27 November but drafted before the *modus vivendi* was rejected. Morison 74. Rear Admiral Edwin T. Layton, U.S.N. (Ret.) et al., *And I Was There* (New York: William Morrow, 1985) 210-11.

Thomas C. Hart, and Lieutenant General Walter C. Short, and stressed orders from the President: *Japan must commit the first overt act.*[19]

On 29 November Konoye, backed by the majority at a top-level conference in Tokyo, begged Tojo to "proceed . . . without war."[20] The argument was futile. At that meeting the militarists passed the final resolution for attack. Tojo instructed the diplomats to continue negotiating. They were not told of the decision.

Gulbas and Armijo were packed and waiting to go home. Jopling wangled a pass to Fort McKinley to see Lucy. It would be their last time together before the top blew.

The commanding officer of the 26th Cavalry told McCahon nostalgically that he'd "sure like to have a cavalry review once again. But I don't have a band that knows one."

McCahon did. "We'd played a lot of 'em in the old days. So we did one for the 26th. It may have been the last cavalry review ever done in the army."

It was the last of a lot of things.

Tokyo, 1 December: "Climb Mount Niitaka." This was the signal the commanders of the striking force awaited. Zero Hour was set for 8 December.[21] The attack could still be canceled if America eased toward a *modus vivendi*.

Washington, 3 December: Government Intelligence intercepted instructions to Nomura to burn all codes except the one needed for the last section of a fourteen-part message. That afternoon Japanese personnel were seen burning papers behind the Embassy.

Luzon, night of 3-4 December: Men on the 2-6-8 reported alien planes over the island, and American reconnaissance planes spotted a large Japanese convoy moving south.

---

19 United States. Cong. *Report of the Joint Committee on the Investigation of the Pearl Harbor Attack.* 79th Cong. Washington: U.S. Govt. Printing Office: 1946, 199-201 (hereafter cited as *Pearl Harbor Report*). *Pearl Harbor Hearings*, 14:1083, 1389, 1407 and 17:2666. Layton 210-11.

20 *Pearl Harbor Hearings*, 14:1406 and 20:4012-13. Morison 77-78.

21 7 December U.S. and Hawaiian time, 8 December (beyond the International Date Line) in Tokyo and the Philippines.

Cheltenham, Maryland, 4 December: "East Winds, Rain." This was the war message for which the naval receiving station had been monitoring since 28 November. Authorities immediately relayed it to the President.

Washington, 6 December: Roosevelt, in a final quixotic gesture, appealed personally to Hirohito for peace. The message died in the Emperor's hands. That afternoon the first thirteen-part section of the long "pilot message" to Nomura was intercepted. The President read it that night and turned to Harry Hopkins.

"This means war," he said.

MacArthur ordered a full alert, and Wainwright remarked an increased tension at his headquarters, but for most of the men it was a typical Sunday. Hutchison watched the afternoon polo match. "Wainwright sat between my legs. I was drinking Scotch and soda – not a worry. We beat the Manila Polo Club that had just beaten the Australians."

Peck and Sage strolled to the Clark Field theater where they munched buttered popcorn and watched a Dick Tracy serial.

In the field, Jack Fleming wrote a letter to Janie. Some of the men talked lazily about having a party that night, if someone could get some booze.

That night Baldonado heard strange sounds through his earphones. "Unidentified aircraft," he reported. An immediate order crackled back: "Shut down and report to camp." Corporal Glen Farmer, on the Battery F switchboard, held off a blackout while B-17s took off. He didn't know their destination.

Hutchison was duty officer for his unit that night. "It was a boring situation, so I loaded the Jeep with Coca-Cola and rum and took some to all my platoons. It was just another night of alert and not alert. This party lasted until nearly daylight."

Toward morning Corporal Walter Johnson, at his station, listened to music on a homemade radio. Suddenly an excited announcer broke in. Johnson gasped. He grabbed the phone. "Tell the Captain –" his voice sounded like a stranger to itself. "Tell him – they're bombing Pearl Harbor!"

BOOK II

BATTLING BASTARDS

"On December 7, 1941, when the Japanese unexpectedly attacked the Philippine Islands, the first point bombed was Fort Stotsenberg. The 200th Coast Artillery (AA), assigned to defend this fort, was the first unit in the Philippines, under General of the Army Douglas MacArthur, to go into action and fire at the enemy, also the first one to go into action defending our flag in the Pacific."

General Jonathan Wainwright
December 1945

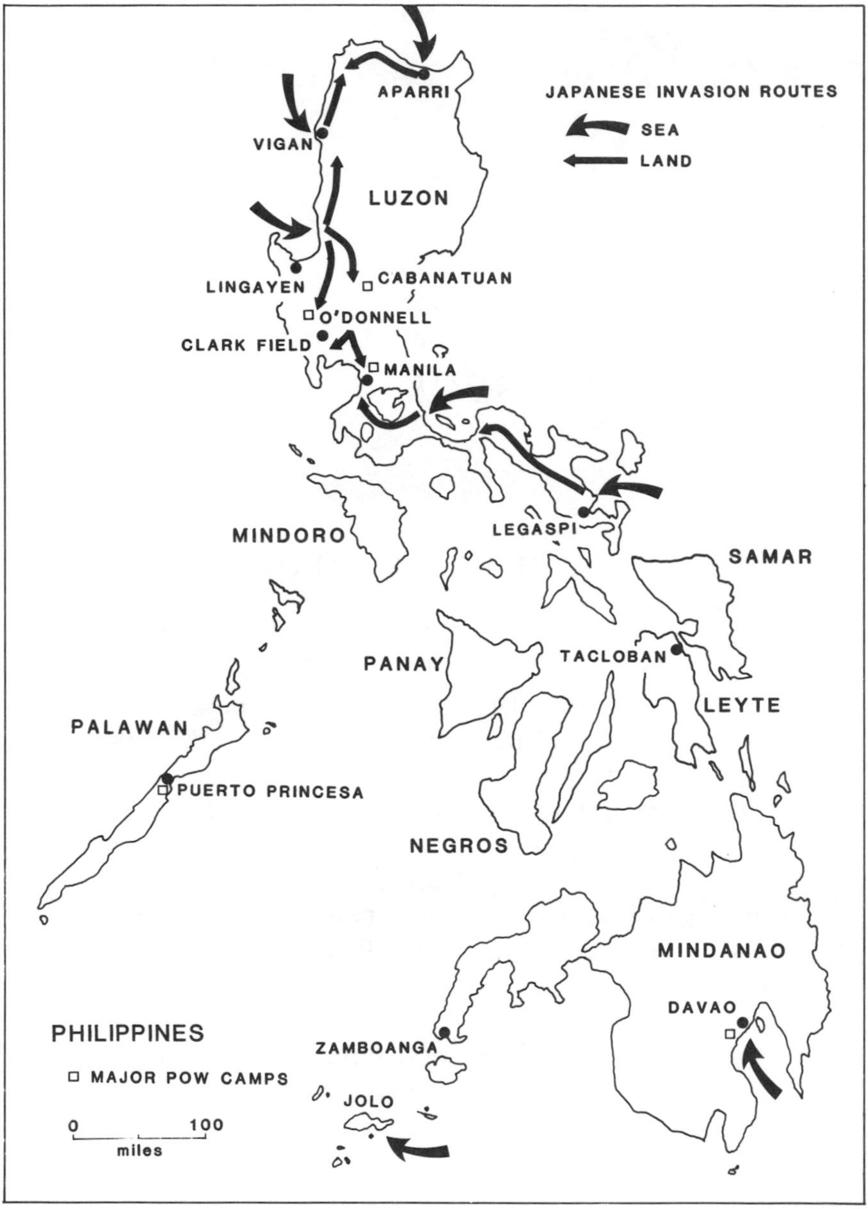
APARRI
JAPANESE INVASION ROUTES
SEA
LAND
VIGAN
LUZON
LINGAYEN
CABANATUAN
O'DONNELL
CLARK FIELD
MANILA
LEGASPI
MINDORO
SAMAR
TACLOBAN
PANAY
LEYTE
PALAWAN
PUERTO PRINCESA
NEGROS
MINDANAO
DAVAO
PHILIPPINES
ZAMBOANGA
MAJOR POW CAMPS
JOLO
0
100
miles

– 5 –

THE DAWN COMES UP LIKE THUNDER

"We heard they'd hit Pearl Harbor and Clark Field was being bombed. But it was peaceful. I thought, 'This is a hell of a war.'"

– Sergeant Jack Finley –

"AIR RAID PEARL HARBOR. THIS IS NO DRILL."

The intercept jolted the radio operator at Naval Headquarters in Manila from routine boredom at 0230. Admiral Hart had the news by 0300 and broadcast it to the fleet, but failed to alert MacArthur, whose headquarters personnel learned it from a commercial broadcast half an hour later, about the same time Corporal Johnson was relaying it to his captain. Not until 0530 did the general receive official notification from Washington: War had begun. Almost simultaneously Air Commander Lewis Brereton requested permission to bomb Formosa. Prepare but wait, he was told.

As Japanese bombs hurtled into Pearl Harbor, Japanese naval pilots, scheduled to hit Clark Field at the same time, cursed the thick fog that had settled over Formosa. Grounded until it lifted, they had lost all chance of surprise. They paced by their planes and pled for the gods of Holy Nippon to clear the fog before American bombers hit them first.

Deployed in the field, Batteries G and H, unaware of bombs and broadcasts, were still trying valiantly to kill the last of the rum. Hutchison stretched out in his tent, mused that he'd given his boys a pretty good party, and that they deserved it. It was 0430.

At 0500 someone shook him, and a voice sliced through his euphoria. "Hutch, we're at war!"

Daylight was graying the field when Steen went off duty. The Japs had hit Pearl Harbor, his relief told him. "I'd never heard of Pearl Harbor, but at the guard shack the radios were all on and the news blasting, and I thought, 'Well, hell, the war's started,' so I ran to my barracks and started waking everybody up. Didn't realize how serious it was."

Sergeant Jesse Finley did – he'd fought in World War I, and knew the meaning of foxholes. "Dig," he ordered his men. They griped, but they dug.

The day shifted into gear and the radios alternated music, news, and conjecture. "At this time," Don Bell blurted, "Clark Field is being bombed." At his command post close by the bomb-release line, Finley's son, Jack, Sergeant of the Guard, looked out. "It was peaceful, and I said, 'This is a hell of a war!' I took the phone, with an extension cord, to a little ravine where I could get in case we were bombed, measured out my line, and went back to my radio."

Only two radar sets operated in the Philippines, but air watchers wired or phoned into the Nielson Field Interceptor Command. As reports of enemy flights began to flood from the north, B-17s and pursuit planes were ordered aloft. All morning they circled in clusters at different altitudes.

On Formosa, Japanese nerves grew tauter as the thick fog continued to swirl. Concluding from a message intercepted at 0800 that they would be attacked within two hours, they began to issue gas masks.

At 0925, Brereton, still pleading to attack, chafed in Manila at a report of Japanese bombers over Lingayen Gulf. They were few, however, overflew unimportant targets, and turned north.

By 1015 the Formosan fog began to clear, and 108 twin-engine Mitsubishi bombers revved up their motors. "*Banzai!*" the pilots shouted above the roar, taxied, rose like a swarm of killer bees, and peeled south.

The Regiment watched, waited, and wagered when they'd be hit.

Corporal Juan Manuel 'Bob' Chavez returned from early church – it was a day of obligation. "We're at war," someone in the orderly room told him. Bob, from Cochiti Pueblo, came from warrior stock. Commandeering a truck, he ferried his machine gun and ammunition to his foxhole and prepared for action.

A few straggled in from off post. Sergeant Willie Burrola's malfunctioning gun was on its way to Corregidor for repair. "We went to Angeles and raised hell, and in the morning we were at Stotsenberg waiting for our gun. It never even got to Corregidor."

Romero rode in that morning in a horse-drawn *calesa* loaded with soldiers, and noted the frantic activity. "What the hell's going on?" he demanded.

"Get your gear, Chief," yelled a buddy. "We're at war!"

Senter heard it when he came off duty from tracking enemy aircraft. "We listened on my old ham radio to reports from San Francisco and Manila, all gung-ho – going to set the world on fire."

Overhead the planes kept circling.

HONOLULU BOMBED! proclaimed Manila headlines. From KMZH Don Bell broadcast reports as they came in. The men listened avidly but, knowing Bell's predilection for the sensational, some discounted it. Louis Mendoza laughed it off as a "bunch of bull." James Gunter thought it "some kind of soap opera." Merle Kindel was stunned, but shrugged that "Pearl Harbor's a long way from here." Jonathan Burns heard it in the mess hall, but paid little attention. He had a meal to prepare.

John Johnson made the ice run early, and found Manila chasing its tail. Radios blared and shrill-voiced newsboys hawked extras. Trucks raced troops to guard water, phone, and fuel installations, and air raid sirens shredded the air with false alarms. "We heard Pearl Harbor had been bombed, and then that it hadn't, and then it had. We just picked up the ice and headed back for Stotsenberg."

Aldrich heard it in the shower. "We slipped over to the radio truck to listen, and then to our duty stations. Everybody was buzzing with excitement. 'We're in the soup now.'"

Sakelares was off duty "listening to my radio in my bunk, and I heard they were overhead, so I blew my whistle and called the guys outside. They lined up and wondered what the hell I was doing. I said, 'We're under attack,' and they laughed at me."

Out in the field, Shillito awoke with a monstrous after-party headache, and the news didn't help it any. "Of all days," he grumbled, "for a war to start!"

Supply Sergeant Earl Harris thought he should issue the gas masks that "a week or so before they'd gotten us out in the middle of the night to draw. Our training masks were used up, so they gave us these, but our orders were not to issue them, to put them in the store room." Harris set about getting permission to pass them to the troops.

The morning jerked along. Moods of quiet alternated with bursts of excited speculation, and they hung suspended between peace and war, in a strange isolation. It was a little like swimming under water.

In the turquoise sky the planes kept circling.

The small enemy force reported earlier had loosed a few bombs and turned back; the main attacking force winged its massive way undetected. They were approaching the Luzon coast as the all-clear signaled the B-17s to land, refuel, and load on bombs for the strike MacArthur had just authorized.

By 1130 the Americans were on the ground. Pilots ran for a quick lunch while the planes were gassed up; crews began to load the three-hundred-pound bombs. Almost precisely as the last B-17 had landed, the first Mitsubishis roared over the northern coast. Reports began machine-gunning into Interceptor Command; pursuit planes took off from Nielson Field to cover Clark.

Clark was under attack, the radios shrilled. Ojinaga looked up. "That's crazy!" But when he tried to phone Captain William Schuetz, the wires were dead.

Foy, at the Battery H command post, was having the same trouble. "We couldn't get through to Clark. It seemed like some of the wires were crossed." They didn't learn until later they'd been sabotaged.

Interceptor Command ordered all planes aloft for incoming attack. They didn't know that Clark Field never received the warning.

Across the world in Albuquerque, New Mexico, Janie Fleming came home from church. "I knew the boys were on alert – the last letter John wrote was from out in the field. We were – I guess – preparing for war. Gertrude Finley picked me up and we went to her mother's, where she and her baby were living. After dinner the telephone rang and someone said to turn on the radio. The Japs had just attacked Pearl Harbor and Fort Stotsenberg!

"We were absolutely speechless, scared out of our minds. We felt like the world was coming to an end. And then we didn't hear from them again. That day began a living hell for all of us."

The men still laughed at the false reports, but it became uneasy laughter. Foy got "a funny feeling, like somebody knew more than we did." He kept on trying to contact Clark Field. So did others. By 1210 every fighter on Luzon was aloft, except those on Clark. The warning hadn't come.

Rhea Tow scanned the skies. "A Navy plane circled in, talking to the tower. They passed the word that Jap bombers were headed our way and to stand by, but 'Don't fire until fired upon.'"

Maybe not, growled John Gamble, but his guns would damned sure be ready. "The Japs can't do anything to us!"

Lee Roach was right by the runway. "We just sat around our guns waiting for them mothers to come, and waiting for the chow truck."

Arthur Smith fiddled with his height-finder, and checked his instruments that weren't even hooked up yet. Manuel Armijo laughed at him. "I've got nothing to worry about," he said. "I'm going home tomorrow."

So was Gulbas. "Come get me if my call comes," he told a buddy and started for the PX: He fancied a carabao steak.

Pilots began to return from lunch. The air roared as P-40s revved their motors. Someone whistled "Frenesi" off key.

East of Mount Arayat, an echelon of Mitsubishis peeled off for Iba. The rest, flashing like needles through the gauzy clouds, streaked toward Clark Field.

– 6 –

FIRST TO FIRE

"One minute you're at peace, and the next you're being bombed. It's a big transformation, from peace to war. And it's quite harrowing."
– Sergeant Nicholas Chintis–

Foy was still trying to contact Clark Field when they heard the drone.

There were fifty-four of them in two perfect V-formations, "so high they looked translucent" to Sergeant Arthur Baclawski. Clark Field spread naked below. "Hey, look at the Navy!" someone yelled, and they began to cheer. The drone grew to a roar and then the raucous wail of the air-raid siren cut through the din.

"Navy, hell!" shouted Romero. It was 1235.

Standing in chow line, Banegas saw "a beautiful cloud of white planes. Then little black things started falling and we thought they were leaflets. We started running toward them." As they fell, they glinted in the sunlight.

Villaseñor heard a noise "like newspapers in the wind, and then a forest of brown mushrooms. I fell on the ground, and I kept bouncing in the shock waves."

Harrington dived into a ditch, straight into a rifle barrel. "Get that damned Springfield out of my face," he yelled.

Something hit Sakelares and his leg began to swell. "Some damned fools were standing out there firing pistols. And I fired a little, too."

Bill Gurulé thought it "good fun, like hunting rabbits. We didn't know any better."

Huxtable was eating. "My mess kit flew off the table when the first bomb hit. I dove out and crawled under the barracks. Every time a bomb hit, I'd bounce." He quickly discovered he lay on a bed of angry red ants.

Drake and Baldonado rushed from the canteen, Drake with a beer. "I'd only had one swig. I jumped in the ditch and Pepe landed on top. I wasn't mad about the bombers, or Pepe nearly crushing me to death, but, damn it, he made me spill my beer!"

Explosions rocked the ground, and between geysers of flame men ran like ants. Smoke poured black from the line. Aldrich "suddenly knew fear for the first time. You get a strange metallic taste in your mouth. I didn't know what fear was until that day."

Burns crawled under a kitchen shelf. The dishes above him rattled like machine guns.

Harris had just gotten permission to issue gas masks. "They were packed in tin containers, and we were opening them and stacking them in the truck when the thing hit."

In the showers, McCahon "grabbed my helmet and hit the floor, naked as a jaybird except for that tin hat," while Lucas "ran for the commodes and thought, 'What am I doing here – three feet off the ground and don't know where to go?'" They grabbed some clothes and ran for their troops.

At his command post in the field, Finley watched horrified. "The bombs just marched up the field. I grabbed my phone and ran, got tangled in the wire, and did two flips."

Chintis was eating at his battle station. "The pork chops went one way and I went the other. And I thought about those chops for the next four years. Then I thought, 'Those guys are trying to kill me!' That's when I got mad."

Arvil Gale "threw my mess kit straight up – even the chocolate cake. Then I did another stupid thing – I stood up. Concussion from the next bomb knocked me on my can."

The mess truck finished serving Battery E. Privates Douglas Sanders and Roy Schmid joked a little with the gun crews and started back across the field. Suddenly Munsey found himself "tackled and thrown into a foxhole as the first bomb exploded. It was a direct hit on the mess truck and both fellows were killed. One was my good friend."

Foy heard the swish of bombs and "then all hell broke loose. They decimated our planes, and we couldn't hit them. We didn't even fire the 37-mms. The 3-inch guns tried, but they couldn't reach that high with those old powder-train fuzes. Their maximum range was 27,000 feet, and the Nips flew just beyond."

He and Hutchison sat out the bombing in a carabao wallow, smoking big cigars. Hutch remembered the polo game the day before and mused on the hell-and-heaven differences in life.

Behind the bombers streaked the Zeros, darting, strafing, darting skyward again, and for the first time Adolfo Hernandez saw "that old Rising Sun under their wings, and knew we was at war."

They could see the pilots grinning from their cockpits. Shock turned to fury, and the big guns opened up. Wellington Hollingsworth and James Chaney brought down the first Japanese plane in the Philippines. Furiously firing the 37-mm., they were quickly out of ammunition. Dodging strafer bullets, Edras Montoya sprinted thirty yards to the trench that held their shells, raced back, and continued feeding them ammunition.

At the fort, Lee Pelayo ran for his rifle. "Strafers were everywhere, and us shooting with our damned automatics. I had on coveralls – unbuttoned – and Melvin Waldrop's Browning threw two shells right in my pants. A strafer was coming at me, and I thought, 'That sonofabitch got me!'"

Running for his unit, Wallace 'Dub' Phillips "bumped into a couple of water-cooled .50-caliber guns. I stayed and helped. The strafers would dive for the revetments, then turn back right over us. It was a beautiful place to get them. You could see the rounds entering their aluminum skins."

Steen ran across the motor pool. "Floyd Johnson dived under a truck and blood started gushing from his head. I thought they'd hit him. Pulled him out – and hell, he'd only hit his head on the rear axle." From then on he was 'Bloody' Johnson.

Demetri Doolis dived under a tank car, "but it smelled hot, so I got out and looked. It was hundred-octane gas. I got the hell out to a hillside. There was a fellow with a BAR, scared to shoot. I said, 'Give me that thing,' and I wrapped the strap around a branch and emptied the clip into a Zero."

Lucas got to his men just as the strafers hit. "We formed a line in a trench dug for a water pipe. Those with automatic rifles turned them wide open, and those BARs were shooting the tops of our buildings down, and the telephone wires."

"If there'd been a smart Jap," said Burrola, "he could've swooped down that ditch and killed us all."

As smoke rolled over them, someone yelled "Gas!" The men in some batteries had masks, but few had taken them seriously. 'Pappy' Graves reached in his carrier and pulled out a bottle of gin. Worthen's was stuffed with candy. "What'll I do?" he yelled.

"Well," said Sergeant Dick Carpenter, pulling his own mask on, "you can't crawl in here with me, 'Fat Boy'!"

Finley, in his shallow trench, had only a training mask, and it leaked. "I didn't know what to do. A Filipino came running and yelled, 'Stay here and you'll be killed,' and took off hightailing. And I was right behind him." When Finley returned later to retrieve the telephone, his trench had been gutted.

Harris was still opening gas masks, "in this grass shack, with planes strafing back and forth, a row of barracks at a time. They missed ours. We thought the smoke and fumes were gas – and here I sat with all these masks unopened, and our men out there in the field."

Gamble raced across a clearing in a Jeep, but halfway through the strafers hit it. Enraged, he ran the rest of the way to his battery, flame haired and flame tempered, yelling to his boys to "Give 'em hell!"

Confined in the post hospital with minor infections, several men from F Battery demanded their clothes. When the orderlies refused, Mike Pulice's adrenalin rose. He had to join his battery, he insisted. They'd be having hell.

They were. Pilots poured from the mess hall and raced to their planes. Strafers swept the field and cut them down. Some made it. The 200th tried to cover the P-40s, but they had little chance against the swarming Zeros. Steen watched, helpless. "The runways were so cratered only two or three got off, and we hit one in the smoke and confusion. He went down in the field, but he crawled out."

Another wasn't so lucky. John West watched, anguished, as a pilot, parachuting from his burning plane, was machine-gunned in midair.

James 'Red' Hunter, an indifferent peacetime soldier, became a fury in combat. "Get the hell down," he shouted to Sergeant Paul Womack. "Trying to get yourself killed?" He shoved Womack aside and began feeding shells into the gun.

Womack, freed, raced for a burning plane. As he dragged the pilot out, his arm took a bullet. Blood drenched his shirt. Phillips ran toward him. Womack waved his bloody arm and grinned. "Look," he yelled. "Purple Heart!"

Near Charley Ross's entrenchment, "[William] 'Shorty' Coleman ran to a crewless gun, cut a fuze to zero timing, and shot one out of the sky – just by himself. He made sergeant right there."

Bob Chavez manned his gun alone the entire battle.

Steve Alex learned quickly about firing procedures. "We had never fired our 37s until that day. We pressed on the foot pedal, and didn't know those things exploded at the cut-off of air. A leaf almost would set it off. The Japs dived low, and we fired at a low angle, into little revetments of bamboo and dirt, and the bamboo slivers sticking up detonated our shells. We were blowing holes through our trucks and tents. Well – we learned that day."

So did Niemon. "We had our ammunition half buried in black sand. We felt so smart, getting it out of sight. But the first time we fired, the vibration caved in all our ditches, and we had to dig out all the shells."

It also buried Lalo Ramos. Primitivo Peña dug him out.

Shillito noted grimly that "the bombers came directly down the track where we'd seen those odd strings of fires at night in the field. I doubt that it was coincidence."

Don Harris manned his radio in a hole. "My platoon sergeant kept vaulting over the sandbags dodging a plane that came at him from one side and then the other. Once he looked down and said 'Harris, are you scared?' I said, 'You're damned right I'm scared!'"

So was the kid who came running to Hernandez with his hand clapped to his neck where he'd been hit. "I pried his hand loose, and then I began to laugh. He'd been stung by a bee."

In the hospital, the boys from Battery F still couldn't get their clothes. "To hell with it," snorted Pulice, and as one, still in their pajamas, they dashed for the door.

At Fort McKinley, before communications completely broke down, someone handed Lucy Wilson a telegram. Was she all right? Dan Jopling wanted to know. She had no way to answer.

The wounded began to arrive. "We worked around the clock. It was pure hell, seeing all those patients with limbs and parts of bodies missing, and all sorts of hideous wounds, having to wait in line to get into surgery."

It made them sick the way the planes, lined up on the ground, were bombed in place. The 200th motor pool fared no better. Their 150 trucks, parked with military precision, made a beautiful target.

The 200th had not set up all its equipment, and what they had was defective or outmoded. It would plague them the rest of the war. The powder-train fuzes could not reach the high-flying bombers, ammunition was corroded, and most of the ancient shells were duds.

Hutchison checked the 3-inch guns, "which had been certified as being personally inspected. The shell cases were green with corrosion. Every time we fired a shot, they had to be cleaned to go into the breechbox, and we had to break the frozen fuzes with a wrench. We had World War I weapons, and our modified ammunition had too much muzzle pressure for the guns to withstand." Resultant muzzle bursts injured several men. Later, on Bataan, one killed Sergeant Felipe Trejo.

Boyer found it "not unusual to fire ten rounds on the 37-mm.s and have only one burst. The rest were duds. We didn't say much, except for a little cursing that we couldn't do more. It didn't hurt the morale – just made us work a little harder. What hurt more was the order, for economy, to fire only ten rounds. It can take that many to adjust your firing."

Earl Harris felt pure disgust. "The 37-mm. was obsolete before it was built. Our machine-gun ammunition was made in 1918, reinspected in 1929, and issued to us in 1941. We had to polish the corrosion off with steel wool before we could get it in the belt. The guns were 1918. The mounts were jury-rigged during World War I, and they didn't work."

Sergeant Rhea Tow's "range finders and control box could not keep up, so the gunners would swing that sucker around. I stepped on the platform behind the gun and grabbed the seats. Every fifth projectile was a tracer, and I adjusted those by swinging the gun or tapping the assistant gunner on the shoulder to speed or bring it up. 'Kentucky windage,' we called it." When that didn't work, they unhooked from their central control system and depended on the gunners.

"When the barrel on the 37-mm. got hot," Gale found, "it got caught in the recoil position and the collar wouldn't let it go forward. You weren't supposed to fire guns the way we fired them. After a round or two you were supposed to fasten up – 'Hey, everybody, hold the war up, we gotta cool our guns!' We had to pump water down through the barrel to cool it."

Despite all, the 200th kept cool and kept firing. When the Taos warriors in Battery H shot down a Zero, Romero watched him fall. "He landed in a rice field, not too far. That was the first dead Jap I ever see. We run for that burning plane and drag him out, and then we all line up and pee on him."

For over an hour the Zeros swarmed, and Foy wondered why they didn't crash among themselves. Then suddenly the roaring receded, the Zeros turned back toward the China Sea, and the men in the blackened ruins were sealed in the eerie silence of new-made ghosts.

The attack had devastated Clark Field and destroyed or irreparably damaged nearly every plane. Shaken, the men looked about at the carnage and at each others' blackened faces, and they examined their own first response to war.

The burning field seemed strangely quiet to Aldrich, "except for sudden explosions, and wounded horses screaming in agony. We were standing around in shock, when John Gamble came running towards headquarters, dirty, sweaty, his pistol slung low on his hip, cowboy style, and he looked meaner than hell. Colonel Sage asked him how things were, and he snapped to and saluted, and grinned a big grin.

"'Fine, Sir,' he answered. 'Fine. Couldn't be better!'"

Suddenly strains of music wafted raggedly through the air. It marched closer. "The old gray mare, she ain't what she used to be, ain't what she used to be . . . . " Down the street, led by their jaunty warrant officer, swaggered the Regimental band.

"It sounded so artificial" to Finley, "after going through all that. But it brought us back to our senses. He knew what he was doing, whoever's idea it was."

It was McCahon's. In the tarnished light of smoke-filtered sun and fire, he looked around and started for headquarters. "Colonel, I think it's time for some music!"

Sage agreed.

"The old gray mare, she ain't what she used to be . . . . "

A plane roared over. The old gray mare fractured into a few shrill neighs and the musicians hit the ditches. Rifles aimed and bullets flew, until they recognized one of their own P-40s, limping back from somewhere, alone.

The plane sought a bomb-cratered runway, the band crawled out, and the martial parade resumed. It wasn't very good music, McCahon admitted, but it had spirit. One man was too nauseated to play. "That's all right," McCahon said. "Just march!"

They began to pick up the pieces. Those in the jungle started filing in. Communications crews went to work repairing the lines. Jesse Finley saw his erstwhile grumblers digging fox-holes with gusto. Burns checked his kitchen; inside a large ice box huddled a terrified Filipino.

Planes burned along pock-marked runways. Hangars were twisted masses of metal. Buildings blazed or smoldered, smoke blackened the air, and through it flew burning bits of debris. Lee Roach saw "planes afire and people afire and bodies burned to a crisp." Fire trucks and ambulances wailed into the night.

At the hospital, Fred Brewer helped Chaplain Howden care for the wounded who kept streaming in. Once he looked out at the polo field in front, "where we'd held a match only yester-day. Today holes pitted the field. The score was still up on the blackboard."

"We had underestimated the enemy," Lucas knew. "We said the Japs didn't have good bombsights and they couldn't see. That's eyewash. These pilots had bombed in China and Manchuria. They were seasoned troops. They'd learned tricks we never heard of. We were so sure we could handle it. It's a shock to learn you can't."

Many felt disgust. Why, they asked, had not Washington adequately defended the Philippines? Why had America not built the strength that would have repelled the attack?

"Simple," Captain Cash Skarda shrugged. "We were not on the priorities list."

They weren't then, or later.

The waiting was over, the war was on, and the Regiment had gone into action immediately. Despite outmoded weapons and bad ammunition, they scored five confirmed hits that first day. They had, as General Wainwright would later affirm, been the first unit in the Philippines to fire.[1]

A few had panicked at first, as Lucas saw in the mess hall. "They had thrown their trays straight up. Mashed potatoes and gravy stuck to the ceiling, and food was all over the floor. Well . . . that's how you make veterans."

---

1 General Jonathan M. Wainwright, in a speech at Deming, New Mexico, 11 December 1945.

* * *

That night the Regiment split.

Except for one machine-gun platoon sent over from Corregidor, no antiaircraft protected Manila. The 200th, too small to defend Clark Field, was the only AA unit on Luzon. That afternoon Colonel Peck got his orders. A third of the Regiment, under his command, would repair to Manila.

The men assembled, and those so ordered grabbed their gear. That evening they boarded trucks and rolled into the dark. The Provisional 200th CA (AA) of Manila, later christened the 515th, was America's first war-born regiment.

Those who waved their buddies off felt a sudden loneliness, and tears streaked more than one face. They turned back toward their barracks.

Somewhere, before the thin blue notes of Taps floated over the silent post, someone played a Kate Smith record, and that refrain would become an unofficial anthem through the dark years ahead, and "God Bless America" the last cry of dying men. Now it echoed through many minds as they waited for sleep. "Stand beside her, and guide her, through the night with a light from above . . . . "

– 7 –

SOUTH TO MANILA: THE WAR-BORN 515th

"What are you guys doing in a foxhole? Don't you know this is an open city?"
– Captain Paul Schurtz –

Hutchison never did get back to the BOQ. There was the party and then there was the war, and then it was dusk and the officers were told to split the batteries. Hutch would go to Manila with the new regiment – five hundred men and twenty-four officers – as soon as they could pull out. "So we flipped a nickel for first choice, then chose men." Peck and his staff had gone ahead.

It meant promotion for some, and personnel changes. It also stretched both regiments thin, especially when, the next morning, the 200th got orders to send an additional ninety-six troops to man 'half-tracks' – 75-mm. self-propelled guns – that had arrived minus crews. "A little major with a clipboard," told Phillips to grab his gear, "and from then on I was a half-track operator. The only time I saw my friends again was when we'd run into them during the campaign."

The 200th – too few to begin with and now divided to cover two targets – suffered further depredations when several of its ex-cavalry officers were transferred to the Philippine Scouts (26th Cavalry) and several more to Air Warning and Quartermaster units. From the first day, the versatile New Mexicans served in many capacities.

Of the original eighteen hundred men and officers in the 200th, only eleven hundred remained at Clark Field.

En route to Manila, Peck found roads and bridges clogged with Filipinos fleeing the city, their cars or wagons or handcarts piled with the accumulations of human lives. It was dark when they reached the Intramuros – the walled City east of the docks – where they twisted through narrow streets to MacArthur's headquarters. There Peck met Colonel William F. Marquat of the Coast Artillery Command, with whom he worked out battery assignments, and dispatched Majors Virgil McCollum and Howard Hazelwood with MP guides to meet the incoming batteries at the Rizal Monument and to guide them to Port Area.

The blacked-out convoys from Fort Stotsenberg crept through the moonless night along the debris-strewn road, and finally into Manila, black lumps in a night as thick as ignorance. Sometimes sentries shot at them. Somehow, truck by truck, they found the monument.

The artillery awaiting them at Port Area was as outdated as that they had left at Clark Field, and the ammunition as ancient. The guns were still crated, and packed in Cosmoline – thick grease that would take hours to remove, even had they had cleaning supplies. There was no communications gear. One of the 37-mm. guns was broken, and there were no parts with which to repair it. Trucks for transporting matériel strayed somewhere across the city, so it was morning before some of the batteries got their weapons.

Lucas was appalled to find the same old equipment he had turned in at Fort Bliss. "Two of the trucks still had '200th' chalked on them. We'd turned in the worst we had. In one, the glass was all missing and the whole interior burned out.

"None of the trucks had any gas, so we started filling fifty-five-gallon cans by hand, tipping the barrels. They had no spouts, and we didn't have time to make a stand, so we spilled a lot. If anybody had smoked, we'd have blown ourselves sky-high."

All night they sweated on the docks, battling to get the guns cleaned before the next attack. They heated water in drums, swabbed the insides of the barrels with soap and whatever they could commandeer for rags and ramrods, and cleaned the rest with gasoline.

There were no searchlights, so Lucas helped draw equipment for other batteries. When, after two hours he had only signed for two trucks and a searchlight generator, with fourteen still to go, he and the ordnance officer agreed to dispense with military proprieties and "just move it out."

As they drew their weapons, those who could pulled out for their assigned areas, to clean them when they got there. And as they smashed crates and heaved drums and scrubbed and loaded, without rest and without food, a grim President was asking a somber Congress to declare war. It was just past noon in Washington. One lone Congresswoman voted nay.[1]

At home, New Mexicans listened tense-jawed. Proprietors turned up radios in stores, or out on the sidewalks, where crowds gathered quietly. School children filed into auditoriums to listen. No one needed to be told it was a "day of infamy," but they wanted to hear it enunciated. Few families in the stricken state were without friends or family in the 200th.

The men on the docks in Manila had no radios. They didn't need Washington to tell them they were at war.

They were still fueling trucks and generators when the planes roared over. The artillery was still inoperable, but a few machine guns and rifles opened fire, and every Filipino with a popgun trained it on the bombers.

At Nichols Field, Battery H had just found its position. Just as Skarda started across the bridge, "the Japs hit. Bombed the living hell out of it. I made the mistake of standing up and got my nose torn up. I learned how to get in a hole after that."

Lingo was close behind. "We took cover as best we could in the ditches along the road. After the bombing, a lady sent us cleaning supplies for our weapons. We were scared to death, and hungry, and tired, and we couldn't fire the guns until we got the Cosmoline off."

---

[1] Representative Jeannette Rankin of Montana, who had also opposed a declaration of war in April 1917.

Hutchison ended up at the Manila Polo Club, where a Mrs. Baldwin "sent us sheets and kerosene in her Packard, and later Mr. Baldwin arranged for us to have full use of the Club shower and locker rooms and pool, and he offered us the Packard Motor Company in Manila to repair our trucks."

When Battery C arrived at daylight, Ross "fell on the ground and took a nap. We'd been bombed and strafed at Clark, and again at Manila, and we hadn't slept all night. We were exhausted. Then we got barrels and built fires, but before we could clean those old guns, here came the Japs. We tried to fire and knew we couldn't."

Battery B set up between Nichols and Nielson Fields. Then, to the disgust of Doolis, "here came the commanding general of Nielson, raising hell – imagine, two prime targets, airfields with planes – and he's chewing out Lieutenant Henfling about *us* being there and making *him* a target!"

G Battery was detailed to protect gasoline and oil installations along the Pasig River; Private Amador Lovato was delighted to find himself stationed at the San Miguel Brewery. Chintis set up behind a copra plant. Gale was outside the Malacañang Palace.

Glen Farmer, in Battery F, drew the choice position – "Right in front of the Manila Hotel! They'd bring us food out on silver platters, and those rich dudes in there paid for it. We thought this war was going to be A-Okay!"

Lucas, scouring Manila for searchlights, mustered three; then, looking for the carbons necessary to operate them, he found a warehouse full, "not only of carbons, but all kinds of searchlight equipment – spare parts we didn't even know existed." A timely air raid solved the problem of locked doors by blowing out the side of the building, after which "we loaded all the searchlight apparatus in the Philippine Islands onto two trucks. Later, on Bataan, I told Corregidor if they needed any spare parts, I had 'em!"

At dawn Colonel Peck met a boat from Corregidor bearing ammunition for both New Mexico regiments – the same obsolete fuzes, and nowhere near enough. That was all, he learned, unless supplies arrived from the States. There were no cooking provisions, no picks or shovels or sandbags, and "very little signal and engineer equipment, which we needed most."

There was never enough transportation. Telephones, wires, and switchboards were almost non-existent. "We had only one observation scope per gun battery," Peck recorded, "and the eye pieces on them were not good."

Senter found no radio paraphernalia. "I don't know how we did it. But we picked up that old dilapidated stuff, got it working, and were firing at the enemy within twenty-four hours." When the attack hit in mid-afternoon, Battery G was ready – the first to fire in the battle-born regiment that would become the 515th.

While the New Mexicans set up to defend Manila, the Navy was pulling out. On Admiral Hart's orders, Task Force 5 had cleared Manila Bay before night fell, and headed south to join the Dutch, who, Hutch snorted, "never fought a decent war in their lives."

The troops made do with what they had. Reinforcements, they knew, were coming. Seven ships, escorted by the heavy cruiser *Pensacola*, steamed toward Manila with planes, artillery, and ammunition.

But on 9 December Washington ordered the convoy back to Hawaii, and turned four troopships en route to Manila back to San Francisco. MacArthur was not told, nor was he informed of the secret Roosevelt-Churchill accord to 'get Hitler first.' Instead, Marshall radioed him to expect "every possible assistance."

The next day the *Pensacola* was redirected to Australia, and on the twelfth Marshall apprised MacArthur that reinforcements were on the way via Brisbane; but Hart, in a stormy session with the General, refused to bring the convoy to Manila. The supplies never arrived.

On 10 December, Japanese assault forces landed on Luzon at Vigan and Aparri, preparatory to a full-scale invasion, while fifty-four bombers and twice that many fighters divided to hit Nichols Field and Manila Bay massively.

Skarda's platoon seemed to draw the bombs, whatever position they took, though, Peck noted, "a drink or two was all they needed to put them into shape for the next raid. Each time the Japs came over they gave them hell."

Digging in was difficult. Lingo found it "like plowing through chewing gum," and within two feet they hit water. That was doubtless why the cemetery where Hutchison's platoon set up was built above ground, but it discomfited his sergeant. "What," he asked, "if a bomb hits and throws corpses all over everything?"

An Air Corps lieutenant who joined them was killed in the raid. "There wasn't a mark on the body. No blood. Just a little slit under his heart. One piece of shrapnel had gone in." After the raid, Hutchison sent for a hearse and jumped in to direct the driver. Suddenly the planes returned.

"Stop this damn thing!" yelled Hutch. "A hearse is no place to be in an air raid!"

For two hours Manila reeled under one of the deadliest attacks of the war. The gun crews fired valiantly, but for the most part ineffectually, at the bombers that wheeled just above their range and devastated Cavite Naval Base. Across the bay, Niemon watched the radio tower fall, and Ross "saw them hauling dead and wounded in by the truckloads." Five hundred died. A shifting wind spread flames until the whole yard blazed out of control. Desperate fire fighters checked the inferno just short of the ammunition dump.

From the top of the Marsman Building, Hart viewed the destruction. That night he ordered remaining surface craft south – Manila, he wired the Chief of Naval Operations, was no longer tenable. MacArthur thought otherwise.

With the Navy gone, Manila became a cacophony of shrilling sirens and tolling bells. Horns blared. Traffic snarled and bulged. Terrified humanity fled the city for the provinces, or the provinces for the city, and the chickens, pigs, and dogs they lugged all contributed to the din.

Every gun-toting Filipino shot at windmills, and though they fired at figments, they often hit flesh. MacArthur ordered a civilian cease-fire, which lessened, but did not quash, their zeal. Lieutenant Eddie Kemp took care of potshots at Battery D by threatening to machine-gun the houses whence they came. The shots terminated.

Cavite continued to burn. Blackouts increased looting. Supplies dwindled, prices rose, and businesses sold for cash only. The Army bought up all available vehicles, food, clothing, radio and telephone equipment, and medical and surgical supplies.

At the end of the week most of the nurses at Fort McKinley were sent to Sternberg Hospital. Lucy was detailed to Holy

Ghost College, which they set up as a hospital. Throughout the city, first-aid stations were set up and bomb shelters built. Manila girded for a long campaign.

Rumors clustered like gnats: American ships approached Manila Harbor; Japanese ships approached Manila Harbor; fifth columnists infested the city; a great Japanese landing force had been decimated at Lingayan Gulf; and a pilot named Colin Kelly had dived into and sunk the battleship *Haruna*.[2]

Lack of manpower nagged Peck like toothache. The cooks had to serve on some of the gun crews. Officers filled sandbags and helped on KP. But they kept the guns firing. They were relieved somewhat on the eleventh when the regiment received a hundred cadets from the Philippine Military Academy. Too small to handle the heavy shells, they were assigned to searchlights.

The battery found it a blessing like smallpox – those who survived became immune. Few of the cadets spoke English. All shared a cherubic confidence that the equipment was *Americano* magic that needed no maintenance. They were untrained, recklessly enthusiastic, and inclined, when they felt the urge, to shove the war aside and take a nap. Lucas turned them over to Lieutenant Leonard Skiles, who "did a fabulous job, using enemy aircraft as training targets, and turned them into a positive asset."

The Japanese pushed inland along the northern coast, simultaneously landed a force at Legaspi in the south, and quickly seized the railway terminal and airfield there. By this time only twenty-two P-40s remained, and a sprinkling of P-35s and P-26s. Of sixteen heavy bombers, only seven could fly offensive missions. American air operations were limited to reconnaissance.[3]

At noon on the twelfth, hundreds of enemy planes hit Manila and airfields over Luzon. Peck watched with Marquat on the Intramuros wall as they roared over, just a ghost's shade beyond the AA guns' range. Battery D managed to reach one.

---

2 It is ironic that America's first popular Pacific war hero was canonized for sinking a non-present ship. Kelly, attacked by a Zero, manned his shot-up B-17 and thereby allowed his men to parachute free of the stricken plane, until it crashed near Mount Arayat.

3 Morton 95.

It fell out of line, straightened, and then went down over Fort McKinley.

In the night, a crew arrived from Fort Stotsenberg to man two radio height-finders Colonel Marquat had located and turned over to Peck. With them came badly needed officers, headed by Lieutenant Colonel John Luikhart, a tough old World War I infantryman who became executive officer of the new Regiment. Morale vaulted.

After another angry session with MacArthur, Hart ordered the last of his command out of the Philippines. Only a few insignificant surface craft, twenty-seven submarines, and Hart himself remained. MacArthur protested to Marshall, and Stark enjoined Hart to cooperate "when practicable,"[4] but British-American conferences that commenced ten days later played the 'Beat Hitler First' reprise. Unfortunately, MacArthur was never apprised of these conferences, and continued to believe plans for reinforcements were progressing.[5]

Daily bombing raids became as routine as C-rations, though small incidents broke the monotony.

The medical detachment scrounged a red panel bakery truck, on which Sergeant Orlando Stevens proudly painted "Ambulance 515th CAC," after the ad hoc regiment received notification from the War Department on 19 December of its official birth and title.

Behind the copra plant, Chintis got a new weapon. A crew from the plant's machine shop, disturbed at how little protection the 37-mm. gave him, built him a shield and mounted it. (Later, going into Bataan, men eyed it curiously and asked just *what* kind of gun was *that*?)

To connect Peck's headquarters with MacArthur's, about a block away, communications sergeant Donald Kedzie was ordered to install a telephone line. "That's all the instructions we got. So we threw a line onto the roof, climbed up, and crossed buildings to MacArthur's headquarters. We lowered ourselves to a balcony, pushed open the french doors, and hooked up the phone." They then proceeded to examine MacArthur's war maps, and were voicing their own comments, when a door flew open.

---

4 Morton 151-52.

5 Douglas MacArthur, *Reminiscences* (New York: McGraw-Hill, 1964), 121.

"My God!" gasped an astonished colonel. "How the hell did you get in here?"

"From the roof," they said.

"It's hell, too, Sir," added one, "to climb buildings toting rifles – Sir." They'd sure like some pistols, he said.

The amazed colonel disappeared. In a moment he returned, carrying a clutch of old .45s, and quietly handed one to each man. They didn't learn his name.

During the blacked-out nights a persistent light gleamed from a window of the Palace. When a worried Al Suttman approached him, Bond could not countermand his orders not to disturb the residents. "But," he said with a quick wink, "if I hear a shot, I'll understand."

A couple of minutes passed. Then a rifle barked one terse syllable like a drill sergeant's order. The light disappeared. After that the Palace stayed dark.

At the air fields they cannibalized the mutilated B-17s of their air-cooled machine guns, 'twin fifties' which could be rotated on tripods, and fired singly or simultaneously – when they could get ammunition.

On the Pasig River, Shillito reported roman candles lighting the evening skies, and remembered the line of fires at Clark just before the attack. Senter warned his captain of flares "where there was no reason for any, unless they marked a target." They never caught the senders of these strange signals.[6]

On 19 December – the day the 515th was christened – the Japanese bombed Del Monte Air Field on Mindanao, and on the twentieth landed at Davao. That same day the south-moving detachments from Aparri and Vigan joined. On the twenty-second Lieutenant General Masaharu Homma's Fourteenth Army landed at Lingayen. The main invasion had begun.

During the night of the twenty-third another large force landed on the south coast, and then began a giant pincers movement, to converge on Manila. With its loss, Homma believed, all of Luzon would fold.

---

[6] Similar signals were sent from Nichols and Nielson Fields before the initial attack. Allison Ind, *Bataan: The Judgment Seat* (New York: MacMillan, 1944) 107-12.

MacArthur's strategy was to hold the beaches as long as possible, and then to fight delaying actions while his main forces retreated into the Bataan peninsula. From there and Corregidor he would "cork the bottle" of Manila Bay until reinforcements arrived.

It was Christmas Eve in Manila. Flames roared from Port Area. Bombs crashed. Trucks and buses clotted the streets. USAFFE headquarters was evacuating to Corregidor, the Air Corps to Australia, and Asiatic Fleet Headquarters to Borneo. Traffic began to surge toward Bataan like a tidal wave. Phone lines were jammed. Nobody could find anybody. Organization raveled like frayed burlap. Men crated what they could and burned the rest. The Philippine Air Corps torched Zablan Field. Philippine President Manuel Quezon spoke an emotional farewell amid detonating bombs, stepped onto the interisland steamer *Mayan*, and disappeared toward the Rock.

At Holy Ghost, Lucy Wilson grabbed a few items after "a phone call alerted us to be ready to retreat and take only what we could carry in our hands. In a little while a bus came for us. All day we jumped into muddy ditches when Jap planes flew over. We got to Limay about midnight and someone opened a can of beans. It was the best Christmas dinner I ever had."

The 515th was ordered to guard the vital Calumpit Bridges six miles south of San Fernando, over which all northbound travel had to pass into Bataan. These road and rail arteries spanned the gorge of the Pampanga River and must be kept open at all costs. Batteries B, C, F, and G began to move out.

It took all day. They had only enough trucks to move one battery at a time. By dark, Batteries B and C were deployed on the north side of the bridges, G and F on the south. Luikhart commanded these forces, while Peck remained with those still guarding Manila.

In the north, a few exhausted Philippine Scouts with a handful of grenades and gasoline-filled Coke bottles held off Homma's advance while Wainwright dug in on the Agno. Phillips set up his half-track as a road block for the rear-guard action and wondered when he'd see his old regiment again. Beyond that he didn't ask.

Those still in Manila that Christmas Eve tried to get last cables home – where Christmas still came. Each man could send ten words free, courtesy of McKay Radio Station. Perhaps the most welcome message was Ramón Garcia's: He didn't know that the week before he'd been reported dead.

Chintis, not wanting to alarm his family with the realities, wired wishes for a "Jerry Christmas and Jappy New Year."

A battery at a time, they crawled through the streets as the enemy neared. Hoping to spare further lives and property, MacArthur declared Manila an open city. Despite the declaration, the bombs kept falling. During one heavy raid, Greeman looked up from a foxhole to see brother-in-law Paul Schurtz strolling jauntily down the cratered street, "What're you guys doing in a foxhole?" Schurtz grinned. "Don't you know this is an open city?"

In Quezon City a real-estate man named Brown invited Senter's platoon for Christmas Eve dinner. "It was the last civilized meal we had. We ate ham and rice and looked down on Manila, heard the sirens, saw fires everywhere.

"Then we pulled stakes on the 2-6-8 and moved into the Intramuros where they assigned us to drive trucks. Unfortunately, they were empty of food."

A locked brake and a wrong turn caused them to miss the rest of the convoy at the Rizal Monument. They turned back. "Our truck was the only thing moving in the whole city. Bombs were falling all around. As we got to the Intramuros, a string went right over us and hit the water. We finally just followed the rest of the traffic out."

Hutchison told Battery H to scrounge before they left Nichols. "So Graef and Foy looted the quartermaster supplies and loaded our trucks like Ringling Brothers Circus. They put up bamboo poles, wrapped rope around them, and piled up so much stuff that we didn't have to draw rations till February."

On the south side of Nichols, Skarda heard rumors that MacArthur was evacuating Manila. "We hadn't been informed, so we nosed around and found the engineers were mining the field to blow up the runways. We got the hell out, got down the road a few miles to bivouac for the night – and that's when they blew up Nichols Field."

Bombs fell continuously over the burning, exploding city as the last of Battery A frantically packed equipment. All night at Fort McKinley they loaded the few trucks they could requisition, not sure some of the antiquated vehicles could make it. Daylight just grayed the smoking sky on the twenty-ninth as

Lieutenants Skiles and Limpert headed the motley convoy toward Bataan. Headquarters batteries were close behind. Lucas pulled out in a scout car after all the troops had left Manila.

Of Old Two Hon'erd, only a few badly wounded remained in Manila. A few hours before the New Year dawned, as the enemy closed in from two directions, the last of the hospital patients were loaded from the burning Port Area onto the USS *Mactan*, a small steamer bound for Brisbane.

She was the last American ship to leave Manila.

– *8* –

THE ROAD TO BATAAN

"Around Christmas, which we were unable to observe either by religious service or a proper meal, we were ordered south to Bataan, a place we had never heard of, but would never forget."
– Sergeant Neal Harrington –

Harrington awoke in a foxhole the morning after the attack feeling as if he'd been reincarnated as a leftover. He dragged himself out and scanned the still-burning ruins of Clark Field. Men from other batteries began to appear, trying to comprehend the devastation.

Earl Harris found the tires burned off all the guns in his battery. Worse, "there were still drums of gasoline and bombs in our fuel dump, lying around in the burnt-off cogon grass. We put on gas masks and started through it, and ran into dumps of bombs we didn't know were there. None of them exploded, but some of the gasoline did."

Rumors bred like cats in spring. Gurulé heard "our G-2 had intercepted messages that by morning the Japs would effect a parachute drop in our immediate area. We dug in and waited."

What came over at first light was a lone reconnaissance plane. They called him 'Photo Joe,' and they would learn to know him well.

They stripped the mangled B-17s of their fast-firing, air-cooled 'twin fifties' and built carriages on which to mount them. Withdrawing to the jungle, they pitched tents, concealed their equipment, and awaited further developments.

The bombers came over daily at noon, and each day the batteries fired and moved their positions. Chaney's unit built dummy aircraft and dummy fields, "to fool the Japs, and it worked. Every time we got one built, they came in and took care of it."

During one raid, machine-gunner Harold Hubbel ran out of ammunition and raced for a trench. An exploding bomb blew him fifty feet into the air. With both legs paralyzed, he pulled himself to the trench, where he lay for three hours before the medics could get to him.

A swarm dived beneath the clouds toward a group from Steen's battery, assembled at the mess kitchen. "I hit the ground under a tree. Some guys ran under a little grass shack – God knows why. A bomb hit right over it and glanced off. It made one big fireball – shredded the hut to a pile of rubble.

"When the planes left we ran over. Jack England – my buddy – was lying on his back. I grabbed his arms – tried to pull him out – and he was like a sieve. He started coming apart.

"God – I got sick – I had to take off. He was my friend – we'd been real close. Later on you get toughened up to that. But the first time is – it's rough."[1]

* * *

[1] Killed also by this same bomb were Arthur A. Micheli, Patrick Guest, Terecino Jaramillo, and Clifford Grafton. Badly wounded were Hugh Nance and James McKenzie. Frank Nieto, a battery cook, lost an arm. After this raid of 11 December 1941, Battery A moved its mess kitchen deeper into the jungle.

Life in the hills became routine.

They continued to post guards at the fort. Patrolling one night in the eerie, deserted garrison, Harrington froze when an Igorot tribesman suddenly and silently appeared, "barefoot, wearing only a loincloth, and carrying a spear. I belatedly challenged him, but he made a peaceful sign and disappeared into the inky blackness."

They accustomed themselves to the new life of daily bombing and sudden death. Chaplain Howden, an Episcopal minister in civilian life, knowing the largely Catholic regiment would feel steadier with a priest of their own persuasion, found one in Angeles who visited regularly thereafter.

Band members were assigned new duties. McCahon became an intelligence officer the day he ran into Sage behind the stables. "Jim," said the colonel, "I'm going to make you a second lieutenant."

McCahon protested – he made more money as a warrant officer. Well, Sage countered, he'd make him a first looey. McCahon agreed. "Then I kicked myself. If I'd held out for captain, I could have gotten it that day."

On Christmas Eve the 200th got its orders and prepared to withdraw to Bataan. After foraging in barracks, kitchens, and quartermasters' depots, they loaded food, clothing, spools of communications wire. Fred Almeraz found a cache of rum. Then they padlocked the PX and began to roll south, young, buoyant, and confident.

MacArthur shared their optimism, confident that, once on Bataan, his detailed knowledge of the peninsula would offset Japanese superiority in weapons and numbers. Meanwhile, Washington assured him, reinforcements were on the way.

As Wainwright in the central plain, and Jones in the south, fought delaying actions, the main body of troops withdrew into the peninsula. Two bridges were vital to the retreat. At Calumpit the north and south roads met and turned toward Bataan. Guarding this bridge, until the last of the Southern Luzon forces could cross and gain San Fernando, was the 515th. One bomb could have destroyed the bridge across the chasm and aborted the retreat, "and if we're not hit it'll be a miracle," said Jesse Finley. Farther down, at Layac, the 200th defended the single bridge over the Culo, the last barrier into Bataan. Once the troops crossed over, the engineers would blow the bridge behind them.

North toward Calumpit, like a great centipede, crawled a column of rolling stock – trucks and ambulances, guns and huge prime movers, ox-drawn carts and yellow Pambusco buses, and on the edges, in the roiling dust, trudged families, many barefoot. They pushed hand carts, and they carried those too old to walk, or too young. The civilian populace fled with the army.

Hernandez wondered if they'd make it. "The road was narrow, and crowded. Everybody was trying to get to Bataan. But we had to stay on the road. If a truck or prime mover went off in those rice paddies, it sank in the mud. We lost several like that."

The snarl in the twisted streets of San Fernando, where the north and southbound forces met, was an MP's nightmare. The jam backed up for miles, naked to the attack that could come at any moment. One enemy flight did appear, but its target was Manila, and the exposed army below watched, incredulous, as the silver planes roared on.

In Washington, the British Prime Minister watched the American President light the great Christmas tree. "This is a strange Christmas," said Churchill quietly.

The men filing toward Bataan thought so, too. "We'll be lucky to make it through midnight," said Jesse Finley. They could encounter Japanese troops at any time.

Battery G did. Shillito's platoon had just set up on the south side of the Calumpit bridges, and Chintis was laying wire on the road, when a convoy approached. Thinking it one of their own, several ran toward it. Then they saw the Rising Sun. They ducked into a bar ditch as the trucks rolled past.

"Don't stop till I say," Schurtz told his driver as a flight of strafers dived their way. They came close, but Almeraz followed orders. The second pass came closer. "Keep driving!" said Schurtz. Not until a third attack aimed straight for them did Schurtz yell for the convoy to "Hit the ditch!"

From his gully, Almeraz looked up. There lay Schurtz on his back in the road, camera in hand – taking pictures.

Down the line, Ross spent the night under a bamboo hut, a can of C-rations his Christmas dinner, pigs and chickens his messmates.

Steen, driving with blackout lights, "topped a hill, and there in the valley below, we saw the most beautiful sight. The trees were lit up. Glowworms – millions of them – you could outline every leaf and limb. It was a Christmas Eve we couldn't believe."

Gurulé couldn't either. His group made camp, sang some carols, and slept. Toward morning he awoke. The tree above him glowed brilliantly. He lay in the ghostly light, thinking it a dream, before he roused the others.

"A sure-nuff Christmas tree," drawled one. "And we're the packages – all wrapped up for the Emperor."

To the north, in the central plains, Phillips fought as part of Wainwright's rear guard. "We'd set our half-tracks along with the tanks as a roadblock. They'd withdraw the infantry, then the artillery, and while they set up another line, we'd sit there until we made contact with the Japs, fire barrages to hold them up, then move back of the line again."

By Christmas morning Wainwright had withdrawn across the Agno.

Colonel Sage set up regimental headquarters at Hermosa, just inside Bataan and south of the critical Layac bridge. The Christmas bombing was the first of many.

McCahon worried about one young soldier there. "A nice kid. Seemed afraid of everything – until after New Year's. Then suddenly he was a different man – not afraid any more, did any job that had to be done. Seems his GI insurance didn't go into effect until January first. He just didn't want to get killed before then."

Hermosa was where Sakelares stole a tank, "a little British flat deal, without its tracks. Mendoza put them back on, and we were riding about town. But we were from Deming, and so was Colonel Sage. He'd refereed our games, and he knew us. So he sent some MPs to arrest us. Asked if we'd stolen it. I said nobody was using it, but he took it away from us. Next day he was riding around in it. That's what rank can do!"

As the troops filed into Bataan, the New Mexicans guarded those vital bridges. Japanese air attacks hit every day, while their ground forces pushed on the heels of the withdrawing troops. While those from the north streamed over the Layac bridge, guarded by the 200th, the South Luzon forces raced Homma's advance troops for Plaridel, to control the Calumpit bridges, which the 515th covered for the retreat from the south. Orders were to clear by 0600 New Year's, when the bridge would blow.

On 26 and 27 December, Batteries B and D of the 200th arrived from Clark Field to relieve the 515th, who were to pass through the elements guarding the Layac bridge, to Pilar, to guard the air strip there. "Get to Bataan," Hazelwood said, and handed Bond an old Standard Oil map. It was all they had.

Skarda's battery set up at Orani, where "a secret pursuit strip was set up, covered with rice straw. It looked like an abandoned field, nothing but stubble lying around. And of course our guns were camouflaged. We stayed there about two weeks, and then went on and gave the infantry air protection. After two or three weeks of that, they pulled back to the Pilar-Bagac line, and moved us down to Cabcaben."

Through the night of the thirty-first, the troops filed over Calumpit, with the bridges due to blow at 0600. Jones's forces, holding Plaridel, would cross at the tail, with only demolitions engineers behind them. That morning Batteries B and D shot down two more dive bombers, and farther down, in a rice paddy, Armijo's platoon got another.

"We weren't supposed to shoot at lone planes, but we were bored. Along comes a two-motor job, and I was playing with the height-finder and took a reading. Gamble said, 'Oh hell, fire three rounds.' I saw daylight right through the red ball on the wing, and down it came. It was Schuetz's birthday, and I said, 'Have a happy one, Captain – here's the present I promised you!'

"Then the big shots ordered us out. We heard next morning there was nothing left of that rice paddy – they bombed the hell out of it."

Those not on gun crews drove almost continuously between Bataan and Clark Field or Manila to pack in supplies for a long siege. Day and night columns shuttled with food and medicine and supplies. The men drove in pairs; one dozed while the other drove.

Steen had just reached Balanga when Boyer asked for volunteers to return to Clark, "to pick up the communications guys and the ones that were going to blow the ordnance field. Jeff Wysong and I got there about daylight, started rounding up gear and winding the lines on spools. We hadn't had anything to eat since the day before, so about noon we pooled our money and bought candy bars for Christmas dinner."

Earl Harris picked up gasoline, radio parts, and the wheels they had lost off their guns during the retreat. "We'd had to leave them, to set up at the bridge. So we went back and rewheeled where we could, and got guns. They strafed us, and we had to make several trips. But we got the guns.

"Then, before the bridge blew, Regimental Headquarters sent all the available trucks to Manila. When we got there, the regulars told us we couldn't fill our trucks with food – it wasn't regulations. And the next day they blew up the whole damned thing!"

Walter Donaldson led the last convoy back to Stotsenberg. "It was a no-man's land. We loaded seventeen trucks with clothes and shoes. I couldn't find any food. A machine gun could've wiped us out."

Despite the seeming confusion, the retreat was a highly organized maneuver. The thinly stretched 200th covered the retreat of three infantry divisions – "hedge-hopping," Niemon later learned, "with the 31st Infantry. We sighted by the North Star and moved at night. We established our line and dug a pit, so the gun would depress and shoot low at tanks like field artillery. We put sandbags on the outriggers to keep the guns from bouncing. We were too tired to dig foxholes for ourselves."

Don Harris, laying communications wire late one night, looked up to see "trucks upon trucks coming down the road – Japs. We were behind the lines. We got our captain and took to the back roads. Left the wire there."

Harrington's convoy "slowed to a snail's pace. Thousands of refugees fled, some walking, some with carts, all frightened. The road was so narrow in places, if two trucks met, one had to back to a passable point as the other crept by."

Ross, towing a heavy gun, was crowded onto a soft shoulder. "The gun capsized, but it came uncoupled and didn't pull me over. We went back in a couple of days. They were strafing us, but we salvaged the gun."

As Albert Gonzales watched, a Filipino tried to jump onto a bus. "He fell off, and the bus started rolling back – it cut him right in half. All I heard was a grunt. We just kept going. We had to."

During a raid at Layac, Ragsdale saw Melvin Reid fall. "When we got to him, he had a big hole in his pocket. But he had a deck of cards in it. A piece of shrapnel had gone halfway through. It didn't kill him – but it ruined his cards. "

At some little barrio – Myrrl McBride didn't know its name – "We ran into Japs. One of our men was killed, and I got a little shrapnel. After that we hid out and traveled at night."

At the tail end of the procession from the south, Kedzie "went through a village where a platoon of Jap soldiers were lined up at attention. We stared at them and they turned and stared at us. They must have infiltrated across the river – the main body crossed later. We passed through burned villages all the way."

Strafers hit a barrio just ahead of J.O. Lightfoot. "Those shacks were burning to beat the devil, and the Japs flying over. We fired a 3-inch gun – against orders – and scored a hit, and we started down the road again. Got to the barrio – houses blazing on both sides. We was loaded with ammo. We threw tarps, leaves – anything – over the gas tank and floor-boarded it through. The flames blistered our skin. But we made it."

Close behind, Montoya rolled through a barrio and, seeing a priest outside a church, made the sign of the cross. The priest returned a sign of blessing. "Seconds later the front of our convoy was hit and some of our troops killed, but they missed us. We went around the burning trucks and passed through."

As they snaked into Bataan, dust rising behind them in gray sheets, the morale of the New Mexicans buoyed. Villaseñor "knew we'd win – reinforcements were coming." Gurulé felt "exhilarating moments – in a sense we were having fun. Help was coming, and if in an odd moment we suspected not, we wouldn't acknowledge it – even to ourselves." Baclawski "knew we didn't have much of a chance, and nobody was going to get us out, but we didn't worry much about it." And many, like Chintis, "still found the war hard to believe. We were just kids."

They sang, old favorites, and new ones they made up. They painted slogans on their guns, in Spanish, or English, or a mixture of both.

Ike Garrett "got the tail end of a quartermaster job. Stole a truck plumb full of stuff out of it – including a fifty-five-gallon barrel of alcohol. We cut it with water, and burnt some sugar to give it a flavor." They kept in fine spirits all the way to Bataan.

San Fernando was the siphon. Here, nine miles above Calumpit, Routes 3 and 7 joined. Through here all troops from Manila and most from the north had to pass. Here began the final road to Bataan. Here one well-placed bomb could have mangled the retreating lines, especially when, by the twenty-seventh, the traffic had backed up for miles in both directions. And still the streams kept coming. By midday on the twenty-ninth the MPs had begun to move the bloated mass. At mid-afternoon Japanese bombs hit the railroad yards heavily. Fires gushed. A burning ammunition train burst into a series of explosions. An oil-storage depot blew. Screams rose above the planes and horns and blasts as burning debris hurtled into the snarl. Drivers abandoned their vehicles, and movement stopped until the harassed MPs could re-man the rolling stock.

Somehow they unclotted the choked channel and pushed the trickle to a flow. Somehow they marshaled the forces through San Fernando.

Through the long New Year's Eve men filed. Down the line, Almeraz fell to the ground exhausted. "But the Japs were close, and Lieutenant Lutich woke me up. 'Fred, let's go,' he says. 'The batteries at Calumpit need more trucks to move their guns.'"

They arrived shortly before dawn, loaded the last guns for Batteries B and D, and awaited the demolitions detachments. The last of the men shuttling for supplies trickled through. By 0545 all but one platoon of demolition engineers had crossed. Wainwright extended the time until 0615. The New Mexicans prepared to roll.

John West nearly didn't make it. "The rest pulled out, but the phone line got messed up and they couldn't get to us. They finally sent a command car and told us to get loaded and get out. We got out one end of San Fernando as the Jap tanks were coming in the other."

McBride, helping to evacuate people from a barrio, "grabbed a bottle of rum from a little open-air stand. It was New Year's Eve, and we polished it off. I leaned against a tree and went to sleep. The Japs were coming, and the battery loaded up and rolled. The cook truck was last. They threw me in it. The Japs were firing right behind us."

At 0615, New Year's Day, Wainwright gave the order. Jagged masses of steel hurtled through the air. The corpse of the Calumpit bridge groaned and buckled and settled into its river grave. On flowed the Pampanga, deep between the defenders and the advancing Japanese army.

Willie Tillman, who'd just made it, watched his friend Tommy McGee, who hadn't, swim the wide expanse.

Homma entered Manila on 2 January, but he had failed in his primary mission. MacArthur's army was safe and intact. Homma, intent on his Manila objective, had perceived the American strategy too late. "If the Japs had bombed out a couple of bridges at Calumpit," Skarda noted, "our war would have been over."

But the Americans had held the bridge and were across. The 515th had chalked up thirteen confirmed hits, the 200th, twenty-three.

* * *

All roads converged at Layac Junction to cross the long wooden bridge that spanned the Culo River, the last barrier into their stronghold. Elements of the 200th still guarded the crossing as the weary men trekked into Bataan. As Gunter, driving Major William Reardon, approached it, three dive bombers came at him.

"Sit still," Reardon drawled. "They've never hit a target yet." Not a bomb hit the bridge.

Batteries coming from Calumpit passed through to the Orani field to relieve 515th Batteries C and G. On the night of 1-2 January, the 200th quit the Hermosa command post and passed through the Pilar area, defended by the 515th, to a new bivouac immediately south of Limay. McCahon, scouting in a jeep, had found a site atop a promontory overlooking Manila Bay.

Peck moved his headquarters and ammunition dump to Orion.

Mendoza, ferrying guns and trucks, was still in Hermosa on New Year's Eve. "I had some candy and cigarettes, and four live chickens. I gave 'em to a little Filipino boy named Manuel Agustin. 'Make chicken,' I told him, 'and bring me a piece.'

"He said, 'you got washy-washy?'

"I said, 'Yeah, I got washy-washy,' and gave him my dirty clothes, with the Golden Gate T-shirts I'd bought in Frisco. He took me to church later, and I gave the priest some C-rations. Then they shelled us that night, and we had to move." Mendoza left without his washy-washy. He didn't know he'd see Manuel Agustin again, in a strange circumstance.

Bataan seethed like a witch's cauldron as soldiers and civilians streamed in and milled about and wondered where to go. Convoys sought their units and units sought their bivouac areas. Vehicles towed heavy equipment in crosscurrents of knotted traffic. Men were numb from lack of food and sleep.

On the night of 5 January the last of the army passed through Layac Junction, and across the bridge, as Wainwright staged the final withdrawal across the Culo. Here Phillips found old friends and set up his half-track alongside their guns.

At 0200 the bridge blew.

As the last troops crossed, Sage and Peck reconnoitered to

Mariveles to plan positions. Here also Peck delivered to Lucas a Christmas package from home which someone had brought from Stotsenberg. It contained an electric fan and a box of moldy candy.

The 200th and 515th had accomplished their mission in a manner worthy of their tradition. The retreat had succeeded in large part because of the AA defense of key bridges and crossroads along the way. For this and subsequent actions the Regiments would one day receive Presidential Distinguished Unit Citations.

Now they dug in for their next mission, the protection of Bataan and Cabcaben airstrips – for the present, to defend the seven P-40s that still flew, and, for the future, those promised planes to come.

The Battle of Bataan was about to begin.

– 9 –

"VERY SOON NOW, JOE"

"The Voice of Freedom kept telling us, 'Hold out for two more days. Help is on the way.' We could have taken the truth. But they lied to us."
– Sergeant David Johns –

Steen awoke New Year's morning in a dark jungle with someone yelling in his ear. He grabbed his rifle. "The guy had found a candy dump a few feet from our truck. Cases and cases! We were half starved, so we started stashing. I buried a case of Mounds in my foxhole.

"Ordnance jumped our captain. He didn't know anything about it. But they found a case somebody'd stowed in the back seat of his command car. They crawled all over him! But they never found mine."

* * *

As Steen and his buddies stocked their foxholes, the armies girded for battle.

North of the demolished Layac bridge, Homma's Fourteenth Army poised for the final mopping up, a two-pronged advance down either coast, in which they would annihilate the defenders as they progressed. The men on Bataan, they believed, were the weak remnants of a chaotic rout.

But what Homma believed a disorderly flight had been a masterful withdrawal. Fil-American forces had gained the strongest defensive position on the island, burned or blasted 184 bridges behind them, and sustained fewer casualties than the enemy.[1]

MacArthur's main position, the Abucay Line, stretched thinly twenty miles coast-to-coast across Mount Natib from Mabatang to Mauban. The mountain itself, considered impassable for an advancing army, lay undefended. Eight miles south, the rear position extended from Orion to Bagac. General Wainwright and Major General George M. Parker, Jr., commanded respectively the west, or I Philippine Corps, and the east, or II Corps.

The peninsula was a natural fortress. Mountains crowded almost into the sea to guard the narrow western coastal plain. Thick growth camouflaged the ravine-slashed earth, and mysterious paths known only to the dark children of the jungle wound through the tangled mass. A narrow dirt 'highway' followed the west coast to Mariveles and continued up the west side to Moron, and a cobblestone road cut east and west across the valley between the two mountains to connect Pilar and Bagac. These offered the only access into Bataan. It was a well-chosen bulwark, and MacArthur knew the terrain intimately.

---

[1] The Japanese numbered over 2,000 dead and wounded. (Lt. Col. Yoshio Nakagina testified to the larger figure of 4,500.) Though Wainwright lost 12,000 of his original 28,000, these were largely desertions of untrained Filipino troops; actual casualties were small. Jones lost 1,000. Morton 230 & n. Japanese testimony later conceded that the withdrawal fooled them completely. "We thought the Americans were cowards at the time," Lt. Col. Monjiro Akiyama testified, but "I have come to believe it was a great strategic move." MacArthur *Reports* 16, n. 29.

What the gods had wrought the men on Bataan improved. They drove stakes and stretched barbed wire and planted mines in shallow graves. They dug gun emplacements and foxholes, and where they lacked shovels and picks, they dug with bayonets and scooped with helmets. Where the natural camouflage of jungle was cleared for road or paddy or field of fire, they made their own, of branches or cogon grass or rice straw.

MacArthur's troops numbered nearly 80,000, but only 27,000 were trained soldiers – 15,000 Americans and 12,000 Philippine Scouts which included the 26th Cavalry, a highly disciplined group, who, in Skarda's eyes, "made the West Pointers look like rabble." Shillito found them "the most professional of us all," and Graef noted that, "though there weren't many of them, and their artillery was left from the Spanish-American War, they could put a shell in a barrel at ten miles."

The rest of the Filipinos were untrained, ill-equipped, and confused – "recruited from street corners," Earl Harris observed, "given a paper helmet, and maybe a rifle."

Trained or not, those 80,000 had to be fed, and so did the 26,000 civilians packed into Bataan. Tons of food were left at Clark Field, Stotsenberg, and Manila, but clogged roads, milling confusion, and the urgency of time spelled the deciding factor of Bataan: There was not enough food.

On 5 January all men went on half rations.

They were short of ammunition, of medicine and surgical supplies, of clothing and shelter halves and mosquito netting. There were never enough vehicles, or the gasoline to drive them. But morale was high. They were through retreating. They were ready to fight.

On 4 January MacArthur radioed the Chief of Staff a plan for running the blockade in submarines, to bring in the vital food and ammunition. Marshall forwarded it to Australia, and King ordered Admiral Hart to assist. Hart made no craft available.

MacArthur pled again. Marshall backed him fully and urgently, and set a program in motion. His deputies flushed a few ancient vessels from the Australian coasts, and the men who manned them spit at logistics and dared the dark sea where enemy predators prowled. A few pushed through – enough to spark hope in the embattled men. Enough to prove, heartbreakingly, that a properly mounted operation could have broken the blockade.

But the gods in Washington, pledged to 'Get Hitler First,' had cast the die. On 3 January the General Staff of the War Plans Division labeled such an operation unjustified in terms of strength.

No one told MacArthur.

Would the Filipino common soldiers stand and fight? the Americans wondered. Most feared they wouldn't.

Kedzie found them "willing but untrained field workers. They'd never worn shoes. They knotted the laces and carried them around their necks."

"Half," Ross estimated, "didn't know which end of a damned rifle a bullet came out of. We used 'em to relay ammunition. They'd just stop – 'But Joe, I'm tired' – and they'd run off and take a nap."

Adolfo Hernandez tried to persuade them to camouflage properly. "But they'd flash shiny things, and make trails through the jungle. They came and went as they pleased. They wouldn't take the war serious. But they sure was comical – especially one called Santu."

One quiet day, Adolfo was sunning his feet (it relieved jungle rot) and laughing at Santu's sexy rendition of a Marlene Dietrich torch song. Suddenly, "Joe, here they come!" Hernandez pulled on his shoes, leaped for his machine gun, and began to fire. A hot shell fell into his unlaced shoe. He froze on the trigger – firing, kicking, jumping in pain.

After the raid, he examined an egg-sized blister. Santu erupted into laughing spasms. "Joe, I seen you fire that gun lots of times," he whooped between cackles. "But this is the first time you ever fired and did the jitterbug!"

But whatever their failings, one fact weighed with Ike Garrett: The Filipinos did not surrender. "The average Filipino was just a civilian with a rifle. He could've thrown it down and disappeared into the jungle. But he didn't. He stayed and he fought."

* * *

On 9 January at 1500 hours, the massed Japanese artillery opened up on the Abucay line. The Battle of Bataan had begun.

Assuming the supposedly disorganized Fil-American forces would flee before them, Colonel Takeo Imai's 141st Infantry pushed down the east coast, as Colonel Susumu Takechi's 9th cut through the tangled crags of Mount Natib to encircle Parker.

But Parker's line was farther south than the Japanese supposed; it was neither fleeing nor disorganized; and the Filipinos, green but gritty, were ready to fight. Imai's forces drove straight into the jaws of Parker's artillery, and the Fil-Americans fell on them like hungry piranhas. When it was over, two-thirds of Imai's men lay dead or disabled, and Takeshi was lost in the crags and chasms of the mountain jungles.

Homma began to reinforce his positions, MacArthur to redeploy his. Three times the enemy assaulted the Abucay line. Three times the defenders hurled them back. But Japanese night attacks and heavy air bombardments chained the Americans to round-the-clock duty; and sleeplessness, malaria, and half-rations charged high fees. Ammunition was running low. An American counterattack failed.

On the west side, Colonel Yunosuke Watanabe's Infantry occupied Olongapo, seized Grand Island at the entrance to Subic Bay, took Moron, and broke through at Mauban.

Across Bataan the line began to crack.

On 22 January MacArthur ordered withdrawal to the Pilar-Bagac line, where, he radioed Marshall, "I intend to fight it out to complete destruction."[2]

As quickly as the airstrips at Cabcaben and Bataan Fields were completed, the New Mexicans set up to keep them open for the planes they awaited from Australia, and to guard the seven battered P-40s that constituted the Bataan Air Force as of 26 January. That night, with fragmentation bombs lashed beneath their wings, those seven labored down the runway, headed for Japanese installations on Nichols and Nielson

---

2 MacArthur to Marshall, 23 January 1942. Morton 295.

Fields. One crashed and burned on takeoff. The rest wrought immense damage – but now there were six.

Japanese planes came over every day. McCahon set up outposts to spot incoming aircraft. "I had two or three men who'd phone to me on top of the mountain near Cabcaben, and I'd relay the information to the batteries. We also set up a code for our own planes, so we wouldn't be firing on them. We maintained this twenty-four hours a day."

Chaplain Howden, tall and gaunt, made his way from battery to battery, holding services, distributing the few books Sage and Peck requisitioned from Corregidor. He scrounged candy, soap, and cigarettes for the troops, and he and his assistants wrote home for the men, or encouraged them to, and tried to get the letters out on the occasional submarine that nosed its way into the harbor. And, screened in a thicket from sight of circling planes, Howden built a bamboo chapel.

Base Hospital 1, first at Limay but moved to Little Baguio when the troops fell back, and Hospital 2, just south of Cabcaben, served the increasing stream of sick and wounded as best they could. Surgical teams in continuous shifts battled to keep abreast of the endless line of patients on litters outside the makeshift surgery.

Lucy Wilson was just going off duty when an officer stopped her. "Do you know a Lieutenant Jopling?"

She nodded.

"Would you like to see him?"

"You bet!" She followed him to a cluster of cots. "Dan had dengue fever – breakbone fever, we called it. He was there a week, and when I got off work we'd sit on the beach and talk and watch them bomb and burn Manila."

Homma, desperate to end the Philippine campaign quickly, planned an amphibious attack on the west side below Wainwright's lines. From there, detachments would attack Bagac from the rear as others pushed above it, seize the port of Mariveles, and cut off supplies from Corregidor. Accordingly, on 23 January the Japanese effected the first of five landings that began the three-week Battle of the Points.

Wainwright augmented his thin forces with a makeshift infantry of planeless airmen, shipless sailors, Marines, and Philippine Constabulary, some of whom crammed a crash course in riflery as they moved to their new positions.

Batteries G (200th) and B (515th) were assigned to this defense. At Saysain Ridge, just south of Bagac, Battery G set up in bamboo so dense that Sage and Peck, hunting the position, nearly missed them. Nor could they see the sky above, or the planes whose bombs crashed into the thickets around them.

Finally they found a platoon, just as a raid hit. Peck "went over the top of a bank. The bombs followed me just a few feet over my head, and hit down below. The gun crews gave them hell all the while."

At dark that same evening, Battery B, moving to its new position, found the road at Agoloma Point blocked by a large landing force. Doolis, dodging bullets in the back of a truck, saw Captain George Henfling, in charge of the convoy, "running up and down the road trying to decide whether to go ahead – he didn't know how big the landing was – to get cut off, to lose his men and equipment, or disobey orders and go back. Tracers, machine guns, 75s, 155s were all firing over our heads, and the Japs were firing back, hitting right among us.

"Right in the middle of all this damn action, one of our cooks stood up in a truck and started hollering, 'Captain! Captain!' Finally Henfling stopped. 'What in hell do you want?' he snapped.

"'I want to know who issued that live ammunition,' the guy says. 'Some sonofabitch is gonna get killed!'"

They pushed to a beach. There Lingo saw General Wainwright, "with his M-1 and a bandolier of shells, leading the troops in the landing area as the Japs came ashore. If we didn't repulse them, we'd be cut off without any way to get back. We had no food, no maps, no compass, and a one-way road."

Just above the beach, Alex set up his 37-mm. "We'd come down into a clearing and fire almost flat level at the beach line, then pull up on a knoll in the daytime and spot planes. The Japs saw a lot more activity than there was. We only had two .50s and two 37s.

"The first plane we hit came in low, and we hit him in the gas tank. He went into the drink right by us. They doubled and tripled, and we did a lot of firing. We learned later they thought us ten times our strength.

"Then we ran out of ammunition."

They were also running out of food. Doolis, in charge of the kitchen, "drew twelve cans of salmon, eight of milk, and about ten pounds of bread, to feed a hundred men for a whole day. The captain said, 'Get to the food dump and get what you can.' I told him who I wanted with me, and he asked, 'Why him?' I said, 'Because he's the best thief in the outfit.' He helped us stay alive.

"The Japs fired their artillery every two hours, and between shellings we'd jump out of our foxholes to stir the slumgullion."

The enemy began to scatter and barricade themselves in the caves that hollowed the cliffs along the shore. There was only one way to blast them out. Men descended with fifty-pound boxes of dynamite, lit the fuzes and hurled, then jerked the ropes, to be hauled up seconds before the charges detonated.

On the night of 1-2 February another large flotilla headed toward Quinauan Point. As the black shapes loomed in the light of the full moon, torpedo boats off the coast and artillery from the shore opened fire, and from Cabcaben the remaining P-40s, each with six fragmentation bombs lashed onto improvised bomb racks, struggled to gain the air. Directed by Lucas's searchlights, "they'd fly north to get enough altitude to drop their bombs, head for Subic, let 'em go, and get back to refuel and reload and go again."

Beset by planes, torpedo boats, and coast artillery, barges began to sink, and the rest to turn back. Gurulé "could almost feel the peninsula shake with all the cheering."

They weren't gone yet. Landing in the Silaiim area behind Wainwright's lines, they again threatened his rear. Many infiltrated in the dark.

When three were seen skulking about Battery B's kitchen, John Johnson grabbed his rifle. The prowlers ran toward the latrine, where a friend of Doolis's was relieving himself. "It scared the hell out of him, and he ran back and scared the hell out of us. We didn't know how many there might be.

"We fanned out, with some Philippine Scouts, and gave the BAR to Johnson – he was the biggest. Somebody got one, and then somebody hollered at me, and I stumbled, just as a Jap bullet zipped over my head. We got him, too. The Filipinos dragged him out by the heels, with his guts dragging about four feet behind. We said 'He's dead now – for God's sake, put him in a tarp.'"

Battery B had another problem, and that was Buster Wilkerson. Buster snored so loudly someone had to keep watch and prod him intermittently lest he give away their position.

One morning Gurulé looked up to see Japanese faces peering from a balloon just beyond firing range. As one crew fired a diversionary barrage, another slipped behind the lines and aimed. The balloon crashed to the ground.

By 7 February Wainwright had pinned the Japanese at Silaiim Point. His troops drove back an attempted rescue, and as the Fil-Americans broke through, the beach erupted with Japanese plunging from the cliffs into the ocean. Corpses, rapidly rotting in the tropic heat, littered the sand.

Despite the never-surrender code of *Bushido*, some swam back. But they were few. "They were good soldiers," Graef conceded. "For a Jap to die fighting was to go to glory. We were glad to help them along."

On the twelfth a last Japanese counterattack failed, and within several days the exhausted Americans cleared the area completely. The Battle of the Points was over. Wainwright's warriors, at the cost of approximately seven hundred dead and wounded, had destroyed two entire battalions of Japanese infantry – some eighteen hundred men.[3]

While the amphibious troops stabbed the coast, others pierced a gap in the I Corps line and set up two deadly cells behind Wainwright's lines. As the Fil-Americans fought to cut them off, a third salient, trying to unite with the Upper Pocket, threatened Wainwright's flank. Against this, Major General

[3] At Longaskawan, Japanese dead 300; Fil-American dead 22, wounded 66. At Quinauan, Japanese dead 600; total Fil-American dead and wounded nearly 500. At Anyasan, Japanese dead 900; Fil-American dead 70, wounded 100. Figures according to Morton 308, 312, 324.

Albert M. Jones on 4 February launched a three-week offensive known as the Battle of the Pockets.

Meanwhile, as the Japanese penetrated the American lines, dusky Igorot warriors were penetrating theirs. Black as the night through which they crept, the small natives lobbed ancient spears and modern grenades, and silently glided on to rupture another advancing Nipponese line.

From battalion headquarters, Harrington watched them roll north in army trucks, spears in hand and eyes agleam, anticipating slant-eyed victims and the bags of rice the *Americanos* would give them for the proof they brought back.

Ross watched them return. "They had missed a few years' head-hunting, but I guarantee they caught up. They'd come back with ears and heads on poles. They went barefoot and naked, and they could maneuver around and blend in with the trees. They eliminated a lot of Japs."

By mid-February Fil-American troops had pushed out the last remnants of Japanese. Of the 1,000 who had penetrated the lines, 377 limped back. Their 20th Infantry was almost totally annihilated. Of its original 2,881 men, an estimated 650 remained.[4] Most of the casualties were incurred in the combined battles of the Points and the Pockets.

Bataan was safe, for the moment at least, from the west. It was a beautiful, terrible triumph.

The Japanese were not beaten. As the armies battled on the west side, bombs fell almost constantly on Cabcaben and Bataan fields, and in the east sector Lieutenant General Akira Nara, trying to reach Limay, hurled his strength three times against Parker's II Corps. Three times they flung him back.

Wounded men glutted the hospitals. From the operating shack Lucy Wilson "saw the bombs dropping, and from the explosions we could estimate when the next load of patients would arrive." The shortage of medical supplies grew critical. "We had nothing to treat gangrene. They would slit the wounds wide open and we'd try to put gauze or nets over them to keep the mosquitoes out and let the air in. It's awful to see

4 Morton 345.

somebody's arms and legs all swollen, and gashes cut through that. A lot of them had maggots in them.

"Men bled to death. We had no blood – nobody had any to donate. I tried to feed one man whose lower jaw was missing – just his tongue hanging out. He couldn't swallow. We couldn't make any intravenous fluids, because we had no filter. So those with abdominal wounds, or like this man with no jaw – they just starved to death.

"Sometimes we'd work forty-eight hours before stopping. We'd get so tired, and we were so hungry. It's a thing you never forget."

In San Fernando, General Homma faced a humiliating reality. The Japanese war plan had been phenomenally successful, except in the Philippines. Of all Tojo's commanders, only he had been halted. His west-coast offensive had failed. He had failed to take Limay. He had failed to break the Orion-Bagac line. What remained of his Fourteenth Army was rife with malaria and dysentery.

Tojo seethed in Tokyo.

Homma could, with time, starve the defenders to defeat; but Tojo, he knew, would never countenance a further slowing of his timetable. A new offensive would require more men and matériel, but it was his only alternative.

On 8 February the disgraced Homma requested reinforcements (two earlier appeals had been refused) and ordered a withdrawal to rest, regroup, and await fresh men and arms.

MacArthur, too, had repeatedly pled for reinforcements. When, on 13 January, Philippine President Quezon charged America with abandonment and Roosevelt with broken promises, the General relayed the message to Washington, and on the fifteenth repeated to the troops the President's assurances that "Help is on the way . . . . Thousands of troops and hundreds of planes . . . ."

But none had arrived when, on 8 February, Roosevelt broadcast that thousands of planes were destined for Europe. The infuriated Quezon told MacArthur he would request immediate Philippine freedom, surrender, disband the army, and neutralize the Commonwealth.

Again MacArthur relayed the message – he too distrusted Roosevelt's 'Europe first' policy – and again the President promised immediate relief, enjoined Quezon to stay on Corregidor, and forbade MacArthur to surrender "as long as there remains any possibility of resistance." The General replied tersely that he had no intention of surrendering.

But Marshall had already begun to feel out MacArthur about evacuating officials, and hinted at a transfer of command for MacArthur himself, should Bataan fall. MacArthur ignored the inquiries. But Marshall's meaning was clear: Washington had written off the Philippines.

Logic told McCahon they would get no help. "But we talked about it. 'Very soon now, Joe. V for Victory,' the Filipinos would say, and we'd say it too. 'Very soon now, Joe.'"

"Hundreds of planes and thousands of men!" Almeraz read the leaflet in his foxhole. "So here we were, watching for it – and sure enough – here came a big flight. Only it was Jap bombers."

The enemy also dropped leaflets, which the men put to good use – they made fine toilet paper. They listened to the Voice of Freedom, but Harrington thought "the Jap station at Manila had better music – even though they loved to play 'Waiting for Ships that Never Come In.'" Then – Farmer found it good for laughs – "they'd say, 'GI Joe, turn down your rifle, put a white flag on it, and march to freedom!'"

Morale stayed high. McCahon never saw Sage when he wasn't optimistic. "We were going to get out, he'd tell us. The last people they'd sacrifice would be the men on Bataan, because they needed men with combat experience. I don't know if he believed that. I didn't.

"Still there was always a feeling of hope. Life doesn't give up hope. But anyone with a logical mind knew we weren't going to get help. We were going to be annihilated."

In Deming, New Mexico, they posted letters at the Teapot Dome Cafe. The billboards had been blank for over two months, when finally in March a message came, and hope blazed. The date and origin had been censored, but the guts came through:

"All's well!" pledged Gurdon Sage.[5]

The boys in the foxholes of Bataan grew gaunter, and they alternately shook and sweated when the malaria attacks came. But they'd pushed the enemy back, and help was on the way. V for Victory!

"Very soon now, Joe!"

---

5 Deming *Headlight*, 6 March 1942

– 10 –

"NO MAMA, NO PAPA, NO UNCLE SAM"

"January, February, and March saw our position deteriorate from bad to worse to serious. We were trapped on Bataan still waiting for reinforcements, but soon we realized that none would come. The war in Europe was more important. Still our morale was high. We were determined to make the Japs pay a high price to defeat us."
– Captain Jack Boyer –

Photo Joe visited every day in his low-flying craft with its noisy engine that churned, they said, like a Maytag washer. A battery from each regiment went forward to shoot, to force him higher and spoil his pictures, and then to move to another position. Until orders came down to stay hidden and cease firing, "We shot him down several times." Tony King thought he had more lives than a cat. "We got him, and the P-40s got him – but he, or his double, always came back."

Those who saw the big dogfight never forgot it. Captain Jesús Villamor took off to get aerial photographs in an antiquated Philippine Army training plane – unarmed, slow, and low-flying, covered by the six P-40s of the Bataan Air Force.

Across the bay, Villamor snapped his pictures and headed back for Bataan Field. As he shot for landing, six Zeros, alerted by Photo Joe, streaked from the clouds. The P-40s dived for the intercept. Below, Merle Kindel felt his throat close. He knew how unmaneuverable a P-40 was at low altitude. But suddenly, unbelievably, the Americans began to climb.

"Then we saw the great fight. When we realized we were in the line of fire, we started ducking behind trees as they dived." Cheering, they counted: One . . . two . . . three Zeros went down. A fourth burst into fire and plummeted, and a fifth, vomiting smoke and fire, crashed out of sight.

Photo Joe turned north and clattered away.

The last Zero and a P-40 chased each other in and out of cloud, then disappeared. Later, search crews found the twisted guts of both planes.

Six Zeros for one P-40 . . . .

But there was none to replace that one.

Later the troops called this the quiet time, in contrast to what came after. They knew a massed Japanese offensive would come, with fresh troops and planes and tanks and heavy artillery, but their spirits were high. They had stopped Homma once, and they'd do it again – when their own reinforcements came.

Meanwhile, they grew accustomed to the monkeys' chatter, and the curious iguanas that crawled about. Sometimes an Igorot, stealing through the night on his own mission, would click together the little sticks he believed would frighten off spirits. Through the jungle noises the troops listened for that of approaching man. Every sound could be a sniper.

While the monkeys jabbered they felt safe. But when the little creatures quietly disappeared, they knew the dive bombers were approaching, and they grabbed helmets, and looked toward foxholes.

Doolis, asleep one moonlit night in a banana grove, heard a clang. Something hit his chest. "I thought a Jap had bayoneted me. It was a monkey. They'd seen the glitter of the pans we hung to dry, and hit at 'em. The noise scared them, and they ran – right over us!"

On guard duty up a canyon, Aldrich found it strangely quiet. "Just a few bird noises. Even the artillery was silent. It was a bright night, and we had a poker game going. As I crossed a patch of moonlight to get a cigarette, a bullet smacked the tree just above my head. I hit the dirt as the report echoed. Then I got mad – the sonofabitch was trying to kill me!

"Bob Witt and I started through the shadows after him, madder than hell. We never did find him."

For entertainment they listened to radio propaganda from the Japanese station in Manila, or the Voice of Freedom from Corregidor (which most also considered propaganda). Sometimes they could get KGEI in San Francisco. It helped. Without mail from home, their feeling of isolation intensified. They were alone on the planet.

Bond found humor in the leaflets the enemy dropped. "They had pictures of naked women, and they read, 'Come over to our side – look what we've got!' Some of the guys sold them for souvenirs."

Garrett's friends still had the barrel of alcohol they'd liberated on the retreat. "We set that jug in the middle of the motor pool, for everybody to dip out of. We still had half of it left when they found out about it, and the medics came and got it. But we stayed pretty happy there for about a month."

Starvation and disease were deadlier than the enemy. Malaria and dysentery hit hardest, and dengue fever added its victims. Deficient diet unleashed scurvy and beriberi, and tropical ulcers ate into men's flesh. Rations were cut and cut again.

The stench of dead Japanese in the surrounding jungle hung everywhere. So did that of straddle trenches, inadequate for the growing number of dysentery-plagued men. Bloated green flies spread the diseases. Bodies in the streams polluted the water, and there was too little iodine or chlorine to decontaminate many canteens.

Boyer watched battle fatigue gnaw at his men. "We were under combat conditions twenty-four hours a day. We were shelled daily. There was no letup. In other theaters men were in the lines for a period and then rotated to the rear. But on Bataan there was no rear."

The two base hospitals tripled their capacities. Cots and 'dog pallets' – mattress covers filled with bamboo leaves – spread over the hills. Jungle paths connected the 'wards.' Clearing stations filled and overflowed, and units established their own. The critically ill and wounded were ferried, mostly at night, to the rear hospitals.

A single P-40 risked terrible odds to fly to the southern islands for medicine – the 'Quinine Special,' they called it. It helped, and the doctors were pitifully grateful – but there were thousands with malaria.

Doctors Richard Riley and Julian Long built a regimental hospital in a bamboo thicket. The medical detachment seemed never to rest. In exploding bombs and flying shrapnel, with dwindling supplies, they tended the men in the batteries. Often, they had also to man the guns.

Mostly the sick stayed on duty, fired between malaria attacks, or during them, and tried to heal themselves.

Hardest hit were the men from the 515th on the west side. In a mosquito-infested swamp, in direct line of fire, they were cut off from any relief. Of Battery B's ninety-six-man complement, Lingo once counted sixty-five down with malaria and dysentery. Another time Peck recorded only nineteen fit for duty. But they kept the battery firing until the end.

John Johnson manned his gun until they sent him, protesting, to the hospital. He came back fuming. While gone, he'd missed his month's pay.

By mid-February the batteries had deployed around the perimeters of the two fields whose precious planes they guarded. "For ten days we cut our way through the jungle," Peck wrote, "trying to find roads and locations for the batteries."

The fields were unimpressive but vital. Bataan Field was a flat, graded canyon against the Mariveles slopes. Paralleling it, Cabcaben, built on a former rice paddy, consisted of two dirt runways, short, downhill, and terminating in the bay. Barges from Corregidor tied up at the jetty east of the field, which became a hive after dark when the supply trucks came and went.

One morning at the dock Bond reported bodies washing in – about thirty-five, Peck estimated, Filipinos, "tied to timbers with barbed wire and ropes. All had been killed, some stabbed and shot." It was an apparent attempt to frighten the natives into submission. If so, it failed.

Daily air raids became so routine that Roach quit bothering with foxholes. ("If they hit you it was an accident.") Gamble, shading his eyes from the sun, stood in the open and directed his gunners. James McCormick ran some line during one battle, then found a foxhole and slept through the entire raid as a gun fired directly over him. He never heard a shot.

Frequent night raids kept the exhausted gun crews on constant duty, and the flares the planes dropped to light their targets kept the rest fighting fires.

McCahon, who as G-2 reviewed the figures, felt the batteries were remarkably effective, despite exhaustion and their few and faulty shells. "We could fire three shots, make corrections, fire three more – and that was all. Often they wouldn't even explode. It was a miserable situation."

A lull it may have been, but Tillman was hit twice. When the rear wheels were blown off his truck, he bailed out, only to get a bullet through one leg. As soon as he was released from the hospital, a sniper hit him in the other.

Alvin Sharp suffered a lighter wound. As three bombers came at him, Steen saw him run for the jungle. No one knew a barbed-wire fence stretched in his path. "When the dust settled, old Sharp came crawling back, blood all over, and torn to pieces. We thought he'd got hit.

"He looked at himself, and then back at the barbed wire. 'I can't understand it,' he says. 'I only went through that fence once!'"

* * *

Men on the half-tracks performed perilous missions. Phillips scrambled about, deliberately raising dust to draw Japanese artillery fire in order to locate their positions. Then Old Two Hon'erd could blast back, with a howl accompanying each salvo: "Tojo, count your men!"

A friend of Phillips, "a little cowpuncher from Battery C named [Lonnie] Slaughter," drove for their colonel, whom he ranked next to God. "He threw away his GI shoes, got back into his cowboy boots, and wore an old campaign hat. He or the colonel neither one wore a tin hat.

"They were checking the forward positions when the Japs dropped some mortars, and the colonel got some shrapnel – nothing serious, but a lot of blood. Back at the guns, Slaughter was ripping open the colonel's shirt, checking him out, raising hell. 'You dang fool,' he'd say. 'Ought to know better. What'll we do if you get killed?' The colonel just grinned."

They all did double duty. By night Aldrich hauled ammunition, and the men swept behind him with bamboo fronds to cover his tracks from Photo Joe's sight. By day he typed National Service life insurance policies. No one knew the ship carrying the policies would be sunk.

Boyer became S-3 (Planning and Operations Officer) at Regimental Headquarters, and when they began to slaughter the cavalry horses and mules, he hauled rations to the batteries at night. On the return trip he drove wounded men to the hospital. "One was named Reese [Clay], and we were coming down Cabcaben Field when the Japs started bombing and strafing. We had to race the full length, and Reese was lying in back looking up and hollering, 'Faster, Captain, faster – they're catching up with us!'"

Greeman, detached to the Quartermaster Corps, found himself counselor to younger men who, for one reason or another, were transferred to his unit. "One boy came in one night scared to death. 'You'll be all right,' I told him, and I talked to him awhile and assigned him to temporary guard duty, to kind of calm him down.

"He went out that night, and about half an hour later we heard a shot. He'd killed himself."

Jim McCahon and Tom Taggert doubled as messenger boys one night when Sage handed them an envelope to deliver at a certain landing where a boat was expected. They arrived at the deserted dock before daylight.

Soon a captain appeared. "What are you doing here?"

"We were told to meet someone."

"Get out before seven. That's when the Nips bomb."

"We're supposed to meet someone."

The captain grew testy. "There's nobody coming."

"We're supposed to meet someone."

"If anybody comes here that I don't know about," snapped the captain, "he's got to be a mighty important person. Mighty important."

As day began to gray, a barge thumped against the landing.

Out stepped General MacArthur.

Jim saluted, handed over the envelope, and stepped back. A car suddenly emerged from the jungle, the General stepped inside, and the group sped off. Only Taggert, McCahon, and the nonplused captain remained.

"Tom," grinned McCahon, "do you suppose that was a very important person?"

The captain was still standing blank faced as they roared off.

Life became routine. They ate twice a day when they were lucky, scrounged for extra food, and bathed, when they dared, in creeks. They went in pairs, one to stand guard while the other washed himself and his clothes. One day, as Aldrich relaxed in the water, "Huxtable grabbed his .45 and went into a western gunman's movie pose. He scared the bejesus out of me. I thought 'Snipers!' and dived under a tree. He'd found an iguana lizard."

They laughed at little things. When Don Harris's captain visited the slit trench one morning, a Philippine artillery unit directly behind them fired. "They hit a tree by the captain and splattered stuff all over him. He pulled up his drawers, charged back there – hauled off and hit their captain.

"The next morning he was called up to explain his actions to General Wainwright."

Shortages grew acute. Hungry men grew hungrier. Bedding, tenting, and mosquito netting dwindled. Uniforms grew tattered, underwear shredded, and shoes wore thin. Lack of cigarettes sapped morale.

The nurses donned coveralls – white uniforms were visible from the air – and the only size left for Lucy Wilson was a forty-two. She weighed seventy pounds, the seat hung down behind her knees, and she often tripped trying to walk.

Gasoline and ammunition ran alarmingly low. Hernandez, in charge of four machine guns, only had ammunition for one, but he dragged all four, believing reinforcements were coming.

"Each battery," wrote Peck, "was allowed three gallons of gasoline a day – one and a half for the battery power plants, which had to be started just before the Japs came over, and one and a half for the ration and water trucks, as water had to be trucked for drinking."

The greatest drain was food.

Starvation slowed healing in the men Lucy tended. "That's what defeated us. We got no supplies – nothing. It's a miracle they held out that long – all that heavy work, twenty-four hours a day, with hardly any food." They ate crickets, and leaves off trees, and some, not knowing what they ate, died of food poisoning.

Mess and supply duties assumed prime importance. Ross hauled rations for his battery. "We'd get a hindquarter of a mule or horse, with the hide still on it, maybe a few bottles of catsup, and half a dozen cans of pineapple for the whole battery. They threw it all in the same pot and cooked it – and we were damned glad to get it. The rice had worms, and we ate those too, because they had protein."

They killed the horses, and then the mules, and they hunted carabao until there were no more. They boiled scorched rice for coffee, and mango leaves for tea.

Skarda "could haul a two-day food supply for five hundred men in my jeep, and still have room for three men to ride."

Donaldson went with Skiles one day "to see why in thunder we weren't getting anything. A normal day's supply should fill a two-ton truck. We got one little case of Pet Milk for the whole regiment."

Half rations shrank to quarter rations, and two daily meals to one. When Greeman learned of unharvested rice fields in the no-man's land to the north, "we decided we'd gather it at night, from under the Japs' noses.

"We did pretty well until they noticed the rice disappearing, and took after us one night – laid down a real barrage. They didn't get anybody, but we sure retreated!

"Then we broke a stone in our rice mill. The Filipinos told us there was one at Pilar, so Bill Sterns and I went through the Jap lines one night and stole it – unhooked it and lugged it back through the lines. Lord, it was heavy – but we got it, and kept on hulling our rice."

Living off the land was natural for the desert-bred New Mexicans. John West grew up knowing "if an animal eats a plant, humans can too. And anything that's bitter is generally poison too. A lot of those jungle plants were good. The inside of the male palm tree is like cabbage. We ate elephant ears, and caught little fresh-water shrimp in the creeks – and you can get a lot of fish with a hand grenade." (Graef swore that's all the grenades were good for. They were too unreliable to risk on an armed enemy.)

"We got to killing all the carabaos. We weren't supposed to," but James and the boys of Battery F branded 'US' on them. "We ate wild hogs till we found out they were eating out of the slit trenches. And mangoes – I've seen guys in the mango trees, with the Japs strafing and bombing – and they'd just stay up there gathering mangoes."

Wild chickens were skinny and hard to catch, and ammunition too precious to waste – though Bob Mitchell, with shotgun shells 'borrowed' at Nichols Field, and Earl Harris, with an old .22 caliber practice rifle, shot a few tough birds. Boiling a raven once, men from Battery H decided "Old Crow was better to drink than to eat." Iguanas were hard to find, but were prime meat. So were the snakes that grew fat and succulent in the jungle.

They began to eat worms and grasshoppers. Many thought monkeys tasty, though Almeraz found it "like cooking a baby," and Ragsdale quipped that they looked too much like his father-in-law.

Sometimes while hunting, they came, horrified, upon dead or dying Philippine or American soldiers dangling from ropes that tied their hands behind them. Their bodies were scarred with burns, bayoneted, many horribly mutilated, their penises crammed into their mouths.

Always they watched for the snipers that tied themselves in the trees. McBride and Cimerone had just bagged a chicken one evening when "snipers started shooting. We jumped behind some mango trees and finally spotted one. We shot him and got the hell out." Hunting was good that day, they reported. "One chicken and one Nip!"

Then the food was gone. The trees were stripped and the jungle cleared of animal life. An occasional steamer slipped through to the southern islands and returned with rice, but the forays were rare and the load meager. Then, in early March, the *Don Esteban* was sunk. It was the last boat.

Years later, shortly before his death, Jefferson Lightfoot sat reminiscing. "How could you keep going," someone asked, "with nothing left to go on?"

His eyes looked into the past. "We had one thing," he said softly:

"Courage."

The Indians were top-notch shots, and their keen vision enabled them to spot the elusive game or the skulking sniper. One warrior regularly hunted Japanese scalps, and Ragsdale watched him sneak silently into the night, eyes gleaming, and knew he would return by morning, with trophies.

The Indians made invaluable plane spotters. "They could spot Jap planes a good five minutes before I could see them," marveled Finley. "They could tell how many were coming and where they were coming from." The searchlight crews relied on their keen hearing to spot planes at night.

Perhaps their greatest value lay in relaying messages. Foy swore his was the best communications unit in the army, "because I had the boys from Taos. They sent it in their own language – the first Indian group to do that. The Japs tapped our lines and tried to break our code, and when we were captured, they asked what kind we were using. We never did tell them it was the Indians." Their success on Bataan led to the wider use later of the famous Navajo Code Talkers.

Different tribes spoke different languages, worked in teams, and were transferred from battery to battery. They even confused each other.

They also caused consternation in other units. Earl Harris was on duty one night when "nothing much was going on, and the Indians from Taos were talking. An ordnance outfit near us heard them – and sent a runner racing through to tell us we had Japs on our line!"

In the Luna Grocery the women of Deming bought their coffee (twenty-nine cents for a can of Maxwell House) or chose a ham (thirty-three cents a pound) with a sense of guilt, paid their ration stamps, and wished they could share with their starving men. They chatted over the turnips (two bunches for a nickel), but it was small talk. No mother asked another if she'd heard from her son, because too few had, and when those precious messages filtered through they were posted for the town to read. They would no more hoard news than they would hoard sugar, for each letter fed hope to all the rest.

The quiet times between attacks grew longer, and the hunger got worse, and so did the loneliness.

Sakelares often climbed a hill. "I could see Corregidor, and Manila across the bay, and I'd sit on that hill and watch the sunset."

They heard the jungle around them, and the water washing on the shore. The strums of guitars filled the evenings with a soft Spanish folk tune or a lively "El Rancho Grande," or a lonely cowboy ballad, and reminded the New Mexicans of home. So did the insistent cadence of drums, transcending time and space, to which the Indians danced their prayers and chanted their repetitious warning: "Better scram, Tojo, Better scram, Tojo . . . . " Frank Franchini still had his violin, and many lay awake in that strange waiting time to listen as the sad, sweet notes of "Intermezzo" rose in the eerie nights.

The waiting, they knew, was nearly over. Soon the big fireworks from the north would begin. Already there were signs.

They braced to meet it.

With what?

– 11 –

"THOSE DAMNED NEW MEXICANS"

"We had Mass in the jungle, and afterward I said to the priest, 'Father, I sure feel sorry for those poor devils on the front line,' and he looked at me and said, 'Son, you are the front line.'"

– Private Vicente Ojinaga –

The truth first glimmered in February when the thirty-second President commemorated the birthday of the first with a fateful 'fireside chat.' The men on Bataan, starving for more than food, knotted around the radios and listened for words of hope.

This was a global war, the President reminded them. *The Pacific was vast, the distance long*. A few eyes collided, then glanced quickly away. *The capacities of the democracies were strained*. Yet America was sending billions in aid to Britain and Russia. *The situation was desperate*. Tell us about it, Franklin. *And we must realize the great sacrifices that must be made . . . .* They knew then who that sacrifice would be.

Nick Chintis knew. "I knew while I was listening who he was talking about, and it was me. I was one of the lambs. Bait. But – it didn't bother me. I figured somebody had to do it."

Jim Chaney knew. "The Pacific would have to wait. And we knew what the end would be. We couldn't last too long without food and ammunition."

Gerald Greeman knew. "And when the President said we were sending stuff to Russia and the British Isles, a lot of men asked, 'Why not the Philippine Isles?'"

"We're the battling bastards of Bataan," the men began to chant. Journalist Frank Hewlett had penned it and it caught on.

We're the battling bastards of Bataan;
No mama, no papa, no Uncle Sam;
No aunts, no uncles, no cousins, no nieces,
No pills, no planes, no artillery pieces.
And nobody gives a damn.
Nobody gives a damn.

On the day he made the speech, the President ordered MacArthur to Australia to assume command for the Southwest Pacific. Approached earlier by Marshall, the General had three times refused to go. Now it was a terse Presidential order.

Soon thereafter boats began to cluster across Manila Bay, and reports of barges offshore sent both 200th battalion headquarters batteries to defend the beaches. Barrages from the gun batteries seemed to deter the enemy, however, for they made no attempt to land on the eastern shore.

On 3 March a Japanese flotilla appeared in Subic Bay. Captain William Dyess loaded his P-40 with a five-hundred-pound bomb on a contraption only he and God had any confidence in. The other three P-40s followed with thirty-pound loads. Lucas watched them fight for altitude. "You could hear the motors laboring to get into the sky. The field went downhill into Manila Bay. They'd circle over the water, trying to climb, and finally disappear over the mountain."

They made several runs that day, and by dusk those four ancient planes had sunk both large transports and several smaller ones. What remained of the armada was pulling out.[1]

But the price of glory ran high. Lucas watched the planes return in the thickening dark. "Landing from the sea, they flew straight into the land uphill. In the dark, they'd run out of runway and crash into the mountain. We lost three planes that day."

Now there was one.

Sometimes it seemed to the gaunt and ragged men that the newscasts from the States mocked them with boasts of unprecedented production of planes and tanks and guns – for the Allies. But they shrugged and took it, and the spirit and closeness of "those damned New Mexicans" became a legend on Bataan. The tougher it got, the closer they stuck together.

"Well, good God," snorted Garrett, "we was all raised together. Those others might be all dog eat dog – but we took care of each other."

"We're a special outfit," Bond tried to explain to an officer from another unit. "We're Anglos and Mexicans and Indians – and *amigos*. We look at a man for what he is."

The New Mexicans, used to drouth and dry river, accepted the inevitable. Chintis "tried to put it in perspective. I knew what was coming and how it was going to go." Garrett "didn't like it much, but we understood." Ragsdale even found humor when Roosevelt compared Bataan to the Alamo – "where they all got clobbered. We used to joke about it."

"There was some bitterness," Chaney conceded, and Lingo heard a few opinions that "many of the weapons and men sent to Europe should have been sent to the Pacific – that our war was just as important as the European war." As for the Russians, many felt, like Pelayo, "We should have whipped the hell out of them too!"

Few wasted time thinking about it at all. Arvil Gale, though he felt betrayed by false promises, "was concerned with two things – staying alive and keeping my men alive." Don Harris

---

[1] Between 30,000 and 40,000 tons were estimated sunk. Ind 318.

"just watched for those damn planes and scrounged for food and dug foxholes. I don't think any of us thought about the outside world."

On MacArthur's departure, General Wainwright became Commander of U.S. Forces in the Philippines (USFIP), and in the ensuing reorganization, ordered the formation of Groupment "A," a provisional brigade, pending approval of the War Department, to comprise the 200th, the 515th, and a small Philippine searchlight unit. Colonel Sage would command the groupment, and Colonel Memory Cain would take charge of the 200th. Colonel Peck retained command of the 515th.[2]

"I came through," MacArthur announced from Australia on 18 March, "and I shall return."

Reactions varied. Many felt relief that the only man capable of working the miracle they needed had gotten out to work it. Others believed he had been pulled out for other missions, that this was final proof that Washington had abandoned the Philippines.

Some felt let down, but others believed he was moved for a reason. To many, unaware of the Presidential ultimatum, he was the general who ran away. Rumors buzzed and bred – that MacArthur had smuggled out gold, that he had taken a staff of servants, and all his household possessions – all untrue, but the hard-pressed soldiers knew only what they heard. Some of the jokes were bitter. "I shall return," quipped men as they headed for chow line or latrine.

Some remained bitter; others, with time and knowledge, mellowed. Heinz Rhee, years later, still thought him "an arrogant bastard – but a damned fine strategist."

---

2 The creation of the Provisional Brigade meant considerable shuffling of personnel. Major J. H. Hazelwood became Executive Officer of the Brigade, Major William G. Reardon G-3 and Supply Officer, Captain A.M. Melendez Adjutant and Personnel Officer, and Captain Thomas Taggert Intelligence and Commander of Headquarters Battery. Regimental Commanders Peck and Cain put certain personnel in for promotions, which, in the shortage of time, never materialized.

"MacArthur represented the United States to the Philippine people," argued Skarda. "His famous words, 'I shall return,' kept the Filipinos resisting. And don't let's forget – the old man made good his promise."

The Japanese, though dismayed that the big quarry had escaped, made the most of it, broadcasting that the Americans were leaderless, that their general had deserted his garrison. On 18 March Japanese planes dropped beribboned beer cans behind the lines, containing copies of Homma's ultimatum to Wainwright. Accept "honorable defeat," he warned, or suffer terrible losses in the mass offensive he would launch had Wainwright not surrendered by noon of 22 March.

Signs of a massive buildup proved this was not empty bombast. The lone P-40, flying reconnaissance in daylight and smuggling quinine at night, reported increasing activity behind the Japanese lines. The enemy was masking the buildup by intensifying front-line activity.

Patrols from both armies met and skirmished increasingly. Snipers clustered more thickly in the trees, and aimed particularly at officers, who began to wear their rank concealed beneath their helmets. Increased air attacks concentrated on the position of the 200th and 515th, their only opposition.

Acts of heroism were commonplace. When a cave-in buried seven Filipinos, Benson Torres, in the middle of a raid, dug them out and saved every one. Bond later recommended him for a Silver Star, but it was passed over. "Few men in the Regiment," Bond observed, "got any medals unless they were dead." (Or promotions, either, some added.)

There was rarely a letup. Men crawled from one foxhole only to hear the alert and dive for another. During one raid, Ragsdale heard "a tremendous thrashing in the bushes, and yells for help. We ran over and found Del Frate. He'd been looking for a foxhole – and fell into a straddle trench."

Fires, it seemed to Harrington, ignited everywhere. "They dropped incendiary bombs to try to burn us out. Some of the fires were close to our 3-inch ammunition caches, and it was nip and tuck trying to douse the flames."

* * *

On 22 March Homma made good his threat and opened a massive artillery bombardment, which became Rubel Gonzales's most vivid memory of the war. "The Japs bombarded off and on all day. Then there'd be a lull, and at sunset they'd open up that artillery. They did that every night. We called it the evening blessing."

On 1 April Homma, reinforced with troops newly arrived from Singapore, opened the heaviest barrage yet. The world rocked to the roar of artillery and diving planes. Starved, weak, and facing annihilation, the troops determined to sell every inch dearly. Preparing to hold on indefinitely – they didn't know how, but they'd still be "first in spite of hell," they vowed – they began to build shelters for the approaching rainy season.

John Moseley, a tech sergeant with architectural experience, drew plans, and the men willed themselves strength and went to work. Hernandez, roofing a shack, had a malaria attack and fell from the building. As soon as it passed, he was back on the roof.

Though Hutchison doubted they could last long enough to use the shelters, he set up the lumber detail to fell trees along the river bed – the only place they dared clear lest they lose their cover. Up a hundred-foot bank, carabao dragged the loads the men were too weak to handle. They used banana leaves or *sawali* for roofs, and bamboo for floors, walls, and bunks. They salvaged nails from bombed-out houses, and augmented them with wooden pegs. Their frontier heritage served them well.

They grew daily more haggard, their eyes more hollow. An early version of Tokyo Rose urged them to give up the fight, and offered sex, solace, salvation – and steaks. The Voice of Freedom, still insisting that "help was on the way," spurred them to "hold out a little longer."

Earl Harris learned from a Los Angeles broadcast that Wainwright's forces had just gained a stronger position, "when the truth was, the Japs were running our ass off."

McCahon kept a copy of a pre-war *Reader's Digest*. "One article said if the Japanese navy ever attacked ours, it would be at the bottom of the ocean within four days. And there I sat on Bataan, surrounded by Japanese!" Jim, like most, could still laugh, though it had a grim ring.

Shame and disgust stabbed like a bayonet through the New Mexicans when an officer, accompanied by a sergeant and a private, deserted. Finley couldn't believe it. "We were going to fight to the last man – those SOBs actually took food from the battery, and went to the hills to save their own necks."

That was the same officer, Hernandez remembered, who had threatened them at Bliss. "'The first guy that runs away in the face of the enemy,' he told us, 'is going to get shot. By me!'"

Their common shame was a common bond. The New Mexicans stood shoulder to shoulder more sturdily. Long after, when the war was over, Sage called together the officers who had returned. All agreed there should be no court martial: Why hurt his family? That, too, was part of the spirit of Old Two Hon'erd.

But none spoke to him again.

They prayed in their foxholes, and when they could, held services in the jungle, often to the din of bombs and shells, with an ammunition box for an altar. They celebrated Mass when a Catholic priest was available – with luck, their own Father Braun. More often, they were served by regimental Chaplain Howden, who, when the gasoline was gone, made the rounds on foot. "Always jolly," Armijo found him. "He came to our battery every day for a rosary, and then he'd hold services for the others. He gave all of us hope."

West remembered how once, after a fierce barrage, Howden appeared at Battery B's emplacement. "We'd been fighting hard, and we'd moved back a little. It was still dark, and we were sitting around talking, and Chaplain Howden came up. 'It's Sunday,' he said, 'and I'm going to preach you a sermon.' And just then the sun came up. Right through the trees, it made a circle of light around him. I can't describe it, but we all felt it. Everything just hushed."

*   *   *

At Base Hospital 2, Lucy saw Dan whenever he came to Mariveles for supplies, and they could snatch a few minutes. "That's when he asked me to marry him. And I said, 'No way, in this God-forsaken place!'

"Then finally I said, 'All right. Next time you come we'll get married.'"

In lieu of a ring, Dan found Lucy a carved ivory bracelet. "But I got so skinny that when we operated the bracelet would drop down in the surgical field, and I had to quit wearing it."

At Cabcaben, 'Jop' invited his friends to the wedding.

"*What*?" Bond was incredulous.

"It's legal," Dan answered. "There's a Philippine official who'll sign the paper. On Friday."

"I'll be there," Bond promised.

He wasn't, though. Neither was the groom. General Homma and the gods of war had other plans.

In the end they fought as infantry.

The big push began at 1000 on 3 April, Good Friday, with the greatest artillery barrage of the entire campaign. For five hours howitzers and mortars pounded them, while heavy bombers pulverized to rubble the defenses of Bataan, incendiaries ignited the dry thickets of cogon and bamboo, and Zeros strafed the fleeing men.

At 1500 the Japanese infantry and tanks advanced, thrust through a gap on the east side, and by dusk were in position to assault Mount Samat, the center of the defense line. By dark on the fourth, Homma's army stood poised at its foot.

"It sounded like a tremendous thunderstorm" to Lucas. "The skies to the north were lit like day with artillery fire. Then the Philippine line began to break, and soldiers were streaming south. They said they were going to Corregidor."

Harrington heard that "NCO volunteers were offered commissions to go forward and stiffen Filipino troops. But Sage wouldn't buy it. He'd lost enough men to other units."

That evening, Captain Reynaldo Gonzales led Battery F, 515th, forward to cover the II Corps artillery. A gun was immediately blasted to rubble along with several trucks. James saw a friend fall with a bullet through his forehead as he passed shells to his gun crew, then watched as, minutes later, a shell tore the entrails from another.

Pulice was blown from his foxhole and sent to a base hospital – "one of the lucky ones," he said – where he was still quartered at surrender. "Meanwhile, we trained our guns on the road against tanks, as the Japanese advanced. There was no use trying to shoot planes."

Easter dawned with the roar of the resumed barrage. Bancgas "felt safest where the priest held service. The Japs shelled and shelled, and dive bombers were everywhere, but we felt protected in that little spot."

The assault on Mount Samat began at 1000. Shortly after midday the Japanese gained the summit, soon cleared the southern slopes, and controlled the strategic point. The Fil-Americans had lost two divisions.

Wainwright, with great misgivings, ordered a counterattack.

On 6 April the defenders, starving, sick, and exhausted, mounted their last attempt to regain the peak and reestablish their lines. They knew the odds, and they took the gamble.

But Homma held the cards. Moving quickly, he blocked the planned assault on the east, overwhelmed an initially successful push in the west, virtually annihilated the center, and gained more ground.

By dusk on the sixth, only a short line on the San Vicente River stood between the enemy and the bay. They could not hold out long.

Batteries B (200th) and G (515th) were sent with other elements to fill the gaps as field artillery and infantry. As they moved forward, Earl Harris's men instructed Air Corps troops in basic riflery. "We showed them, 'this is the trigger and this is where you put the bullets,' and that's how we went to the front." These were, Harrington commented wryly, "the same regulars who had lorded it over us at Clark because we were only National Guard."

Battery G was quickly overrun. When the Japanese broke through the infantry line, about half a mile in front of Rhea Tow's position, "we turned our guns down on their tanks. I sent all the men except myself and two gunners back into a little arroyo behind us. The Japs jumped into our parapet with us, but the boys behind us fired their small arms and we turned them back. We finally got our gun back to Cabcaben, but it didn't do us much good – all the ammunition was gone."

Chintis found himself in a forward position and under direct shelling when he pushed ahead to take some battery pieces from directly under Japanese noses. "Heroism was just daily stuff. Protecting the front lines? Hell, we *were* the front lines!"

During a particularly heavy shelling, some left their guns to run for cover. Wad Hall stuck to his. So did Chintis. Shillito manned his alone until Walter Upchurch ran up, and the two kept firing as shells hit around them and bombers dived. "Our other gun was maybe a hundred yards off, and silent, and while we were firing, a lone figure jumped out and came running. It was Kenneth Coffey. He'd been taking a nap when it started and didn't know what was going on. He raced over and fed us ammunition."

As II Corps withdrew, the forward batteries of the New Mexicans were ordered back to Cabcaben. B and G made it, but Gonzales failed to get word until afternoon of the sixth. By that time the line had broken and Battery F was left on the front line, still firing its remaining three guns. With bombs and mortar shells falling about them, and trails blocked, Gonzales knew he would need skill and courage to extricate his men. He prayed for both.

The batteries on the west side still held, and still fired. Something kept them going. They faced the end, and they knew it, but when Steve Alex neared Akin Youngblood's platoon, his friend grinned and flashed the old V-for-Victory sign: "We're still on top!"

Despite a large cross made of sheets that clearly marked it, Base Hospital 1 was twice bombed. Its wounded were evacuated to Hospital 2, where Lucy Wilson, swathed in her size forty-two coveralls, worked almost without rest on Colonel Jack Schwartz's surgical team. Bombs hit about them continually, and shells exploded. With each detonation the lights wavered and the makeshift wall of vines and Nipa shook.

Demoralized men streamed past. The lines had broken, they reported. Only God knew what was happening.

Or where Dan might be. Lucy concentrated on the wounded and dying men, and on the dwindling, then non-existent supplies of medicine, of anesthesia, and even of soap. She willed her numbed body to keep going and her numbed mind not to speculate.

Enemy planes concentrated all day of the seventh on the New Mexicans, and "a number [were] injured," Peck wrote. "But that didn't bother. We were getting plenty of hits."

During the battle a priest appeared, and Ojinaga set up an altar at his gun section. "After Mass I said, 'Father, I sure feel sorry for those poor devils up on the front line,' and he looked at me and said, 'Son, you are the front line!'

"A friend said, 'You understand this religion – why don't you pray to Santa Rita' – the patron saint of the impossible – 'and ask that nobody in our battery gets hurt today?'

"Nobody get hurt? And the Japs almost on top of us? But I went into the jungle and prayed. Just for that day.

"The bombs were dropping, and they tore a gun apart, and we had to fight a big fire at the ammunition dumps, with the Japs dive-bombing, and shrapnel flying everywhere. Several Filipinos got killed.

"But nobody in our battery got hurt. Not that day."

That day Colonel Sage was notified that Groupment "A" was now officially born and christened the Philippine Provisional Coast Artillery Brigade (AA). He was named Brigade Commander with the rank of Brigadier General.[3] Its life would be short, but in the forty-eight hours before its untimely death, the Brigade would serve as both artillery and infantry, and it would earn the proud distinction of being the last organized unit on Bataan to surrender.

That afternoon, Captain Thwaits from Battery C, the farthest north, reported many men headed south through his position. "Set easy," Peck told him, "and await orders."

---

[3] Battery A, 2d CA (PA), a small Philippine searchlight battery which had formed part of the provisional Groupment "A", was not included in the Brigade, which comprised solely the 200th and 515th – the original elements of 'Old Two Hon'erd.'

Peck himself was far from "setting easy." There was still no word from Battery F, cut off when the II Corps fell back. Everywhere the lines were disintegrating. The enemy was closing in.

Late in the afternoon, the 'lost' men of Battery F began to pull into Peck's headquarters area, led by an exhausted but exultant Gonzales. He had saved his battery.

The Brigade – Old Two Hon'erd – still stood, gaunt and ragged and terribly hungry, but intact and ready to fight. Where, in what manner, or to what end, was for gods and generals to say. The men awaited orders and the next shock of battle.

To the north the artillery began again.

BOOK III

TAPS FOR 'OLD TWO HON'ERD'

"A terrible silence settled over Bataan about noon on April 9. It deepened with the coming of the night . . . . Bataan was something dead that lay up there two miles across the dark water.

"If there is anything worse than a battlefield that shakes with explosions and the cries of men it is one that becomes mute and dead and just sprawls there dead and broken and exhausted. That was Bataan on the night of April 9, 1942."

General Jonathan M. Wainwright,
General Wainwright's Story
(N.Y.: Doubleday & Co., 1946.)

The clearing in upper right is Cabcaben Airstrip. The men of the 200th and 515th took their last-stand positions on the wooded ridge above it on the night of 8 April 1942 to await the last fatal attack. (Source: U.S. Naval Historical Center Operational Report, U.S.S. *Hornet* CV12, 1 Dec. 1944.)

– *12* –

"THEY STOOD ALONE"

> *"You come down to the inevitable. MacArthur was a brilliant commander – but you don't fight bear with a buggy whip."*
>
> *– Captain Cash T. Skarda –*

In the lonely desert of decision, Wainwright paced on the Rock. The situation was critical, King relayed. Surrender might be his only choice. But Roosevelt had forbidden surrender "as long as there remains any possibility of resistance."

There wasn't much.

Hell itself was only an anteroom for Bataan in those last hours. Communications were a shambles. Commanders lost whole units, and each other. The clots of retreating men Thwaits had reported on the seventh swelled on the eighth to a rout. Fires ignited by incendiaries roared through the smoke-hung jungle and licked at fleeing men and ammunition dumps and artillery emplacements.

Lucas watched the troops stream by. "When the line broke, it really broke, and they were destroying the artillery as they came. They were almost running, as fast as they could go."

By late afternoon the men of the new Brigade (they still called themselves the old 200th), positioned at their guns, watched as the trails and the coastal road disgorged dazed men, and as tanks and trucks and artillery converged on Mariveles.

Battery C was bombed continually, wrote Gamble, but fired at every flight. "The Nips put 15 bombs right in on top of my battery that day, but everyone stood to his post. One bomb burst on one side of the kitchen, and the fragments tore holes in the pots and pans. Another burst on the other side. Most of our surplus clothing was destroyed and fire broke out which had to be extinguished. Two other bombs hit among our .50-caliber machine guns. I was in the pit of one when a bomb hit so close the walls of the tent caved in and banana trees were blown about 200 feet in the air and fell in the pit on top of us. They caught fire and we had quite a time getting it extinguished. One bomb hit near a C[ommand] P[ost] and bomb frags punctured the captain's bed and the bunks of [Jack] Ellis, [Joe] Allen, and mine. Another hit about 50 yards from the director pit and showered dirt. I thought the director was going to overturn on us. It weighs 800 pounds.

"We shot down four planes that day. Two other bombs dropped in among our 3-inch guns. Another hit almost on top of the height-finder. Another hit a few yards from the power plant.

"One man [Homer Spensely] had four toes blown off and a deep penetration of the right hip, rupturing an artery. I ripped his pants with a knife and with my hands pressing the flesh stanched the flow of blood and held it so for an hour or more. The plane that dropped the bomb dove in on us and cut loose a stream of fire, but we had some 'bloody luck of the Irish' and we were not hit.

"Soon I had Spensely in a goon car and headed for Base Hospital 2. I was back at the battery within 40 minutes. Captain Turner was pounded while he was on his way to get a doctor. A bomb frag got him just over the kidney, and he went to the hospital also."

Hernandez ran between the 3-inch and machine guns, firing each in turn. When warned to "cut it out," he paused long enough to yell back that nobody was going to strafe *his* battery, and then resumed his sprint.

Armijo "was praying like I never prayed before. Something happened – I don't remember exactly – and I came to about forty feet from my foxhole. My helmet was gone, I was bleeding through my mouth, my nose, my ears – and I was scared. Captain Sherman said to get to the medics.

"I crawled past a bunch of dead Filipinos, all busted up. I finally got to the medics, shaking so bad I must have seemed loco. Pat Varela[1] gave me a glass of alcohol, and then another. By the time he'd stopped the bleeding, I was drunk, and started getting brave again, and said, 'Hell, I'm going back to my outfit.'" Almeraz, dousing fires, pulled him into a foxhole.

Montoya, sent with other reinforcement troops to the malaria-beset west side, found it "a huge burning furnace. It was dense jungle, but after the bombing, cross-firing, shelling, and fires, trees were sheared. All that was left was black ashes and dead bodies."

Ralph Rodriguez "got malaria so many times I lost count. We were living on nothing but hope – we had a lot more hope than food." Sent back to the east side, Rodriguez ate a portion of a horse someone had stolen, fell asleep, "and didn't even wake up when the Japs shelled the area. When I did, nobody was around, and the trees and bushes were nothing but sticks. How I survived, I don't know."

As the Japanese closed in, the medics had to leave some of their medication. Rodriguez returned for it after midnight, "and got back about 0400 with the Japs on our heels."

Phillips was still in the mountains. "We had eight half-tracks on a little road. The last day our colonel's aide started tearing up pieces of grass and told us to draw. The colonel said, 'You guys with the long straws load everything you can haul on the trucks except the ammunition. Leave now, and take your chances.'

"Those of us with long straws said we weren't going. It was late afternoon, and he said, 'They'll be here by dark. This is not

[1] Incorrectly spelled Barela in army records.

a discussion. This is an order. At least some of us will have a chance. Now get those trucks and GET OUT!'"

The Japanese were advancing unimpeded toward Mariveles on the East Road on the heels of the fleeing II Corps when, about 1800, Captain Anthony George phoned King's headquarters. Japanese troops were within five miles of the 200th positions, he reported.

King ordered George to ascertain the exact location and strength of the enemy, and called Sage to stand by: He would have orders within the hour.

He did. Destroy all antiaircraft equipment that couldn't be moved south or used as infantry, King ordered. The Brigade would form the last line of resistance on the ridge south of Cabcaben. Well, Peck thought, he and Luikart had served in infantry during World War I. It wouldn't be the first time.

Communications lines were gone, and regimental commanders sent runners to notify the batteries. The 515th would proceed to Cabcaben, and the 200th, at Bataan Field, would follow as soon as possible. They would destroy antiaircraft guns and range equipment, take their rifles, and meet on the road west of Cabcaben at 2000.

Gamble had just returned from delivering Spensely to the hospital when Armijo brought the order to Battery C. As darkness settled, "we sabotaged our guns and assembled the battery to retreat by Trail 20 through the jungle. Japanese could be heard firing on Bataan airfield just one mile below us. We had no time to lose . . . ."

Battery F, barely back in position after its difficult retreat, geared up to march again.

"Take a canteen, a belt of ammo, a rifle, bayonet, and one blanket," Ross's sergeant ordered. "We're in the infantry now."

Orland Hamblin tossed his rifle to a friend on a truck, turned away to get his pack, turned back to find the truck gone. He started marching to meet the enemy without a rifle.

Sakelares buried the safe, with the payroll, in the jungle. Tony King buried something more precious to him – his saxophone.

Like old cavalrymen who must shoot their horses, the men wept as they destroyed their guns, then moved up the ridge. Boyer was at Regimental Headquarters "getting ammunition and sending it up to the men when the order came to destroy our weapons. Battery D had a 2-6-8, and I was to see that it was destroyed and would not fall into Jap hands. It was big as a boxcar.

"We broke everything we could break with sledge hammers, and before we destroyed the guns, we shot into this thing and blew it up. Then, on the guns, we'd put a round into the muzzle, fire, and burst it." Boyer's saddest duty was to burn the flag. Men wept, and he turned his own brimming eyes away.

By 2000 all equipment (except that of Battery B, 515th, which was ordered to Corregidor) had been destroyed. The batteries began to converge. The road near Cabcaben swarmed with buses, trucks, tractors, fleeing infantrymen, and men staggering from wounds, exhaustion, and lost hope.

"Where you going?" they asked the New Mexicans.

"To the front."

"God help you!"

Hamblin marched against the retreating tide sans rifle, until he "liberated" one from a Filipino, "moving so fast in the other direction, I figured he wouldn't have any use for it anyway."

Theirs was the only outfit going forward – "infantry on the spot," McBride said. "A noncom handed Cimerone and me the first grenade we ever held." They climbed the ridge, forced into the ditches by the fleeing traffic, and there they deployed to form the last line. Other units were to join them, but they never came. Without infantry training or proper weapons – a few machine guns, a handful of grenades, and their Springfield rifles – they knew they faced annihilation.

Into the mouth of hell strode the Two Hon'erd.

The old special *esprit de corps* surged, and they began to sing. "Praise the Lord, we're out of ammunition . . . ."

Battery B on the west side was ordered to haul what equipment they had to Mariveles and release it to the 60th CAC to be ferried to Corregidor. All night, while shells from the Rock thundered over their heads, they mustered their last strength to move the guns south. At Mariveles the jam of vehicles, of shocked, bewildered men, and of civilians had grown so thick they were locked in. And still the jungles disgorged men into the glutted tip of Bataan. There was no way they could push against it.

Sometime around midnight, weak with malaria, Jack Finley collapsed into the roiling dust in a near coma. Almost immediately a searing pain struck deep in his ear. Springing up, almost delirious, he screamed and ran. Someone threw him to the ground.

Lingo came running. "I touched something with my knife – and discovered a two-inch centipede. Finley was nearly crazy with this thing stinging him so we hauled him to a Filipino doctor. He poured some peroxide in the ear. It eased the pain some. And it floated out the centipede."

Last to arrive on the ridge were those batteries from Bataan Field. By midnight most of the Brigade – minus the two west-side batteries, a few detached squads still trying to get through, and Battery C, which didn't arrive until nearly 0400 – was strung along the battle line.

Sage returned from King's headquarters about midnight. He and Peck sat on a couple of five-gallon cans and talked of what the morning might bring.

At 1130, still faithful to his orders, Wainwright ordered Jones's I Corps to attack. Impossible, said King. No way, exploded Jones. King rescinded the order. After a terse staff conference, concluding there was no way to stop the Japanese from reaching Mariveles, King made his decision. Knowing he would face court martial if he lived, he refused to sacrifice any more men for a hopeless cause. With tear-glazed eyes he announced that he would start forward at 0600 to surrender Bataan. It was his own decision, he stressed; Wainwright was not to be informed. He would not nail his commander to this cross.

All night Corregidor fired the big guns whose shells sounded like freight cars, and the din was augmented by blasts that rocked the earth as ammunition dumps began to blow. Warehouse commanders, previously alerted, received demolition orders about midnight, and the night sky geysered with exploding rainbows that assaulted heaven and fell back writhing and roaring.

Through the long night Boyer and Skarda burned papers and buried what would not burn. Then they poured their last gasoline over what was left of the 2-6-8, and finished it off in a wall of flame.

Lucy Wilson was in the operating room when she got orders to pack immediately. The nurses were being evacuated. But tomorrow, she thought almost irrelevantly, she was to be married. She looked at the men awaiting surgery – critical cases. What about them?

They would follow.

Wearily she removed her mask. "But by the time I got my surgical gown and gloves off and got to the nurses' unit, they'd all been sent out but two. Most of the vehicles were gone, so they put us on a dilapidated garbage van. We were supposed to be at Mariveles by midnight to catch a boat for Corregidor."

The old truck, headed for Base Hospital 1 where the rest of the nurses would wait as long as possible, stalled repeatedly, caught again, and lurched on. Then the explosion of a giant ammunition dump stopped all traffic. Lucy, the driver, and the two other nurses sat numbed. The inferno blazed around them.

By the time it burned down, midnight had passed, and they had missed the boat. At some time during the night, the ancient garbage truck had quietly died, and as dawn approached on what would have been Lucy's wedding day, they were still several miles from the bay. "So we hiked to the shore to wait for a boat. Or the Japs. And I wondered if Dan was dead or alive."

Others were trying to get through, too.

Steen, ordered to get his searchlight to Mariveles, sent a man for water. "He came roaring back around sundown and said, 'The Japs are at Bataan Field – we can't get through.'

"So we started out that night, about seventy of us. One guy led the way with a flashlight. It was pitch black, and we each grabbed the belt of the guy in front. I was toward the tail end. We finally stopped on a hillside and went to sleep.

"Then all hell started breaking loose. An earthquake! It tossed us all over that hillside. At first we thought they were bombing us. After it stopped, we counted off, and there were only sixteen of us – the rest had gone. We started figuring what to do next."

Senter headed for Mariveles with his 2-6-8 in a searchlight truck. "Barefoot Filipinos were streaming by from the front. Poor devils, they were in bad shape. They kept climbing on the truck, until it was dragging, and we had to push 'em off to move at all. We got on Mariveles Mountain about midnight, and I went to sleep under a truck.

"Then the quake hit, and that old truck started rattling. We went back down to see what was going on, and an MP stopped us – said they were going to blow the dumps – and sent us zigzagging in the other direction."

Mendoza was working on a truck in the jungle when a runner found him. "The Japs have broken through," he yelled. "Get the hell out. Pronto." The mechanics heaved a fifty-five-gallon can of gasoline onto the truck. Mendoza fired his BAR into the rest of the motor pool's fuel, and they started south. In the process he sprained his ankle.

"Trucks, buses, soldiers, Filipinos, children – everyone was headed south, and wreckages blocked the roads. I grabbed my BAR and a load of ammo and left the truck, but an MP stopped me. They were blowing the dumps.

"Here came a colonel and some nurses he was trying to get to Corregidor. They'd run out of gas. I poured some from my drum into five-gallon cans. Then I couldn't walk any farther. My foot had swelled big as a balloon. The colonel took the cans and I limped back to my truck."

James was trying to get to Cabcaben. "The dumps were blowing up, and shells going all over, and the Japs right behind us, and then that earthquake on top of it all. In the morning we stopped at Hospital 2. They had a big cross of stones, painted red, and I laid back against it to rest."

Aldrich was among the last to get to Cabcaben. "We were still at Bataan Field waiting for orders, when a shell hit our ammo dump, and we knew the Jap artillery would be there soon.

"Late the next afternoon we got orders to move. The gun batteries started destroying their weapons and we loaded the regimental records and our barracks bags onto a truck, which took off at top speed. We never saw it again.

"We followed on foot along the mountain top. Shrapnel from the dump was still flying, and we could hear the clank and squeal of Jap tanks on the road right below us, and sporadic small-arms fire. We took cover in the rain forest, moving fast and stopping briefly to discuss our situation in whispers.

"About dusk a loud blast ahead, and an explosion behind, made us hit the dirt. A '75' mounted on a half-track was firing over us. 'Don't shoot, we're Americans!' we yelled. They told us to shut up, waved us on, and continued firing. At a cross trail an MP told us to keep moving – the Japs were right behind.

"In the night we stopped for a ten-minute rest – that's when the quake hit. Then we went on. We had to join the regiment by sunrise. Later the clouds broke and the moonlight enabled us to angle down the mountain toward the bay.

"The road was jammed, and at one stream the vehicles were mired in deep ruts, and we got caught in a vehicle-pushing detail for two hours.

"Finally they let us go on. We didn't know where we were, or where the regiment was, and we kept yelling in the dark, 'What outfit are you?' At last someone answered, 'Two Hon'erd!' We dropped on the ground and fell asleep."

After Burrola deployed his men, he and his corporal started down the road with an empty flour sack, in search of food for his men. "Nobody had any. But we took the Filipino soldiers' ammunition. They didn't need it – they were going the wrong way.

"We distributed it to Battery D, and then spent the night looking down at that field and wondering how we were going to stop tanks with rifles."

The old order had ended. The 111th Cavalry had sired the 200th, and the 515th, and eventually the Brigade. They had been accredited with eighty-six confirmed 'hits' on enemy planes – fifty-one for the 200th, thirty-five for the 515th. Actual numbers were probably much larger.

They had been first to fire when the war began in the Philippines. They had successfully guarded the bridges at Calumpit and Layac Junction, and they had kept open the strategic points for the retreat into Bataan. There they had defended the air strips so that not one of those few precious planes on Bataan had been lost to an enemy bombing.

Theirs had been a key role in the Battle of Bataan, which in turn had been instrumental in saving Australia from attack and in slowing Japanese advances in the Pacific, to make possible MacArthur's triumphant return, and eventual victory.

Now they were infantry. The last hours of the Battle of Bataan neared. It would soon be Taps for Old Two Hon'erd. Louis Morton has said it best:

> ...There was no chance that the 1st Philippine Constabulary would reach General Sage before daylight, and little possibility that any of the retreating troops could be organized in time to be placed on the line Sage was trying to establish near Cabcaben. Nevertheless, orders were issued directing the 26th Cavalry to fall in on the right of the Philippine Provisional Coast Artillery Brigade (AA). The cavalrymen evidently did not receive these orders and when the artillerymen, a half hour before midnight, occupied the last remaining line, *they stood alone*.[2]

The men on the ridge watched for dawn, and looked from their foxholes at the open field below, across which the Japanese tanks would roll at first light. They could see the enemy's campfires winking in the jungle just beyond, and could hear their laughter. They awaited the battle they knew would be their last. And they were very, very tired.

Shillito's platoon was positioned on the far north end. He took the end of the line, where a trail headed down into a canyon that ran to Cabcaben. The enemy waited just below. Daylight would come soon enough.

He lay across the path to sleep.

---

[2] Morton 452. Italics are mine.

– 13 –

WHITE FLAG FORWARD

"I saw a Jeep flying a white sheet and carrying U.S. officers heading north. This, I thought, had to be it."

– Sergeant Neal J. Harrington –

Shillito awoke suddenly. Someone had just stepped over him. He tensed, opened his eyes cautiously, and saw Major Paul Schurtz descending the trail. He called softly.

King was surrendering, Schurtz told him. At any moment a Jeep flying a white flag would pass through to try to make contact with the enemy and arrange a cease-fire. Avoid combat, King ordered, unless fired upon.

Down the line tension crackled as dawn began to quicken. Ragsdale looked across the canyon. "We couldn't see any Japs moving yet, but we knew they'd be coming with tanks, cannon, everything. And we had nothing but 1903 Springfields. We'd all be dead by noon."

Rumors of surrender began to buzz, and as battery commanders got the word, the rumors turned to fact, and white flags began to stipple the ground. Then Woodrow Hutchison heard the rumble of tanks, "like distant thunder. We kept standing there with our white flags, but the Jap tanks kept coming and they kept shooting and shooting, so we thought maybe the battle would keep going. And we had nothing that would penetrate armored vehicles. It was almost lights out."

Schurtz started down the path. Alone, unarmed, carrying a once-white T-shirt on a bamboo stick, he crossed to meet the enemy. They fell on him screaming, and began brutally to club him with their rifles. Somehow he got them to acknowledge his white flag. They ceased firing. Paul Schurtz had stopped the tanks and saved his battalion.

Planes were another matter. As the sun rose, Aldrich saw a white-flagged Jeep pass north through the line. "Then suddenly we heard the whine of a dive bomber right on top of us, and two bombs hurtled toward us. We dove for a hole, and explosions rocked the ground."

Peck had just ordered Stiles to issue emergency rations. "Bombs were being dropped all over the area. Some hit the Battery D position. Its guns were put out of commission the evening before, but the bombs did more work on them [and] also set off what ammunition the battery had, and for a couple of hours plenty of shells were flying around our headquarters."

Hamblin, carrying messages between units, noticed that a small, frightened monkey began to trail him. "He kept as close to me as possible and would look up and watch the planes. Every time a bomb exploded he would chatter his disapproval at me."

The Jeep that passed the 200th line into enemy territory in the early light carried Colonel E.C. Williams and Major Marshall H. Hurt, who hoped to arrange a meeting between King and the Japanese area commander, Major General Kameichiro Nagano. It was a touch-and-go mission through hostile soldiers before they made it to Nagano's headquarters. The general agreed: He would arrange a parley.[1]

[1] Major Hurt's diary, as recounted in Calvin E. Chunn, *Of Rice and Men* (Tulsa: Veterans Pub. Co., 1946) 6.

Not until 0600 – about the time the envoys passed through the line – did the appalled Wainwright learn, too late, of King's decision.

Japanese planes continued to pour death from the skies.

Shortly after 0900 two Jeeps carrying King and his officers passed through the line. Driver Lonnie Weaver from the 200th drove him, dodging bombs and strafers for two hours on the three-mile trek.[2] Alternately swerving and diving into ditches, they arrived at 1100, mud-splattered but whole.

Colonel Motoo Nakayama, Homma's senior operations officer, met them. Where was Wainwright? he demanded: He would accept the surrender of all Philippine forces or none. It took some persuasion before he agreed to discuss that of King's command alone. Nakayama denied all requests for terms. He would accept only unconditional surrender.

Would his men be treated as honorable Prisoners of War according to Geneva Convention stipulations?

"We are not barbarians," Nakayama said stiffly.

At 1230 King surrendered his pistol in lieu of a saber, and with it, he believed, all his forces. Nakayama accepted it – but only, he later averred, as King's personal surrender. Each unit must report separately before he would order a cease-fire. It sat poorly with him that Corregidor still held out.

It was a bitter draught for MacArthur. Only five days earlier he had reminded Marshall of a prior plan for a counterattack from Mindanao and offered to rejoin the command and take charge of the operation himself.[3] Washington refused.

---

2 On the earlier mission, having abandoned their command car in heavy traffic, Colonel Williams found a Jeep and driver at Kilometer 155 (close to Sage's headquarters) who drove him to meet Nagano, back to King's headquarters, and presumably remained to drive King to surrender. Although unable to verify the identity of the driver, the author, relying on statements given her by members of the Brigade, feels justified in stating that Master Sergeant Lonnie M. Weaver, of Deming, New Mexico, and assigned to Sage's headquarters, was that driver. The account of finding the Jeep is from Hurt's diary in Chunn 6.

3 Radio MacArthur to Marshall 4 April 1942. MacArthur *Reports* 21, n39. MacArthur *Reminiscences* 146.

"No army had done so much with so little," he pronounced in Melbourne, "and nothing became it more than its last hour of trial and agony . . . ."[4]

"Bataan has fallen!"

In Deming, shocked families gathered in Mrs. Fleda Colvard's living room, as others were doing in every community in New Mexico, quiet and white faced, willing the radio to tell them more.

Senator and Mrs. Dennis Chavez visited a mother in her tiny adobe home. "I do not have ten cents to buy one of those [War Bond] stamps the Government sells," she told them. "But if my three boys in the Philippine Islands have to die, I will be satisfied with the three candles that I have burning."[5]

Ragged reports limped through that some had escaped to Corregidor. But of how many, or who they might be, there was only silence.

While King and Nakayama negotiated, a single Zero landed on the strip at Cabcaben, taxied down the Brigade's line of fire, and stopped directly in front of Gamble's machine gun, "a simple and sure target." Temptation tingled every man's trigger finger, despite the no-fire order.

"We officers knew it was a test to determine if the Americans were sincere in their proposed terms of surrender. But did each and every man so understand? The stress was intense with the Nip tanks drawn up on the opposite side of the field. The firing of one single shot upon that plane would signal the Nips to move forward and wipe us out."

Discipline held. The pilot taxied and took off.

Still Old Two Hon'erd stood alone. By 1000, Peck noted, "the Japs had gotten around to our left flank, which the units that didn't show up were supposed to occupy. The Japs were

4 John Toland, *The Rising Sun: The Decline and Fall of the Japanese Empire, 1936-1935* (New York: Random House, 1970). Bantam Books edition 335.

5 Cf. Senator Dennis Chavez, 31 January 1944. 78 Cong., 2d Sess. Cong. Record, U.S. Govt. Printing Office: 1944.

now in our left rear. About this time planes appeared, seemingly to get the attention of their own Japs, flying back and forth and wagging wings."

Shortly after noon King's Jeep returned: The surrender was final. All officers and men would report to the command post and stack arms. They would turn over all vehicles to the Japanese within thirty minutes – an impossibility, Peck protested, in their scattered state. It was the first of many unreasonable orders.

Japanese planes continued to bomb. There was nothing the Americans could do.

"We have surrendered." Defeat swept like a virus down the lines. Men began to destroy their weapons, then congregated with buddies to discuss whether to surrender or try to escape to the mountains.

Gale had been out searching for food. "When I got back to Battery G, and they said, 'The war's over – we've been surrendered,' I cried. I never liked to lose a ball game, and I damn sure didn't like to lose a war."

Despite orders, James did not destroy his weapon. "I loaded it and fixed bayonet and hid it. 'Chief' [Homer] Yahnozha waved a torn mosquito net to surrender, and the dang Japs opened up and killed a bunch of Filipinos. Me and that Indian beat it back to the brush like two scared cottontails.

"I was laying where I'd hid my rifle when this tank came around a curve, and a Jap was standing in the turret. I drew a sight on his chest.

"'You shoot,' Yahnozha said, 'and they'll streak through here and kill us every one.'" Reluctantly James eased the rifle back to its hiding place.

I Corps still held in the west. About midnight on the eighth, Steve Alex, acting 'exec' for Captain Albert Fields, lay down for the first time in three days to sleep.

At 0300 Fields, just back from I Corps headquarters, shook him awake. "It's all over, Steve," he said. "Tell the men to start destroying their equipment."

Alex drove the one remaining car along the moonlit trail. At Youngblood's platoon, men sat cleaning husks from moldy rice salvaged from a nearby paddy.

"Why's it so quiet?" asked one.

"We're tossing in the towel. We've got to blow our heavy equipment. We have about two hours."

With one truck left, and twelve shells, it wouldn't take long, Youngblood told him, and, following him to the car, flashed the old V for Victory sign as Alex drove off: "We're still on top!"[6]

Surrender, however inevitable, was a shock.

Burrola was numb. "We knew we were lost – how can a rifle stop a tank? But we were ready to keep fighting."

So was Aldrich. "We were prepared to sell ourselves dearly that day. The Japs didn't know how lucky they were when King surrendered! And we were sure that even if they did surrender us, it would only be a month at most before the Yanks would be in there."

Ojinaga remembered his father's parting words. *Don't ever dishonor your country.* "*We* haven't surrendered," he cried. "And we're not going to!" He wasn't given the choice.

Alex thought of Dick Catlett cursing bitterly, and Elmer Worthen crying like a baby, and wasn't sure all his men would obey the cease-fire order.

Don Harris knew it was inevitable. "It's terrible to surrender. But you've got Japs running down your neck, and you haven't got any food. You're out of ammunition, and you've got guys sick with all kinds of diseases. It was the only thing we could do, or none of us would have come back. Not one man."

They were stoic and brave and tough. They were also young and scared and humiliated. "It was the most letdown feeling" Pelayo ever had. Chintis was crying, "but it wasn't from fear – it was from humiliation."

---

6 The foregoing and other accounts of the last days of Battery G, 200th, are excerpted from an unfinished manuscript written by Stephan H. Alex, which he has graciously given the author, in addition to an excellent interview, to use in this volume.

Ross saw a lot of tears shed. "A lot. Men you wouldn't have thought would ever have come that near to falling apart. But we did."

"If the help we'd been promised had only come," Lingo reflected, "it would have been a different story. It was a black, black day. To have to lay down your arms, and watch that pile grow high – it breaks your heart."

Donaldson "couldn't believe Uncle Sam was militarily so down. If we'd had food and ammo the Japs never could have taken Bataan. There's just so long a man can go without anything to eat."

West "was wondering if we were going to get to stay together. You were more afraid of being by yourself than anything else."

It worried Boyer, too. "Nothing in our training prepared us to be prisoners. But still, men did not lose their morale or spirit. We began to look for friends – to help each other, and to buddy up again. Though we were in shock, we still had that old feeling for each other."

Mariveles was a milling mass.

On the beach, Lucy ducked strafers until "a small interisland steamer picked us up and got us to Corregidor. And there I watched them bombing and shelling Bataan and wondered what was happening to Dan."

Thousands were trying to get to Corregidor.

"There's tanks coming up the road and they're strafing everything," McCollum told his men. "You're on your own. Surrender or try to get away."

Almeraz chose the latter. "One guy swam to a Navy interisland boat and they hauled us to a ship. We got bombed and strafed. That's a hell of a feeling – no solid ground, no foxhole. I just lay flat on the deck. Late that night they got us to Corregidor, and the next morning I got assigned to B Battery, 60th Coast Artillery."

Phillips got to Mariveles about two in the morning. "By this time Bataan had collapsed. We were discussing what to do, when a guy walked up and asked what kind of outfit we'd been with. We said, 'Artillery,' and he said, 'Good. Walk out that door and keep walking.' A couple of minesweepers were waiting, and we started for Corregidor."

Irving Gulbas and Norbert Roessler reached an antiaircraft station past Mariveles Bridge. "They loaded us on a truck and drove across the airstrip to where they were destroying everything, and I jumped off. I had a sack of food. I said, 'Norbert, guard that – I'm going back for the rest of the fellows.'

"When I got back the last boat had gone to Corregidor, and Norbert, too – with my food! We didn't know what to do. I said, 'I'm going to swim.' From what I'd seen of the Japs, I'd just as soon risk it. So we swam.

"About a thousand yards off the rocks, beach defense opened up on us. They thought we were Japs. Finally they stopped shooting and sent out a barge and fished us out. 'Tell your gunners,' I said, 'they couldn't hit the broad side of a barn!'"

Some headed for the mountains. Banegas, separated from his group in the dark, "heard some Japs talking, real close, and backed out the other way. About sunrise I found some other Americans, and we started out.

"Suddenly a whole bunch of Japs with bayonets jumped us, and lined us up to search us. I had a knife in my pocket that I forgot to get rid of. I eased it out and let it slide down my pants leg and covered it with dirt with my foot. They didn't find nothing.

"But the poor fellows with Jap souvenirs, or money – they killed them right there."

McCahon and seven men were surrounded on Mount Mariveles. "We decided to go north and fight as guerrillas. We ran into one little Nip who asked what we were doing.

"'Going north,' I said.

"Well, there were seven of us and one of him. 'Go ahead,' he said.

"But in the morning we met a large contingent of Japs. They cleaned us out of everything, while their officers looked on."

Pepe Baldonado, his brother Juan, his buddy Gonzo Drake, and about thirty others, started for Mount Mariveles. When

Juan became too ill to walk, Pepe urged Captain Sadler to go ahead with the rest – he and Gonzo could tend Juan. Sadler refused. When Juan was able, they started out again. Once over the mountain, Sadler told them he would surrender. The rest were free to do what they would.

Gonzo and the Baldonados stayed with their captain.

On the way down the mountain they passed a series of waterfalls, along which bloomed orchids so lovely that Gonzo gasped. "I gathered about three bushels of those blossoms, lay in the middle of them, and just squiggled. I felt like Mrs. Astor!"

It was Gonzo's last luxury. At the bottom of the mountain, "we surrendered to the hugest, most ungodly Mongolians" Pepe ever saw.

When Doyle Decker's position was overrun, "Sergeant [Clinton] Wolfe and I escaped, to find ourselves behind Jap lines. About an hour later Nano Lucero and two others from Battery B joined us.

"As soon as it was light, we headed toward Mariveles to rejoin our troops. About noon we learned that the Americans had surrendered, and we decided to head for the mountains.

"Five of us traveled together for several days, until two left, leaving only Wolfe, Lucero, and me." Three men alone, among thousands of Japanese, they started north.

Jack Finley, sick with malaria and in intense pain from multiple centipede bites in his inner ear, remembered a conversation with his father some months ago. "If Bataan falls," the old sergeant said, "we have plans to escape. Do you want to come?"

Of course he did. "But Dad was sixty miles away on the east side. I hoped he'd make it." It would be eighteen months before either learned the fate of the other.

On the west side, men filed into their command posts with their sick and wounded, stacked arms, and waited. Japanese planes circled just above the tree tops all morning. Alex and his friends pooled their food for a last substantial meal and watched the sun drop into the China Sea.

"I thought of the home I would probably never see again, and knew the other fellows' thoughts were like mine. A few were bitter, but most were uncommonly calm, like men I later saw facing Jap firing squads. Despite a feeling that crept into my mind sometimes that we had been betrayed, I felt proud to be an American. At a time like that, if you felt patriotic, it wasn't flag waving. It was the McCoy.

"I knew then that, even if we didn't live to see it, the Yanks would be back. Somehow we knew, too, that it would take years."

– *14* –

"A HELL OF A HELPLESS FEELING"

> *"I can't give you men much advice. Just always remember you are American soldiers, and act like soldiers at all times. Someday our troops will be back. Use your heads, for God's sake, and stick together – no matter what happens."*
>
> *– Captain Albert K. Fields –*

Munsey started down the road. "Before long I passed a food dump and started to take some. An MP said he had orders to shoot anyone taking food. We ignored him, ate some, put some in our packs, and started walking again. The woods were burning on both sides of the road. I felt more alone than at any time in my life."

The Brigade was the only intact organization left on Bataan to surrender as a unit, and their hosts vented their anger over the entire campaign on its commanders when they reported in mid-afternoon. Why, screamed the furious Japanese officer, were they so slow? "Speedo! Speedo!" he shrilled. Those words would goad their victims for the next three-and-a-half years.

They were not honorable prisoners of war, the Japanese declared, but captives, who, until Corregidor and the other islands surrendered, would be treated as war criminals and denied all protections of the Geneva accords. Later, after those forces did surrender, the Japanese asserted they had never signed the accords.[1] The brutalities would not cease; nor would Tokyo release lists of prisoners. It would be over two years before the stricken families would know if their sons and husbands still lived.

Within the Brigade, battery commanders ordered rations distributed before reporting to their captors. What little food was left, they vowed, their men would get. Unfortunately, too few were close enough to food caches for many to benefit.

As they filed into Cabcaben, McBride had never felt so miserable. "We were hungry, we were regimented, we had to surrender to the Japs. It was a hell of a helpless feeling."

Above all they felt the humiliation. It was, declared one, "the most degrading thing I ever did, to lose my last semblance of a soldier, lay down my arms, and just surrender."

Brewer watched the Japanese tanks roll in. "They had pistols ready, and I expected to be shot. But they started with stealing jewelry, watches, cigarettes – anything of value." And, Ross learned, "if you had the wrong thing, you got clubbed with a rifle butt."

They took Huxtable's gold-framed glasses and snatched his class ring from his finger – his bride had placed it there before he left. He was glad they didn't slice off his finger with it, as they did to some.

---

[1] The Japanese had attended the Hague Conference in 1907, and had signed the resulting agreement, by which they were bound to abide by specified conditions of humane treatment for POWs. Japan attended the Geneva Conference of 1929, which amplified the provisions of the Hague Agreements, and the head of their delegation did sign the convention, though Tokyo did not ratify it. They did, however, pledge in February 1942, through the Swiss government, to adhere to its provisions *vis-à-vis* POWs. Additionally, regulations issued in 1904 during the Russo-Japanese War by the Japanese government itself, and still nominally binding, listed in detail the specifics for the humane treatment of POWs.

Nor were their commanders exempt. Told to put their clothing and personal effects in a command car, Sage, Peck, and Cain did so, with assurances that it would be delivered to their prison camp. As Peck turned to fill his canteen at a nearby well, "a nice Jap drew down on us with a rifle, then departed with our car and baggage. We never saw any of it again."

A Japanese noncom jerked Cain toward a group of prisoners, "made me open my mouth, and looked at my teeth. He held a pair of pliers." Apparently Cain's two tiny gold fillings were too small to interest him, for he kicked him and shoved him aside. "I saw him pulling the teeth of several American soldiers. The pliers had blood all over them."

Aldrich, marching by the open-turreted tanks, "saw the commander with a pistol in one hand and a grenade in the other, its pin string clamped in his teeth. Jap planes flew back and forth. We heard small-arms fire, and bullets whistled through the trees. Filipinos with bleeding wounds begged for help as we moved past. But the Japs motioned us to keep moving."

Marlin Sartin found himself looking into machine guns that "looked three times as big as they were. The Japs took what they wanted and then throwed us into a field where we spent the night like a bunch of cattle." There were no latrines. They were given no food or water. Confused men sought their outfits. Only Old Two Hon'erd had any unity left.

They masked their qualms with banter. When John Johnson asked his lieutenant for the ten dollars in pay he'd missed while hospitalized, Melvin Millard grinned. "The Japs relieved me of the payroll yesterday," he answered.

"Well," quipped Johnson, "didn't you tell 'em it was a penitentiary offense?"

How, all were wondering, would they be treated? Johnson expected the worst. "The Japs had a reputation along those lines. But they'd dropped pamphlets saying we'd be treated by Geneva Conference rules."

James felt a small hope when a Japanese officer approached him, seemingly friendly, showed him his UCLA class ring, and asked in perfect English if he knew of a road from behind Bataan Field to the west side.

"No, sir," James lied blandly. "I've never been there."

"Don't fear the Japanese," the officer said. "They will treat you well."

I hope he's right, thought James. "Tell me," he asked, "which was hardest to take – Singapore or Bataan?"

The officer's face hardened and he stalked away.

Shillito learned about Japanese 'humanity' quickly. "When I saw a Jap corporal stand a Jap private at attention and start slapping him brutally, I knew we were in trouble." So did Sakelares, when he watched a Japanese sergeant calmly shoot down one of his own men.

Foy learned firsthand. "When I surrendered Battery F, they asked where our guns were. I said, 'We lost 'em,' and they began to wallop us over the head and knock us down. One of General King's aides told them to stop. It didn't do any good. From the start they disregarded the surrender agreement."

The Japanese, it seemed to Donaldson, enjoyed brutality. "A whole cavalry unit chased Jack Lewis and Wad Hall – ran 'em down with their horses – just for fun."

The Americans wept, or cursed – some vomited – to see men murdered for failure to obey orders shrilled in a language they could not understand. Grinning guards plunged bloody bayonets into lifeless or dying men again and again. Some they dragged off, and only agonized screams came back to their helpless comrades.

Cain watched a wounded Filipino soldier, his upper body in a cast and body brace, try to climb onto a truck. Clubbed off, he tried again. "The same Jap guard jerked him off, jerked his brace off, and the blood just spurted. The poor devil stood there crying." On his third attempt, "the Jap put his rifle against him, fired, and killed him. I saw seven heavy trucks, driven by Japanese, drive over his body. I turned my back and sat there fifteen or twenty minutes and heard an almost constant stream of trucks run over his body. When this convoy had gone through, the Japanese herded us down the road. All that was left of this body was a pile of plaster of paris, bones, and hair in a pool of blood."[2]

---

[2] This and other quotations from Colonel Memory H. Cain are excerpted from testimony he gave before the War Crimes Tribunal and kindly given the author by his granddaughter, Lindalie Lein Halama.

Charlie James was one of eight lined up to be shot – he didn't know why. "The firing squad knelt, and loaded, and aimed, and the officer had his saber up.

"They say when you're waiting to die, your whole life passes through your mind. Mine didn't. I was wondering if it would hurt when the bullet hit.

"There was an old gray-headed colonel with us, and he said, 'Throw out your chests, boys. We can take anything these slant-eyed sons-of-bitches can dish out!' Well, I threw out my chest. But my knees were knocking!

"But that Jap officer never brought his saber down. They never fired. Maybe he was just trying to see if we'd cry or beg, and when we threw out our chests, he knew we wouldn't. Maybe that saved us."

The heat was terrible and men were crazed for water. Hank Lovato was finally allowed to fill his canteen in the river. "It was dirty, filthy water. A lot of guys died from drinking it. We had some iodine pills to purify ours. Then they herded us into a big square for the night. We had to sit, close together, in a sort of fetal position. If you stood, you got shot."

Niemon and Pulice were captured at Base Hospital 2, when the victors began to pilfer its meager supplies. Not wishing to be encumbered by sick and wounded men, the Japanese left them there until after Corregidor surrendered.

In a tent for malaria and dysentery patients, Niemon heard the looters swarming outside a full day before they ventured inside. "And when they did, they wore gauze masks. They were scared to death of catching our diseases!

"Every time Corregidor fired, we jumped into foxholes. The Japs had a ring of guns around us that Corregidor was after. Some of our men got killed by shrapnel, and one night several with amoebic dysentery were killed in the latrine."[3]

* * *

3 Wainwright ordered his gunners to avoid the hospital area. The deaths occurred on 22 April as the result of misfires. James H. and William M. Belote, *Corregidor: The Stirring Saga of a Mighty Fortress* (New York: Jove Press, 1984), 118-19.

At the command post near Bagac, Alex had just finished eating when ten American officers crashed through the brush. "Some were shot up pretty badly. They were carrying two captains who bled profusely. When we heard their story we dashed for our stacked arms."

The ten had disarmed, gathered at their designated point of surrender, and were cooking a meal when a Japanese patrol, without warning, opened fire with automatic weapons. The unarmed Americans dropped to the ground, then dragged the badly wounded into some brush, treated them, and escaped to Battery G's position.

After this grim story, those at the command post waited tensely until a Filipino courier arrived with orders for Fields and his officers to proceed to a certain bridge where a Japanese officer would meet them at 0300.

There a squad of Japanese lined Fields and the others up, after which, Fields later recounted, "a saber-rattling Jap officer strode in like a ham actor trying for a grand entrance, and let loose with a bellow and a string of gibberish. He soon worked himself into a foaming rage and ran up and down the line, slapping the Americans."

Such performances, they soon learned, were standard, and, Alex believed, "the most trying treatment any Americans ever had to take, all during our imprisonment. Other than controlling our tempers, we had one alternative – death. And there were many who took that way out."

Fields returned at dawn. He was to take his battery to Bagac and await orders there. "I can't give you men much advice," he told the troops. "Just act like soldiers at all times. Someday our troops will be back. Use your heads, for God's sake, and stick together – no matter what happens.

"I want every man shaved and bathed. And put on those 'Manila khakis.' It won't be for what we intended, but we'll feel better."

They bathed in a dirty stream and donned the clean uniforms they had saved through the ragged times as a symbol of faith, to wear when they recaptured Manila. "We knew we'd take some of the joy out of the Japs' victory if we looked like we hadn't taken too much of a beating. Of course we couldn't hide our sick and wounded, but we could look and act like Americans.

"As we rolled onto the Bagac road, I felt we were losing the last handhold of anything American. From now on it would be Japland."

At Bagac, Don Harris was assigned to a bridge-building detail. "They stuffed us into a carabao corral. You couldn't sit, you couldn't lie down. We took turns squatting. Most of us had to stand all night. So I was glad to get out of that place and go bridge building.

"They beat the devil out of us. We were carrying those heavy timbers, with the Japs always after us to move these things, to get the bridge built. Speedo!"

At Cabcaben, Woodrow Hutchison was forced to act in a Japanese propaganda film. "They had their photography corps in there by the hundreds, on every tank, winding up their cameras to get shots of their great capture. They kept us there two or three hours."

That afternoon the Japanese massed several hundred men from the 200th and 515th in front of four 105-mm. artillery pieces, which they began to fire at Corregidor, thinking the Americans' presence would deter the Rock from returning fire. It did not.

Several rounds hit the corner of a nearby schoolhouse, and in its yard, within a few feet of another group of prisoners penned inside. When they failed to explode, it ran through Earl Harris's mind that "maybe Corregidor, knowing we were in the line of fire, had purposely not set the fuzes. I later learned better. They just didn't go off."[4]

Sakelares was being herded to the field. "Suddenly the Japs opened up those 105s right over our heads. The Americans started shooting back and we started running – I knew better – and Colonel Cain grabbed me and dumped me in a hole, where I should have jumped in the first place." The explosion knocked Cain to the ground.

---

4 Corregidor fired very few shots. After they had destroyed a battery of Japanese 75-mm. guns on the beach, Wainwright ordered care in firing where Americans might be. Most of the shells seem to have come from a gunboat in the bay. Belote 118-19.

In front of the guns, Lucas felt "like we were looking right down their muzzles. They'd fire and just clear us, and then we could turn and watch the shells land on Corregidor and explode. We thought Corregidor was firing back, but it turned out to be a gunboat firing 3-inch shells.

"The first pulverized a *sawali* home. The next hit between the house and us. About then I saw Sage on the road pointing his finger down at a little Jap officer. Suddenly he turned toward us and yelled, 'Take cover!' Then the third shell hit. It jumped over us and hit a machine gun. Blew it to pieces and killed the crew."

When Sage yelled, McCormick bent down to grab his musette bag. "Just as I stooped, a shell whizzed over my back – I could feel the wind – and I raised up and looked behind me, and there was a Jap standing there with the whole side of his face blown off."

Art Smith "suddenly felt my left side all blood and flesh. I thought this was it, and looked down at my arm. But I hadn't lost it – all those guts and blood was from one of those Japs blown apart on that gun."

Men scattered. Lucas ran toward some P-40 revetments on a hillside, "slid into one, and found some of our boys in there. One said, 'Captain, what are we going to do?' I certainly didn't know. 'If you've ever prayed,' I told him, 'you'd better start now!'

"That wasn't much to say, but I suddenly felt like I was on a picnic. Maybe it was just shock, I don't know. But as far as I'm concerned, that was a prayer, and it was answered. I had completely lost my fear."

Some of the shells fell at Base Hospital 2, and the shrieks of terrified patients rose with those of exploding shells. One ward was badly hit. So was the red stone cross where Charlie James had rested not many hours before.

Prior to their final assault on Corregidor, the Japanese conducted interrogations. How many troops were on the Rock? How many guns? Where was the tunnel connecting it with Bataan? And where, they demanded, was the rest of the artillery? They could not believe such a small group, with so few guns, could have dealt their planes such a drubbing.

Taken to Balanga for questioning, Sage and some of his officers were clubbed along the way; then, after sleeping on the floor of a small room, they were interrogated one at a time. Chaney's inability to answer some questions, and his reluctance to answer others, angered his interrogator. "He tried to beat it out of us. He hated Americans – and he'd been educated at the University of California."

Cain's questioner, after several evasive answers, also grew testy. How many guns did Cain have firing when he surrendered? he demanded.

"I said, 'None.'

"'Did the Japanese Air Corps destroy all of them?'

"'No, sir.'

"'Then why didn't they fire?'

"'Because I destroyed them.'

"This was my first introduction to personal contact with the Japanese. The interpreter then proceeded to give me one of the damnedest beatings I ever had. I was dizzy and sick at my stomach when he got through. I was bruised and cut on my cheekbones and bleeding."

Huxtable saw officers at Cabcaben "slapped around by Japs wanting to know where the rest of the men were. They were convinced that we had ten times the men and artillery that we did."

It was an accolade, of sorts.

That afternoon they were ordered to attention as their captors raised the Japanese Sun. They had fought a good fight, they knew. They had, for four months, held off an enemy vastly superior in numbers and arms. They also knew it was not those numbers that had defeated them, but starvation. "With a ham sandwich," they liked to say, "we could have held Bataan forever." That, and something to shoot.

"We'd given them more than they expected," Chintis knew. "We hadn't disgraced the uniform. But I still couldn't quite comprehend – me – giving up."

Neither could Glen Farmer. "And as they hoisted that old Rising Sun, a big knot came in my throat and I couldn't swallow. We knew then we were under them. From then on."

Banegas felt a chill. "I knew that was it. That whether we lived or died, it was all over. And I couldn't fight for my country any more."

– 15 –

DEATH MARCH

"Men were covered with their own filth, eyes were blank and we were like walking zombies. We had seen men drown in human excrement; bodies laid open by bayonets; heads cracked by blows from gun butts. The days and nights became progressively more nightmarish. Our brains, bodies, and souls were numb, and we were no longer human."
– Corporal Cone J. Munsey –

When the shells hit at Cabcaben, the men scattered like shrapnel. Almost immediately the Japanese began to round them up, and Kindel found himself herded onto the road to begin what history would call the Death March. "They told us we would walk to a camp called O'Donnell. I didn't realize how far it was. Or how long the years would be."

The New Mexicans sought each other out, and their strong bond grew stronger. Medic Salvador Garcia helped those whom he could. "But the 200th and 515th were my brothers,

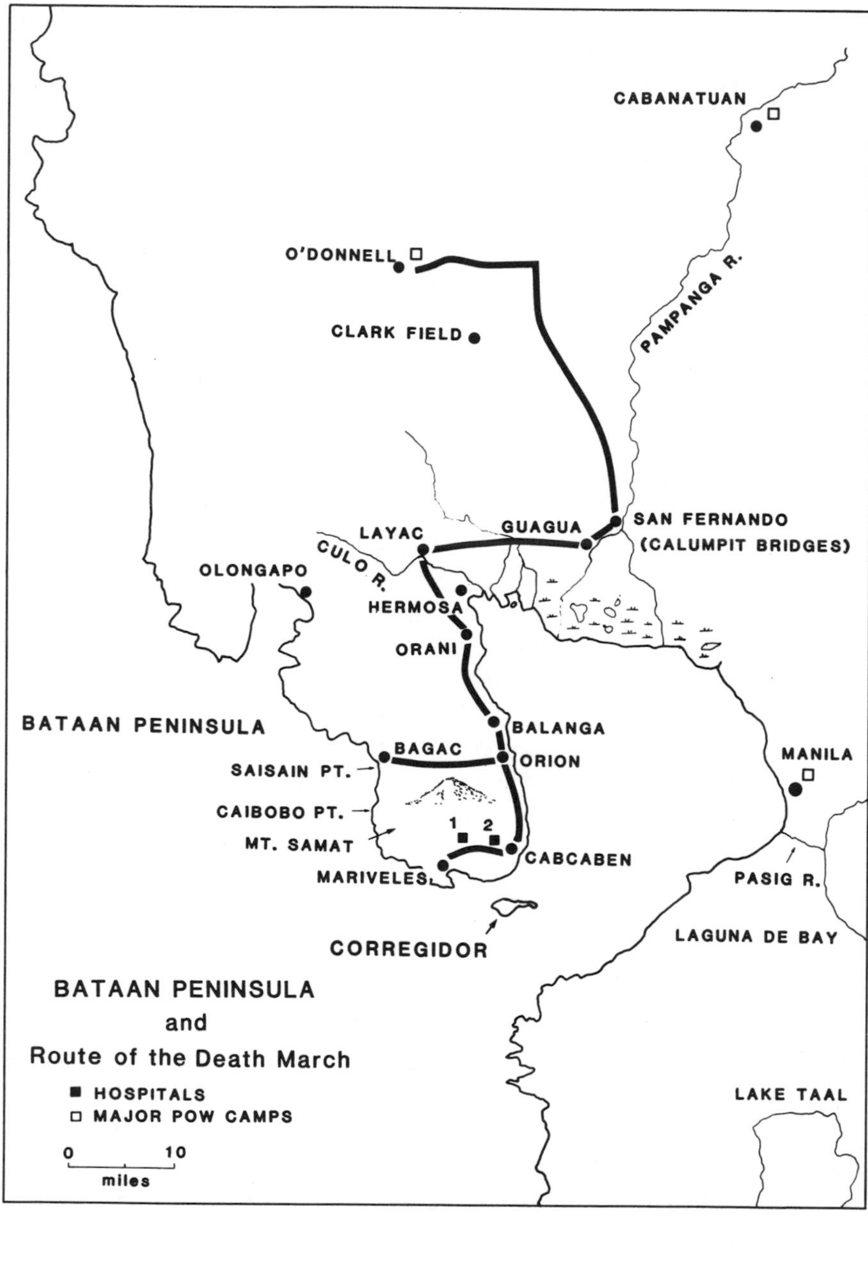

CABANATUAN
O'DONNELL
PAMPANGA R.
CLARK FIELD
SAN FERNANDO
(CALUMPIT BRIDGES)
GUAGUA
LAYAC
CULO R.
OLONGAPO
HERMOSA
ORANI
BATAAN PENINSULA
BALANGA
BAGAC
ORION
MANILA
SAISAIN PT.
CAIBOBO PT.
MT. SAMAT
1
2
CABCABEN
MARIVELES
PASIG R.
LAGUNA DE BAY
CORREGIDOR
BATAAN PENINSULA
and
Route of the Death March
HOSPITALS
MAJOR POW CAMPS
0
10
miles
LAKE TAAL

and that's who we helped first. Guys from other outfits talked about how we stuck together."

The Death March was in reality not one, but many marches, as groups filed in from the jungles to join the main trek north. Crossing from Bagac, Alex saw "hundreds of fetishes that marked Japanese graves. The ground was still covered with the decaying bodies of Americans and Filipinos who had fallen in battles weeks before. To the Jap, the only thing worth burying was another Jap – the stench was, it seemed, irrelevant. This was our first lesson in Oriental psychology."

At Orion they joined the main march. "They put us in a small space, sitting upright, and those who couldn't sit were either bayoneted or thrown to the side. Fields was one of those – he'd been so sick. I saw him go by. He was still alive – and that Jap wouldn't let me get to him."

Major General Yoshikata Kawane, charged with clearing Bataan for the assault on Corregidor, apparently planned to provide food for the prisoners, and transportation for part of the march. But a combination of logistics, ingrained hatred, and fury over the loss of time, men, and face in the Bataan campaign prevented his plans from materializing. The Japanese press further inflamed this fury. "To show them mercy is to prolong the war!" proclaimed the *Japan Times and Advertiser*.[1]

Further, the fanatic Colonel Masanobu Tsuji, without Homma's knowledge, ordered the execution of all Bataan captives. Though some senior officers refused to comply, others, conditioned to unquestioning obedience and a code of vengeance, encouraged the slaughter.

Thousands would perish on the March.[2]

---

1 As quoted by Toland 344.

2 No one will ever know how many died on the Death March. Allowing for those killed in the last battles, those in hospitals, and those who escaped to the hills or to Corregidor (and no records exist for any of these), perhaps 70,000 started on the March, of which 10,000 were Americans. Approximately 9,000 Americans arrived at O'Donnell, according to Colonel John E. Olson, who was Personnel Adjutant for the camp, and is probably in the best position to know firsthand. He estimates a total number arriving as 50,600, though any figures from the Filipino side of the camp are based purely on conjecture. John E. Olson, *O'Donnell: Andersonville of the Pacific: Extermination Camp of American Hostages in the Philippines*, 1985, 13.

* * *

Duration of the March varied. Some walked through in three days, with few stops or none; others were penned for days in the fields.[3] They marched in columns of fours, in groups of about one hundred. Truckloads of southbound Japanese troops kicked or clubbed them as they passed.

Bayonets prodded Aldrich along. "We were denied food and water, and made to march at a gait that kept the Japs with us at a dogtrot. When they were replaced by guards on bicycles, we were pushed faster. And that was when the hot sun and the lack of water and food began to take its toll, and guys, already weakened by disease and hunger, began to fall by the side of the road."

Arthur Gilcrease marched "until it looked like nobody could make it any more. But if a guy fell, the next guard would run a bayonet through him and leave him to bleed to death."

Hank Lovato, doubled up with cramps, "got to the side of the road and fell, holding my stomach. Here came a Jap with his bayonet. I moved quick. That bayonet slashed down. I got up and ran, stomach or not, and he came after me hollering. I ran till I got in the middle of that column."

A fortunate few escaped the March when an estimated 375 men and officers were loaded onto trucks and sent ahead to ready the camp. The first group rolled out late in the afternoon of the ninth and arrived at O'Donnell about dawn.

Boyer, Bond, and most of Battery G were picked up later by trucks returning to the rear for supplies, and driven to San Fernando.

Though they fared better than the marchers, Woody Hutchison found it no joy ride. "Every time we met a southbound unit, we'd pull over to let them pass, and we'd get some licks. One stopped his tank and started beating us over the heads with his long-handled crank. Another group gouged us with bayonets."

---

3 Olson indicates that as far as can be ascertained, the last prisoners arrived on 23 April, nearly two weeks after they set out. Olson 21.

Gamble's lip was split with a stone "about the size of my two fists" hurled by a passing Japanese soldier.

Occasionally they encountered a humane guard. On the first truck with Lucas, "Bill Schuetz was perspiring profusely. The guard gave his fan to Schuetz. Bill fanned himself, thanked him, and handed it back, but the Jap said, 'No, no, you keep,' so Bill stuck it in his musette bag." Schuetz would pay dearly for this rare kindness.

Boyer's group spent the night in San Fernando in a cavalry corral. "Exhausted and hungry – we hadn't eaten for several days – we lay down in the mud and manure. In the morning we were packed into small steel boxcars, so tightly that everybody had to stand, and the doors were closed and locked. The heat and stench were overwhelming. We all had dysentery, and had no control. As we had had no water for several days, we quickly became dehydrated. Those who died, died standing up. Detraining at Capas, we walked the remaining [seven] miles to Camp O'Donnell."

There they were searched and robbed of most of their remaining possessions. A few were bound and led off, to where, no one knew.

Inside, they discovered there was no food. Those who had salvaged a few cans pooled and shared until some rice and seaweed arrived several days later.

They built fences, erected guard towers, repaired pipes, set up kitchens, and otherwise readied the disused Philippine Army training camp for their comrades who would soon begin to stumble in.

Those who marched tried to carry what they could, but as they grew weaker they began to drop bedding and clothes. Doolis started out with his helmet. "But if you had a helmet, they'd beat hell out of you, or kill you. So you put on your fatigue hat if you had one, or anything you could find to cover your head."

The guards seemed especially to enjoy jerking off the men's dog tags and flinging them into the jungle.[4] But they seemed

[4] This is one reason for the post-war nightmare of trying to recover and identify bodies.

also to fear anything supernatural, so the men with religious medals often saved both them and their attached dog tags. Many also kept their rosaries, and the Indians salvaged some of their jewelry by convincing their captors that turquoise was sacred.

Ralph Rodriguez lugged a bag of medicine. "It got heavy on the third day and I nearly pitched it, but Pat Varela protested, so I hung onto it to San Fernando. Then I felt like needles were pricking me, and I hollered to Pat and fainted. When I came to, Pat had my bag."

They began to limp and then to hobble. Mendoza pushed forward on his swollen ankle, and Virgil Sherwood marched barefoot and bleeding – it was that or the bayonet.[5] Ross was nearly as bad off with new shoes. "The first night I took them off, and like never to have gotten them on next morning, so I kept them on after that. I made that whole march on raw feet."

Pepe Baldonado, carrying his sick brother on his back, "walked barefoot with blisters on that hot pavement, till finally the blisters broke and I was walking on blood."

They marched through a shadeless, burned-out land of charred stumps, and their throats closed from roiling dust and palling smoke. Their numbers grew, and as they neared Balanga the columns bloated like a serpent that has swallowed whole his prey.

Conditions worsened. As they neared each barrio, Doolis anticipated shade. "But they'd march us to an open gully and stand us at attention, up to two hours, to show their superiority. They were trying to impress the natives. Then they'd march us to the other side of the village and do the same thing."

James watched for cane fields. "When the guards weren't looking, we'd run and get some, then duck back in line – chew it and spit it out, and the guy behind you'd get it and chew it again."

Worse than hunger was thirst. Free-flowing wells along the route tortured Ross. "But if you tried to fill your canteen you'd get shot, bayoneted, or busted on the head with a rifle. Every

[5] Sherwood made the March twice. At San Fernando he escaped, was caught, and as punishment taken to Mariveles and forced to make it over again – still barefoot.

few miles they'd put fresh guards in. Sometimes they'd make us run. And we'd try – but, Christ, you can't run when you're starved to start with and dying of thirst."

LeMoyne Stiles believed the Japanese "the most inhuman people on earth," as he saw "men driven from water and slashed with bayonets, their mouths swollen and hysterical looks on their faces. Then an eight-hour sun treatment during which some gave up and drank from streams. Natives had crapped in them. Men's bodies lay in them, and all kinds of refuse and carabao dung."

A man in front of Montoya was shot as he dashed toward a well. "He got his water, though. The blood was pumping out of his chest through the bullet hole. He pressed a cloth to it and kept on marching."

During one stop, West spread his poncho under a spout and collected enough water for his own canteen and those of his friends.

The Indians, used to long treks in the southwestern deserts, taught their white brothers to suck a pebble in the daytime and save their water for the night, when it better satisfied.

Mad for water, many raced for the ditches or carabao wallows, filled with blood and refuse. Doolis came close. "But my buddy would say, 'Go on, you goddamned sonofabitch, drink it – die – go on,' and I'd do the same for him. And we didn't drink any of the water."

Those who had iodine shared it. Ross got a few drops in his canteen. "I guess it worked, because I drank water so thick you almost had to eat it, and I didn't die."

One man drank from a stream, then began to cry. "I'll be dead in three days," he sobbed. "Look there." A body, already blackened by the sun, lay in the water. He'd seen it too late.

Thousands poured into Balanga, where some – perhaps a third – got a spoonful of *lugao*, a watery rice gruel. Men rushing to fill canteens in the Talisey River were beaten back. Guards screamed orders made comprehensible by energetic thrusts of their bayonets, and herded them into corrals.

There Armijo saw an American general bludgeoned to death. "And two other Americans were murdered that night, just for getting water. They had the empty canteens on them when we marched by their bodies in the morning."

Homma, headquartered at Balanga, later claimed he neither saw nor heard of any unusual cruelty on the March.

Balanga, Orani, Lubao: One place was like another to Hank Lovato. "They were all filthy. Men had been shot, maybe had an arm hanging off, or heavy sores, with no way to take care of them."

James slept in a corral at Balanga, in the horse manure. "Somebody had a nightmare – started hollering – and the Japs started firing. Some guys ran up trees. I hugged the ground."

Cain slept on a concrete floor in a building which had holes in the ceiling, through which the Japanese, billeted above, "urinated and defecated on us. I got one defecation in my face."

Ross stayed in a compound where "they ran through all night with fixed bayonets, screaming and hollering, and we didn't understand Jap. We knew we were supposed to do something, but we didn't know what the hell it was."

Baldonado was caged in a barn. "The Filipinos had been there ahead of us, and they had diarrhea. The body waste and maggots were ankle deep."

Late at night McBride stumbled into a carabao pen. "Someone built a fire, and here came a Jap with a big can of water. We thought we were going to get a drink. He poured it all on the fire."

Screaming Japanese awoke Harrington. Someone had tried to escape, or the guards thought so. "Two Japs were shining flashlights in my eyes. I feigned sleep. Had I opened my eyes or moved, I'd have been a goner."

At Orani, Gamble "spent a hard night on the grass-covered ground of a war-battle cemetery where the dead had barely been covered with dirt. The stench was sickening. The dead bodies were so close to the surface that the moisture from them made dark splotches on the grass and the flies and insects were so thick they swarmed upon us."

Some marched steadily, without overnight stops. McCormick walked "five days and six nights, or maybe the other way around. I don't remember." Aldrich, suffering sunstroke as well as malaria, knew he'd been walking in his sleep when he regained consciousness with rain on his face. He was licking his lips for the moisture.

North through Hermosa they tramped, across the rebuilt bridge at Layac, on to Lubao. The guards grew more brutal. Men faltered and fell in increasing numbers. Many along the way lay headless.

James passed a bayoneted Filipino "setting on the ground, with blood gushing from his stomach and neck." Montoya saw a corpse, "sitting like he was alive, with his hands extended like he was begging for food."

Lingo watched, helpless, as "a Jap colonel jumped from a car swinging a thick bamboo pole. He hit one fellow who couldn't get up. The blood started pouring, and he begged, 'Please don't,' and then just keeled over."

Ferron Cummins, a New Mexican with friends in the 200th, was bayoneted in the leg for helping one. "I had two close friends removed from my arms and shot. Another close friend went insane and dived headfirst from a bridge to a dry rock bed below."

Passing Japanese soldiers smashed the jaw of a man ahead of McBride, who, to protect his own face, slanted his helmet forward. For this "impudent and defiant gesture," the guard jerked McBride's arm over his knee and dislocated the wrist.

Bill Evans never got used to the sound of a bayonet entering a body, "an exhalation of air such as when a guy gets punched in the gut. Then, there is that unreal sound of a blade passing through bone and gristle. The Japs developed a great taste for that sound . . . ."[6]

Fellow New Mexican Winfred Stroope collapsed. "A Jap hollered at me and pointed his bayonet. I just opened my coveralls and showed him my chest and yelled, 'Stick it right there, you yellow bastard!'

"He couldn't understand that – thought I should be afraid. I would have been if I'd had enough sense, but I was too weak

---

6 William R. Evans, *Kora!* (Rogue River, OR: Atwood Publishing Co., 1986), 12.

and sick. He drug me under some trees, brought me water, and that night put me back in the ranks. He was one of the good Japs – if there is such a thing."

During the five days Don Harris walked, "they liked to tempt us with food and not give us any. They'd stop by artesian wells, and if guys ran for water, they killed them. I've seen many men bayoneted, just for trying to get a drink of water."

Munsey "could see it, smell it, hear it, and could not have it. The guards would drink and taunt us with it, but they would not let us have any." Often they were made to stand by the wells for hours.

Earl Harris saw "some guys who had done something to anger the Japs tossed into a latrine pit. When they'd struggle up, the Japs hit their hands with rifle butts. Until finally – they didn't come up any more."

Three men with Lightfoot were found with Japanese money. "They made them dig holes, then stood them on the edge and shot them, and told the Americans to throw dirt on them. But one wasn't dead. He kept trying to climb out, but the Japs said bury him anyway. One American rared back and hit him as hard as he could with the shovel, so he wouldn't be buried alive."

A friend of Salvador 'Baja' Garcia's suffered a like fate, but without the preliminary of a firing squad. "He had dysentery and malaria, and the Japs made some Americans dig a hole, and then pushed him in and told the guys to throw dirt on him. He was still trying to push out. One of his buddies had to hit him with a shovel. And he ached over that for the rest of his life."

"It wasn't a quick honorable soldier's death with a bullet through the head or a bayonet though the heart," wrote Ragsdale years later. "No man dropped out of the march line until he was too weak and exhausted to continue and his buddies were too weak to help him any further. Once he fell out, the Japs gathered like a pack of coyotes around a carcass.

"The first bayonet usually found the testicles; then a couple through the upper arm muscles; then a bayonet through each calf. Each Jap tried to outdo the others in inflicting pain without killing the man.

"Then they would cut his penis off, pry his mouth open with a rifle barrel, drop his penis in his mouth, and leave him to die. Very few who died on the Death March were lucky enough to be shot and die quickly."

Strength drained from Finley, sick and still in intense pain from the centipede bites in his inner ear. "Three of us got separated from the Japs and were going up the road by ourselves. I was passing blood, and cramping. By sundown I couldn't go any farther. I told them to go on, and I crawled into some weeds. They left me a canteen of water.

"The sun was just setting when a Filipino came and said, 'Come with me, Joe. I can get you to Corregidor!'"

It was a note of hope like reveille. With food and medicine, he might yet survive. Finley pulled to his feet to follow his unknown deliverer.

In the shadeless stretch into Lubao, men grew crazed for water. Many had become too dehydrated to urinate, and when finally they did, pain seared them. Tongues and throats puffed like cotton, and those few who got a taste of water were often unable to swallow it.

Many went berserk. Earl Harris saw a Filipino "attack a Jap barehanded. The Jap knocked him down three times before he shot him – which was, for a Jap, quite a bit of restraint."

Alex "saw men who were perfectly sane when they began the March go hopelessly mad before we reached San Fernando."

Never had the spirit of Old Two Hon'erd proved stronger. The March took on a sacramental quality, and a single, almost palpable heartbeat seemed to sustain them.

Mendoza saw a buddy fall in a ditch. "His face was in that filthy water. I picked him up and covered his face with grass. He was my friend. I made the sign of the cross, and said, 'God let you rest in peace,' and we marched on."

When a comrade seemed ready to fall, buddies on each side supported him as long as their own strength allowed – Ross found himself "almost dragging some to keep going at that pace" – and they shared their canteens. When Munsey sagged, two Navajo friends, John Begaye and Sam Nez, supported him the rest of the way. Tomás Cisneros and Gregorio Villaseñor carried Paul Schurtz into San Fernando and found him a spot in the shade.

John West and his friends "carried one of our boys from Carlsbad the last few miles, taking turns. You'd get so hot and tired you just had to quit, only you couldn't. We made it with him, but he died later."

James kept going. "But I knew if I'd fall and say, 'Battery F, 200th,' one of 'em would come over, or try to."

Norval Tow's buddy "dropped and they bayoneted him. I was alone. So I walked without any rest breaks till I caught up with Rhea and the Silver City guys."

Rhea's group hadn't found it easy to stick together. "The Japs were always trying to cut groups apart, and we got split several times. But we managed to get back together, and we stayed together. It was the only way you could make it."

Through the barrios, the people helped them. A surreptitiously flashed V for Victory or the hummed strains of "God Bless America" strengthened them as much as the cone of sugar or the banana-leaf packet of rice tossed into the ranks, or the precious bottles of water left along the roadside.

The people in Lubao wept to see the staggering men, and tried to pass them food and water, despite the rifle-swinging, bayonet-wielding guards. A man gave his hat to Lightfoot. A little girl tossed Tow a green tomato and a cone of sugar. Brewer got a plate of fish and rice from a couple with children, who hadn't enough for themselves.

An old woman brought water and darted back into her house. Cain watched sickened as a guard dragged her out by her hair, and cut off each of her ears, and then her breasts. He threw the bloody pulps into the column, and left her to die screaming.

When a Filipina, about eight months pregnant, passed a rice ball to a friend of Drake's, "the guard ran up screaming and jabbed her in the belly with his bayonet – right through the fetus. She fell, and he bayoneted her again in the heart. Then two other Japs came up, and one took out a hunting knife.

They ripped her clothes off – cut her belly open – dragged that fetus out, held it up, and laughed like the fiends of hell.

"I had to turn my back. I had nothing to vomit, but I heaved until my socks came over my kneecaps."

In the last stages of emotional and physical exhaustion, they stumbled toward San Fernando. When Aldrich felt he could go no farther, he smelled the sweet smoke of sugar factories, knew it was San Fernando, and summoned his last strength.

Montoya, his endurance gone, prayed for help, and decided to escape or to die trying. Not knowing that he had only to walk one kilometer more, he watched for his chance.

Nez and Begaye still kept Munsey going. "Men were covered with their own filth, eyes were blank, and we were walking zombies. We had seen men drown in human excrement; bodies laid open by bayonets, heads cracked by blows from gun butts. The days and nights became progressively more nightmarish. Our brains, bodies, and souls were numb, and we were no longer human."

In the teeming rail center they were corralled to await transportation to the prison camp called O'Donnell.

Baclawski was penned in a wall surrounding a collapsed building. "There was one faucet and a long line of guys trying to get water. There were no latrines. Flies everywhere. Most of the men were sick, a lot with dysentery, and had no control."

A small Filipino boy came into the yard where Poe was confined. "He'd been shot through the shoulder, and our Dr. [George] Colvard dressed his wound. That little kid brought us rice. That's all we had to eat for five days."

Latrines were nonexistent, and the prisoners walked and slept in a mire of excrement. Green flies gorged on the filth and swarmed over men and food, and those so far free of dysentery escaped no longer. Some spent days in these sties before they were herded to the depot.

As Mendoza waited to entrain, "a Spaniard came up in a white sharkskin suit, and said he could get me out of there if I'd come with him and join the guerrillas. The Japs weren't bothering him, and I thought maybe I had a chance – I was dark and could have passed for a Filipino. But I couldn't speak Tagalog. So I decided I'd take my chances with the Americans. Then they loaded us into those boxcars."

Some of the cars were wooden; most were of steel, "seven-and-a-half or eight feet wide, and twenty-eight or thirty feet long," Cain testified, "not very high, and hotter than an oven." Each car was crammed with one hundred men.

Banegas could barely breathe. "Fellows started suffocating, passing out, dying. Finally they opened the doors a little. The guard was watching from the top. We'd go through a station and the Filipinos tried to give us food. Once I grabbed a little basket of eggs and we ate them raw. But I hadn't eaten in so long I almost died that night."

Aldrich, at a half-open door, "felt a blow to my chest. It was a baked sweet potato! I passed half of it out and ate the other half. It was like lead in my stomach. It was the first food I'd had on the entire March."

The heat mounted. The stench was awful, and it grew worse as men vomited and, afflicted with diarrhea, lost control. Lightfoot had an attack, "and I was about to blow up. One of the guys said, 'Well, stick it out the door and let it go!'" But few could get to a door.

At Capas they stumbled, gulping air, on legs so numbed many could not stand. Some pitched forward dead.

Cans of water like small shrines lined the road as they marched the seven miles to Camp O'Donnell. A few guards let them drink. Most kicked over the pails, and the men watched the water trickle into the dust.

Outside the fence they were searched again. "Get rid of anything Jap!" The word passed down the line – men had already been shot for possessing what the guards assumed they had rifled from dead Japanese.

Some had bought food at San Fernando and accepted change in Japanese 'invasion' money. Lingo swallowed a nickel. Pelayo shoved a handful of *pesos* into the mud. The small map Sakelares carried (there was always the thought of escape) would have meant sure death. Angel swallowed it.

Here they learned the fate of five of their officers and eight enlisted men, all from the Brigade, who had gone ahead on trucks:

Hazelwood had a pocketful of *pesos*. Schuetz still had the fan the guard had given him. Both were jerked up, beaten, and trussed. "I have money!" Hazelwood yelled to warn the others.

Oliver Witten chewed up his money. Sage threw a metal disc from the first plane the Regiment had shot down, was caught in the motion, and beaten over the head. Lucas saw them swoop on Eddie Kemp. "He had Jap propaganda leaflets – souvenirs. I'd lost mine when they bombed my truck. But Eddie had kept his." So had Raymond Thwaits, Sergeants Barney Prosser and John Keeler, and an Indian boy from Gallup.[7] Reynaldo Gonzales arrived in the second convoy and yelled to Boyer to save him a place, that he'd be along soon. But he, too, had some invasion *pesos*.

They marched them off, hands shackled, and the guards returned carrying the ropes that had bound them. The next morning – 14 April – Frank Sarracino saw them in the guardhouse with thirty or forty other Americans. Later that morning the men in camp heard gunfire.

That afternoon Cain and a corporal were sent for water. "On the way back, they showed us twenty or thirty American Army officers and men, dead. In this group I recognized Captain Kemp and Major Hazelwood lying face up in a sort of common grave or pit." He and the corporal were told to cover them with dirt. "I had known Kemp and Hazelwood intimately for fifteen years. Hazelwood was like a younger brother."

Those who had ridden awaited those who hadn't. Shillito saw the first formation coming. "They marched them through the gate and kept them in formation, and some died standing there, before they even broke formation. And then is when we learned about the Death March."

---

7 Colonel Cain, from whose testimony much of this account is taken, was unable to recall this man's name. There were apparently five other enlisted men from the Brigade executed in this group, but the author has been unable to ascertain their names.

Boyer stood appalled. "Men we had seen just before the surrender, you could hardly recognize now. And they had nothing. Those of us who rode still had knapsacks. So we shared with them, and then we all had nothing. We'd look for New Mexico men as they staggered in, and we'd take them to our barracks and try to clean them a bit with what little water we had."

Chintis, watching for friends, saw a flash of purple and gold – his college colors. "By damn," he yelled, "here comes a Mustang!" It was Elmer (no longer 'Fat Boy') Worthen.

Gamble met each group. "Each day we would anxiously look for faces of our comrades as they marched past the Nip headquarters. There were the sublime, the ridiculous, the tragic, the comic, the sad, and even the lighthearted. There were those almost Godlike in their bearing, in their stoicism, and in their consideration for their fellow soldiers.

"But little did they know of the hell and misery and death in a Japanese prison camp."

Jesse Finley met each group and asked those he knew if they had seen his son. Lingo, who had seen Jack collapse by the road, dreaded the question. "I said yes, I'd seen him, and he should be along. I was lying – I knew he wouldn't."

Jesse watched until no more came. He turned back from the gate.

– 16 –

"ALL THAT IS HUMANLY POSSIBLE"

"The hope of going further is just not there any more, so you figure if you've got to go, you're going out in a blaze."
– Private First Class Wallace R. Phillips –

Corregidor held out until 6 May. To those who had crossed from Bataan, unaware of their comrades' March, it seemed at first a reprieve.

Gulbas mistook Malinta Tunnel for heaven when they brought him "a pack of cigarettes, a cup of good Stateside coffee, and a bowl of canned peaches."

Meuli stumbled ashore in the night, found a foxhole, and awoke at dawn to find himself beside his old friend Jack Fleming.

The boat Phillips crossed in "picked up men wounded in explosions at Mariveles. They were floating on planks, and their friends swam alongside pushing – with sharks in that water. One fellow looked dead. He was in shock and his thigh was broken, so his foot kept rolling off the plank. A corpsman aboard gave him morphine. He lost his leg, but his friends made him an artificial one.

"An Indian named Bluebird picked me up on the beach, took me to his battery, and I had a bath and clean clothes – his fit perfectly. He kept laughing and telling me what a sorry-looking mess we were!"

Those on the Rock were shocked at the condition of those from Bataan. Captain Benson Guyton of Battery D, 60th CA, found them "skinny, gaunt, shell-shocked, exhausted, and most of all hungry."[1] Though most of their surplus was gone, they were still eating relatively well on Corregidor, and glad to share their largesse.

"Our flag still flies on this beleaguered island fortress," Wainwright radioed Roosevelt when Bataan fell. So long as the Rock denied Homma the use of Manila Bay, the Japanese had not yet won the Philippines.

Hope flared briefly with the news of the Doolittle raid of 18 April: Americans over Tokyo! But it was less a siege than a symbol. It offered no help for Corregidor, and every man there knew the inevitable outcome; but they would sell the Rock dearly.

The pulse of the island was the rock-hewn Malinta Tunnel, whose twenty-five concrete-reinforced laterals housed USFIP headquarters as well as those of Harbor Defenses, quartermaster and gasoline stores, and the hospital. Batteries of antiquated but effective 10- and 12-inch guns bristled around the island's periphery, manned by the 60th Coast Artillery, and to these the New Mexicans were assigned.

Most of these units already had full complements, and when Senter was directed to a 2-6-8 unit, the captain refused to accept him. "He said he wasn't going to feed me. Finally the captain of Battery E said, 'Son, you've gotta eat,' and took me."

---

[1] Lt. Col. Benson Guyton, USAR, in a letter to the author, 16 February 1987.

Almeraz had barely reported to Battery B on the morning of the tenth, when the men looked up to see a silent observation balloon looming above them. After that, 'Peeping Tom' came daily. "They directed fire from that thing, and could hit anything on the island. They knocked out our gun, but we finally got it fixed."

Gulbas found his old friend, Lieutenant Louis Lutich, just as an air raid struck. "I hit a foxhole, and men piled in on me. Louis only got halfway in when a bomb came crashing. I had gravel all over my face, and I could see blood, and I asked, 'Who got it?' It was Louis. They rushed him out and I high-tailed it to Malinta." Lutich was alive, but he lost a leg.

Artillery opened up from Bataan and Cavite on the twelfth, and intensified on the eighteenth with the arrival on Bataan of ten 240-mm. guns, which pounded them massively and continually for the next twenty-four days. Battery Geary, leading the return fire the first morning, played havoc with the Japanese 7th Tank Regiment. But the old fact of obsolete equipment and limited ammunition loomed as ominously as Peeping Tom, and the gun emplacements in six batteries were quickly disabled.

Like moles, the men in the batteries tunneled for ammunition storage and shelters. Almeraz spent his twenty-first birthday "wheel-barreling muck." Gulbas, in charge of digging Battery D's tunnel, "was scared to death, and pushing so hard to get that thing dug that somebody said I was bucking for promotion. 'Listen,' I said, 'they're going to lob in a shell and bury us alive unless we break through for air.' I was taking a breather outside when a shell hit and a piece of shrapnel caught me. They threw me in a pickup and took me to Malinta. Next day [Norbert] Roessler told me a shell had caved in the tunnel. But they'd dug through in the night."

Phillips was sent to hospital with malaria. "I was really out of it, but they loaded me with quinine. By the third day I wanted out of that tunnel – it was like being trapped. I was weak – could hardly walk – but they gave me some quinine and let me go.

"When I got back to my battery, my gun had been hit and the man taking my place had lost his foot."

By 28 April Homma was ready to invade Corregidor. His amphibious forces were massed; he had captured detailed maps of the Rock; and, having destroyed or reduced to practical impotence most of the antiaircraft batteries on Corregidor, he controlled the air. He could have starved the Americans out by June; but, humiliated by the long resistance on Bataan and pressed by Tokyo, Homma had no intention of waiting,

On the twenty-ninth he opened up with the most massive artillery barrage yet. Over 10,000 shells battered the island that day. Whole cliffsides collapsed, sending billows of dust into the smoke-heavy air. Observation stations, a searchlight plant, and gun emplacements were wiped out. Communications were severed. A direct hit blew Willie Tillman's machine gun from under him and killed several of his buddies.

Senter ended up in Battery Way. "It had been abandoned for several years, and the Japs had hit two of the guns and cracked the powder magazine. They sent us out from Battery E to take over those 12-inch mortars." Reactivating the outmoded guns under artillery fire, they had to adapt whatever shells were available. Breech loading and firing were complicated and hazardous, and the impact of the resultant explosions shattering.

The Japanese shock when the supposedly silenced battery went into action was enormous. So was the delight of the Americans on the beaches. Then, rallying, the enemy concentrated on Battery Way until they had destroyed two of the guns (and Senter's hearing, permanently). The men of Battery E sweated all night to repair the two remaining guns. By morning they were firing again.

After two Navy PBYs braved the blockade to fly in some quinine and 740 mechanical fuzes from Australia, Topside batteries gave the Japanese another surprise when they brought down three planes on the next flight over. It was like aspirin for terminal cancer, but it eased the pain momentarily.

* * *

"SITUATION HERE IS FAST BECOMING DESPERATE," Wainwright wired MacArthur on 3 May. The few antiaircraft guns still operative were without height-finders, directors, or communications. Men under fire continually repaired telephone lines. Beach defenses were under equipped, and, except for the Fourth Marines, the only men with infantry combat experience included a few overage World War I veterans and the ill and exhausted men from Bataan.

The watcr supply grew critical. Reservoir levels had dropped, the power plant was inoperable, and diesel oil to run the pumps nearly depleted.

In Malinta Tunnel, Lucy Wilson grew pallid. As air-raid lights flashed red warnings, the nurses steeled for new influxes of wounded. With each detonation the arched ceiling trembled, bottles fell from shelves, and lights flickered or went out entirely. Dust swirled, and they covered their own and patients' faces with dampened gauze.

With the blowers off during each attack, the smells of death and blood and superating wounds, and of latrines overflowing from ruptured plumbing, nearly choked them. Flies droned and varmints crawled.

The twelve laterals filled, and the hospital expanded into three more. Recuperating patients were rushed out prematurely to make room for newly wounded. Those who died lay until the chaplains could bury them in the night.

Wainwright began to evacuate key personnel, important documents, and nurses from the doomed fortress. Some left on the PBYs that had flown in the medicine and fuzes. Lucy was not among them, but on 3 May she was told to be ready to leave that night by submarine.

Back in the ward, she chatted with Dan's old friend, Louis Lutich, then learning to hobble on an improvised leg. "I told him I wasn't going, that I was tired of retreating, but he said, 'Get out and go on,' that I couldn't help Dan by staying, and he'd want me out."

That night, with eleven other nurses, a civilian wife, and a dozen officers, Lucy stepped onto a small craft that churned them out to a hulk looming black in the cloud-draped night.

She was the *Spearfish*. Quickly and quietly they boarded, to head through the mined waters for the open sea and Australia.

She submerged just as the clouds parted, and the moonlight revealed her silhouette against the fires and explosions of Corregidor. Japanese patrol boats raced after her.

She was the last ship out.

On 5 May, under cover of heavy barrage, the first wave of Japanese landing craft was spotted approaching the north shore of Corregidor's tail.

Gulbas saw the red lights flashing in the tunnel. "That meant if you're assigned to beach defense, get to your station!" Gulbas wasn't so assigned, but, determined to get out of the hospital, he crawled out to a foxhole with an acquaintance who was. Under cover they shared a cigarette. It was spookily quiet.

"Then we heard them coming, hollering and screaming. It started an hour or so after midnight, and by morning they raised their flag."

Despite contrary currents and tremendous losses of men and landing craft, the Japanese established a beachhead and landed tanks and artillery. The main party headed toward Malinta, seized Battery Denver, and established a line. Beating back American attempts to regain the position, they directed artillery fire at the tunnel's west entrance, and awaited the second, larger wave of infantry, tanks, and artillery.

Almeraz was one of four left on his gun – "a Jew, an Italian, an Anglo, and me – a Mexican – all huddled under the carriage." The Anglo in this miniature melting pot told the rest to get out. He had to man the telephone.

"To hell with the phone," Almeraz said. "The sergeant's gone, the corporal's gone, and we're going to get hit!" The shells kept moving towards them, and knocked out a nearby gun. "We're next," Fred said.

"We heard the gun report then, and two of us dived in a trench. One guy ran across an open space toward a big gun, and caught a leg full of shrapnel.

"Then the shelling stopped, and here came the bombers. We ran back to start firing, but they'd hit our gun. There was just a big crater. So we started for the Tunnel."

Shrapnel hit Tillman in his machine-gun nest. A shell knocked out another of Battery Way's mortars. They kept firing the one that remained.

Phillips and Bluebird, at Middleside, "didn't know what was going on down there, but we knew things were bad. We were cleaning our small arms, and a fellow called 'Hawkeye' said it for all of us. 'If I'm going,' he said, and the tears were streaming down his face, 'I'm going to take a bunch with me!'

"The hope of going further is just not there any more, so you figure if you've got to go, you're going out in a blaze."

The forts in the bay fell one by one, until only Fort Drum still fired. A second landing force approached and defeat was inevitable. Wainwright must sacrifice thousands of lives, or surrender.

"Tell the Nips," the agonized general ordered at 1015 on 6 May, "that we'll cease firing at noon."

Then commenced the last rites. Men in the Tunnel scurried frantically to destroy records, codes, equipment, and money. From outside came the continued crackle of small arms and the thunder of artillery, and the dead and wounded piled in at a terrifying rate. Battery Way still fired its one remaining mortar until, shortly before noon, the breechlock froze, and it fired no more.

Wainwright prepared his report to his President, to be sent before they smashed the radio equipment. It was his heaviest duty.

"With broken heart and head bowed in sadness but not in shame . . . ." He began that message, soon to be flashed to a stunned world. "Please say to the nation," he concluded "that my troops and I have accomplished all that is humanly possible and that we have upheld the best tradition of the United States and its Army . . . . With profound regret and with continued pride in my gallant troops, I go to meet the Japanese commander."

Phillips, for one, was not ready to surrender. "When we got word to destroy our weapons, we couldn't believe it. You'd think it would be a godsend – a reprieve. But we felt almost betrayed."

They smashed their weapons and filed toward Malinta. They heard the last Taps float over the Rock. They watched the Stars and Stripes slide down the flagpole, and they saw her burn as the white flag ascended. It was high noon. Those who had not wept before, wept now.

To forestall renewed hostilities and a sure massacre, Wainwright assumed command of the remaining forces in the Philippines and ordered their surrender. It was the only condition Homma would accept. On Mindanao, Brigadier General William F. Sharp, to avert a retaliatory massacre of the 11,000 captives on Corregidor, passed the order down. It took a month to effect the surrender of all the outlying islands.[2]

In the meantime, the Americans on Corregidor were held hostage under miserable conditions. The nurses, with their patients, remained caged inside Malinta. The rest were marched down to the 92nd Garage area, a former seaplane base on the south beach.

"There were no latrines. It was a mess, with the heat and all that cement. They didn't care whether we ate or not. They put up a rope and told us not to go beyond it." Phillips saw several men shot trying to get to water.

"They took small details to get water for the rest. One evening we were going up a steep incline – there were cables through pipes for a guard rail – and a Marine carrying a couple of sticks with canteens laced in them was just ahead of us. He set the canteens down, stepped over the cable, and poised there an instant. Then he did the most beautiful swan dive and disappeared into the darkness.

"We took his canteens and got the water and went back."[3]

Almeraz thought his brain would burst in the sun. "We got blankets, or pieces of tin, or whatever we could find, to make a little shade to crawl under. The stink of dead bodies was terrible."

---

2 Chynoweth on Cebu surrendered on 15 May, Christie on Panay on the 20th, Cornell on Leyte and Samar six days later, and the last of the islands, except for a few small and remote pockets, on 9 June.

3 The Marine's colonel got permission to hunt for, and found, his body. He reported him killed in action. "There was no discussion," Phillips reported. "I thought it appropriate."

Phillips, detailed to clean out a bombed barracks for Japanese officers, was able to steal food. "A young Jap lieutenant who spoke English showed us a food dump. 'But don't overdo it,' he said, 'or we'll all be in trouble.' So we'd put a pound or so of rice in our pants legs and carry it back to the others.

"There were a few good ones along the way, like this lieutenant, who made it possible for us to survive."

Few details were that pleasant. The Americans were forced to gather the bodies of Japanese to be cremated. Only later were they allowed to bury their own dead, and it was a hasty, shallow matter, in rock, and without adequate tools. Chaplains were not allowed to compile rosters of the dead.

Meuli was marched down from a Topside detail several days after the surrender. "The dead Japs had all been picked up, and all we could see were dead Marines along the shore. It was a sight you can't forget."

Finally they were ferried to Manila and marched to the old Spanish prison of Bilibid, circuitously, to flaunt them before the Sunday crowds.

They hauled Tillman, still recuperating from shrapnel wounds, from the hospital, "and just throwed us on a little old boat. About a mile off the shore they kicked us out in the water. If it hadn't been for some good buddies, I'd 've drowned, 'cause I had one arm taped to my side, and I couldn't swim anyway."

The Battles of Bataan and Corregidor were over.

For twenty-seven days after Bataan fell, as food and munitions ran low, as water and hope dried up, they had clung to the Rock with taloned will. Like Bataan, of which it was an extension, the tale of Corregidor inspired a nation.

The doomed defense was not a futile fight. Depending on a fleet that never came, the sick and starved defenders, ill equipped and outnumbered, had cost the enemy dearly in men and time. Those on Bataan had decimated the Japanese Fourteenth Army and caused Homma to requisition land, air, and naval forces needed elsewhere, and those on Corregidor had smashed the Fourth Division, on which Japan had relied for offensives in New Guinea and the Solomons.

A soldier's return to the battlefield: Jack Aldrich, left foreground, inspects bombed topside barracks of Corregidor, July 1987. (Courtesy: Marcello B. Gerez, photographer, Philippine Government Department of Tourism.)

Some of the old gun emplacements still lie in quiet ruins on Corregidor. (Courtesy: Marcello B. Gerez, photographer, Philippine Government Department of Tourism.)

They had denied Homma the use of Manila Bay. From the Rock they had intercepted messages and provided valuable intelligence regarding Japanese plans and deployments.

They had slowed the Japanese advance in the Pacific by six months, protected Australia from attack, and enabled MacArthur to mount the offensive that would win eventual victory in the Pacific.

The New Mexicans had done their own large part,[4] and when finally they were driven to a surrender not of their making, they could report with pride, "Mission Accomplished."

When once their story was told, it rolled like an anthem through the land. The battlers on Bataan and the eagles on the Rock gave hope to an embattled America, and pride for her children to come. For theirs is the stuff of epic: It is such annals that impassion Man's will to renew the covenant of his fathers, that his Republic shall live, in glory and in honor.

4 Because the 200th had gone *in toto,* and the state was thereby represented so heavily in the Philippines, New Mexico suffered more casualties per capita than any other state in World War II.

BOOK IV

GUESTS OF THE EMPEROR

"Your letter . . . strikes close to my heart. There is little I can tell you of the men of the 200th and 515th Anti-Aircraft Regiments that you do not already know. They have written their own immortal record in the bloody transcript of Bataan. I knew them well and loved them greatly . . . . If I live I shall return to save them."

– General of the Army Douglas MacArthur,
in a letter dated 9 February 1943
to Dr. V.H. Spensley –

APARRI
VIGAN
CORDILLERA CENTRAL
LUZON
BAGUIO
LINGAYEN
LUZON
MAJOR POW CAMPS
CABANATUAN
PAMPANGA R.
O'DONNELL
CLARK FIELD
SAN FERNANDO
HERMOSA
MARIVELES
MANILA
CORREGIDOR
LAGUNA DE BAY
LAKE TAAL
LEGASPI
MINDORO
0
50
miles

– 17 –

"WE ARE ENEMIES FOREVER"

"We were all in the same kettle, and there you go back to the individual. The quickest way to gauge a man's character is through his stomach. Hunger brings out the best or the worst in him. I saw some who just couldn't cope. And some were really noble, were still part of the human race."
– Sergeant Nicholas Chintis –

Steve Alex was among the last to lurch through the gate of Camp O'Donnell. "Gentry and Chintis found me – sat by me several days and dripped water in my mouth. They brought me back to life."

Each day the New Mexicans who survived the March scanned the ragged wraiths who stumbled in, and, finding one of their own, pulled him toward the area they occupied. Earl Harris saw many die almost as they gained the camp. "We'd bed them down wherever we could. The next morning, those who could move, would. A lot couldn't. They'd just been going on determination. They were walking dead."

Those still conscious enough to perceive never forgot their welcome to O'Donnell. Each new group was forced with stick and bayonet onto the parade ground, stripped, searched, and robbed again. Those who fainted lay unconscious in the sun; their friends tried to cover them with bits of clothing.

Then the camp commander, an overage reserve in saggy shorts, strode out with all the arrogance of the incompetent, climbed onto a box, and began to screech. He was Captain Yoshio Tsuneyoshi – soon known to the Americans as 'Baggy Pants.' In a tirade which mounted in fury, he inveighed against all Caucasians (and especially Americans), whose evils would cease forever when Japan won the war. They were not prisoners of war, but captives. Whether they lived or died was of no concern. Any slight infringement of his rules would command instant death.

"We are enemies forever!" he shrieked. "Japan will fight and fight and fight if it takes a thousand years! If you try to escape you will be shoot. I would like you all be killed. Only the benevolence of the Emperor permits you to live. You are guests of the Emperor!"

"Well, then," muttered Hernandez, "the Emperor must be a very poor host."

Munsey began to look for water. "We had dreams of a bath, washing our clothes, and having plenty of water to drink. We discovered one spigot running a slow stream. It was here that it finally sank in that staying alive was at best a long shot."

O'Donnell sprawled like a slattern on a rolling plain of cogon grass. Except for their own quarters, the Japanese made no effort to restore its wind-scalped Nipa roofs, to build latrines, or in any way to ready the camp. Eventually Tsuneyoshi ungraciously spared the Americans a few tools for repairs.

The Capas road split the camp into American and Filipino sides. On 15 April units were designated areas, but as men poured in, these spilled into one another.[1] Early arrivals slept in tiered bays that lined the central aisle of each barracks – five to a bay. With neither bedding nor flesh to pad their bones, sleep on the bamboo slats was almost impossible. At first they were too exhausted to care.

The barracks filled and still men staggered in. Knighton crawled under a building. Schmitz slept in the open. With the onset of the rainy season, rivers of mud inundated both. Wherever they slept, vermin crawled.

On 27 April Tsuneyoshi, to break up unit cohesion, ordered a new organization based on prewar occupations, a move so inefficient it was never fully accomplished. Despite reorganization, battery officers began to collect their own men, and the New Mexicans clung stubbornly together.

Boyer and Lucas were each assigned a 'sick barracks' – a risky charge, they found. One of Lucas's charges, shot through the neck, "couldn't drink – the water ran out the bullet holes – and he was delirious. We had to keep him in the barracks or he'd get shot – and so would I."

On 10 May the Japanese moved most of the senior officers to a separate camp at Tarlac, leaving only a staff of several colonels, including Cain, and General Sage, who, at King's suggestion, was named commander of the American camp – "an honor," wrote Gamble, "in which all the 200th and 515th rejoiced."

Discipline grew harsher. Villaseñor was beaten because he forgot his number in Japanese, James for awkwardness with a Japanese saw. Stiles saw a man beaten for wasting a bite of rice, made to stand in the sun for hours, handed a saber, and told to disembowel himself. When he refused, "they cut his fingers and made him sign a paper with his blood."

---

[1] American personnel figures cannot be exact, because of the circumstances of the March, the conditions at O'Donnell, and the disorganization of both Japanese and American commands. Those of the Filipinos were even more chaotic. Tsuneyoshi expected from 20,000 to 30,000 prisoners to occupy a camp designed for a maximum of 10,000. Between 50,000 and 60,000 arrived; of these, close to 9,300 were Americans. E. Bartlett Kerr, *Surrender and Survival: The Experience of American POWs in the Pacific, 1941-1945,* (New York: William Morrow & Co., 1985), 60.

Colvard, asked to operate on a Japanese general with a ruptured appendix, agreed; but when told he would be held responsible for the patient's life, refused to perform surgery under that condition. "When he came back," Cain testified, "he was the worst beat-up man I ever saw."

"Life became," for Chintis, "a day-to-day process of surviving. And that's where the real strain and drain began."

Though Tojo's "no work, no food" policy was not official until 30 May, it was maliciously observed from the first, and many seriously ill men died who could have survived with adequate food. Those able to work had little more, and Tsuneyoshi refused to allow the Philippine Red Cross or the Bishop of Manila to distribute any.

Without water to wash their mess kits, Gamble licked his clean, "though we would have licked them anyway. After some weeks we began getting a few grains of salt. We guarded each grain. I saw men go mad for lack of salt."

They lived on rice. Never enough, boiled to a saltless paste called *lugao*, it crawled with weevils and worms. "But," shrugged Gamble, "they were the only meat we had." Rations were issued by the head, and it became common practice to keep their dead several days before reporting them, in order to collect their rations.

Despite the risk, men on outside work details tried to smuggle food and medicine into camp; and, being Americans, they devised ways. Charlie James nursed Frank Martin until Frank was well enough to forage. "Then at night he'd sneak under the fence and crawl to the Japs' side, fill his shirt with sweet potatoes, and crawl back in. Next day we'd boil up a *quan*."[2]

After Corregidor fell, they acquired some flour – a staple the Japanese rarely used – and with it a carabao for each four thousand men – not enough, wrote Gamble, to serve as meat, "but in a weak thin broth with a few *camotes*[3] and turnips –

2 From Tagalog. *Quan* refers to any bit of food that could be added to the ubiquitous rice or cooked into a stew. Some of the mixtures were masterpieces of invention. Anything delighted the starved men, and the anticipation of a *quan* kept many a man's hope alive. The word grew to mean the can in which it was cooked, or the kitchen; used as a verb, it denoted the cooking, or the hunting for food to cook.

3 Native sweet potatoes.

what a feast it was! We almost wept for joy." They concocted an oven from a steel barrel, laid it over a fire pit, and, with the flour, cooked "one thick biscuit for each man in our brigade. There was a renewed spark of life. Men showed an occasional grim smile.

"All knives and razors were taken from us, but they began to show up with the coming and going of outside details. Men fashioned mess kits from bamboo poles. The pioneer spirit was coming to the fore."

The dehydrated men panted for water. Though two artesian wells served the camp, only one was operable until after 1 May, when the Japanese finally allowed the Americans to install a pump. A five-eighths-inch main sporadically gasped near-boiling water through a single tap. Eventually two more spigots were connected. The pipes leaked. Moreover, the Japanese irregularly cut off the supply, and thousands of men stood hours in line, often to find the tap dry when they reached it.

Foy "saw men just fall over. We'd haul 'em into a barracks and get a little water from the front of the line. By then, some weren't still alive to drink it."

About a mile from camp wormed a slimy stream, into which the latrines filtered. Crazed for water, some eluded the guards to drink the scum. Most who drank died.

Determined to get water to the hospital area, John Gamble and Tony Montoya cut the end from a fifty-five-gallon drum to fill for bathing the patients. "We had to get permission to carry water from the river, and all we had were five-gallon cans. But we took out details, swinging cans from bamboo poles. Of course we boiled the water." In three weeks Gamble "washed more than fifty pairs of shitty pants and bathed over two hundred men."

When finally it rained, the men stood in the deluge, absorbed it through their pores, and thanked God.

Sakelares found the filth "the roughest part of the whole thing. Nearly everyone had dysentery. There was feces everywhere you stepped. And a lot of men without shoes."

The planks across the slit trenches, slimy with excrement, caused men to slip. Many fell into the troughs and died before anyone could get to them. Armijo and Roessler "used to help each other to the latrines. One would faint and the other would keep him from falling in."

For toilet tissue, Gamble gathered old office papers. When they were gone, "the men used grass and sticks, and then they started picking leaves off the few bushes. We had to keep them from climbing trees and stripping them of what little shade we had." Always "there were long rows of men over the trenches in an agony of dysentery, and another long line of pain-wracked men waiting their turn with curses and grimaces. Sometimes they simply couldn't wait."

Green flies bred by the millions in the open latrines, and Boyer, forty years later, could "still hear, not the hum, but the roar of those flies." They ate with one hand and with the other tried to keep the flies from crawling into their mouths and noses. Maggots swarmed everywhere.

Rain-filled holes stagnated quickly. Hank Lovato "cleaned off the scum with a pole, and we washed and shaved. One Gillette blade shaved a hundred guys."

Rain brought bane as well as boon, Banegas learned. "Our camp was below the cemetery, and when it rained the filthy smelly water and the blood washed out, and then the sun would come out and we could hardly breathe. We were living in a nightmare."

Men began to die. Spurred by filth, starvation, and hopelessness, an army of diseases galloped through the camp – dengue fever, yellow jaundice, night blindness, tunnel vision. Sores ate into flesh and worms gorged on the putrescence. Men tore shreds from their clothing to keep the flies off. A friend of Penix Fletcher's remembered an old frontier remedy, "and we urinated on the sores. It was the only cure we had."

Nearly all had worms. Gamble "saw men cough, partially disgorge a worm, and pull it from their esophagus." Doolis "gagged until I threw up a worm eight or nine inches long. And the damn thing wiggled at me."

The big killers were dysentery and malaria. Together they were usually fatal, but when one followed the other, men often survived. Lucas found cerebral malaria the most heartbreaking. "Men scream and thrash, and all you can do, without medicine, is tie their hands and feet until they're out of their misery.

"Doc Riley gave me some medicine for one man. I couldn't find him in the barracks. I stumbled over something outside and I knew it was a man. I squatted and called his name. He didn't answer. It was an eerie feeling. The moonlight was bright, making dark shadows, and frogs were croaking. I put my hand under his shirt. He was cold and clammy. I took Doc back his medicine."

Gamble found many "so weak they passed out four or five times a day. One passed out in the chow line each meal for two days. The third day he died while I held his head in the bend of my arm."

When they could do nothing more for a man, they laid him in the shade beneath the buildings to die. Earl Harris saw "one man carried down there three times. The maggots got in his sores and cleaned them out. And the guy survived."

The last resort was 'Saint Peter's Ward' – a hospital with no medicine, no beds, and no way to clean. Corpsmen slipped in the excrement that covered the floor. Evans "felt almost as much pain for the doctors and medics as for the patients . . . . Men [were] lying there with maggots crawling in and out of their asses, and the guys were still alive and trying to communicate."[4]

"The whole camp," wrote Gamble, "was a ghostland of half-gone men." He heard "the groans of agony during the night" and ached because "there was nothing to relieve their suffering. The odor of dysentery was sickening. These men needed help as no men ever needed it, yet few could be persuaded to help them."

It hurt him "to see West Point graduates fail in their mission as officers so miserably. Our Guard officers were much more human and sympathetic." To the doctors of Old Two Hon'erd,

---

[4] Evans 38.

"too much honor cannot be paid. Colonel Colvard worked day and night at the hospital, and Major Riley and Captain Long did man-killing work at man-killing hours."

Lucas wept when Japanese officers came to inspect, "and left that lousy hospital laughing." Pleas for medicine, bandages, and surgical equipment, for food, cots, and bedding only angered the Japanese, although eventually, Gamble recorded, they did receive "a little iodine, a few rolls of bandages, and a few injections of dysentery serum."

When a representative from the Philippine Red Cross, escorted by 'Baggy Pants' and a Japanese doctor, came to inspect, Cain and Colvard pled for supplies. The Filipino offered to bring "equipment and medicine for a 150-bed hospital, including beds, linens, and mosquito bars," for which, Cain testified, the interpreter "hit him across the face with a sheathed saber, knocked him down, and said, 'You get into automobile, you talk too much.' We never secured any medicine, never got any beds or equipment."

On another occasion, Cain and Chaplain Alfred Oliver begged permission for the chaplains to contact Filipinos for medicine, citing the Geneva Accords and the prisoners' desperate plight. "I know about the Geneva Convention," shrieked Tsuneyoshi. "All I want to know about the Americans are their names and numbers when they die."

What medication they had was smuggled in. Though many sold these treasures, the men of the 200th shared with their *amigos*. When Johnson "conked out at muster, Durwood Wright gave me twenty quinine pills he'd picked up on the March. He gave them to whoever needed them. Then, when he got it, he'd run out. And he died."

Harrington found some quinine "minutes before the surrender, which I slipped into O'Donnell and gave to Lieutenant Shamblin." Later, when dysentery hit Harrington, Shamblin came to the hospital looking for him. "I was lying naked in excrement, so wasted away he didn't recognize me, and I was too weak to call out. Later Doc [John] Farley discovered me and found me some sulfa tablets."

Chintis, at the gate of O'Donnell, "had seen a big hospital field pack, and got it inside – it had syringes, morphine, quinine – and took it to Doc Riley, and he and I worked together after that."

Rodriguez was not so lucky with his pack. Having struggled with it to O'Donnell, he sank exhausted. "I wrapped the handles to my arm while I slept. But somebody cut the straps and took it."

Other units marveled at how the New Mexicans cared for each other. When Bond contracted pneumonia, boys from his battery shared their rations and pulled him through. When Ojinaga sickened, a friend got on a work detail, hoping to bring him back some medicinc. "But the guerrillas attacked his convoy – and they killed my best buddy."

When Doolis nearly died, his friend joined a detail "to steal me some food. They brought him back three weeks later with cerebral malaria. 'My buddy's dying,' I told Captain Long. 'Can't you find some medicine?' He did find a little – but it was too late."

The stench of death hung over O'Donnell. From the Filipino side first, Shillito saw "a constant stream of two-man crews, with poles and a blanket stretched between them, carrying the bodies – we'll never know how many. And the Americans soon began to follow."[5]

Lucas "walked into the barracks one morning and saw a man in a bay facing towards the feet of the other four. I swatted at his bottom and he didn't move. I rolled him over and he was dead. I shook the next man and he was dead. I looked at the next one and he was dead. Three from one barracks in one day. And this was an everyday occurrence."

---

[5] Figures are unreliable. No one knows how many perished on the March, and many died unrecorded beneath the barracks and were found only after the camp had been evacuated. Probably one of every six of the estimated 9,300 Americans who reached O'Donnell died. Kerr 65. The Philippine toll may have reached 22,000. "Report on American Prisoners of War Interned by the Japanese in the Philippines," prepared by the Office of the Provost Marshal General, 19 November 1945.

Don Harris was conscious of little but death. "They died so fast that the bodies lay stacked like cordwood before we could bury them. At first we tried digging individual graves, but that didn't work, so we dug big pits. Then the rain began and the bodies would float. We'd try to weigh them down with dirt and they'd come up. And at night the dogs would scavenge."

All who had strength served on burial detail, to dig or to join the long file bearing their comrades' bodies on bamboo shutters. Graves dug the night before filled with water by morning. Banegas tried to "grab the hands and feet and throw them and run, because the water would splash and spill out. They'd float, and we'd throw mud in. Some were standing or sitting, and their legs stuck out, and we'd have to jump in and tramp them down."

West "tried to make the details for our own bunch, though we didn't have much control over it. But in the 200th we always tried to bury our own."

Alex "didn't recognize one bloated guy, but I saw his dog tags. It was Rexell B. Coffindaffer, from my outfit. I got him by the leg and his skin came off in my hands, like a chicken. It was sticky and I couldn't get it off. I've had a hell of a time eating chicken since."

Sakelares "buried some good friends. We'd hoist a man on a litter after he was bloated. The skin busts open and pus runs out. We loaded ten to fifteen a day on our shoulders, and all this stuff dripping on you. We'd throw 'em in a hole. And if he was your buddy, you tried to drop him easy, because he was your friend."

Besides burial detail, there were water and wood details, and, for the lucky ones, kitchen details, where they might steal a little extra food. Others went to various parts of Luzon. They vied for these jobs – anything to escape O'Donnell.

Gamble watched groups leave "to work as mechanics, or to salvage war plunder, or to build bridges or roads. Many returned sick, and many died. Some were beaten, shot, or bayoneted when they became so weak they fell to the ground."

Waldon 'Jack' Burchfield's crew was ordered to build a road, "with a basket and a hoe – through the jungle. The monsoon started and we all got yellow fever. Most died. They drug what was left of us to Bilibid."

Arvil Gale went to Tarlac to build a bridge. "The Japs never got one truck over it! The rains washed it away – we saw to that. A bunch of GIs together are mean sons-of-bitches. We sabotaged everywhere we could."

Life reduced to simplest terms: One survived or one died, and many chose to die.

Theirs was a sorry plight, Gamble wrote. "We received no mail, nor could we write home. We had no cigarettes, no books, no magazines. Snaps of wives, children, sweethearts, or friends had been taken by the Japs. There were no lights; we were in total darkness from nightfall till dawn. Most were sick in mind if not in body, and the mental condition was an incubator for body ailments."

The news of Corregidor's fall further trampled morale. "Some turned to religion. Men could be seen standing, sitting, or kneeling, counting their rosaries and praying. Some moved their lips, others mumbled, and some just stared.

"Poor devils. Some became so religious they wouldn't kill the flies and didn't want anyone else to. Some quit cussing. They became religious in every way except doing a kindness for others. Many sat inertly while a fevered comrade suffered for a little water. I saw men on the way to the latrine stagger and fall while others passed by without an offer to help. They simply did not give a damn."

McCormick heard men say, "'I'm going to die next week,' on a certain day. I don't know how a man knew. Maybe that's when he wanted to die. It was easier than living."

Chintis "saw many die because they wanted to. And I saw many fight through it. We all had the same food and lack of medicine. It all boils down to the individual."

As McCahon grew weaker, "a feeling of complete peace came over me, and I wasn't tired any more. I realized I had given up – I was dying. As soon as I resolved to live, the exhaustion came back. I never lost it again, because I was fighting for survival."

Foy never lost faith. "If you didn't believe your country would get you out of there, you'd never make it."

Doolis "never heard any of our boys ever cuss the United States. I saw men give up and die, but not from losing loyalty to their country – or doubting its loyalty to us."

Many believed the desert rearing during the Depression years helped them survive. Macario 'Max' Villaloboz "grew up tough. When I was twelve I was herding sheep for twelve dollars a month. And I punched cows." Johns "grew up on a ranch and knew what work was from daylight till dark." Gunter's family "was oil-field folks, and we learned to take care of ourselves. What brought me home? I guess – hope. I knew if I could just hold out, Uncle Sam was going to come."

West "just wasn't ready to die. We helped each other – no way could a loner make it. And then – the Lord had something to do with it."

"On June 1st, 1942, the first group began to march to Tarlac," wrote John Gamble. They were leaving O'Donnell – even the Japanese admitted the impossibility of remaining – for Cabanatuan. Only the desperately ill and a skeleton crew to care for them remained.

"Though men had only meager equipment to carry, some fell by the road. Those with no canteens could carry no water. At Capas we were loaded into boxcars, caged like animals. Many fainted from suffocation . . . . " They left as they had come.

Soon after O'Donnell was evacuated, Colonel James Duckworth's medical team from Base Hospital 1 joined the skeleton crew, who had by then largely cleaned the camp and buried the decomposed bodies they had found beneath the buildings. Even so, the incoming men were stunned at what they saw, and they wept to see the pitiful gratitude of the patients when they saw medical and surgical equipment – and beds. It was the team's first hint of the hellhole that had been O'Donnell.

Here, in a three-month period, over fifteen hundred Americans and Filipinos died from disease, starvation, and brutality. Today a concrete cross marks the spot. Poured from a sack of cement the remaining Service Group wheedled from the Japanese, its words read simply:

IN MEMORY OF THE AMERICAN DEAD
O'DONNELL WAR PERSONNEL ENCLOSURE 1942
OMNIA PRO PATRIA

– 18 –

BLOOD BROTHERS

"I pulled myself up. I decided then that if I was going to die, I'd die on my feet."
– Sergeant Winston Shillito –

They had not been long at Cabanatuan when McBride heard martial singing, and a company of Japanese guards marched in with "the long-haired bloody head of a Filipino dangling from a bamboo pole. They set this up at the main gate." The warning was effective. So was the formation of ten-men 'blood brother' groups: If one escaped, or attempted to, the other nine would be shot.

At Cabanatuan they were reunited with the prisoners from Corregidor, who wept to see the feces-smeared skeletons from O'Donnell. Senter "didn't even recognize old buddies from Bataan. Then I learned what the poor devils from my regiment had been through."

Cabanatuan comprised three camps, a few miles apart in the treeless plain. The Japanese occupied Camp 2, in the center; Camp 3, with ample water and fair conditions, housed most of the prisoners from Corregidor for a few weeks, until they were eventually moved to Camp 1, which became the largest POW camp in the Orient.

Lucas found it "the same kind of camp we'd left. One water spigot for the whole camp, and an American engineer working on the pump to keep it running – or trying to. He'd get it started and it would give out." The barracks were the same thatched huts, their five-man bays so short the men's feet hung over. They wondered which tier was worse. Those above must drain their sapped strength to pull aloft; those below caught the excrement that dropped through the slats from the dysentery-wracked men above.

On 15 August the last personnel from Camp 3 arrived. Colonel D.J. Rutherford was commanded to organize an American headquarters,[1] and 200th Colonel Memory Cain, as Executive Officer, to compile detailed information on every POW and have ID tags cut by the next morning – an impossible task, Cain explained, especially with 2,700 in hospital, many delirious.

Unsatisfied with the completed report, the interpreter burst into a prolonged tantrum and beat Cain senseless. He was still ranting when Cain regained consciousness.

"As I gathered my senses and my eyesight came back, I steadied myself by the desk. He hit my hands with his crop and said, 'Stand at attention!' I stood as best I could for one hour and fifty minutes as he raved." He continued to beat Cain. The session resulted in temporary paralysis of both Cain's hands and a foot, the loss of three fingernails, a knot on his head "as big as three goose eggs," and headaches that forced him to resign as executive officer.

* * *

[1] Rutherford was named CO in June according to Kerr 96, but Lieutenant Colonel Memory H. Cain, his Executive Officer, testified that Rutherford did not arrive from Camp 3 until August. He was later replaced as CO by Colonel James Duckworth, M.D.

"Last night," Gamble wrote, "a fellow escaped from Building 3 and got food. They caught him trying to sneak in. They're going to shoot him, I hear."

After three men escaped from his detail, Doolis was lined up with the rest as the Japanese officer "took every other man till he had thirty. One was a twin, and his brother remained. We never saw them again."

The strongest deterrent was the ten-man system. To guard their own, many of whom were crazed with malaria, the Americans set up perimeter guards inside the double fence. Doolis saw Japanese guards on the outside "put food to tempt men – sick men – to crawl under the wire, and then they'd bayonet them."

One night, just as a perimeter guard urinated into a sewage ditch, three officers, trying to escape during a monsoon, passed under him. The sprayed officers yelled and several men, Gamble among them, came running. "The American guard called 'halt' and Sergeant [Mario] Tonelli, a former Notre Dame All-American,[2] made a flying tackle and brought one down. They pulled their rank and demanded to be released.

"The ruckus attracted the Nip guards, [who] beat up the officers and kept them tied up all that night and the following day without food or water. At sundown they were led out and shot."

Cain tried to secure the release of three others whose minds, he pled, were befuddled by malaria. Lieutenant Colonel Shigeji Mori, the Japanese Camp Commander, refused. An interpreter told him the men were beaten "very hard with a big club, many bones are broken." Two days later, horribly mutilated, they were hauled from camp in a carabao cart. Two were shot, the third beheaded.

Often the Japanese forced the entire camp to witness executions. The helplessness hurt Ragsdale worst. "At one execution, it took several volleys. A man had fallen to his knees, and someone yelled 'For God's sake, shoot him – he's not dead!' And there was nothing we could do."

---

2 Tonelli was a member of the 200th.

The 'sun treatment' took various forms. Men were stripped and tied facing the sun, often suspended from their wrists, which were tied behind them, a position that dislocated the shoulder. Passing guards held lighted cigarettes to their flesh. Sometimes men were nailed in small boxes, with tiny air holes. The heat mounted, along with the stench of their own excreta. It usually took a man two or three days to die.

Kedzie saw one group, hung by their hands, "slowly clubbed to death. Finally the Japs cut them down, hung them on posts, and turned out the camp to watch while they gave them 'honorable military executions' – after they were already dead."

"Last evening," wrote Lieutenant LeMoyne Stiles, "Private Connell escaped to a small barrio, where he was detected. The Nips beat him, breaking both arms and legs. Then they bayoneted him in the legs, stomach, and neck. One bayonet through the head tore out his eye. Then they beat his head in with a club." The mutilated body was displayed for the camp to view.

The public executions often produced the opposite effect from that intended, when acts of courage braced their comrades' resolve. Armijo remembered Tommy Long, who, just before he was shot, spit in the Japanese officer's face. Gilcrease drew courage when a friend refused a blindfold. "They shot and he fell to his knees. They shot again, but before he died he yelled, 'God Bless America!'"

Many alleged 'escapes' were only quests for food. Jim Argeanas and Tom Hunt sneaked out several times to bring medicine back, until Argeanas was hospitalized, and Hunt went out alone. It was Tommy's last trip: They caught him coming in.

"Nobody," Ross averred, "could understand the Japs. You never knew what the hell they'd do next."

When a friend of Heinz Rhee's was caught smoking on farm detail, "the guard grabbed his cigarette, broke his arm with his stick – and then gave him one of his own cigarettes."

Finley saw a Japanese officer kill a member of his own drill squad, "an old fellow who just couldn't keep in step, and the officer pulled his pistol and shot him. They have no feeling for animals, either. I saw them working horses that had been shot in the head."

"'Charlie Chaplin' went on a rampage today," Stiles recorded. "He beat one man for half an hour for no known reason. His face was a bloody pulp. He turned on another and cracked open his head." He broke a hoe handle over a third for "laughing"; then, learning he was only squinting, "he got friendly and gave him two packages of cigarettes."

Banegas was sentenced to die for an escaped blood brother. "They lined us up and said it was our last chance to tell where he was. That gun barrel looked like a cannon. I wouldn't stand close to the others because I was shaking. I didn't want them to know how chicken I was.

"But they found him. His fever was so high he didn't know what he was doing. They dragged him to a faucet – opened his mouth and filled him with water, then started jumping on his belly. The water poured out. They kept on till they killed him."

Other times the 'water cure' was effected by a hose up the rectum. The performance always evoked thigh-slapping laughs for the Sons of Heaven who gathered to watch.

For lesser punishments, finger- and toenails were pulled out with pliers, or sharp sticks were inserted beneath the nails. Men had to stand at attention with five-gallon cans of water on their heads, or kneel and sit back on bamboo rods behind the knees, which cut off circulation. Any small movement brought a rifle butt crashing on the head. They endured common beatings with the razorlike edges of sliced bamboo.

When Mendoza, shaking with malaria, crawled into a ditch, "my buddies covered me with burlap sacks. A Jap yanked me out and beat the living hell out of me. I prayed, 'Lord, give him all the power you can, so I can just die.'"

When a friend of Ragsdale's refused to salute the Rising Sun, "they beat him and beat him. Each time they knocked him to his knees, he got up, or they pulled him up. Still he wouldn't salute. As one started to swing, this guy spat on the Jap flag. They beat him unconscious.

"Then for days they tried to make somebody salute that flag. They never could. Maybe it was foolish to take that kind of beating over a piece of cloth, but – we were Americans. We were captured, but we weren't whipped!"

* * *

They devised ways of 'stabilizing the Japs.' Officers acted as intermediaries. When a guard began to beat a man on his detail, Lucas ran to the spot "to put on a good show. You'd yell at the man and jump up and down and raise hell. You'd swing your arms and jump and scream and hit the air, and he'd fall back. That appeased the Jap and saved the man a beating. But you had to be fast. If you gave the Jap time to really get mad, he'd beat the man and you too!"

Unable to pronounce their names, the men nicknamed their guards: Liver Lips, Greaseball, Long John Silver, Big and Little Speedo. Ragsdale called one "Hammerheaded Sonofabitch, until we were advised to change it before he found out what it meant." Cyclops supervised sick call, and beat those whose fever he could not feel through the thick gloves he wore.

Skarda earned notoriety the day he outran Air Raid, in charge of farm details. "He'd beat the hell out of you with his sawed-off pool cue. Fractured skulls, broke arms, legs, and ribs." When Banegas collapsed at work one day, Air Raid laid open his back with a steel rod.

Donald Duck sounded, when angered, like the famous movie actor for whom, they solemnly told him, he was called. He strutted importantly – until the real Donald Duck stood up at a showing of American movies, to which the guards flocked. When Don Harris reported next morning, "he was waiting. We knelt with rods behind our knees and he went up and down beating the tar out of us. We never called him Donald Duck again – not to his face!"

Men soon began to die at an alarming rate. Cabanatuan was divided into three parts, the Japanese sector in the center, through which all must pass, escorted by an officer with a white flag, to gain the hospital area. Only a hundred a day could go; many died awaiting permission.

James Hamilton, obtaining admittance data, asked a soldier his name.

"He can't talk," answered another weakly.

"Why not?"

The reply was terse and logical. "He's dead."

Dysentery killed half a thousand before June ended; July took about 768.[3] In the fenced-off area, curtains of green flies billowed; men crept painfully and left behind them trails of blood; and there were no medical supplies to ease their misery. Rodriguez saw men "just lie down and die. It hit sudden. At night you'd be talking to a friend, and in the morning he'd be dead."

After a few weeks, Chintis "looked around at my blood-brother group, and there was only me and one other guy alive."

Lucas sent men to hospital "only if they couldn't take care of themselves, and just lay in their filth. We'd lay them until they died in Zero Ward," so-called "because zero percentage would ever come out."[4]

Cain recorded seven men in his Regiment who died the morning he was admitted.[5] The Japanese refused them burial for several days. They had no shovels, they said.

Early in June, Lucas summoned Dr. Long for "a boy whose throat was swollen, in great pain. Long took one look. 'Move him out of here, NOW!' Then he told me what it was:

"Diphtheria."

Within days it was epidemic. Despite warehouses full of serum, Mori ignored the doctors' pleas. When the Bishop of Manila brought a large supply, Mori sent it back.

Lovato watched friends die. "Sometimes the doctors had to cut their throats to let them breathe – and some would still die. They got a little antitoxin, but they ran out. Men just choked to death."

Greeman found Father Braun in the diphtheria ward. "He got word to the Bishop of Manila through the Filipinos who came to our fence at night. The priests combed the city and

---

3 Kerr 94-95.

4 Skipped when numbering the buildings, it was later designated 'Zero,' the reason forgotten because it was so appropriate a name.

5 Privates Matias Armijo and Manuel A. Aguilar of the 200th, Adonaiz Cordova, José Fajardo, and Eutino C. Medina of the 515th, and Sergeants Charles W. Oles and Joe D. Smith, both of the 515th. "It was apparent," Cain testified, "those men died from starvation, dysentery, malaria, and abuse."

smuggled us serum. Not enough, so we drew straws. I was paired with the Father, and he won, but he said, 'Give it to Gerald.' I would have died except for him."

Finally, in August, Mori allowed a modest amount of antitoxin and serum into camp. Deaths from diphtheria and malaria slowed. But malnutrition now took its toll in running sores, impaired vision, and beriberi. Pellagra and scurvy loosened nails and teeth.

Niemon wrapped his festering sores in rags to keep out flies. "They'd lay eggs and we'd get maggots in the sores. Our eyes couldn't stand the light. We made cardboard blinkers, like glasses, with a pinhole to see through. And of course we all had beriberi."

Lucas watched its progress. "With dry beriberi, every step is like walking on needles. If a fly lit on a toe it felt like you'd stuck it into an electric socket.[6] With wet beriberi[7] you can't pass liquids, so you swell. It works up your legs into your stomach and you look pregnant. When it gets to your heart, the pressure stops its beating."

Ross "swelled so I'd fall flat on my face or back. The doctors had no medication. They'd slit your stomach and draw the stuff out with a hose."

Doctors performed several appendectomies without anesthesia. Banegas held men while doctors "scraped pus from sores with a stick. Those poor fellows screamed, but it took the rotten stuff out."

It took a crowbar to pry out Schmitz's infected tooth. Hauled in a cart back to his lumber detail in the rain, he developed lockjaw. His buddy tried to feed him, and finally persuaded the guards to return Schmitz to the hospital. There a doctor scrounged serum to loosen the jaw, and pried out another tooth.

---

6 Many of the men, when interviewed some forty years later, said they still suffered pain (from nerve deterioration) and they still slept, even in winter, with their feet outside the bed covers.

7 So-called 'wet' beriberi is actually edema.

Dr. William Bleuher, with a drill powered by a foot-pedaled bicycle-like device, ground out a tooth for Aldrich and filled it with a melted-down Philippine *peso*.[8]

A few doctors were self-serving. Armijo saw a psychiatrist steal food from his patients. When a man on Earl Harris's wood detail (all of whom smuggled in medicine) contracted malaria, "they told him only one doctor had quinine – for a price. This guy had just turned in to the hospital several thousand tablets – and now he couldn't get any without money."

Most doctors, however, were dedicated, and in this group those of the 200th were noteworthy. Julian Long seemed never to rest, and Dick Riley sacrificed his own life by giving medicine that could have saved him to men he felt needed it more.

West and Banegas aided the overworked medics. West assisted one doctor in surgery. "And I washed rags – we used 'em over and over – and I worked with the patients. One kid lay buckled up so long he couldn't straighten his legs. We worked with him for months before he got so he could walk. And I read to them in the moonlight. Their favorite was a Thorne Smith book – *Night Life of the Gods*."

Someone carved a chess set, and Banegas played with the patients. "I told jokes – anything to get their mind off home. One kid was crying, 'Mother, get me out of here!' My own eyes got full of tears. I wanted my mother, too. But he was younger and couldn't hold it back."

That was when Banegas composed his *corrido*[9] to an old Mexican tune. "They made a guitar with carabao guts for strings. The Japs wouldn't let us sing, but we sang *corridos* anyhow, and 'El Rancho Grande.' And even the Japs liked it."

Above all, the men of 'Old Two Hon'erd' looked after their own. Harold Knighton sent quinine tablets he'd found on the March to his buddy. When malaria struck Knighton, he had none, "but Jonathan Burns sneaked me food, and quinine too."

---

8 Aldrich kept the tooth 48 years. Much later, in Albuquerque, he and Bleuher marveled over its durability. Both agreed it was "a damned fine job."

9 *Corridos* – folk ballads – are an important part of life among the Hispanic population of the American Southwest, and are composed and sung with guitar accompaniment on any or no occasion. Lorenzo Banegas and Ruben Flores, at the time of this writing, still entertain with this very popular one at Ex-POW gatherings.

Sakelares found Aldrich "dirty and blacking out. He hauled me out in the rain and bathed me, and when I got better, he got me a kitchen job, swatting flies. It meant more food."

Baldonado, carrying stolen food to the hospital, stumbled over a buddy, "laying naked in the sun by a stream. His anus was three inches big, and maggots crawling in and out. I wet my T-shirt, cleaned him up the best I could, and put that shirt on his butt."

Bond found Don Harris in Zero Ward and "gave me what-for to get up and out. I was dying and I didn't care, and I said, 'Dow, if I get out of here I'll kill you.' Years later I went to see him in Taos, and he said, 'I'll be damned – you're back to keep that promise!'"

Bond laughed about it for years. "Harris was laying in phlegm and I told him to clean it up. He said he'd beat holy hell out of me. But I saw a Jap guard coming, and if anybody spit or defecated, he'd make them eat it. I couldn't let that happen to Harris."

Lucas relied on Fred Swope to get water for the sick barracks. "He'd take canteens and wait, sometimes all night – and with both kinds of beriberi. But every night he got water for the men. And never complained."

Many refused to go to hospital. When Shillito could not stand at morning head count, "somebody held me up. I knew I was in the same condition I'd seen guys just before they died. After head count they laid me down. I pulled myself up.
I decided if I was going to die, I'd die on my feet. I walked around that barracks all that day and the next, holding on to the posts. And I started to get better."

"A woman's here. Having a baby!" In this stinking death hole? "A Filipina – she wanted an American doctor." A hush tiptoed through the hospital, a kind of quiet awe; and, when told the baby was born, smiles lit the faces of the old-young men. Even here, a life had happened.

Torrential rains made burial detail a nightmare. As the river rose, "it floated out our dead," and Phillips "tried everything to identify them in the marshy mass graves. If we could find a bottle, we'd write who was there, and try to keep it close to the bodies."

When he could, Burrola "pulled grass and covered them a little, for some decency. But it was monsoon, and the Japs were wet and angry. They'd make us throw them in, all tangled. They'd float. Some held them down with shovels while others threw in mud. We'd slip and fall into those stinking graves. The water was green with maggots."

For months the Japanese allowed no services, no chaplains at the cemetery, no means to register deaths. Some twenty-five hundred had been buried before they allowed one chaplain, late in 1942, to accompany burial details.

As Garcia and Armijo carried a buddy to the cemetery, he sat up. "Garcia yelled, and that damn Jap took off like a ruptured duck!" Hernandez wondered how many they did bury alive. "They was all skeletons – you couldn't tell. We'd bury 'em like they was found, under the barracks, out at the latrine."[10]

With the arrival of Red Cross supplies in late November, 1942, hope surged through the camp. The men knew nothing of the long negotiations before the *Gripsholm* sailed with diplomats and a hold loaded with food and medicine. Nor did they know it would be another year before a second shipment would get through. They only knew they were not forgotten.

Food and vitamins, while they lasted, worked miracles. The death rate slowed. Sight returned; sores healed; and the doctors had anesthetics, antiseptics, and medicine for the desperately ill. Men wanted to live again, and their pitiful joy long outlived the material substance.

Conditions improved briefly. Mori let them set up a commissary to handle native produce, and in January he initiated a new project, the Farm. But by March the Red Cross food was gone. Commissary prices inflated. It was June before the farm produced, and then the prisoners reaped only a few radish

---

[10] It was reported that Jacob Morgan, a Navajo from Battery H, was actually covered over, when a slight movement or bubble in the mud caused his friend to disinter him. On regaining consciousness, Morgan demanded angrily, "Whatever sonofabitch has my shoes, better give 'em back!" Morgan later died.

or *camote* tops their hosts spurned. Rations were cut and the disease rate climbed again.

"We are always hungry," wrote Stiles, "like starving animals with their mouths watering and eyes bulging. Twice a week we get dry salted fish. The last two issues have been spoiled, covered with maggots, and stinking." When a delegation approached Mori, he said he wished to keep them too weak to resist. No Filipinos could donate food, and anyone seen talking to one would be severely punished.

Life's greatest luxury was a *quan*. Anything they could pilfer – a snake, a grasshopper, a turnip – they pooled. They ate 'pig weed' and boiled guava leaves for tea. Gamble once got some fish paste, "made of heads, fins, scales, and tails." Rank, he admitted, but food.

"The Japs stoned wild dogs to death. Wad Hall got 'em and we had dog loaf," which Don Harris found tasty. When a cat with kittens appeared, West's buddy boiled cat and litter.

Those who drove trucks smuggled food. A friend of Foy's "worked in the Jap kitchen and when he could, he'd sneak us fish heads. We ate them behind the barracks and buried the evidence."

Donaldson, ordered to shoot a sick horse, "stole the head and we boiled it. [Major James] McMinn even ate the eyeballs."

Stealing became a fine art. One evening Garcia cast a longing eye on the chickens in Colonel Duckworth's quarters.[11] "We bent pins like fishhooks and baited them with stolen corn and threw it over the fence. The chicken would swallow, we'd yank, break its neck, and pull it out. We *quanned* ten chickens that night!"

Kitchen and wood details were more or less permanent; others varied daily. They exploited every opportunity. Sherwood used his position as Mori's driver to smuggle news and messages. Villaloboz punched small holes in the salt sacks he hauled so others could reap the leakage; and "when we cleared Clark Field, I stole a sack of flour. It was full of worms, but them tortillas was sure good!"

[11] Colonel James Duckworth, then American CO at Cabanatuan.

Friends tried to get friends on 'good' details. When Aldrich returned from Bilibid, "'Toots' Tixier and Bob Lucero grabbed me at the gate, got me assigned to their special-duty barracks, and got me a job on the 'Duck Pond' in the Jap compound. We fed the ducks, stole eggs when we could, and built a little dam. I began to get my strength back, and eventually got on the wood detail. That was work – hard mahogany and dull axes – but it gave the best chances for smuggling."

Skarda "talked the Japs into letting us buy food off the natives. We'd buy two cans – eat one and sell the other. Interesting way to make a living, but it beat hell out of starving to death."

It expanded into a barter system. Those on wood detail became purchasing agents, and those with money bought, sold, and traded. Tobacco became the medium of exchange. "Nicotine for protein! Protein for nicotine!" rang from the chow lines.

Rhee traded for some rice flour. "What I did not know was the 'flour' was foot powder. We ate the hot cakes anyhow."

In August the interpreter announced that they were no longer captives, but prisoners of war, and in October officers began to receive a small stipend. Privates and noncoms on details were paid ten and twenty *centavos* a day in near-worthless 'invasion money' printed in Manila. A month's pay would almost buy a package of cigarettes.

Most stood in pay lines only to have their cards stamped and filed. When Aldrich asked the purpose of this ritual, the paymaster grinned. "We buy you Japan War Bonds! When Japan win war, you buy lice paddy, be big honcho!"

Private enterprise flourished. McCormick saw masses of Philippine counterfeit, "slipped to men on carabao details, folded inside canteens. We made money in camp, too, from notebook paper. The commissary was running 60,000 to 70,000 *pesos* a month, and the Japs never could figure where it came from. They knew we were making money – they'd come search for the stamp. But they never found it. It was over at the radio shack."

Japanese guards, who dared not report venereal disease to their own doctors, turned to the Americans for sulfathiozole. Garcia was glad to oblige. "We got tooth powder from the Red Cross boxes and started making pills. We shaped them with a hollow razor handle and sold 'em at night for five *pesos* a pill." Pelayo and Garrett made their 'sulfa' from cornstarch. Stamped with a carbine shell, they looked professional.

Boyer had contacts with the Masonic Lodge in Manila. "They'd cash our checks and send the money in through details. Bond and I sent it back out for medicine for our men. We never met the people, or knew who they were or how the contacts were made."

It was likely through one of two operations conducted by American women, who collected money, medicines, and messages which they pumped into the camp through highly organized pipelines. Margaret Utinsky ('Miss U') worked through vendors who slipped funds and mail into the produce bags they sold the carabao details. Claire Phillips, code-named 'High Pockets,' allegedly because she transported messages in her brassiere, worked out of her Manila nightclub. Masterminding the activities was Ted Lewin, an American gambling king known throughout Southeast Asia.

On occasion Mori let Father Buddenbroch into camp, probably because he was a German citizen and a supposed ally. Concealed in enormous pockets inside his cassock, the boisterous priest carried medicines, letters, and money.

Inside camp, Lieutenant Colonel Edward Mack and Chaplain Robert Preston Taylor organized agents. This network functioned until May 1944, when the Japanese seized and tortured Taylor and other ringleaders, executed civilian intermediaries, and threw 'High Pockets' and 'Miss U' into Santiago Prison. They tortured Father Buddenbroch until he died.

The largest undertaking was the three-hundred-acre farm, which ultimately employed three thousand men.

Lightfoot's detail cleared ten-foot cogon with three-inch knives. Niemon, barefoot in the stubble from the cut grass, attacked giant termite mounds, higher than a man. "This clay gumbo stuck to our picks, and we had to scrape it off between strikes. We only wore g-strings, and the ants would attack us."

The man next to Gunter "dug up a bunch of mice, and ate them raw. I understand they shot him."

As Huxtable swung at his mound, "a cobra stuck his head between my bare feet. The pick went one way and I went the other. But the Japs said to catch it – they wanted it to eat. It had to be captured alive. We became quite proficient at capturing cobras with a forked stick and a gunny sack. For a live cobra, we got cigarettes.

"The Nips killed them themselves. They wouldn't let us, because if you hit a cobra wrong, the venom entered its blood stream and poisoned the meat. They'd skin them and hang them from their belts." They reminded Niemon of red bicycle tubes.

They called it 'Farmer Jones detail,' and hauled water and human fertilizer in five-gallon cans. Baclawski tilled "with hoes or picks. If you lagged, a Nip laid a bamboo 'vitamin stick' on you. Rest period consisted of five minutes of calisthenics."

Villaloboz plowed. "They thought us Spanish guys was from Mexico and still drove oxes. Soon as those carabao see a water hole, they drag you into it and stay there all afternoon."

Bond and Hall found a colt. "Our guard said it was his. Hall told him what a good cowboy he was, and how I used to rope steers, so we got the job. The Jap brought milk. We'd feed the colt one can and drink the rest, till one morning we found the colt dead. We didn't know what the Jap might do, so we smeared phlegm from the hospital on its nose and said it died of distemper."

"Farm detail is getting rougher," wrote Stiles in July 1943. "They beat men unconscious, then kick and beat them some more. They work men inhumanly. Had six of us carrying heavy boards from the new farm to the old. Our muscles knotted, we staggered, and two men collapsed. Our shoulders were so bruised and cut we could hardly get back."

Stealing was hazardous but not impossible. They risked beatings to fill canteens with beans, or stuff pig weed beneath their hats. One New Mexican, sighting a guard, hid a banana in his g-string, but in his haste, wedged it longwise. "Ah so!" The guard grinned at the obvious protrusion. "Big man!"

When Gamble saw a fellow officer reach through the fence for a piece of okra, "a Nip guard shot him twice, and as he lay dying, crying for help, drove away any who sought to succor him. A dismal cold swept through camp."

Somehow they maintained their morale. It was not easy. Doolis, walking duty in the rain in a borrowed poncho, heard a "hello" through the fence. "I nearly fainted. It was a guard impounded from Singapore – he'd never been to Japan. He gave me five cigarettes. I said, 'I'll be right back,' and took them to Zero ward. I don't know why – I wanted cigarettes, too. But it made me feel good.

"Going back in a cloudburst, I walked into a slit trench up to my neck. Took me half an hour to claw enough mud away to get out. I was filthy. I took off the poncho and let the rain wash me and it off, and I sat there and bawled like a baby."

Religion nurtured some. At first they prayed covertly. Foy met friends for a rosary behind the rabbit hutches. Eventually the Japanese allowed weekly services, though all sermons had to be approved and delivered as censored. The chaplains converted several barracks into chapels and fashioned rough crosses of bamboo. Father Buddenbroch brought sacramental necessities from Manila.

The chaplains shared details with the men – the Japanese considered spiritual duties extracurricular. In the fields, seemingly robust despite the emaciation of his large frame, Father Braun attacked physical obstacles the same way he had built a church on the Mescalero Apache reservation in New Mexico, barehanded. He chopped wood for cooking, and when the men could steal corn, he made them hominy.

The Japanese attitude toward religion was unpredictable. After the long ban on services, in 1943 they surprisingly allowed a Memorial Day ceremony at the cemetery, and sent a wreath.

"They were scared of anything religious, so when they gave us notebooks and said to write our thoughts, I drew a big cross on mine. A week later they took the notebooks. Some guys had written their thoughts, and were brutally beaten." Drake told the guard his was a religious book. "He saw the cross and dropped it like a hot potato!"

* * *

"Five more days till Yuletide," wrote Gamble in 1942. "It's a pity men have to die just before the holiday. Five more were carried out this morning. We're singing Christmas carols. They remind us so poignantly of home. But we'll make the best of it. We certainly won't have to complain about the commercialism of our Xmas! It would be nice to get even a card – anything from home."

On Christmas Eve, Baldonado recorded "the most beautiful midnight Mass I ever attended. The night was quiet. The moon was full and the stars bright. The altar was decorated with shrubbery and lit with candles. I offered my Holy Communion to Mother, Dad, the kids, and especially to Juan."

Another year passed, another holiday approached, and hope flagged. "'Peace on Earth, Good will toward men,'" wrote Stiles. "If only it could be. This is my third Christmas away from home, and a lonelier one I haven't known. A strange nostalgia has invaded the camp.

"Dreamed last night that I was home in Albuquerque, and I tried to get Mary on the phone, but couldn't get the right number . . . . Too much reminiscence is no good, but it sure is hard not to do. Merry Christmas, Little Sweetheart. I love you."

Some began to keep diaries, at risk and in secret, as small notebooks became available at the commissary. King detailed his halcyon days on the *Coolidge*, kept his journal sporadically, and filled it with musical notations. Chaney filled his with the poetry of homesick men. Bond's was a catch-all for logs, lyrics, and letters to his Pearl, which he knew he could not mail. Many composed recipes and menus. And everyone collected State-side addresses of buddies – in itself a testament of faith in a free future.

A small group of minstrels salvaged a few guitars and began to stroll at night through the darkened camp to make men smile again. Schurtz organized 'sing alongs,' and on the hospital side, Gamble formed the 'Dysentery Quartet.'

Father Buddenbroch brought instruments from Manila, and in time the officers got permission for the men to form bands. Included were trumpeter Jim McCahon, sax-master Gonzo Drake, and a number of 200th guitarists. Skits came next. Tall, gaunt Chaplain Howden made a memorable Red Riding Hood, and Villaloboz won seven cigarettes for "The Prisoner's Prayer" (for more rain and less work).

Full-length productions evolved. Under the direction of Colonel O.O. ('Zero') Wilson, the 'Mighty Art Players' utilized all available talent for Wednesday-night band concerts and Saturday plays or variety shows. "We made fun of ourselves, of our officers, and of our captors," and Rhee saw men smile again. "Even the Japs enjoyed them."

The 'Cabanatuan Cats' imitated the big bands with songs the men wrote, and Karl Schroeder (the 200th's former radio professional) MC'd the 'Cabanatuan Hit Parade.' "Bell Bottom Trousers" brought cheers, and "I'm Getting Sentimental Over You" caused hastily wiped tears.

Plays included highly original versions of *Uncle Tom's Cabin* and *Gone With the Wind*, and Colonel 'Zero's' nostalgic script of *Our Town* brought home a little closer. They even, band member Chuck Kaelin wrote, satirized the Axis powers, and got by with it. "I once performed before the Crowned Heads of Europe," boasted one player, "and now before the Sloped Heads of the Far East";[12] and few forgot Gonzo Drake's famous line, "He's slow as the second coming of MacArthur!"

The holiday production of *A Christmas Carol* brought lumps to many throats, wrote Stiles, "and when the choir sang carols everyone stood and sang with them, with all the feeling we had. The crowd stood still for a good two minutes after it was over. No one wanted to leave. I guess it wouldn't have taken much more to have us crying like babies."

"They put on some of the damnedest shows" Kindel had ever seen. "Americans can do anything when their backs are to the wall."

* * *

12 From an unpublished tribute to the entertainers written by Charles Kaelin, a copy of which he kindly sent the author.

They fed on rumors and waifs of news, the two usually indistinguishable, but it didn't matter – it kept them going. The convoy was on the way; Germany had surrendered; they were to be exchanged. Whether they believed them did not matter – to repeat them was an act of faith. One day a rumor of freedom would come true; if not this one, the next.

Always there was the hastily flashed V for Victory, surreptitious, but irrepressible.

They learned gratitude. "After going a year and a half barefoot," Harrington "was issued a pair of second-hand shoes – something I had always treated as a matter of fact. How little we appreciate our blessings until we find ourselves without them."

Gamble closed each day's entry with a prayer of thanks that "we can still find sunsets, constellations, the ever-green horizon, the release of laughter, the reality of friendships, the memories of the past, the rumors, the little joys that fall our way – even here."

They kept faith with each other. Stiles noted "an enormous something that only we who have lived through what we have can feel and know – a thing sacred to ourselves. We are no doubt a rough and discouraged bunch, but there is a bond that will hold us together forever."

What brought them home?

"A sense of humor and the laws of chance," said Senter. "I always knew we'd be liberated. We didn't discuss it, but we had little sayings. 'Frisco shore in '44,' 'Frisco dive in '45.' Our favorite was 'Christmas turkey in Albuquerque.'"

"The Americans' great sense of humor," said Finley. "That's how we got through it. We could laugh, no matter how bad things were. It frustrated the Japs. We'd play mock baseball with an imaginary ball, and they'd wonder what the hell we were doing."

"The Nips can't figure us out," wrote Stiles. "No matter how hard they beat us, we take it with a grin, and it really gets 'em. It would take more than the Japanese Empire to kill us."

Aldrich, from his special-duty barracks across from headquarters, got his chuckles watching the guards answer the telephone. "If it was an officer calling, they'd snap to attention, salute the phone, yell into the receiver at the top of their voices, and bow.

"And we made our own fun. At the Duck Pond, I'd hear a cowboy whoop, and my New Mexican *amigos* on butcher detail would dash out swinging their ropes."

Banegas was herding when a downpour hit. "We jumped on the carabao and started running them to the corral. This Jap yelled, 'You crazy fools!' But in Jap 'crazy fool' sounds like '*vaquero,*' which is 'cowboy' in Spanish. He was mad and yelling '*vaquero*' this and '*vaquero*' that, and we started laughing – '*Bueno* – we went up to *vaquero* already!' That Jap got so mad he started hitting everyone he could reach with his stick, but we couldn't stop laughing.

"They used to hit us with pick handles. You'd get purple marks on your back. But we'd count the stripes and say, 'Oh, he's got three, he just made sergeant.' One guy had so many we said, 'He made colonel today,' and saluted him."

Those raised on ranches told tall tales at night in the cowboy campfire tradition. They estimated the size their herds would be when they got home. Otis Yates told Roach, "There were two things I said I'd never do – join the army and pick cotton. And if I ever get out of this mess, I'll probably pick a little cotton!"

They talked of food and fun and the future. "What are you going to do when we get back to Frisco?" Senter asked a buddy.

"I'm going in the first Chinese cafe I find and get me five gallons of rice," he answered. "Then I'm gonna sit on a corner on Market Street and look at that rice and say to it, 'You sonofabitch, you're all mine!'"

Humor and rumor stretched a long way. Jesse Finley was strong on the first – it kept him going the long months when he believed his son Jack was dead – but he didn't much heed the second . . . .

Until the day the gaunt man, recently captured, came to him. "Jack's alive," he told Jesse. "I was sick in the hills, and a guy gave me quinine. Said he was Jack Finley." Jesse wanted to believe him; but the man had been mad with malaria, probably remembered the name wrong.

And then, a year and a half after he'd watched at the grisly O'Donnell gate, Jesse Finley got new life and courage in a strange package. Nestled in a box handed him was a pair of eyeglasses.

He'd ordered no eyeglasses.

The prescription was for Sergeant Jack Finley, 200th Coast Artillery . . . .

In Bilibid Prison.

– *19* –

THE BOYS IN THE HILLS

"I discovered that food and clothes were the only necessities. All other things are luxuries."
– Lieutenant Doyle V. Decker –
(formerly Private, Battery H)

"Joe! Joe – come with me!" A thin curtain parted death from life, and he didn't know which side he was on, or which side the voice came from. But it wasn't a Japanese voice, and whether it beckoned him to hell or Corregidor, Jack Finley figured it was better than where he lay.

Another column of prisoners marched by, but the guards were on the far side and failed to see him. At sunset the Filipino helped him to a hut in a nearby barrio. "I'll be back," he said. "If I find a boat we'll get to Corregidor."

Finley collapsed.

When he came to, the boy was leaning over him. "You got any money?"

"Twenty *pesos*. In my sock." He kept quiet about the hundred sewn in his pants. He slept again. Later, half conscious, he felt hands remove the *pesos* from his sock.

Still later he heard Japanese voices. "My God," he thought, "he's turned me in!" But they were a communications crew laying lines for the siege of Corregidor. They nailed wire to the corner of the hut, but in the dark they failed to see him.

He left at dawn. Down the road he collapsed cramping. "Joe, come with me," a Filipino begged. "Japs inside those houses." He pulled to his feet and stumbled along until the world turned black.

He awoke under a mosquito net, with a bowl of *lugao* beside him, and people clustered watching. He reached toward the bowl, and someone said, "*Americano* is eating rice!" It was the first time, they said, in the three days since Emilio Agustin had brought him to the barrio Santa Teresa.

Malaria wracked him daily, the chills at noon and then the fever. They dosed him with bark and boiled corn silk. It was all they had. "Then it settled in my spleen. I swelled until I looked pregnant, and could hardly keep my balance. A doctor said if I fell and it burst, I'd had it. They boiled cactus and bound it to my stomach with a long cloth till I could hardly breathe – that was one of their 'cures.'"

When he could stumble the few miles to barrio Santa Cruz, Troadia Soriano sent for him. "We started across a field, and I'd say, 'I can't go any farther,' and he'd say, 'just to the next hill,' until he finally got me there.

"They fed me, food like I hadn't seen in a year. Soriano found me quinine, and they hid me in a little house and his wife took care of me. They saved my life.

"Then the rains came, and so did yellow jaundice. They treated me with sarsaparilla and some kind of starch. For two weeks I did nothing but sleep and eat. Finally I could move around and the swelling slowly went down.

"Then the Japs started raiding, and they had spies out, so we headed for the mountains. We'd build little lean-tos in the cogon grass and lie in there. But if they thought anyone was in there, they'd burn the whole damned field down. We kept one step ahead of them. Fortunately, by then I could maneuver.

"We pushed farther and farther back into the mountains to Santa Rita, to Vincent and Arturo Bernia's sugar plantation. They were guerrillas with a big reward on their heads. Mine, too, for that matter – 50,000 *pesos* for any American. I was with them for awhile, and then pushed on into the Zambales Mountains. That's where I found Jack Bart."

Bart had been framed and blamed for a waterfront murder in New York, had spent a year in Sing Sing, ended up in the islands, and was caught by the war. Finley had known him in Santa Teresa. He, too, had fled to the mountains. Now he was dying of cerebral malaria.

It was too late to help Bart, but Finley could help his companion. "Take this quinine," he said. "Get on your feet and turn yourself in – or you'll die out here like Bart." Jack forgot the incident, but this man did not. It was he who, recaptured and sent to Cabanatuan, brought Jesse Finley the first hope that his son might yet be alive.

Jack and Soriano pushed through the mountains, helped along by the tiny Balugas. "They were marvelous hunters. Walking along a trail, suddenly we'd be surrounded. And they had big grins on their faces. But Japs – they'd annihilate Japs on the spot."

In the hills they found the Hukbalahaps. "They were our allies then, fighting Japs, hitting their garrisons. We raided one isolated barrio for food – the people had fled and left their chickens and hogs – and damned if we didn't run into a Jap patrol. The guerrillas hit and ran, and we took off too. Then Soriano and I lived by ourselves for awhile. Once a week we'd go down in the lowlands for rice and chickens, and we'd share with the Balugas.

"We decided to join a Huk sortie to Mount Arayat. The Japs never did take Mount Arayat – the guerrillas kept control. I thought if I could fight through with them, I'd try to push on to the Lingayen Valley, where they said there were no Japs and plenty of food."

Trying to get word to the guerrillas, they pushed through rivers and jungle, through twisted trails and no trails, through noisy birds and silent mystery, and heavy damp where mildew weights the clothes and settles in sores and nothing heals. An infection on Finley's foot became a tropical ulcer.

"I've seen men's legs chewed off by those things. They just eat, and you wonder when it's going to stop. It almost took my Achilles tendon off.

"We came on an American colonel and his friend. But he was scared to do anything, and by then I couldn't walk. The Japs were putting out propaganda, that if we turned in we'd be treated right. The rains were coming. And the Japs had told the Filipinos they'd wipe them all out if any Americans were found in their province. We couldn't risk these people's lives – they'd sacrificed everything for us. So we decided to turn in.

"This colonel wanted me to stay with him. But he was scared of his shadow and I couldn't walk. I needed treatment before that thing ate off my leg. I had no choice."

For a year and half Jack Finley had held out, and survived. With the others, he headed toward the valley, and captivity.

Many guerrilla groups prowled the jungles. Japanese methods, intended to cow Filipinos into submission, increased their determination; and resistance movements, at first isolated and uncoordinated, grew. Escaped Americans formed their own groups or joined the native ones.

Trying to establish contact with the outside, a lone radio cast its voice from a jungle pocket upon the vast Pacific, and somehow reached MacArthur. Colonel Guillermo Nakar continued to beam his messages, dodging stealthily and continuously until, in August 1942, the Japanese found him.

Two months later, two Americans,[1] daring the ocean in a tiny craft, made it to Australia with information of guerrilla activities, and MacArthur, despite inadequate supplies and vast distances, determined to organize an integrated guerrilla network. It seemed to many quixotic.

He dispatched a few submarines to smuggle supplies to the underground in the islands; he reestablished radio contact; and

[1] Captains William L. Osborne and Damon A. Gause.

by early 1943 his agents had built a nucleus of well-defined districts, with designated leaders, and orders to fight only if attacked, to keep low profiles, and to address the main business of gathering and relaying information. Throughout 1943 and 1944 the radio and submarine network grew into a complex system which furnished information vital to MacArthur's eventual invasion of Leyte and Luzon. Not until then could they shed their cloaks of invisibility and join the main action.

For days after escaping the surrender, Doyle Decker and his companions struggled through canyon-slashed, growth-matted no-man's land. When the rice ran out, the captain and the sergeant who had joined them in the jungle disappeared. It was just as well. They were the two (though Decker, Wolfe, and Lucero didn't know it) who had deserted two weeks before the surrender and shamed the regiment.

"So now we were three. We vowed we'd stick together and headed north. Near the foot of Mount Natib some Filipinos found us and fed us. It was our first food in days. Then a captain joined us, and at the Pilar-Bagac road we met three more officers and a couple of enlisted men.

"We found a cache of rice, and there was wild game, and, with the rainy season approaching, we decided to build a shack and sit it out." But mosquitoes descended in malarial clouds. A first man died, and a second, and a third. Finally some Filipinos found them and told of a camp to the north run by an American.

North they pushed for days, battling fear and disease, aided by friendly Filipinos. At length they stumbled into Fassoth Camp. It was June: They had been two months escaping Bataan.

Brothers William and Martin Fassoth, William's Filipina wife Catalina, and his son Vernon, working with the Bernia brothers who had sheltered Finley – and a few Filipinos who washed and cooked – quartered the sick, wounded, and exhausted men until they could move on. In this camp Decker met Bob Campbell, also from the 200th; their friendship was immediate and lasting, and in late August the two started for Olongapo to join guerrillas there.[2]

On the way, Decker's leg suddenly and strangely became totally paralyzed. For days he hobbled with a crude bamboo crutch. Filipinos brought them food. "Those were the hardest days. I knew if the Japs came I couldn't get away. But we didn't talk of failure, and we vowed we'd never surrender."

Slowly the muscles began to function, until he could maneuver – stiffly, but without the crutch. Learning of a guerrilla group in the area commanded by Colonel Claude Thorpe, they set out to find him. It was then October.

Days later they reached the camp. A ragged man stepped from a Nipa hut.

They'd come to report to Colonel Thorpe, they said.

He'd gone.

Gone where?

Wherever the dead go.

"What in hell . . . ?"

Jap raid. Betrayed for 50,000 *pesos*. Sonofabitch didn't live to spend it though.

So where now?

Might try Conner's outfit.

They hid in the mountains for the next few weeks until they found Lieutenant Conner's 155th Guerrilla Squadron, part of the network commanded by Lieutenant Colonel Gyles Merrill. The group comprised six Americans, a few Filipinos who gathered information and relayed it to the Americans, and, according to Conner's roster, two thousand Negritos, former headhunters who controlled the mountain areas.

Decker was assigned to a base station on Mount Banaba, overlooking Clark Field. "We were ordered to confine our operations strictly to intelligence, and not attempt sabotage – though some Filipino units, who could move freely, did. They were farmers by day, fighters by night.

"I tracked troop movements and planes at Clark with field glasses. I had a Filipino who located fuel and supply dumps.

---

2 They left Lucero and Wolfe still recovering at Fassoth Camp, and would see neither until war's end. Wolfe remained in Luzon and married a Filipina.

He was a commercial artist, so it was no big deal for him to draw maps of their locations." Decker relayed information to Conner, eight miles away on Mount Pinatuba, who passed it on to Merrill in the Zambales Range near Olongapo, who in turn, via a well-hidden radio, beamed it in code to Australia.

The pygmy Negritos served as runners for the network, and shared their food. "It wasn't appetizing, but it kept us alive. They grew some rice, beans, *camotes*, and a slimy stuff called *euba*. They dug a root they called *callote* that they'd slice and soak to remove the poison, which, if they failed to get it all out, made you walk like you were drunk. This happened often and lasted for days.

"We ate lizards, wild chickens, frogs, toads, fish, bats, snakes, and rats. Sometimes we got a little pork or carabao, but they thought nothing of butchering a sick animal, so to survive, we asked no questions. At worst, we were better off than the prisoners. I discovered that food and clothes were the only necessities. All other things are luxuries."

Decker spent weeks alone. "I had to move constantly to avoid detection, though I always stayed in sight of Clark Field. We never really knew friend from foe, but we had to trust the Filipinos. Most were loyal, but the 50,000-*peso* reward on our heads was a great temptation to many."

Too great, Decker learned the night he and Campbell were ambushed. "We'd gone to the Lowlands for supplies, got clothes and food for our men. But a Filipino we thought we could trust tipped off the Japs. To make sure we arrived at the right place at the given time, he had us leave an hour earlier than we planned, and had us change carts just before we reached the ambush area while he returned to the barrio."

Then: *"Tomare!"*

Bodies leaped from the night shadows. Moonlight glittered from their rifles and eyeglasses. The driver U-turned the cart. He whipped up the little pony. Bullets spattered like sudden rain. "We bailed out and ran across an open field into a bamboo grove, and laid low while the patrol stalked us. They had killed our driver and the boy with him. He was only seventeen. His great desire was to become an American citizen.

"After walking and running all night, we made it back into the mountains. Only then did I discover bullet burns on my arm and knee. Campbell was grazed, too. I heard the man who betrayed us was killed a few days later."

Decker, alone or with Campbell, made many more such forays in the next two-and-a-half years. "But I never again told anyone when I would leave or where I was going."

Edras Montoya hid in cogon grass after he slipped from the Death March near Guagua until the last of the columns passed by, then inched his way toward a house whose family fed him and hid him in a thicket. There he lay in water, carefully keeping on his dry side the prayer book his mother had given him. After dark his rescuers led him to a hut deeper in the jungle. For three days Japanese tanks and trucks screeched by, and on the third evening a Filipina appeared. She would take him to her husband's camp for escaped Americans, she said. She was Catalina Fassoth.

They walked two kilometers, then rode in a carabao cart through Japanese-infested barrios, where he "lay like a mouse, covered, and hoped in God they wouldn't inspect." The cart could not pass through the last three kilometers of roadless jungle, and Montoya was too weak to walk. Her husband would send for him, Catalina said. He lay under the trees and slept.

Antonio Sanchez found him. For eight months he and his wife Eugenia nursed him in their home through dysentery, malaria, and beriberi. Then it happened:

Five Japanese soldiers murdered an old man at a nearby farmhouse and raped the women. The guerrillas struck back. They accounted for all five. Then, ranging near enemy headquarters, they killed three more for clothes, rifles, and food.

"Soon hundreds of Japs gathered. We heard the machine guns and the tanks closing in. When the moon came out, we left the barrio. The guerrillas reported 150 Japs killed that night – and by the Japs themselves, thinking in the dark they had the guerrillas surrounded."

After the battle, persuaded by food and their girl friends, some lingered in a nearby barrio. Near dawn the Japanese attacked, captured those remaining, and tortured them to a slow death. They began to comb the jungle for the rest.

"We left to higher places, with the women and children. The Japs burned the houses. We saw the smoke and flames. We climbed higher and higher, and the Japs were after us, firing." At length they gave up the search.

Returning to the burned-out barrio, the villagers faced surrender or starvation. Propaganda leaflets promised food and good treatment, and the big-eyed children were crying from hunger. There seemed no choice. Sanchez hitched the carabao he had hidden in the jungle and loaded the children onto the cart. He would settle his family and return, he said.

"With many tears we said *adios*. Lonesome, sad, and alone in a strange jungle among an enemy that wanted to kill me, I prayed to God for courage and strength." Montoya worked his way to the mountain hut to await Sanchez.

Weeks later, Eugenia came alone, "wet, barefooted, her eyes swollen from crying, with a basket of rice and dry fish. She told me her husband, my true friend, was tortured and beaten to death. She slipped out while the Japanese were having a celebration. She took many chances coming, and hoped they were still celebrating so she could sneak back in. 'Pray for me,' she said."

Montoya spent several weeks with a guerrilla band before he decided to take his chances alone in terrain he knew. He returned to the shack, rebuilt it, and installed a rock-and-mud fireplace over which he cooked, using green bamboo joints for pots. He burned the fire continuously, to save his few matches, and to drive away mosquitoes.

With a needle of Eugenia's, and ravelings for thread, he sewed a blanket of two gunny sacks, and made two pairs of shorts from his worn khakis. Those and a ragged T-shirt he wore for the next three years.

He lived on what he could find. "I caught fish in ponds after rains. Once I found a Jap corn and cane field, raided it after dark, and had food for a few days, though I couldn't help worrying about my big barefoot tracks. I found wild fruits and vegetables, but not all year round, and chickens that had run when they burned the barrio."

He hunted before dawn, always on the lookout for venomous snakes and Japanese. From a tall tree he scanned the countryside. "Many times, thinking it was nearly morning, I went down the mountain, cutting my bare feet on rocks and sticks, swarms of mosquitoes sucking my blood, and then found it was not morning. I got very discouraged to return without any food."

He endured malaria, dysentery, toothache, beriberi, and other malnutritional diseases. Cuts became infected ulcers. His prayer book and a Bible Eugenia had given him sustained him through the diseases, the fear, the loneliness – and the worry. "No day went by without me wondering if the Japanese had invaded the United States. Horrible thoughts came that my family were in the same state I was. I prayed that they were alive."

From plane-dropped propaganda leaflets, he read claims that the Japanese had inflicted severe damage on American operations in the Solomons. "This assured me the enemy was not in America, for the Solomons are on the way to the Philippines. My spirit was lifted. I knew that one day the Americans would come."

Early one morning during the dry season, Montoya saw from his treetop lookout some two hundred Japanese marching up the canyon toward his shack. They passed on without discovering his shelter; but three days later they marched back down the canyon, and, close by his position, they fired the dry forest.

"The flames started roaring up the mountain. I got my few things ready to leave. I knew my strength was too low for me to save my shack. I thought of my friends, burned out and tortured and killed. I thought of myself living in a strange jungle alone, no friends, weak, sick, hardly no food, no clothes, no shoes, no tools for building another shack. As the fire roared in the jungle night, I knew I did not have a chance.

"I cried out, 'My God, my God, how much power are you going to give these people?' I stood there crying . . . .

"About fifty yards from my shack the roaring fire died. From miles away I could see a line where it stopped. I was sorry for my words. I had doubted the power of God. There was no need to – I was still alive and I knew the Almighty God was with me."[3]

Guerrilla bands made their presence known to the prisoners in many ways. On a detail headed toward northern Luzon, McBride saw furtive V for Victory signs and gestures he knew meant men and guns nearby. These increased as they traveled north. Once they came on the headless body of a Japanese soldier. At their destination in Lagangilang, high in the mountains of Abra Province and largely inhabited by wild Igorots, Bantus, and Ifugaos, a street barber whispered that guerrilla Major Cushing was gathering recruits. "If there is a raid, stay inside and keep low."

It came that night. "All hell broke out. I heard rifle fire and windows breaking and much shouting and confusion. Trucks were blowing up. In the hall I saw two Nips bleeding on stretchers. Then the firing stopped, apparently when the Japs retreated into a stone building." McBride hid in a closet until he saw daylight through a crack.

The Japanese soon quit this location.

Calvin Graef, sent with a thousand-man detail to Davao Penal Colony on Mindanao, saw Lucky Strike packages lying about and knew guerrillas were around. "We could have taken the camp over, and gotten away. But we had so many sick. We could have lost close to a thousand men. You don't go off and leave people like that."

Some did: When one group of eleven escaped, the rest suffered. Security tightened, brutality increased, and it never let up after that. Like most, Russell Hutchison resented the escapees. "They just walked out and left us there to suffer the consequences. They said later they knew we wouldn't be shot. That's a bunch of damned lies. Our whole barracks was locked in a compound for thirty days, on one ration a day, to await the execution order. We couldn't even speak to each other. Each morning we were taken out, wondering if we were going to be shot."

---

3 The above account is taken from an unpublished memoir written by Edras Montoya, which he kindly furnished the author.

Major Kazuo Maeda, Japanese Camp Commander – less vicious than most, or more concerned to retain his work force – flew to Manila to intercede. "Then came the big morning for our audience. We were scared – had been for thirty days. They always executed for escapes. Troops with their guns stood on either side of the road, and a group of sedans rolled up. Our little old hunch-backed interpreter got out of the first car and passed down the word: Maeda had stayed the execution.

"'Hutch,' said my buddy, 'after this day, if we ever worry about another thing, we're crazy!'"

Over all the islands guerrilla groups coalesced, grew, and waged their own peculiar war. Native drums – the 'bamboo telegraph' – rolled mysterious messages through the thick nights, and prisoners and guards knew the unseen unsurrendered were about their dark work. It seared the nerves of the guards and ignited hope in the prisoners. Sometimes a guard was found dead.

Signs of guerrilla activity appeared in unexpected little caches of food, money, messages. On a runway-building detail at Las Piñas, Aldrich found a note. "On a certain day, it read, they would raid our camp, with enough weapons for us all, and they would guarantee our safe conduct to the unexplored country to the north.

"Then we began to find a little rice or fruit, as if they were proving they were close and could get in. Another note said they'd set up medical stations, and to join them when they raided. We were so excited we talked about it half the night."

The raid never came off, for suddenly the situation changed. American planes began bombing Manila: All guerrillas were about to join a larger battle.

– 20 –

"YOU NOT HERE TO LAZY"

"I swore that I would survive and see comfortable life again. I repeated General MacArthur's words, 'I shall return'."

– Corporal Myrrl McBride –

As details fanned out of Cabanatuan, Old Two Hon'erd began to split, though buddies tried to get on the same crews. Many volunteered gladly – it got them outside the prison fence, and often meant extra food. It also meant bone-grinding, often dangerous, labor.

On Bataan, Ross "climbed down in a canyon and hauled out dynamite the Americans had stashed. It was packed in sawdust and heavy. A lot of guys got beat to death if they moved too slow. And you drop a box of water-soaked dynamite and it'll explode. I fell with one, and a Jap clubbed me. If it had blown, I wouldn't have cared – it would have gotten him, too."

To get food for a sick buddy, Sakelares accepted a wrestling challenge from the officer in charge. "The prize was a can of food, so I volunteered. Came to find out he was a Judo instructor. But I was AAU boxer from Deming High! I said, 'You Judo, I Joe Louis!' I was scared – all the Japs sitting there with bayoneted rifles – but I said, 'What the hell,' and hit him. Knocked him out.

"A Jap sergeant slapped me around and stood me at attention for two hours. Then the officer took me inside, poured some alcohol, and said, 'You dlink!' I said no, I wanted my can of food – I'd won the fight.' He said, 'Amelicans wine, women, song,' and I had to drink it. Next thing I remember was Mendoza dragging me in – he thought they'd really beat me up. Hell, I was just drunk!"

Mendoza drove a salvage truck on Bataan. "We stopped in Hermosa, where I'd left my 'washy-washy' with little Manuel Agustin. The guard wandered off, and I heard a whisper. 'Mr. Mendoza!' There was a little boy, with my Golden Gate T-shirt – my little friend! His parents had been killed. I gave him what I dared from the truck."[1]

The worst of the details sent in 1943 to build runways fell to the eight hundred men assigned to Nichols Field, commanded by the sadistic 'White Angel,'[2] who beat them to mutilation if they failed to meet their work quota, hung them by their arms, or inflicted the dreaded water cure.

Pelayo "saw men beat till they couldn't stand. We'd push those cars up the hills, dig through, push out, dump. After eighteen months I hurt my back. Couldn't walk, so they made me fill papers with dynamite powder. Breathing that stuff, I felt like my head would blow off."

"Two of my boys came in from Nichols Field detail," wrote Stiles. "They have been exceptionally rough on the Americans there. Have killed four men . . . . Bayoneted two at the latrine

---

[1] Louis Mendoza gave Manuel Agustin his Stateside address. He never saw him again. But in 1947, in Deming, New Mexico, he received a letter from Manuel. "My Dear Brother," it began. Years later they were still corresponding.

[2] So called because of the white naval uniform he wore.

because they were too weak from dysentery to make it back to their group."

It was the worst detail Roach ever drew. "Boys would bury a piece of fish to rot, so they'd get sick when they ate it. Some let loaded ore cars run over their legs to break them – anything to get off that detail. A lot died."

Men prayed to be spared the Nichols detail. On his way south to an unknown destination, Aldrich "felt the old metallic taste of fear return. We grew silent, and I prayed for help. Then someone said, 'There's Nichols.'

"We headed for that white gate – and rolled past!

"Slowly we began to talk, and slap each other on the back and, after the stench of Cabanatuan, to enjoy the smells of sampaquita flowers – and fresh air."

Las Piñas wasn't much better. Here too they had impossible quotas. "Sharp objects in the gooey mud made foot injury common as we built runways over rice paddies. When we failed to meet our quota, the Jap honcho jumped on our crew chief, and broke his watch with his stick. The next day he broke his arm.

"We screwed up every way we could. Surveying crews gave wrong readings. We threw loose dirt in the depressions, with no stable base. The runways were never even. We left diesel equipment in the rain."

As the Allies began to win victories in the Pacific, rations were cut and work quotas rose. Men resorted increasingly to self-mutilation. Many a man got a buddy to break his arm with a sledge hammer, while others kept a lookout for guards and prepared a story to cover the 'accident.' Glenn Ream watched a buddy from Zia Pueblo drive a pick through his own foot.

Merrill 'Pete' Pyetski had himself circumcised, for the few days' rest. While recuperating, he noticed Camp Commander Watanabe's chickens straying into the American compound, and mentioned this interesting fact to bunk-mate Aldrich. A spark of genius ignited. "We cut a hole in the floor, lowered a string to a box trap below, and in the night laid a trail of rice from Watanabe's chicken pen to the trap.

"That night we *quanned* chicken."

* * *

David Johns drove a steamroller at Murphy Field. "We were building a runway on a plateau, and a steep hill went down to the river. I had no brakes – just used steam pressure to hold it back, and took it down with a cable. At one sharp curve, I went right into the river. Steam spewed everywhere. Then the cable broke loose.

"What was funny was the Jap guard. He'd been half asleep on the roller box. He came to and grabbed that cable like he was going to stop it, and he was hanging on, sliding down that hill, yelling, '*Putangola! Putangola!*' That's Filipino for sonofabitch!"

When the honcho at Clark Field learned that Art Gilcrease and Grayford Payne were ranch boys, he put them on butcher detail. "We caught a carabao and dressed him out, and saved the blood in a bucket. Then Grayford smeared it on himself and let out a yell. You should have seen the Japs take off – they're scared of crazy people. So while they were gone, we stashed a bunch of meat."

At the garbage dump they found a bony puppy. "We raised that little dog. Shared our rations. Called him 'Hound.' He learned to hate Japs. Too much – he snarled at a guard, and we had to take our little dog out and kill him – they would have tortured him first." It hurt: At least a man knew what he was dying for.

Many were sent on road-building details. When the Japanese on one project in northern Luzon had no luck rustling food in the barrios, Burrola and a buddy persuaded the officer to let them try. "One family cooked us yams and gave us cans of Pet Milk – then gave us rotten vegetables to take back to the Japs! It kept them happy, and they let us go down every day."

Less lucky in the south, Amador Lovato was detailed to clear enormous tree stumps in Tayabas Province. "But we didn't have any equipment, and those trees got a million roots. We couldn't do nothing with just picks and shovels.

"Then the malaria started. Those mosquitoes were so thick we couldn't hardly see. Men were dying – of six hundred of us that went, only eighty survived." Lovato himself was carried to Bilibid with cerebral malaria.

The large circular building that was Bilibid Prison, built in Manila by the Spanish in 1865, now served as hospital, clearing house, and interrogation center. In it also were billeted stevedore details for Port Area, and men awaiting execution.

Here Stroope survived an appendectomy performed by an American doctor with a mess-kit knife. He was returned to live or die in a cell, "dank and dirty, with only cement to sleep on. Besides the pain of the operation, I had malaria and beriberi."

Here also, in another area of the great stone wheel, Finley stood trial for suspected guerrilla activities during his months in the hills. "I was in San Fernando waiting to be transferred to Bilibid when they brought in a couple of fellows they'd caught.

"One – Ingram – was in the same cell with me. We could see across the compound under the shower doors, where they gave the other the water cure. Got him on the floor, ran a hose and forced water in him. Started beating him, jumping on him, trying to make him confess he was a guerrilla. They finally killed him.

"Ingram knew he was next. He was shaking – God, he'd just seen his friend murdered. But then the *Kempetai*[3] came in, gave the garrison soldiers hell, and sent Ingram and me to Bilibid, to the execution chamber.

"We were on trial over a month. They'd ask the same questions over and over. 'You were in the hills?' 'What barrios were you in?' 'How did you get food?' I said I told the people I needed food so I could go turn in to the Japanese. I lied so much I believed it myself. I never gave names – told 'em I didn't know who the people were. Of course, if your stories didn't match, you were as good as dead.

"There were about sixty of us in there. They put red tags on thirty and sent us to Cabanatuan. That's where I found Dad. They took the others to the dungeon pits at Fort Santiago. Lined them up and shot every one. One was a good friend –

3 Elite Japanese soldiers who served as secret police, with authority over both military and civilian personnel.

and he was no more guilty than I was. Maybe his story got twisted. Or the interpreter messed up. Why he was in that group and I wasn't – I don't know."

Harrington, among thousands funneled through the old prison, found Bilibid a madhouse. "We slept on the concrete. Sanitary conditions were deplorable and flies swarmed. Trading, stealing, and gambling sessions were continuous."

The confusion aided Pulice, who, small and dark as a native, slipped in and out of the walls. "A Filipino I'd known on Bataan gave me his ID card, and I'd get medicine and bring it back – they'd let Filipinos in to sell stuff. I'd stay with his parents on a river boat. That's where I got the medicine. If we'd been caught, it would have been Taps. But they couldn't tell us apart."

McBride marched through Manila to Bilibid, "past a night club where an orchestra was playing 'The Missouri Waltz.' We glimpsed men and women in evening clothes. It was a reminder that there were still places left without death and disease. I swore that I would survive and see comfortable life again. I repeated General MacArthur's words, 'I shall return.'"

When McCahon's contingent from Cabanatuan arrived in late October 1942 at Davao Penal Colony on Mindanao, the camp commander greeted them in English, of sorts. "You not here to lazy!" snapped Major Maeda, adding that he had asked for workers, not skeletons, and ordered that they be fed adequately until they were fit to work.

Prisoners captured in the southern islands greeted them, and learned of Bataan, the Death March, and the Luzon camps. Among them the New Mexicans found an old friend and former Guardsman, Colonel Arden Boellner.

Davao seemed like Eden to McCahon. "There were thirty or forty different kinds of bananas, and we got fish or carabao stew, and plenty of rice – for about three months." But when Red Cross boxes arrived in January, Maeda cut their rations, and they stayed cut long after the boxes were emptied. After the eleven-man break in April 1943, work increased, rations were cut further, and then cut again after another six escaped the following March. After each escape the treatment grew more brutal.

"Sugar cane, avocados, papayas, oranges, coffee" – Graef, like most, had scurvy and pellagra – "and we couldn't have any, unless we stole it."

Here the 200th lost its chaplain to starvation. Howden died sharing his food with others who, he insisted, needed it more. His old friend and honorary member of the Regiment, Father Albert Braun, nursed him, administered last rites, and read the funeral service. Someone sounded Taps. The New Mexicans buried their own.

"Planting rice is no fun," ran a native folk song. "Break of day till set of sun. Cannot stand, cannot sit, Cannot rest a little bit." From four in the morning until nine at night, Knighton "plowed in water, planted in water, and harvested in water. We threw it in huge baskets hung from bamboo poles with a man at each end. It was all we could do to pick the thing up – carry it knee deep in water to the little railroad, then push the cars uphill. I often wondered how we'd make it."

So did Donaldson, straining miserably against the train one rainy night. Then a voice rose. "As the storm clouds gather," someone sang, and others joined in. "'God Bless America!' We were all singing, and the Japs were scared – thought we were going to take off and do something. But – there wasn't any place to go."[4]

There were countless extra duties. Pulice hauled water to boil for salt. Knighton unloaded cement. Donaldson carried logs. Greeman sacked rice.

Who knew how to raise poultry? asked the honcho. The chickens were dying. Donaldson volunteered himself and several friends. Mess kits ranneth over! "A Filipino sneaked us fruit, which cured our scurvy. And we stole eggs. When a guard would turn his back, I'd lift one from the nest, and it was down the hatch. I ground the shell in the sawdust."

4 Flying insects ate on them in nighttime hours and, by day, as they labored barefoot in the rice paddies, tiny worms that lurked in the infested waters entered through their soles, and traveled to lay spined eggs in their bladders and intestines. The resultant disease, schistosomiasis, caused tissue damage and hemorrhaging. Many died, then and later. Donaldson, rescued at war's end nearly dead, was flown to the States and saved only after months of drastic treatment.

They slipped food into g-strings or ponchos. In the supposedly empty can he took to the mess to fill for the crew's lunch, Greeman smuggled pumpkins to the doctors for the sick. Mending sacks in a dark corner, each day he watched a guard stash avocados filched from the officer's mess. "Then I'd steal them from him – until the day I was eating and looked up to see his face in the window. He beat the whey out of me."

Stealing progressed from a means of survival to a way of life. Stevedore detail at Port Area offered fascinating possibilities. Ojinaga could fit a few cans nicely in one sleeve of his jacket, and juggle them quickly to the other as the guard inspected one sleeve at a time.

Earl Harris was loading sugar when a troop ship docked. "In the confusion, sugar was falling out of the nets, and sacks were splitting, and we were raking it into our mess kits. They were short of guards, and the American supervisors kept an eye out for Japs while we ripped 'em off. Then the Jap troops joined the melee, and a guy bending down to get sugar would draw back and hit a three-bagger. The Jap wouldn't even look back – he'd fall on his face, get up, and take off! We had a ball that day."

Johns loaded eggs. "We'd go in the cooler, suck out the egg, and put back the empty shell. We got two or three each trip, until they started inspecting – and found the whole top layer in every crate gone. They sure beat our butts! But we'd go out next day and steal something else. If we got by with it, we were that much ahead. If not – hell, they could beat my butt as long as my belly was full!

"Extra guards meant a shakedown. So whoever was at the end of the line would pass what they had to the guys ahead of them, and then start a fight. The guards thought it was the funniest thing in the world to see Americans fighting, so they'd run back hollering, and we'd walk in with the stuff. They never did catch on."

Aldrich and Pyetski, hauling sand for concrete, ran over a small pig. "The Filipino ran out of his hut screaming, the Jap guard leaped out of the truck and beat hell out of the poor guy, and Pyetski grabbed the pig and buried him in our load. By the time the Filipino slumped to the ground, the Jap had forgotten about the pig."

Earl Harris unloaded shiploads of beer. "We drank our share, and when a guy got too much, we held him up and counted off for him. If they questioned us, we said he had malaria.

"One ship had officers' footlockers full of Scotch. We helped ourselves while we unloaded the other stuff. One guy got soused and went to sleep under a lifeboat. When we counted off, and one was missing, the guards went aboard with bayonets fixed. About then he came to, and took off. Down the deck, around the superstructure – twice around, and they were gaining. He dropped to the lighter, rolled down to the cargo, crawled out between the ship and the deck, and got in line. They never could spot him. God, they were mad!"

When another group drank too much beer and found their crates too light, they remedied the situation by relieving themselves into the empty cans, screwing the tops back on, and delivering them to the Japanese Officers' Club.

Unloading rice, sugar, or beans, each man on Earl Harris's crew carried a bamboo tube, which, inserted into the burlap bag on the back of the man just ahead of him, siphoned the produce into a sock concealed in his crotch.

"Our American commander – a Navy captain – built a jail. If a guard caught guys stealing, he'd yell and slap you around, and work himself into a frenzy. That's when the Old Man would run out and grab 'em, throw 'em in the can, and lock the door, so by the time the Japs got really mad, the victims were gone. And the Old Man and the key were hard to find!

"He got by with it because he'd known the Jap commander before the war – he'd worked for a steamship liner Stateside. That Jap was intelligent – he knew the eventual outcome of the war. A lot of them did."

Coral Sea . . . Port Moresby . . . Guadalcanal . . . Bismarck Sea: Battles unknown to those to whom MacArthur had pledged, "I shall return." The Solomons and New Guinea; the Gilberts, the Marshalls, the Marianas. Clash by bloody clash, across the vast Pacific, the Americans struck, bypassed enemy bastions, and isolated them behind new lines. The Japanese began to ship the prisoners from the southern islands back to Luzon, beyond MacArthur's north-pushing path. And since October 1942, following their losses at Midway, they had begun shipping men north to Manchuria, Korea, and Japan itself.

The prisoners were unaware of the swelling tide, but they gauged the winds of battle by the temper of their guards. Each time rations shrank and beatings increased, they knew the Allies had won another battle, and hope surged. Yanks and tanks were coming!

There were other signs. A scrap of rumor; a furtive Filipino grin and a whispered, "Very soon now, Joe!" A native saying became a slogan: "Cheer up, *mi compadre*, you have but small to wait."

Standing in sick line in September 1944, Rhee saw a low-flying craft over Manila Bay. As they watched, another plane attacked and shot it down. The men exchanged glances.

At Clark Field, an arm-waving guard rushed into the American compound. "Get ready go!" he screamed. "NOW! You go Manila. Then Japan!" Something, they knew, was up.

They saw them first at Cabanatuan. Greeman "looked up and saw planes – American bombers, between layers of pursuit planes. Hundreds! A Jap plane was trying to hedgehop away, and right there by the camp a Yank shot him down! An old Jap officer said in a sad voice, 'War is but a means to rid all nations of their youngest and best.'"

But the prisoners' eyes were following the planes. "We looked south to Manila, and the whole thing was going up in smoke." It was 21 September 1944.

On his lonely mountain, Montoya ran to his lookout tree, and from its height saw the stars on American fighter wings and watched a dogfight with Zeros. "They were roaring up and down the sky. Bullets were flying everywhere, but I was too happy to take cover."

Garcia watched them tear toward Nichols Field. "The Japs were having target practice when our Navy dived on them, machine-gunning their runway and planes. They didn't know what happened until too late."

At Las Piñas, Aldrich "heard gunfire and saw the orange arcs of burning planes smear across the sky, and we knew the fight was real. The Japs started screaming to get in the barracks or they'd shoot us. Then a blue aircraft, trailing smoke, streaked over our heads for the hangars. Its wings spouted flame, and the Japs took off.

"We just stood there cheering, though we weren't sure these were American planes, because the insignia had changed. But they were damn sure on our side!"

The next day a second raid hit Clark and Nichols Fields and finished the work on Manila Bay. Smoke and flame geysered from the city, and those close enough spread the word: The harbor was a boneyard of sunken hulls, torn, twisted, some still burning.

"Nips very quiet and reserved," wrote Stiles at Cabanatuan. "Rice rations decreased. Looks like hard days before our *compadres* reach us. When they fly over, they are so near and yet so far."

They would soon be free, many said – the Japanese could not possibly evacuate the islands now. They were tragically wrong. While Manila still burned, their enraged captors began to herd those prisoners still left on Luzon[5] through Bilibid to the docks, and on 1 October a large group boarded the *Haro Maru* for Japan.

Their ordeal was not yet over.

---

[5] As early as October 1942, following their losses at Midway in June, the Japanese had begun shipping prisoners north to Manchuria and Japan.

– 21 –

"NOR IRON BARS"

"Those days of not knowing are unimaginable. The men do the suffering of the body. The women endure the anguish of the soul."

– Jane Fleming Meuli –

"After two years," wrote Stiles on 31 January 1944, "the Japs have finally let some letters in. However, they are only letting about a hundred a day loose, and there are supposed to be fifteen thousand." Two weeks later he opened one from his father, "over a year old, but the only word I have received since the beginning of the war . . . . Can take anything since hearing from home."

In time, another from Mary "was enough to make a fellow decide he'll make it despite the odds. Don't worry, darling . . . . It won't be much longer – it can't be."

Many, he wrote, became disheartened when mail from home gushed with "what good jobs they have, lots of money and plenty of good times"; and when one friend learned that his fiancee had married and had a baby, "he threw up what little chow he had."

Stiles himself suffered a tragic blow, ironically on the day the Americans bombed Manila. Returning from wood detail, elated and sure he would soon be home with Mary, he whooped to find a letter from his father awaiting him. Then –

"Dear Moyne," he read. "So sorry to inform you Mary passed away November 3. Be courageous . . . ."

Dear God, what else? "But I won't go feeling sorry for myself," he vowed. "I'll just pray to God to keep her . . . . A beautiful, wonderful girl, and I consider myself fortunate to have been her husband the short time I was."

They garnered scraps of news any way they could. Schmitz's brother evaded censorship when he wrote from Italy, "We have rolled up the ball of yarn here and we're going on." As they learned the language, they eavesdropped on indiscreet guards. A friend of McCormick's who worked in the repair shop "would short out a Jap radio, tell 'em it needed a part, and while they waited a week or two for it, he'd fix it – and he had the radio."

Much they heard was rumor circulated as news, and much was news circulated as rumor to protect the sources. But, it seemed to Aldrich, news from the Outside "was never in our part of the world. It was always somewhere else, in Never-Never Land."

Occasionally they could fill out printed cards to send home, with blanks to be completed. "Regards to __________" ran one line; Niemon filled in *Laika* and *Kipija*, which meant 'thin' and 'sick' in his family's native Finnish.

Though they doubted the cards would reach home, there was nothing to lose, and many were delivered. They were equally skeptical when, in 1943, the Japanese devised a vehicle for propaganda dubbed "Humanity Calls," wherein chosen POWs could broadcast messages shortwave via Radio Tokyo.[1]

[1] Later a second 30-minute program, "The Postman Calls," was added.

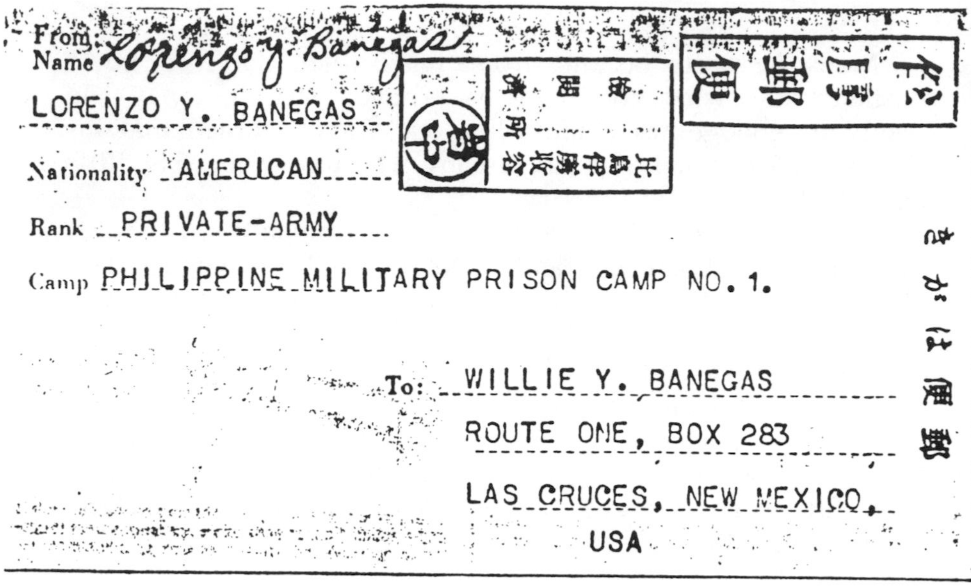

From:
Name *Lorenzo Y. Banegas*
LORENZO Y. BANEGAS
Nationality AMERICAN
Rank PRIVATE-ARMY
Camp PHILIPPINE MILITARY PRISON CAMP NO. 1.

To: WILLIE Y. BANEGAS
ROUTE ONE, BOX 283
LAS CRUCES, NEW MEXICO.
USA

俘虜郵便
比島俘虜収容所 検閲済
郵便はがき

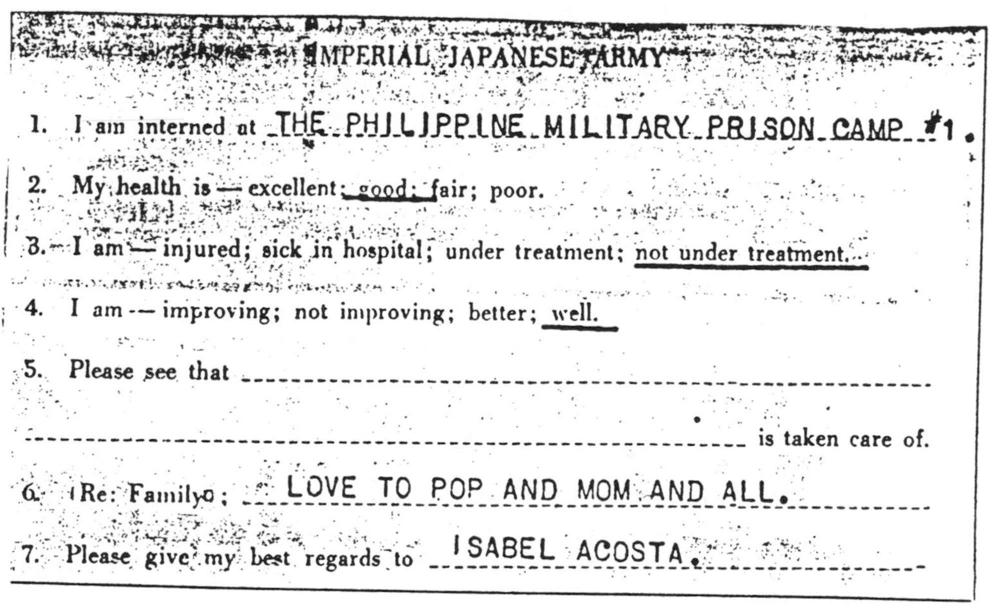

IMPERIAL JAPANESE ARMY

1. I am interned at THE PHILIPPINE MILITARY PRISON CAMP #1.
2. My health is — excellent; good; fair; poor.
3. I am — injured; sick in hospital; under treatment; not under treatment.
4. I am — improving; not improving; better; well.
5. Please see that ______________________ is taken care of.
6. (Re: Family) ; LOVE TO POP AND MOM AND ALL.
7. Please give my best regards to ISABEL ACOSTA.

Prisoners held by the Japanese could occasionally mail cards such as this. Knowing they were censored, and hoping to reassure their families, men seldom marked the responses accurately. (Courtesy: Lorenzo Banegas.)

Munsey's parents received hundreds of letters from people who had heard his message; it was their first knowledge that he still lived. Ross Aldrich, operating a shortwave post at an internment camp for German POWs in Fort Stanton, New Mexico, froze, astonished to hear "Hi, Dad" – in the voice of his son Robert. Bill Reardon's little daughter Jean grew wide eyed over a special "Happy Birthday" from Daddy. And the citizens of Artesia thrilled to hear an orchestra in which – a spokesman read their names and addresses – their own Tony King played.

Despite official warnings regarding the authenticity of the broadcasts, Americans clung to their sets through tides of propaganda for any evidence that father, son, or husband still lived. In Albuquerque, Janc Fleming and six other women organized "Listening Post 200," manned their shortwaves in shifts, and recorded messages relayed from the West Coast.

"The Japs would tell us all the ships they'd sunk, all the planes they'd shot down, all the men they'd killed. They started with 'Miss You' and 'I'll Walk Alone' and all those sad war songs, and to keep us listening, they'd intersperse messages from our men.

"We sent cards to the families, and we took those in town to Mrs. Bradley's, because the broadcast was usually repeated. Sometimes they could hear their own boy speak."

It was the first news many heard. Letters written on Bataan had filtered in for weeks after the surrender, to be reprinted in local papers, and posted on bulletin boards. "Then there was nothing. We clung to every little thread of news, and tried to bolster each other's morale."

It was eighteen months before Jane Fleming learned that Jack was in Mukden, Manchuria. "Those days of not knowing are unimaginable. The men do the suffering of the body. The women endure the anguish of the soul."

"Our time will come," wrote Stiles in May 1944, "if Uncle Sam ever gets off his twat. Sure doesn't look to us like he's done much toward winning this war."

Many at home felt the same. Hurt and angry from the first over the 'Get Hitler First' strategy, New Mexicans formed the

Bataan Relief Organization in March 1942, to demand action in the Pacific. By mid-April the BRO was incorporated and its new purpose stated: "To obtain immediate relief for all American soldiers held as Japanese prisoners of war, their release as quickly as possible, and their safe delivery home." Their pledge: "We will not let them down."

The following year they published their first monthly *Bulletin*, one hundred copies edited and printed by BRO Secretary Paul McCahon. Within another year their circulation reached four thousand, commercially printed and nationally distributed, and BRO membership had grown to over one million, with affiliates throughout the United States.

Headquartered in Albuquerque and led by founder and president, Dr. V.H. Spensley, they barraged the President, the War and State Departments, and the Red Cross with letters, telegrams, and petitions for food and medicine for their boys, and planes and tanks for MacArthur. "For God's sake," Spensley demanded, "send the General something to fight with. Our boys died fighting with bare hands and promises."[2]

"POUR IT ON WASHINGTON" urged the *Bulletin*.[3] Its readers did.

The BRO persuaded the Governor to establish a War Veterans' Information Bureau which, supervised by BRO representative Carl F. Whittaker, gave help to relatives of Japanese POWs and served as liaison between the State Adjutant General and the War Information Bureau in Washington.[4]

When Easter 1944 fell on the fateful 9 April, a Los Angeles chapter requested the President to designate it Bataan Day. Impossible, the White House answered: The President was focusing all energies on Europe. Despite the snub, New Mexico's governor proclaimed Bataan Day, and, sponsored by the BRO, churches throughout America dedicated services to the heroes of Bataan.

---

2 BRO *Bulletin* No. 7, 11 October 1943.

3 BRO *Bulletin.*

4 BRO *Bulletin.*

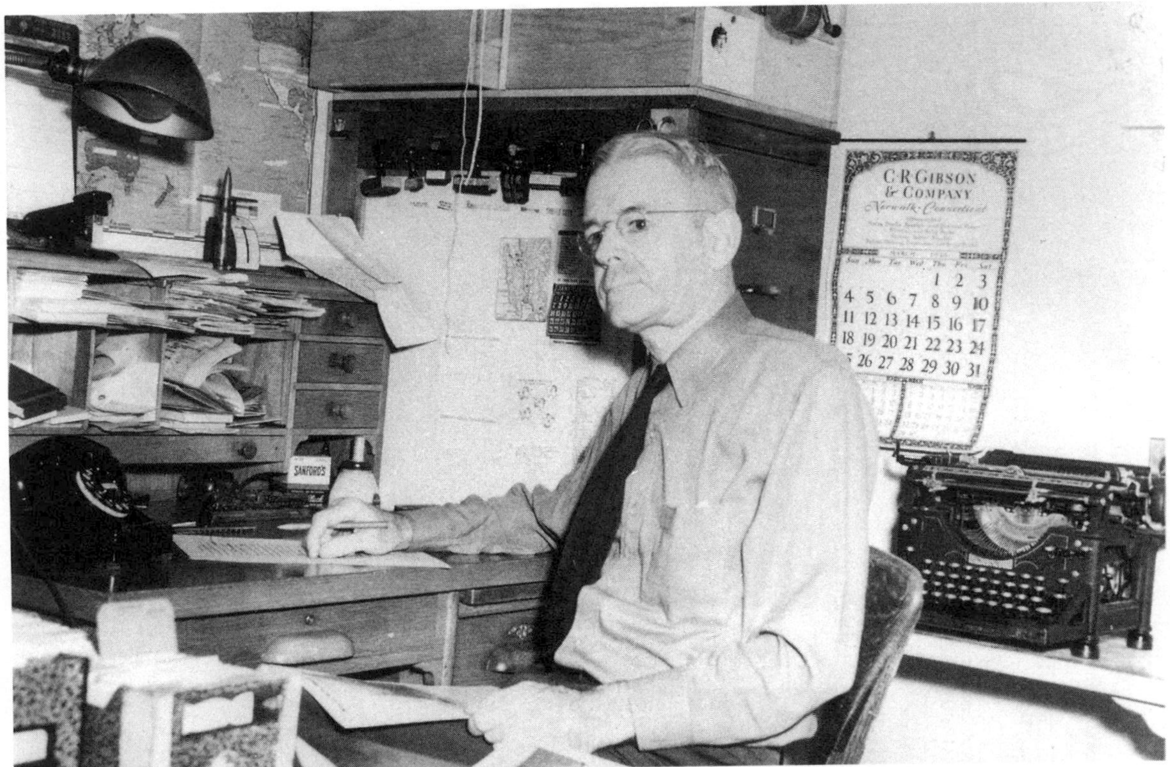

Paul McCahon at his desk in Albuquerque, where he wrote and edited the BRO *Bulletin*. McCahon died just days before his son James was liberated. (Source: BRO files. Courtesy: James McCahon.)

The President led the nation in prayer on D-Day for those on the Normandy beachheads. Why, a mother wired him, had he never asked the nation to pray "when our boys were fighting on Bataan?" and charged him with writing them off, "even as they were told . . . , 'help is coming.'"[5]

On the Capitol grounds in Santa Fe a thousand people gathered on 14 June 1942 to dedicate the old concrete insignia the boys of the 200th had built at Fort Bliss to mark their headquarters, subsequently obtained by the BRO and Governor Miles.

When an art critic deplored the garish colors of "these blobs of concrete" and hoped "this hideous object is only a temporary arrangement,"[6] Adjutant General R.C. Charlton snapped back that it was a tribute to the regiment, "intimate to them and the only thing they left behind."[7]

"It is the handiwork of our boys," bristled the *Headlight*. Its colors were those of the State, its form the Zia emblem, which they "loved enough to lay down their lives for."[8]

The monument still stands.[9]

Spearheaded by the BRO, New Mexico always exceeded its quota of War Bonds. If the state could sell $300,000 in bonds during a drive ending 26 January 1943, they were promised, they could name a new bomber. They doubled the amount. Secretary McCahon reported to the Secretary of War, got an evasive answer, and complained to the Governor that "New Mexico responded nobly," believing "this bomber would go to the Pacific area to directly aid in the eventual liberation of our heroic sons," and requested his aid.

---

5 BRO *Bulletin*, Vol. 11, No. 3, 28 June 1944.

6 Amelia Elizabeth White, as quoted in the *Santa Fe New Mexican*, 16 June 1942.

7 *Santa Fe New Mexican*.

8 Deming *Headlight*, 19 June 1942.

9 Later a permanent flame was added. Each year on the weekend closest to 9 April a ceremony pays tribute to the Regiment before the State Capitol, now officially called the Bataan Building. At this writing, plans are being implemented to move the monument to the New Mexico National Guard Armory in Santa Fe.

Dr. V.H. Spensley, at Kirtland Field on 17 July 1943, dedicates and presents to the Air Force the *Spirit of Bataan*, bought with War Bonds by New Mexicans. Dr. Spensley's son, Homer, was among the thousands who died in Japanese prison camps. Mrs. Arturo Garcia, believed then to be New Mexico's first Gold Star Mother, christened the ship. (Source: Air Base Photographic Laboratory, Kirtland Field, Albuquerque.)

"Do you want to do anything on this?" the Governor's secretary typed at the bottom. Beneath that appeared a penciled notation: "Raise Cain talking to Washington."[10]

Washington heard. At Albuquerque's Kirtland Field, on 17 July, Dr. Spensley presented to the Air Corps the sleek Flying Fortress that New Mexicans had bought, and Gold Star mother Mrs. Arturo Garcia christened her: *Spirit of Bataan*.

Dr. Spensley learned of the death of his son Homer on 4 July 1943, as he prepared to leave for Washington to present a plan for shipping food and medicine to the POWs through Russia. Despite his heartbreak, he and Adjutant General Charlton joined W.B. McCollum, Secretary of the New Mexico War Prisoner Relief Bureau in Washington, and met with State and War Department officials. Carlsbad editor Marcus Griffin dedicated a special issue of the *Eddy County News* to "New Mexico's heroes of Bataan," praised the mission, urged its speedy implementation, and flooded Washington with copies.[11]

Their combined pressures resulted in the deposit in early 1944 of eighteen hundred tons of food and medicine at Vladivostok, to await Japanese acceptance. McCollum flew to Moscow and Vladivostok to aid the process, while the Swiss minister in Tokyo worked in their behalf.

Nearly a year later the *Hakusan Maru* picked up the supplies. Though the Japanese kept most of it, a small portion did reach some prisoners.

Through the BRO, New Mexico's voice was heard out of proportion to its negligible electoral vote. The loudest outcry burst when the War Department, on 27 January 1944, released news of Japanese atrocities. Why, asked a horrified America, were we not told what official Washington had known since the summer of 1942, when civilians exchanged via the *Gripsholm* reported the horrors of the Death March and O'Donnell?

---

10 P.W. McCahon to Hon. John J. Dempsey, 27 April 1943. New Mexico Archives, Santa Fe.

11 *Eddy County News*, 1 September 1944, Vol. 34, No. 6.

Nor was America informed when three escaped prisoners[12] who reached Australia in July 1943 were dispatched by a shocked MacArthur to Washington, where they gave sworn testimony and a detailed report. Roosevelt ordered this and all reports of Japanese brutalities withheld. Only when threatened with British and Australian disclosures did he authorize its release.

Angry at the deception, many refused to accept administrative excuses of fear for the POWs, and labeled it fear of increased demand for action in the Pacific. The *Headlight* resented such suppression, "only to be released in time for the Fourth War Loan Drive,"[13] and Senator Chavez protested that bond sales were not enough. His small State, which had supplied its entire National Guard,[14] demanded "a thousand planes to MacArthur," he fulminated. "No one can prove to a single mother in my State, that it is more essential to send 2,000 tanks to England or Tunisia, than to send 200 to MacArthur."

He read from a flood of telegrams. "'Your refusal to heed pleas of your own hard-pressed troops while . . . aid was rushed elsewhere places [on you] the responsibility for the horrible suffering and death of our sons on Bataan and Corregidor . . . .'[15]

"' . . . We want action in the Pacific.'[16]

---

12 Captain Ed Dyess, Major Stevan Mellnick, and Commander Melvin H. McCoy.

13 Deming *Headlight*, 4 February 1944.

14 Doubtless Senator Chavez did not mean to imply that New Mexico's "entire" National Guard served in the Philippines, but that the entire Guard was sent to combat. Although the bulk of the state's Guard comprised the 200th and 515th, two smaller, but highly effective, Guard units served in the European theater. The 120th Engineers Combat Battalion was, at the time of Senator Chavez's speech, with the 45th Infantry Division in Sicily, and would soon see more action in Italy, and in the final campaign through France and into Germany. The 804th Tank Destroyer Battalion (attached alternately to the 34th and 88th Infantry Divisions) was, while the Senator spoke, engaged in the final fighting in North Africa, and was preparing to join the Italian campaign. Both units served with distinction.

15 Signed Blanche Cain, Fleda Colvard, and Lydia Byrne. Copies to President Roosevelt, Secretary of War Stimson, Secretary of Navy Knox, Senator Chavez, and BRO Albuquerque.

16 Two Hundredth Club, Artesia. Beth King, Secretary.

"'The political chicanery . . . in Washington . . . should be called the Raw Deal instead of the New deal.'"[17]

In September 1943 Senator Chavez introduced a BRO-sponsored bill to give promotions of one grade to all men below rank of colonel captured on Guam, Wake, Bataan, and Corregidor. Secretary Stimson opposed it. "There is no way," he pontificated, "to distinguish between those who, by virtue of having fought to the last, might be deserving . . . and those who surrendered in circumstances under which they might reasonably have been expected to resist."[18]

The Secretary, "speaking of the boys he knew had suffered the agonies of the damned," Chavez charged, "had the audacity" to suggest they might not be deserving?[19] The BRO added its own blistering comments.[20]

He had not meant to insinuate cowardice, Stimson protested. But he still opposed the bill.

Twice Chavez revived SB 1374.[21] Twice it passed the Senate. The BRO, repeatedly and unsuccessfully, sought Presidential approval for its passage in the House. Both times it died in committee. The Chairman refused to bring it to the floor over War Department opposition.

It is impossible to measure the impact of the BRO. Its efforts in the face of Capital odds were gargantuan – and often hopeless. Yet its persistence chafed. A constant burr under the Washington saddle, the BRO proved a major irritant for action in the Pacific, until at last the stream of supplies began to cross for MacArthur.

The BRO also spurred the second sailing of the *Gripsholm*. The American-chartered Swedish liner had exchanged

17 Signed Kathleen H. and Paul W. McCahon. Telegrams and portions of Senator Chavez's speech, 78th Cong., 2d Sess. *Cong. Rec.* 2 December 1943, p. 10322.

18 Secretary Stimson to Chairman Sen. Comm. on Foreign Aff. *Cong. Rec.* 2 December 1943, p. 10322.

19 Chavez, 78th Cong.

20 BRO *Bulletin* No. 9, 28 December 1943.

21 BRO *Bulletin*, September 1944 and February 1945.

diplomatic and civilian personnel with Japanese and Italian ships on 23 July 1943, transferred cargoes of food, medicine, vitamins, surgical equipment, clothing, books, tobacco, and toilet articles, and hoped they would reach the prisoners.

On his trip to Washington in July 1943, Dr. Spensley, besides presenting plans for the Vladivostok shipment, also secured from General Marshall promises to dispense with red-tape barriers to another sailing of the *Gripsholm*.[22] As a result, after a year's delay in New York harbor, she sailed again in September 1943, carrying, along with another huge load of Red Cross supplies, the only boxes families of Japanese POWs were allowed to send during the entire war.

Wives and mothers crammed everything possible within the size and weight limits into the parcels – shoes, food, vitamins. Some wrote messages of hope inside labels. Janie Fleming sent long underwear to Jack. "I embroidered 'Mom' on one lapel and 'Janie' on the other. And then I put on a lot of lipstick and kissed it!"

"Red Cross goods have arrived," wrote Stiles, "and some of the guards are smoking Lucky Strikes."

Gripsholm supplies lay stockpiled in Yokohama and Manila while men starved; distribution, when it did come, was uneven. Some camps enjoyed boxes for two Christmas seasons; others got one parcel the entire war.[23] Some boxes were never delivered. Those that were, were rifled. Munsey "saw a guard trying to get a bar of cheese to lather. He finally threw it down and said American soap was no damned good. We washed it off and ate it."

"Some personal packages in," Stiles wrote of the second *Gripsholm* shipment, which got to Cabanatuan in March of 1944. "Japs have already confiscated one truck load. The dirty yellow thieves. About a thousand men will be without."

---

[22] The BRO also secured at this time, through Senator Carl Hatch, the appointment of a subcommittee to the Senate Committee on Military Affairs, to investigate further relief for the POWs. BRO *Bulletin* No. 6, 9 September 1943.

[23] This is a distinct contrast to the weekly Red Cross boxes distributed to most Allied prisoners in German camps.

Winston Shillito and Nick Chintis, third and fourth on second row, gaze at Red Cross boxes furnished for the inspection. Tree, clothes, and boxes were taken from them after the inspectors left. (Courtesy: Nick Chintis.)

Those who did get boxes were pitifully happy. Keats Begay and Dick Nunn, opening piñon nuts and cowboy boots respectively, cried. Though Rhee "received socks, and I hadn't had any shoes for months, and the mouth harp my mother sent was rusted" – and stamped 'Made in Japan' – they brought love from home. In cold Manchuria, Jack Fleming donned his kiss-brightened underwear, gave a whoop, and performed a lively Cossack dance.

And a handkerchief embroidered with "Daddy" brought James Hamilton "joy beyond belief in this place where it seemed all the world had forgotten us." Some did not get any personal boxes, "and it was heartbreaking to see the expressions on their faces."[24]

The seal between the prisoners and the free world closed tightest when representatives of the International Red Cross or the Swiss or Swedish legations came to inspect. So near, so distant, the men could see but dared not speak.

Chintis knew the Red Cross was coming "when they dressed us up in some old uniforms they'd captured, with ascots to hide our scrawny necks. They had us put up a Christmas tree, and took pictures." Tree and clothes disappeared the next day. The official report: "Three meals, varied menus . . . . Impression favorable."

In Mendoza's camp hospital, "the guards put out Red Cross parcels, canned goods, books, medicine, clothing. They put the cooks in as patients, and hid the sick men in the mine. As soon as the Red Cross left, they took it all away and sent the cooks back to the kitchen." The report was predictable: "Sufficient clothing, good medical care."[25]

---

24 James H. Hamilton, *Rainbow Over the Philippines* (Chicago: Adams Press, n.d.), 40.

25 Photostat of reports dated 15 August 1944. New Mexico National Guard Headquarters, Santa Fe. Reports cited are from Yokohama and Fukuoka 17, respectively, where Chintis and Mendoza were held. These are not isolated cases, but follow the usual pattern of reports following the staged inspections.

For the International Red Cross inspection in December 1943, the Japanese ordered the POWs at Asano Shipyard to erect a Christmas tree, and furnished musical instruments, British uniforms captured at Hong Kong, and ascots to hide their bony necks. Tony King plays the clarinet as Winston Shillito peers over the guitarist's shoulder. Lower right: Nick Chintis and Julius Tecumseh. (Courtesy: Nick Chintis.)

* * *

Lucy Wilson, escaping Corregidor in the *Spearfish*, had pierced the seal from the inside. "I was seventeen days under water, then across Australia on a troop train. Along the way, aborigines cooked mutton stew for us in fifty-gallon oil drums. We sailed from Melbourne to New York, and they said we'd never have to go overseas again."

Then, yearning for news of Dan Jopling, Lucy tried to pierce through from without, attended Flight Nursing school, and in January 1944, returned to the Pacific. "I landed first in New Caledonia. When we heard of any place with a landing strip, I hit it. Always I wanted to get back and find Dan.

"Most of the time we were island-hopping on C-47s, up to the front lines, with ammunition and food. Sometimes we'd have to circle until the firing stopped, and we'd land and load the injured quickly. Some of the soldiers would come up and touch our arms – they just wanted to touch an American woman. If we didn't give them anything but courage, we were the symbol of what they were fighting for.

"Chest or skull injuries affect breathing, so we'd ask the pilots to fly low – sometimes nearly skim the ocean – so they could breathe. We tried to take food for them. They never got much food in the Pacific – it was all going to the European theater.

"We were the first nurses into Guadalcanal – we flew the injured back to hospitals on islands behind us. Finally we got to Leyte – and then Luzon. It was the highlight of my life. I helped to fly out some ex-POWs, and some were from the 200th. I kept asking them all, 'Where's Dan? Where's Dan?'"

They probed the darkness with ingenuity and guts. At Mudken, Steve Alex and John Moseley of the 200th, with two British officers, cranked out a newspaper. "We sifted items from propaganda papers some Chinese smuggled to us, and put clues together. I wrote one- or two-liner blurbs and Moseley drew cartoons. We ran off miniature papers on an old Jap mimeograph machine when the Japs were out of the factory office, and smuggled them out in our wooden clogs. We named it *Nor Iron Bars*.

"The first edition showed a Santa Claus scratching his head, looking at a globe, and saying, 'Egad! Where is Mukden?'"

At Zentsuji, in Japan, Boyer enlarged a map from a small geography book he found, using a grid for accurate scaling. "Work details coming in in columns of four would see a Jap with a newspaper, march around him on both sides, and when they passed, his newspaper was gone! A naval officer translated. They'd talk about driving the Americans off some island, with thousands of American casualties. Then, in a week, or a month, they'd report winning another battle – but we'd check my map, and it would be five hundred miles closer to Japan! So we knew what was happening. We followed MacArthur all the way up."

For years they talked of Russell Hutchison's radio.

At Davao he repaired Japanese Camp Commander Maeda's radio, and a movie projector, and he told the American Camp Commander he believed he could build a radio if he could steal parts. Lieutenant Colonel Kenneth S. Olson immediately assigned him to the machine shop, where he could forage freely.

Hutch began to steal a filament here, a tube there. From old telephones he swiped aluminum diaphragms; in a junked car radio he found tube sockets. He rescued an Air Corps earphone from a pile of burned debris, disassembled it, and buried the parts.

"I got resistors from the movie amplifier, a condenser from the switchboard, and a voltage meter. I mounted a Colgate shaving-stick cover on an old busted vibrator and made me a coil form. I lifted electrical tape and I stole a micron wire and copper for coils, and rubbed it in the dirt to look like scrap, and threw it in the junk bin.

"Then I slowly began smuggling the parts into camp and began to assemble them.

"On my first test I only got static, so I had to break it down and go back to the machine shop. That cost more time. I made a tiny choke coil, and Lieutenant Becket got it into camp in his g-string. But he hadn't wrapped the pigtails, and right in front of the guardhouse a wire began to work into his testicle. He walked half a mile that way. It nearly killed him – but he got the coil in!"

Hutch reassembled the tiny set in a piece of hollowed mahogany four inches long and half that wide. "I cut through one side and put two leads in for my power cable and two out to plug my little radio in. You couldn't tell it wasn't just a piece of wood.

"Finally I was ready to operate."

Hutch set up in the watch shop run by Colonel Arden Boellner, former New Mexico Guardsman and friend. "The first night I got music – I listened several minutes so I could whistle the latest tune to the guys.

"Then I got the news! And when I ran and told Olson – he kissed me!

"We had to keep it secret. Clyde Ely, Charlie Brown, Boellner, and Jack Day, an Air Corps instrument man, worked with me. The guards inspected on the hour, and it took them fifty-five seconds from the gate to Boellner's shop. Charlie sat on a bench facing the guard shed, and Clyde sat on another halfway down.

"When the gate opened, Charlie crossed his legs by Barracks 1, which was Clyde's signal to come from behind Barracks 4, walk past our building toward the latrine, and knock on our window. On that knock, Jack and I dismantled the set. He'd leave with the wood and coil. I'd slip Clyde the radio, wrapped in an old piece of shelter tent. I fitted the tube and head set into an old sewing kit.

"Clyde sat in one latrine and Charlie in the other, holding the radio and sewing kit between their legs, to drop if the Japs came. After the guards left, they'd bury the parts under the barracks, and I'd go brief Olson on the news.

"Newscasts came on the hour, and so did the damned guards – so it was awkward. My best station was Chungking – there were American Air Corps there.

"The Japs said if Americans got close, they'd execute everyone. So the object of the radio was to know ahead, and keep the camp intact, to save everyone when they came. We weren't risking our necks every night just to give out news.

"It was risky. My radio was a regenerative set, which sends out a signal when it's turned on. You can tell in a minute if there's one anywhere, and you can locate it. So I had to be extremely careful. Once they searched Boellner's building. He didn't know what for, but the shakedown lasted two days. I didn't set up till that was over.

"The news was hot then, as the Americans advanced, and Olson had to have news. So I set up in his bed. Suddenly, here came this Jap interpreter to the office, about nine feet away, with a thin wall. I stayed in the bed with the radio, and Olson jumped in too. 'Colonel,' I said, 'we could get twenty years for this!'"

Should they be moved north – which seemed likely as the Americans advanced – Olson wanted the radio with them. They devised an elaborate scheme. "I opened Red Cross cans of corned beef, until I had complete sets of unbent edges to assemble new cans. I soaked off the labels and made a little scale and kapok weights exactly the same as a can of corned beef.

"Everything fit inside except the tube. Day and Boellner enlarged the opening of a cocoa can, fit the tube in, and reshaped it so it wouldn't look tampered with. When the time came, I disassembled my radio, packed it tightly with kapok, centered the weight into two corned beef cans, and soldered the lids back on. I found glue at the machine shop and put the labels back on.

"We had two cans of real corned beef and two with radio parts. Those two I put in an old musette bag. I put a pod of okra in the side pocket so I could identify that bag in the dark. Thank God I did!"

They sailed from Davao on 6 June 1944 on the *Yashu Maru*, their baggage stowed separately. After two men jumped ship at Zamboanga, the prisoners were herded into the hold and the hatches boarded shut. Hutch could no way get to his bag. In Cebu they went ashore to change ships.

"Hutch," Olson whispered that night, "the detail can't find your stuff."

By the time they boarded four days later, Hutch was frantic. "I dropped into the hold, onto all this ratty baggage. Just a tiny light came through the cracks over the hatch, and I was feeling among hundreds of bags for one with an okra pod. It was just luck I found it.

"And the cans had been twisted open!

"But the looters wanted food, I guess, and they'd left the parts." He had somehow to repack them. "Some of the men had somc Red Cross soap, which Olson scrounged, and for two days I squatted in that hold under a little crack of light, in 120° heat, carving out those damned bars of soap! Then I spent another five days packing the pieces inside, and I stuffed the shavings back and reformed the bars. I had only one source of liquid to stick them together – I urinated on the blooming things!"

The choke, too large for the soap, remained, but Dr. Calvin Jackson had a pill bottle. "I don't know what the hell it is," he grinned, "but I'll take it."

Inspection when they passed through Bilibid was cursory, but at Cabanatuan the guards closely inspected Day's cocoa can . . . Clyde's soap . . . Charlie's soap . . . Hutch's soap . . . and handed each one back. But doctors had to pour their pills onto a blanket. Jackson scratched a hasty hole and buried the choke before the inspectors got to him. Two guards lingered, and he had to march on. He noted carefully the spot.

That night, under cover of heavy rain, the doctor crawled through mud and darkness, groped until he located the contraband, and crawled back in. Hutch had his choke by morning.

"We were quarantined in the old hospital side – didn't know for how long, and we'd been without news for a month. I assembled the radio in an upper bunk at the far end of the barracks while Ted Parker stood lookout, and in a few days I was ready to operate.

"Then they said we were moving across into the main camp. I hated to tear it down again, so we stuffed it into a straw pallet they'd issued Olson, and carried the damned thing right past the guards."

* * *

There was another radio at Cabanatuan, he learned from old friend Julian Long, and its operator was also named Hutchison. For safety's sake they never met; Long acted as go-between. Homer Hutchison would continue to operate his battery-powered set, and Hutch would stand by for emergency.

"Then one day they told me to get ready to operate. I needed a power source, so I went to Father Braun. Could I use the small red light over his altar? I asked.

"'Russell,' he said, 'you can use my altar any time you want.' And then he twinkled his eye. 'But if the Japs come by,' he said, 'be sure you're praying like hell!'"[26]

---

26 When Cabanatuan was evacuated ahead of the American invasion, leaving only a few very sick men and medics, the radio was destroyed. It had served its pur-pose.

BOOK V

TO THE LAND OF THE RISING SUN

"More than a hundred mangled corpses that only a day before had been Americans fighting for their lives were piled in long high rows. Those were the men who had held Bataan and Corregidor until they were starved into surrender . . . . They were brave, hard. They were men who made a man proud to be an American. Now they were a conglomeration of butchered bodies . . . . "

– John M. Wright, Jr., *Captured on Corregidor: Diary of an American P.O.W. in World World War II* (Jefferson, N.C. & London: McFarland & Co., 1988), 123. –

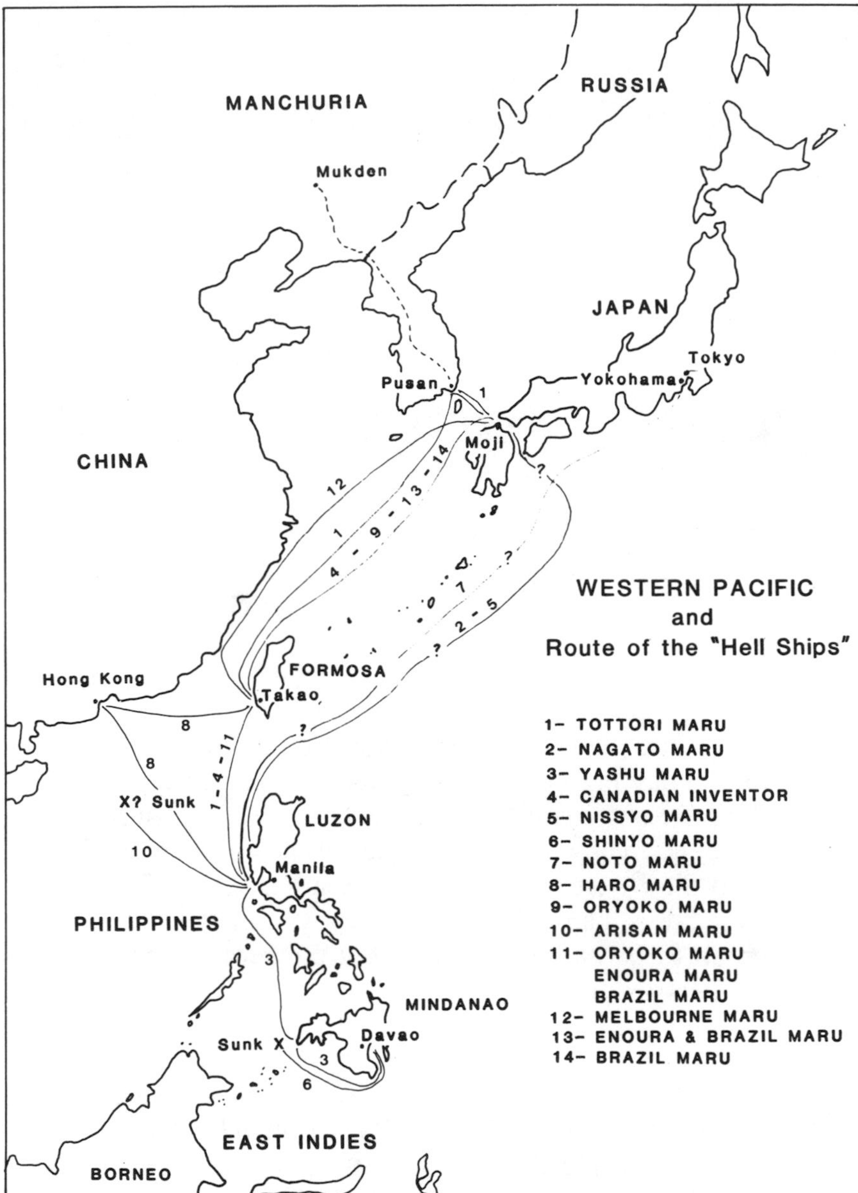

The Hell Ships, to avoid attack, often took more circuitous routes than here indicated. In the absence of existing ships' logs, the routes as here shown are only approximations.

– 22 –

NORTHWARD BOUND[1]

"Men began to panic and tried to form a pyramid to climb out of the hold. In the light of the explosions I could see the faces of the fellows they were stepping on. I hugged a big steel beam and gave myself to God."

– Private Lorenzo Banegas –

While Russell Hutchison hollowed soap in the hold of the *Yashu Maru*, Hamblin clung unaware on the top of a crude latrine which overhung the rail. It was the only space he could find. Then, after the two men[2] escaped in Zamboanga, the guards kicked and beat the nearly thirteen hundred men into two already crammed holds which, Cain testified, "would have accommodated comfortably not over 250."

---

[1] Some of the survivors interviewed are unsure what *maru* they shipped on. The author has tried, on the basis of external evidence, to place them correctly, and assumes responsibility for any inaccuracies.

[2] Lt. Col. John McGee and Lt. Donald Wills, in separate escapes.

They debarked at Cebu – McCahon didn't know why, though some heard they were to repair an airstrip. But when, with no warning, they were rushed to the docks, herded onto a tiny ship, and headed out, "we realized they'd gotten word of an impending attack. We knew then that American troops were getting close."

The Japanese knew it too. Though girding to defend the Philippines, they grew increasingly aware of their ultimate loss. To prevent the recapture of prisoners, and to alleviate critical labor shortages in the mills and mines of Manchuria and Japan itself, they had long since begun to move the POWs out of the islands in unmarked ships – targets for American submarines, whose commanders could not know their own countrymen lay caged in their black and stinking holds.

The *Tottori Maru*, first of the Hell Ships, sailed on 8 October 1942, carrying 1,202 Americans, among them a large contingent of New Mexicans, who, to escape Cabanatuan, had answered a Japanese call for 'specialists.' Gentry and Alex became instant mining engineers, and Shillito an airplane mechanic. So did Wheeler and Chintis, to keep intact their quintet from Battery B.

The old tramp steamer, already crowded with Japanese soldiers, chugged into the China Sea, her holds crammed with Americans, her topside littered with the overflow, who clung wherever they could.

Shortly out of Manila they were attacked. Sakelares, "perched on a winch in a g-string, just sat there and watched the torpedo coming." So did Munsey, "and as it came closer, I felt if this was the way it was to end, I would welcome it." Men penned in the hold began to yell.

Phillips wondered which side to run to. "Then I decided it wouldn't matter, so I went to watch them coming. They were shallow, and as they'd cross a trough they'd make spray. Three were coming at us, and another farther off.

"The captain was watching on the bridge. He was a little fellow, in his navy-blue suit and white whiskers. He waited until he saw the divergence of the torpedoes, then turned and backed into the widest space, so they went on either side.

One didn't miss us more than eight feet. That maneuver saved our bacon. So we applauded – and he turned and bowed!"

Strangely, the attack seemed to lift morale. America, they knew, was still fighting.

Afterward, those on deck were forced into the hold. Then began for Schmitz "a miserable thirty days. Men were sick, and we just had a bucket to use, and they'd spill it pulling it up. If you weren't already sick, you soon got sick in the hold. No air. No water. Men died, and they'd haul them up and throw them over."

As the ship pitched, feces churned back and forth, "and always," Alex remembered, "a dead body or two was floating in it. Everybody had dysentery, and all that stuff was rolling around."

Heat mounted. Oxygen decreased. Men grew delirious. Crazed for water, they heard it lap against the ship. Some drank urine. Some slit the veins of others as they slept, and drank the blood. Some slashed their own wrists and bled to death.

At Takao, Formosa, the prisoners were allowed on deck to be hosed down. A native stevedore slipped four limes to Phillips, "and they were beautiful. My scurvy symptoms disappeared."

There they joined a convoy and headed for Pusan, Korea. Twice engine trouble or American submarines forced them back to Takao, and a wide zigzag course to avoid attack slowed them further. Shillito "saw several ships from our convoy burn, and when we got to Pusan only three had made it." Here most of the Americans were put ashore to entrain for Mukden, Manchuria, though some too ill to go on were left in camp. Schmitz and several others stayed behind to care for them. Over one hundred died there.

In the night, the *Tottori* dashed across the straits to Moji, and thence to Osaka, where the few men left aboard debarked on 12 November. Chintis looked around. "I had lost some of my best buddies. Out of the two thousand who had left Manila, there were seventy-five left." From the quintet who had vowed to stick together, only he and Shillito remained.

* * *

The stench of manure and rotting vegetables greeted the seventeen hundred who descended on 7 November 1942 into the three holds of the *Nagato Maru*.[3] Tom Foy, one of seven hundred in the middle hold, felt lucky. Though it had stabled horses, "the other two contained scrap iron, to be melted down for bombs and shells. The remaining thousand men had to sit on old truck bodies. A lot of them died."

Two tiers of shelves accommodated one hundred men on each of the four sides of Lingo's hold. "I was in the fifth hundred who sat in the middle. A fellow on a side shelf traded off with me. He slept in the night and let me have the shelf during the day. We got one tablespoon of water and a small cup of rice twice a day. We had one small 'honey bucket,' and we all had dysentery, so if you had to use it and it was full, you climbed up five flights to dump it."

Men began to die. "They'd just toss them overboard for the sharks. But as we got closer to Japan," Foy noticed, "they'd just put them in a gunny sack – they didn't want any disease this close to Japan."

Like the rest, the *Nagato* was unmarked. They were not attacked, though they did fire on a submarine off Formosa, and other ships in the convoy were apparently sunk. The men were not allowed on deck until they reached Japan on Thanksgiving Day.

In spitting snow at Moji, in their tropical rags, they were hosed with icy water and sprayed with disinfectant. "They made us stand out there for hours. A lot of the boys caught cold – they were so weak anyhow." Foy worried about those left ill on the freezing docks. Rightly so: an estimated 150 died there.[4]

By the end of June 1944 the Americans had taken the Marshalls, landed on Saipan, and driven back an enemy fleet in the first Battle of the Philippine Sea. The Japanese began mass evacuations of POWs from the Philippines.

---

[3] The battleship *Nagato* had been Admiral Yamamoto's flagship during the attack on Pearl Harbor. Damaged in the Battle of Leyte Gulf, the *Nagato* was afterward used for transport only.

[4] American Ex-POW National Medical Research Committee, *The Japanese Story*, Stan Sommers Pub., 1980, p. 34.

On 1 July Harrington and a thousand others marched through Manila.[5] "Though the streets were packed with Imperial troops, some of the shops played 'God Bless America' on phonographs. We must have been a disheartening sight. After sweating for hours on Pier 7, we were packed into the forward hold of an old freighter of dubious seaworthiness." She was the *Canadian Inventor*, and theirs would prove the longest voyage of all the Hell Ships. "Some cannot even find a place to sit," Harrington continued. "There is scarcely a breath of air in this hell hole."

They sailed on 2 July, but returned to harbor the next day, followed, noted Captain Benson Guyton, "by several Jap warships badly beaten up – near as I can gather, from the naval battle around the Marianas. They had huge holes. One large ship with its forward, three-gun turret muzzles leaning over the side splashing water. A beautiful sight."[6]

For another twelve days they sat in harbor in the blistering holds. After they finally sailed, they were allowed some time on deck, though discipline was harsh. Guyton saw "one Private First Class Mickelson forced to kneel on the red-hot iron deck for hours for smoking at the wrong time. When he was pulled up the skin off both knees stuck to the deck. He died a few months after we reached Japan."

In the bay above his, Harrington heard two officers talking softly in the night "of mutiny, of a loose scheme to seize the ship. The gist was that we greatly outnumbered the guards, who were only lightly armed, and that some of our members were capable of navigating and operating the ship."

The problem lay in where to go. Japanese ships infested the area, and theirs, with faulty engines and few supplies, barely made it from port to port. The difficulties became more obvious when the typhoon struck. For five days the old ship tossed, barely able to churn through the buffeting seas. The discussion of mutiny was dropped.

---

5 Half of this contingent came out of Cabanatuan; the rest were those left from the *Yashu Maru*, recently arrived from Davao, who had not been sent to Cabanatuan.

6 Lt. Col. Benson Guyton, 60th CA (AA), letter to author 16 February 1987.

A twelve-day layover at Takao offered some respite. Lines of coolies loaded salt from barges. In the bottom hold Mendoza watched. "They dropped stuff down, and all of a sudden some bananas came down with the salt, and some brown sugar candy. I yelled, and we started grabbing it as it went down." Later Mendoza and Albert Gonzales managed to break through their hold into a compartment that held bananas and tomatoes, and to spirit them to those who needed nourishment most.

Up the Formosan coast they limped to Keelung, where they anchored for another twelve days. Here members of the local press, refusing to enter the filthy hold, fired questions from above. "Who," they taunted, "is going to win this war?"

"We are!" chorused the men.

On lumbered the ailing old ship, from island to island. By now they had christened her the '*Mati Mati*' – 'Wait Awhile' – *Maru*, because "this old tub's in no hurry."

Overcrowding, starvation, and filth contributed to jaundice and numerous severe skin disorders, for which they had no medication. When an infection swelled to golf-ball size under Harrington's arm, a doctor slashed it. Did he want to examine it later? Harrington asked.

"No, soldier," snapped the doctor. "You're on your own."

Mendoza watched Dr. Thomas H. Hewlett perform an appendectomy on the floor with a razor blade. "I had a little straw mat I gave him, and they laid him there and just cut his stomach open. No anesthetic. Nothing. Sewed him up with an old piece of string. And he lived."[7]

They reached Moji on 1 September, were marched to some abandoned stables – and got their first drink of fresh, cold water in nine weeks. "As we crossed the bay," Harrington recorded, "we caught our last glimpse of the *'Mati Mati' Maru*. No tears were shed." They had been aboard her for sixty-two days.

* * *

---

7 Only one man died on the long voyage of the *Canadian Inventor*, a Corporal Weeks of the 31st Infantry.

"Get your hat, Marvin," said Tom Taggert. "We're going to Japan." Lucas, Taggert, and Frank Turner, who had vowed to stick together, volunteered. Their own Major Winnifred Dorris was senior officer. Theirs was the *Nissyo Maru*, a small freighter, and they sailed the day after the *Canadian Inventor*.

Don Harris knew they invited attack. "She was heavily armed and flying the Jap flag. I had two empty canteens. We were getting no water, but I kept them. I figured they'd help me float a little." As he started down the ladder, a grinning guard jabbed him with a bayonet. "Now you see how we can hurt you!"

The officers examined the hold. "You can't stick fifteen-hundred men in a matchbox and expect them to survive – they won't fit," Lucas protested. The interpreter said they would.

"Our men were sitting with their knees up to their chins, and, my God, we were going all the way to Japan that way! Men on the lower level started passing out. In front they were standing, and the Japs shoved them back with long bamboo poles. When my turn came, there was no room. A vent stack ran under us to the coal, and I pushed it away a little and wedged between it and the wall. I tore a slit in the canvas over it to get my nose in for some air. And the rest kept coming down.

"They finally moved six hundred to the forward hold. Then half could lie down. If one turned over, they all had to. The rest stood all night. You couldn't even fall down – there was no place to fall. It was so hot, and we had no water. Everybody was yelling, and it echoed, a constant roar, the whole trip."

From the man above Don Harris, "sweat ran down on me like a river. A lot of guys panicked – cut themselves and drank the blood. I felt like this was the end."

"Late one night, a few days out, a great explosion rocked us. The sky lit up, and we thought, 'This is it.'" Then silence. Lucas, because he was mess officer, was allowed topside in the morning. "One of our carriers was gone. Behind us an oil tanker lay over on its side burning.

"A sailor from the forward hold said, 'If I ever heard a torpedo, I heard one last night. It went right under us.' We were riding too high to catch it."[8]

Don Harris felt the concussion. "They covered the hatches – there was no way we could have gotten out." Ojinaga felt the ship roll, "and through the cracks the sky lit red. A chaplain said, 'Let's pray for the men in the submarines – they want to go home too.' He started the rosary, and we prayed in the red light."

From a knothole in the latrine, Niemon saw a third smoking ship. "We took turns watching that black smoke, several days. Each day it lagged farther behind – whether it finished the trip, I don't know."

Woody Hutchison could hardly breathe even before they finished loading the *Noto Maru*. Then they closed the hatch. "Within five minutes all hell broke loose. They finally opened one hatch and let us bring out about a hundred who had passed out.

"You sat between a guy's legs and opened yours for the guy in front of you. We used wooden tubs [for latrines], and those in the back had to struggle fifty or sixty feet – half with dysentery. I think about seventy died."

The *Noto*, unmarked, fully armed, and carrying depth charges, sailed straight for Yokohama with no stops. When a terrific blast shook the bulkhead, McCormick thought the ship had blown up. "But it was a dud. The hatch was open, for once, and everybody started up the ladder. But they ran three or four machine guns in and started to fire. That quieted people down.

"They fired depth charges and told us it was an American sub, and they'd sunk it. But if there was a battle anywhere, they always said they won it, so we didn't believe them."

As Aldrich boarded the *Haro Maru*, "the old metallic taste of fear returned. Argeanas, [Charles 'Amy'] Amos, and I were pushed to the back corner. No room to sit and the temperature

---

8 Heinz Rhee, who shipped on the *Haro Maru*, described the sound of a torpedo that misses as sounding "like a toy train off the track with its wheels still running."

shot up. Soon we were dehydrated. And that goddamned ship lay at anchor several days."

On 3 October they joined an eighteen-ship convoy in Subic Bay and proceeded north. The seven hundred men in the rear hold rode on a cargo of coal, the four hundred forward on horse manure. Aldrich estimated the water ration at "about three tablespoons a day, and half a canteen cup of *lugao*. We made fun of ourselves because we looked so ludicrous – just skin stretched over bones. No buttocks, and the anus stuck out behind like a tail. Heads like skulls, with deeply sunken eyes."

The *lugao* crawled with maggots. "That's meat too," reasoned Johns. "The same buckets served as latrines. It gets pretty nasty, but what else can you do? They'd pass that 'honey bucket' around and it would get so damned full, and when they'd pull it up, the poor guys under the hatch caught it." They began to call her the '*Benjo Maru*' – 'Toilet Ship.'

Aldrich strung his blanket between the bulkhead and the boiler. "It was hot as hell, but I struck gold – a plate had buckled on the side, and at night, through the slit, I could watch the stars.

"Three days out we began to hear the ping of good old US Navy sonar. Then explosions. Our convoy was under attack. Before those on deck were shoved below, they saw a large tanker and another ship take hits. There was a huge explosion, and through my slit I saw the sky light up like day."

Men around Banegas "began to panic and tried to form a pyramid to climb out. In the light from the explosions I could see the faces of the fellows they were stepping on. I hugged a big steel beam and gave myself to God. A chaplain tried to pray above the noise. Chavez got topside, and was thrown back into the hold, where six inches of filth flowed around us."

Three days later another attack rocked the ship. In Baclawski's hold, "men were yelling and screaming. It was a seething mass of men moving around like Jello. Some climbed the walls and hung on the struts. One guy preached all night. In the morning, when they pulled the canvas off, a lot were unconscious. Eight were dead."

Around Johns, "guys went pure crazy. Each morning you'd feel the guy next to you to see if he was still alive. If he wasn't, you took his shirt or shoes, if he had any. Then you'd holler topside, 'Get this SOB out of here, he's dead.' But those that were alive – well, we looked out for one another."

Aldrich saw men drink sea water left in the latrine buckets. "Those guys would go insane – leap around like animals – and they'd belch an eerie blue phosphorescence. I thanked God my hammock was out of reach of these monsters. Usually someone beat them insensible.

"A few slashed their wrists and drank their own blood. These usually bled to death. In one or two cases, a deranged guy tried to bite someone's throat.[9]

"In the morning they lowered ropes to haul up the dead. In the roll of the ship they swung slowly back and forth, eyes bugged out, lips drawn back in a hellish death smile. Naked except for a g-string, they danced a strange dance."

Carl Deemer had half a canteen of water. As he dozed, Baldonado saw someone "grab his canteen and start beating his brains out. I was too far away to help him."

When morning lit the hatch, Aldrich saw "a lone figure climbing the ladder very slowly, and as he ascended, a long dark shadow followed him. He had a huge lump on his head, dark like blood. As he climbed in that shaft of light, he turned his head, and I recognized him – from the 200th. It was Carl Deemer. He must have died on deck. He never came back down.

"Gradually things calmed, and the violence of the crazies tapered off. Chaplains told stories, prayed, got people to help care for the sick. We sang. And through those dark days we never wavered in our belief that we would someday go home. The song we sang most was 'God Bless America.'"

"Thirty-two men have died, to date," Evans recorded on 11 October, the day they reached Hong Kong.[10] Those strong enough to climb out were allowed to bathe in the muddy harbor waters. The fresh air made them dizzy and the light hurt their

---

9 Such occurrences were reported by survivors of nearly every ship, and were attributed to the lack of oxygen, whereby men can become crazed and cannot be held responsible for their actions.

10 Evans 114.

eyes, but they luxuriated in their allotted five minutes before they returned to the stinking hold. Of the thirteen vessels Rhee had counted in their convoy when they left Manila, he now saw three.

On the sixteenth, Aldrich heard a commotion. "The Nips rushed the cook detail into the hold and closed the hatches. Bombs began to explode all around us. Klaxons and sirens pierced the air, and machine guns roared on the decks. In the hold, men were yelling, 'Open the hatch,' until hot shell casings from the guns began to fall on them through the cracks."

The raid left the Kowloon docks burning and the harbor ablaze with stricken ships. A freighter off their port side "burned gloriously," Evans recorded. "We all thought it a great performance!"[11]

On 21 October they left Hong Kong to zigzag for Formosa. When they finally debarked at Takao on 8 November, after thirty-nine days on the *Benjo Maru*,"[12] few could walk. Johns "crawled over the side down cargo nets, and waiting launches dumped us on the beach. It was the next afternoon before we could walk. Then we marched about ten miles to a train."

For twelve weeks they worked in a sugar mill with a group of British as starved for news as they. Increasingly frequent air raids gave them the best dispatches they could want: The Yanks were getting closer. Penned inside during the raid, Rhee never saw an American plane. "But the bombs were very close and very big. Every time one hit, the roof raised up several inches, and the door fell out a foot or so. Then it would bang back, and the roof would settle."

On 16 January they boarded the *Melbourne Maru*, and two weeks later dropped anchor in Moji. Since departing Manila they had weathered heat, thirst, and starvation; filth, brutality, insanity, and murder. They had repeatedly dodged torpedoes and bombs – and they had made it. Preparing to disembark, Aldrich, Amos, and Argeanas shook hands and congratulated themselves.

---

[11] Evans 115.

[12] They had anchored at Takao 24 October, remained aboard, and, after a dash to sea on 6 November to avoid an air raid, returned to the harbor. They finally debarked on 8 November.

"At that moment sirens began to shriek. A destroyer launched a seaplane, and our guards rushed us down the gang-plank. A large explosion tore a tanker to bits before our eyes. Fire and smoke gushed. An American sub had been lying in harbor waiting for a proper target!"

On 9 October 1944, a month before the men from the *Benjo Maru* staggered ashore at Takao, Sage and Peck sailed from the same harbor. They had been on the island since August 1942, where, Peck wrote, Japanese newsmen delighted in photographing senior officers herding goats.

In the hold of the *Oryoku Maru*, after one aborted departure, they sat in harbor for two weeks, through a series of bombings, locked in complete blackness, their ship "jumping around" as bombs exploded about them. "No way to get out," he recorded. "We didn't care if the ship was hit, so long as the Japs got what was coming to them."

Their eventual destination, after a layover in Japan, was Chen Chia Tung, 200 miles north of Mukden, in Manchuria.

Many never learned the names of their ships, or misery obliterated memory. The patterns varied little. All were unmarked, armed, and crowded to the limits of human endurance. All were filthy. *Benjo* buckets overflowed. Men lost control, and urine and feces covered the floors. Some ships had bottomless wooden crates lashed over the sides; but time on deck was limited, many were too weak to crawl up the ladders, and during typhoons these proved hazardous.

Food and water were minimal, and the prisoners often found their throats too swollen to swallow when it came.

Madness occurred from lack of oxygen and overdoses of carbon monoxide, or from severe claustrophobia or cerebral malaria. Men howled like wild animals. Some clung to sanity only with guts and backbone. Meuli told a rosary over and over. Friend helped friend.

Typhoons struck. Lightfoot's ship listed "until we'd slide from side to side. If you went topside to use those hog troughs, you had to hang on for dear life." Huxtable's ship stood "practically on end, and when it came down, the next wave crashed over it. Huge logs in the forward hold came unlashed, and we were in the next, with just a thin steel plate between us. Every time we'd start uphill, those logs hit that plate and it would buckle and we thought we'd all be crushed."

As seas calmed, the danger of attack increased, and, at the first salvo, the men looked into machine guns thrust into the holds. James, topside in the latrine line when a submarine was sighted, was brutally clubbed by a guard hurrying him below. So was the man behind him, who later died.

Yet of all his physical agonies on that hellish trip, the wound James never forgot was one of the spirit. Climbing topside to the latrine, he passed the Japanese troops' quarters. "And they were using American flags for blankets. I think that hurt me worst of all."

Men staggered from the ships at their final ports so weakened many could not walk. King "was irrational and half blind for two months." Many were swollen from kidney failure, and those who escaped dysentery doubled with constipation.

Their reception in Holy Nippon was hardly welcoming. Tubes jammed up their rectums extracted specimens, ostensibly to guard the homeland from disease. Hosed on icy docks, many contracted pneumonia, or died of exposure from sleeping in unheated warehouses while awaiting transport. Baldonado slept under a viaduct. Huxtable and Kedzie were paraded through the streets in American naval uniforms, "in front of thousands of people. They told them we were survivors from a carrier they had just sunk." Some groups were stoned. Civilians beat Gilcrease with sticks.

On the docks at Moji, a guard accused someone of singing. Though Finley doubted anyone had, "they were going to make us stand there all night, until someone admitted doing it. So Johnny Burns stepped forward to save the rest of us. They beat the devil out of him."

Most believed the Hell Ships assaulted humanity worse even than the Death March; and, like the March, resulted from deliberate policy. In Takao harbor, McBride saw "Japanese ships with hospital red crosses painted conspicuously on them being loaded with ammunition and guns." Yet those carrying

POWs were as conspicuously unmarked: Prison ships made good decoys.

As American forces closed in, the Japanese utilized men and fuel and ships to transport prisoners. The reason seemed obvious, years later, to McCahon. "The Germans used gas chambers. The Japanese were a little more subtle, and accomplished the same thing. They knew they were going to lose ships – they might as well get rid of some Americans while they were doing it."

They did lose ships, and those whom fate placed on the *Shinyo*, the *Arisan*, the *Oryoku*, and another unnamed *maru*, would tell yet a further tale of horror – those who survived. Five thousand did not.

On those ships that made it through, over three hundred perished, and many more died shortly after arriving. Those who survived clung somehow to faith and fellow feeling. The image rises from those hell holds of a man averting his eyes from the sight of his enemies who blanketed their bodies with his flag; the echo persists of "God Bless America" rising from swollen throats and failing strength. Helpless but not hopeless, these men sustained themselves with God, guts, and something beyond courage.

– 23 –

"THAT NONE SHOULD BE RECOVERED"

I: The Long Way Home: Two Strange Odysseys

"I didn't think I had strength enough to get off that ship. Yet I killed that Jap with my bare hands. Just choked him to nothing. I didn't even figure I had a human being."

– Sergeant Calvin Graef –

'Doc' Colvard and Mike Pulice had not sailed with their buddies on the *Yashu Maru*. Assigned to a detail in Lasang,[1] they worked on an airstrip until increasing bombing raids forced the Japanese to evacuate ahead of MacArthur's returning forces. On 20 August 1944, Pulice and Colvard boarded an unidentified ship with 750 others. Theirs was the last group to leave Mindanao.

---

[1] Ten miles south of Davao Penal Colony, on the coast.

They docked at Zamboanga, where, to confuse American intelligence receiving information from the guerrilla underground, the POWs were transferred under cover of drenching rain to the *Shinyo Maru* as Japanese soldiers from the *Shinyo* boarded theirs.

On 5 September they headed north in convoy, hugging the western coastline. Late in the afternoon of the seventh, the US submarine *Paddle*, off Sindañgan Point, fired two torpedoes into what they believed to be a Japanese troopship.

The men in the hold felt the double impact and the shudder that ran through her, and heard the roar of depth charges. Steel plates buckled and gave, and beams fell. Those not pinned beneath wreckage scrambled for the hatch; guards turned machine guns on any who emerged. From a pile of debris, Pulice painfully worked out a badly shattered leg. He saw Colvard fighting through the pandemonium to treat the wounded on deck, and tried to pull him back. "They're shooting everybody up there," he barked. "Stay down here – after dark we'll try for shore." But Colvard crawled on.

Some made it to jump overboard. Guns from the *Shinyo* and a freighter behind her machine-gunned the men in the water, and a tanker driven aground opened on those who neared the shore.

The ship was listing badly when Pulice, his leg now swollen and partially paralyzed, jumped with Private First Class Victor Mapes,[2] to be washed farther out in the bay. "A Jap guard was out there trying to drown, so we helped him. Drank the water from his canteen, and headed toward the bonfires that marked the shore."

Among the bodies that rolled on the swells, Pulice spied Colvard struggling to help those he could reach. Whether he exhausted himself – he was not a young man – or was shot in the water, none in that carnage could say.

All night Pulice swam with his shattered leg. "By morning I got close in and some Filipinos got me to shore in a dugout, and into the jungle. They never even took me out of the dugout

---

2 Of the 14th Bombardment Squadron, US Army Air Corps.

– they just picked it up and carried it. I'd lost Mapes in the night, but found him in camp." Of the 750 Americans aboard the *Shinyo*, only 81 survived.[3]

They stayed with the guerrillas until MacArthur, apprised by underground radio, sent in the submarine *Narwhal*. "They made three tries. Five of us were pretty badly hurt, and they'd carry us fifteen or twenty kilometers to the edge of this lagoon, and if the sub didn't show, they'd haul us back. Then one night we saw this big black thing come out of the water." Pulice could not climb aboard; they loaded him through a conning tower.

En route to Biak, they passed directly beneath a large American convoy headed for the coming battle for Leyte. "There was complete silence – we weren't supposed to have any kind of contact. After a month on the island they flew us to Brisbane, and finally put us on a ship – for home. And on December 7, 1944, we sailed under the Golden Gate."

On 6 October, acting on information gleaned from Moscow of impending heavy American offenses against the Philippines,[4] the Japanese prepared to actuate SHO-1, the Philippine phase of the desperate defense plan SHO-GO; and they raced to remove all remaining POWs ahead of the advancing Americans.

On 12 October the *Arisan Maru* left Manila with eighteen hundred Americans aboard. Among them was Sergeant Calvin Graef, "feeling low, because we knew our troops were coming." Men began to suffocate almost immediately, and when the guards asked who could steam rice, Graef volunteered. "When we anchored in a cove they took us cooks topside, and we could see we'd gone south."

On the twentieth they returned to Manila.[5] "Our planes had wiped out that harbor. Wrecked ships lay everywhere.

---

3 Although 82 made it to shore, one died shortly thereafter.

4 C.J. Sulzberger, *World War II* (New York: American Heritage Press, 1985), 249.

5 Although Graef did not know it, on the day he returned to Manila Harbor on the *Arisan*, General MacArthur, following intense bombing of Formosa and Manila, waded ashore in Leyte and announced, "I have returned."

Then a typhoon hit, but we took on supplies and headed right out in it. Locked in that hold, men went crazy, and some killed others. They wouldn't let us bury our dead. A few five-gallon cans were our toilets – for eighteen hundred men with dysentery and malaria. The heat was awful.

"One guard was especially cruel. We were begging for water – there was one man we felt we might save if he had some water. This guard took a *benjo* bucket and just dumped that filth down on us.

"We went up to cook twice a day, and we could see our convoy was shrinking. On 24 October we were cooking our evening rice when all the guards started hollering and running and taking the canvas off the forward gun. The two destroyers with us started firing, and I saw torpedoes coming for us. One missed the bow. The next came for the stern. The guards opened their machine guns at us, and we dived in the hold.

"Then a torpedo hit midships, smack dab in that hold. It wasn't loud – it was like you had cotton all around you. The force of the explosion was hardly anything.

"Suddenly I was covered all over with pieces of bodies. I don't know how many were killed, or how long we were down there. The Japs had boarded us in, cut our rope ladder, and evacuated to the destroyer. We hoisted some men to where they could pry a plank off the hatch, and we got everybody out we could.

"The ship was listing badly, and men were going over the side. I headed for the kitchen, drank all the water I could, and filled two canteens. Then I saw the guard that dumped the *benjo* can – they'd left their worthless men aboard. He didn't recognize me – I was solid blood – but I knew him. I didn't think I had strength enough to get off that ship. Yet I killed that Jap with my bare hands. Just choked him to nothing. I didn't even figure I had a human being.

"Then I jumped overboard, and dug some of the bigger pieces of shrapnel out of me. The destroyer, maybe half a mile off, looked like it was picking up survivors, so I started swimming toward it, through huge mountains of waves – the typhoon was still blowing. Then I saw they were pushing men under with bamboo poles.

"I swam with the current. Some men hanging on pieces of wreckage called out, and we tied the pieces together with our g-strings and made a raft. Then I swam out to get two poles – and that's the last I saw of the raft. So I hung onto some pieces of hatch cover.

"During the night a man washed by, hanging onto an old life preserver. It was Don Meyer. He couldn't swim, and said he'd had it. But I grabbed him and said, 'You're the first company I've had – I'm not going to let you go!'

"During the night the moon came through the clouds a time or two and we thought we saw a lifeboat, and in the morning it was still there. I swam and pulled the hatch cover toward it, and Meyer kicked and pushed. Someone inside said, 'Who's there?' and three guys – Cichy, Overbeck, and Wilber[6] – helped us in.

"We were 350 miles off the China coast, though we didn't know that. But we studied the stars and knew which way to go. We had nothing to eat; our canteens had salted; and we had a lifeboat – but how do you get a lifeboat from here to there?

"Then the miracles began to happen. First, a five-gallon keg of water floated by. No top – the bung-hole gone – but we tasted it – and it was sweet! And it had floated twenty hours since that ship went down. Then a box came by, and in it was a sail. We fished out a mast and ropes and fixed the broken rudder. We knocked open a sealed compartment, and in it was a box of hardtack.

"Then off in the distance we saw a Jap destroyer coming towards us. We hid the water and draped ourselves over that boat and looked dead. That destroyer turned its forward guns on us, circled us twice – and left.

"We put up the sails, and three days later we made the China coast. The first thing we saw was a big fishing boat, and we made them understand we were fighting the Japs and wanted to go in.

---

6 Private Anton Cichy, Robert Overbeck (a civilian internee), and Sergeant Avery E. Wilber. Another group of four also survived, were recaptured, and put aboard the *Haro Maru.* Sage listed the following officers from the 200th/515th as having died aboard the *Arisan:* Jack Ashby, Alvin Bayne, O.C. Bryant, Dwayne Davis, Albert Field, Clayton Irish, Hubert Jeffus, Julian Long, Melvin Millard, and Neil Shimp. General Sage's list, compiled in prison camp as best he could from available information, may not be entirely accurate.

"One of them took word ashore in a little boat. They sawed ours up so there wasn't any evidence and put the pieces in with their cooking wood, and they fed us. By morning we were close to a town, and they got us to shore in their small boat.

"We started down the street, naked, and people just pointed. A Chinese guerrilla gave us blankets and took us to a hotel. He told us, in English, that we had landed in the only five-mile area on the Chinese coast the Japs didn't have. This town was surrounded by mountains and the Japs were up at Canton.

"He contacted American forces. While we were getting our strength back, Japs in the next town heard about us and set out in a patrol boat to capture us. But the Chinese knew about it and got us out.

"Meanwhile, the Americans dropped us .45s and carbines and ammo. We sure weren't going to be taken again – we knew that. We traveled in sedan chairs, and walked, and even drove an old ammunition cart for a ways. The longest part was on bicycles. That's when our ammunition came in handy. We were attacked by wild dogs, and by bandits.

"We had a guide, and we didn't stop until we got to Anlung, where the Chinese were building an emergency landing field for B-29s coming back from raids. There were maybe a couple of hundred Yanks there, and we tanked up on good old American chow. We'd get sick and go outside and throw up, and go back in and eat some more.

"In a few days a DC-3 took us to Kunming. Admiral Halsey wanted all the information we could give him, and Wilber and Cichy – they'd been on a detail at Lingayen and knew the emplacements – told him where to get aerial photographs. They got the pictures – and Halsey hit 'em with every plane he had.

"They flew us through Casablanca and Bermuda, and on to Washington, and rushed us to the Statler. We couldn't talk to anybody, and we had on old army clothes, and we went into the lobby about one o'clock in the morning, still carrying those carbines. I guess we looked pretty wild –

"Nobody tried to take them away from us!"

* * *

II. Holocaust At Palawan

20 October 1944: "I have returned!"

So had the Third and Seventh fleets, whose victories of 23-26 October sent twenty-five Japanese warships to the floor of Leyte Gulf, and thereby effectively smashed organized Japanese sea power.[7] American planes and submarines prowled the waters enlarging the toll, and 24 November saw American planes over Tokyo. SHO-1 had failed.

Kamikaze planes, initiated at Leyte, were a desperate measure. So was General Seichi Terada's order covering prisoners: *That none – under any conditions – should be recovered.* That order spawned the last frantic evacuations, and the massacre of those still left on Palawan.

Two days after the Battle of Leyte Gulf ended, B-24s hit the airfield at Puerto Princesa heavily. More raids followed, and when a large American convoy entered the Sulu Sea on 14 December, Garrison Commander Captain Kojima, convinced it was heading for Palawan, thought immediately of his 150 prisoners. *They must not be retaken!*

At noon he ordered them back to camp. As sirens shrilled, they were driven with rifles, sabers, and machine guns into three large covered trenches, built for air raids and open at each end. Around three sides of the barbed-wire enclosure – the fourth faced a sheer cliff that dropped to the beach – armed soldiers took positions as others ran to the first trench and hurled flaming torches into the openings. On top of these they dumped buckets of gasoline.

Fire gushed. Then rose the horrible screams of trapped men. Some fought through the holocaust, to fall beneath the burst of machine guns. Most were burned alive.

---

7 Three battleships, four carriers, nine cruisers, and nine destroyers. MacArthur *Reports* I:223, n 72. Japanese dead in the Leyte campaign totalled 56,263; American dead 2,888. Sulzberger 255.

Hearing the din, Private Alberto Pacheco, 200th CA (AA), peeked out to see blazing men running, saw them cut down with bullet and bayonet. Then the roar of igniting gasoline rocked his own trench.

He took his chance. Dodging the splatter of bullets, Pacheco dived under the cliffside barbed wire and over the drop. Perhaps thirty others made it to the bottom. When the slaughter above ended, the hunt began for those below. Men who tried to cross the bay were shot as they swam. Those hiding in crevices in the crags were dynamited, or dragged out, doused with gasoline, and set afire, one limb at a time.

Pacheco hid with several others in a cave and later in a sewer outlet, ducking beneath the scum each time a searching guard approached. When finally night covered them, they began the four-mile swim across Puerto Bay, and seven hours later he and Private First Class Edwin Petry reached the other side. A Filipino family fed and clothed them and guided them to guerrilla headquarters at Brooke's Point in southern Palawan, whence they were flown to Morotai. A second group was taken to Tacloban. In all, eleven escaped.[8]

Five others from Old Two Hon'erd are believed among the 139 men massacred at Palawan: Lieutenant Tony Montoya, and Sergeants Henry F. Scally, Charles A. Schubert, J.M. ('Jake') Smith, and Jack D. Sprunk.[9]

---

8 The account of the massacre and of Pacheco's escape is based on the official report signed by J.L. Kaufman, Cmndr. Philippine Sea Frontier, to Chief of Naval Ops., 25 January 1945, and containing the sworn statements of escapees Fern Joseph Barta, RM 1/c, USN; Glenn W. McDole, Pfc., USMC; and Douglas W. Bogue, Sgt., USMC; and on the testimony of Edwin A. Petry, Pfc., USA.

9 In the absence of an official roster, the only list, to the author's knowledge, is that given by Barta, McDole, and Bogue, compiled from memory and incomplete. The names of Smith, Montoya, Sprunk, Scally, and Schubert do not appear. Their inclusion here is based on statements provided by members of the 200th and 515th CA (AA).

III. The Perilous Seas

"Men had died in that hold – I don't know how many – just stacked like cordwood. My left ankle and right arm were shattered – the bones were sticking out. I don't know whether they pulled me out or what – but I crawled on that second ship on an elbow and a knee."

– Captain James Walter Donaldson –

On 9 October the last detail departed Cabanatuan for Manila, leaving behind only five hundred sick and disabled men and a few medics. For over two months the evacuees languished in Bilibid while the Americans bombed Manila steadily – an operation they watched hoisted on each others' shoulders and dodging rocks hurled by irate Japanese through the high windows. Not until a typhoon grounded the planes could the *Oryoku Maru* steal into the harbor through the maze of sunken ships, and spirit the last human cargo off Luzon.

Some fifteen hundred Japanese – stranded merchant seamen and civilians fleeing the American advance – boarded the one-time luxury liner. Then the 1,619 POWs filed into three holds on the unmarked, heavily armed *Oryoku*.

"December 13, 1944: Our lucky or unlucky day," wrote Gamble. "The swinging sign at Pier 7 fell, an ill omen to the superstitious." With six hundred others, he found the forward hold stifling. "No ventilation, no water. Packed like men on a bobsled. My squad got nothing to eat. The night was HELL."[10] Those in the midship hold were somewhat better off, but the seven hundred in the rear were forced, with a shovel, into the

[10] Although Gamble buried his diary at Cabanatuan, he continued to write on the back of a letter addressed to Captain James E. Sadler, who died en route to Japan. These additional notes were recovered by Dwight E. Gard after Gamble's death at Fukuoka.

far corners by Lance Corporal Kazutane Aihara – the dreaded 'Air Raid.' Men immediately began to suffocate, and American Commander W.P. Portz pled with Lieutenant Junsaburo Toshino and his hunchback interpreter, Shunusuke Wada, to open the hatches. They refused.[11] An estimated thirty men died that night.[12]

The ceiling above Jopling was "so low we could only stand in a half-crouching position," and they were crammed too tightly to sit. Lack of oxygen crazed many, and "men began to attack their friends, cutting their throats and drinking their blood, and their own urine. In a few minutes the guards began firing into the holds and the screams of the mad and dying were horrible."[13]

The *Oryoku* anchored that night off Corregidor. At dawn they started north and opened their hatches, and the prisoners counted their dead.

About 0830 Major James McMinn "heard the sound of airplane motors, and almost immediately the hatch was covered. We heard the ship's AA guns commence to fire, and shortly after, the first bombs hit the ship. The concussion blew some of the boards from the hatch and we were able to get some air."[14]

The Navy dive bombers from the US carrier *Hornet* returned at thirty-minute intervals all day to strafe and bomb. Despite their own peril, Jopling noted, "there was not one man who did not feel pride in their accuracy, and among the group one could hear, 'Come on, Yanks!'"

---

[11] These three Japanese directly and deliberately caused the deaths of many men. Toshino and Aihara received death sentences at the war trials; Wada was given life imprisonment at hard labor.

[12] Estimate from "The Oryoku Maru Story," prepared by Charles M. Brown, Lt. Col. AUS, Ret., August 1982.

[13] These and other quotations from Dan Jopling are from a letter dated 22 March 1946, kindly furnished the author by his widow, Lucy Wilson Jopling, with her permission to quote.

[14] This and other quotations of Major James McMinn, 200th CA (AA), are from his sworn deposition for the Tokyo War Crimes Commission, kindly furnished the author by his widow, Mrs. Mary McMinn.

American doctors summoned to treat the Japanese found some three hundred dead or wounded topside. Having attended the injured, the doctors reported the inhuman conditions in the holds and asked for water, for which they were beaten severely. Their countrymen, they were told, were responsible.

Anchored that night off Olongapo, all the Japanese except the guards and crew evacuated. The hatches were again boarded, and another thirty men suffocated. Gamble, in the forward hold, "knew we were badly damaged. Men were going mad. Pitch dark. Naked men crawling about in search of a canteen with a few drops of water. Murders – throat cutting and drinking of blood. A man beside me screamed, 'Somebody cut my throat!' Several Americans were shot trying to get out."

"They may be back tomorrow," someone said, and in the dark, a friend of Gamble's heard him answer calmly, "I hope so. I hope they sink this ship."

They did return, at dawn – just after Toshino gave orders to evacuate – and hit with all they had. Still penned in the hold, men began to yell, and to try to crawl out. Captain Ted Parker put a hand on the ladder, and a guard fired. Parker fell dead.

Two bombs caused some damage; then the entire ship shuddered as a third crashed into the rear hold. The explosion killed or mortally wounded nearly 250 men. Wreckage pinned screaming men under its guts. Hutch saw Charlie Brown "within eight feet of that damned bomb. McMinn found him later, wandering around, wounded and grinning – he stayed nutty for ten days. McMinn saved his life."

"We've got to get out!" cried the man beside Gamble, as fear spread toward the forward hold; and again Gamble's voice was calm. "It's more important that they get us."

"The ship was already burning and sinking rapidly before we could come out of the holds and swim ashore." Even then, to Jopling's horror, "the Jap guards opened heavy fire as the men began climbing the ladders, and continued to fire as they dived into the water."

The ship was listing badly before Greeman and Sherman gained the deck, sprinted for the galley, "wolfed down some rice and sardines, and tried to find Paul Schurtz among those pouring from the rear hold. We couldn't see him, so we grabbed life jackets off some dead Japs and jumped overboard."

Another rush of planes dived for the ship; but, as the frantic Americans waved, the pilots pulled from their dives, waggled their wing flaps, and began to circle. The prisoners cheered.

Chaney started up the forward ladder, "so weak it was hard to climb, and harder to swim. We hung on floating debris. You couldn't tell where you were, and if you got off course, Japs in patrol boats machine-gunned you."

McMinn, weak from dehydration and towing Brown against the tide, "used nerve alone to make any headway. A detachment of Jap marines was firing machine guns at us from the shore."

"As it was a considerable distance to the shore, many of us who were able" – Jopling was one – "made trips to and from the ship bringing in men who could not swim or were too weak to do so. When we were finally ashore, we were marched into Olongapo and crowded into a wire-enclosed tennis court."

There they watched as the returning planes finished off the burning *Oryoku*. Late that afternoon she sank. They watched the Americans bomb Olongapo, and, as the planes dived over them with machine guns blazing at installations three hundred yards on either side of the tennis court, they cheered at each hit, as fragments of steel and debris showered into their midst.

They sought friends, exchanged information, and learned of their dead: Dean Craft, killed by the bomb. Paul Schurtz and John Turner, dead of suffocation. Ted Parker, shot in the hold. Gerald Darling, shot in the water.

Near naked on the concrete court, they baked by day, shivered by night. Water was scarce, food scarcer. On the evening of the seventeenth each man received his first ration – two tablespoons of rice. They ate it raw.

At one end they laid the two hundred sick and wounded. They tore the few rags they wore into bandages, and their doctors did what they could. Lieutenant Colonel Jack W. Schwartz, with a mess-kit knife and no anesthetic, amputated gangrenous limbs. They pled for medicine.

"Your planes sank our ships," Wada answered. "You must suffer for the offense of your people."

The other eleven hundred were crushed into a sixty- by eighty-foot space, in glaring sun, though Gamble saw "plenty of shade less than fifty yards distant – fifty-two hours sans H_2O – eight days without food, then only two GI spoons of raw rice. Many beginning to die. Wounds, gangrene, dysentery . . . . "

On 20 and 21 December, trucks hauled them in two groups to San Fernando, Pampanga, where they were quartered in the local jail and a movie house. Rice balls and water cheered many. On the twenty-third, Wada asked the American doctors to select fifteen of the sickest to be hospitalized in Manila. They were instead bound and driven to a prepared grave, where, under the supervision of Toshino and Wada, Japanese officers and guards decapitated and bayoneted all fifteen of the helpless men.

On the twenty-fourth, all who remained were squeezed into boxcars – the wounded rode on top in the broiling sun – for an eighteen-hour trip reminiscent of the nightmarish ride to O'Donnell. Passing a few miles south of Clark Field, they watched American Navy planes bomb the base, and felt grim pleasure. Thinking it now impossible to leave the Philippines, most believed they were headed back to Bilibid. Instead, daylight found them at San Fernando La Union. It was Christmas morning.

As they marched the six miles to Lingayen beach that night, "two or three planes strafed the roads and some buildings" near McMinn. "We flattened on the ground. After the planes had gone, we were told that if we again tried to take cover, we would be shot."

For two days and nights they huddled unsheltered on the beach awaiting another ship; the Japanese were still determined to evacuate them. They learned the heartbreaking irony later: Only thirteen days after they boarded to leave, on this very beach American forces landed on Luzon.

Loading in low tide on the twenty-seventh, they were forced – often pushed – from the pier onto barges twenty feet below. Many were injured, one killed. Most boarded the larger of two ancient freighters, the *Enoura Maru*, the floor of which was covered with fresh horse manure and swarming with flies. The starving men picked through the offal for grains of oats and millet.

The last 236 prisoners filed quickly onto the *Brazil Maru*, and, as American planes bombed a nearby barrio, the ships slipped out in convoy. On the third day out, men aboard the *Brazil* each received a third of a mess kit of rice; on the fifth, some moldy hardtack that crawled with maggots. Five men died on the way.

Rolling in horse manure and their own excrement, sixteen died on the vermin-infested *Enoura*. Jopling lost all sense of time. "Constantly came the cries of men for water. Many were dying each day, and as the Japs had nothing to weight the bodies with, they refused to lower them over the side for fear they would float and submarines could trace our course. The emaciated bodies were stacked about us like cordwood."

Approaching the Straits of Formosa in heavy seas, they heard depth charges and gunfire, and knew they were under submarine attack. Two torpedoes seemed to miss narrowly. On 31 December, in cold that pierced their tropics-tempered bodies, they dropped anchor at Takao, and on 6 January those from the smaller ship boarded the *Enoura*. On the eighth all thirteen hundred were jammed into the forward hold to make room for a load of sugar.

The next day they were hit again. Though the POWs didn't know it, American troops were pouring ashore at Lingayen, and massive raids on Formosa airfields and Takao Harbor covered them from retaliation from the north.

The *Enoura* was still taking on sugar when she was hit. Bombs crashed through the forward hold, ruptured the steel partitions. Another just missed them, gashed huge holes in the hull. Rivets blown from steel plates whistled through the hold and mangled men to a pulp. Plates buckled. Beams toppled on the trapped men. McCahon had just gotten his pittance of rice when "they dropped a bomb right on us. Of four of us sitting there, I was the only one left. That bomb killed Colonel Luikhart."

The man on Hutchison's left "lost his head right above his eyes, and the one on my right lost an eye. We had to cut it out, because the blood supply was severed – and he lived seven days, in that bitter cold, without an eye in the socket. Shrapnel went up Charlie Brown's leg. Clyde Ely was injured. Walt Donaldson had an ankle, wrist, and arm broken. I was the only man on the ship without a scratch."

Over 450 – many of them doctors – were killed or seriously wounded. Those left did what they could. The Japanese refused any help.

"The Nips have just removed our dead from our midst, more than forty-eight hours after the bombing," Gamble recorded on the eleventh. "Nips refuse to give us clothes, bedding, medicine, salt. Little or no water."

Among those working on the large funeral barge, onto which the dead were lowered by nets, was Lieutenant Frank C. Thomas of the 200th. His ordeal is described in part by his fellow officer, Major John Wright,[15] beside whom he worked: "As the net was lowered onto the barge, the winch operator amused himself and the guards by jerking the cable to make the bodies jump grotesquely. The guards laughed when the jerking shook blood and pieces of flesh and parts of bodies on us . . . . "[16]

They ferried the mostly decomposed bodies to shore, unloaded them on the dock, and give their former comrades a final salute. "All the words in the English language," Wright recorded, "could not clearly depict the most horrible work we did today."[17]

"Last night very cold," wrote Gamble on 12 January. "Eight died during night; 918 now alive of the original 1,619 who left Bilibid thirty days ago." Once again the 200th mourned its losses: John Luikhart. Oliver Witten. James Sadler. Allen Walker. William Randolph.

Four days they remained in the hold of the stricken ship. On the thirteenth they transferred to the *Brazil*. Donaldson wondered how he could make it. "My left ankle and right foot

---

15 Coast Artillery Corps.

16 John M. Wright, Jr., *Captured on Corregidor: Diary of an American P.O.W. in World War II*. (Jefferson, NC: McFarland & Co., Inc., 1988)

17 Wright 124.

were fractured, and my right arm was shattered – the bones were sticking out. But Charlie Brown found a piece of board for a splint and wrapped an old dirty rag around it. I don't know whether they pulled me out or what – but I crawled on that second ship on an elbow and a knee."

Shock and exposure killed fifteen the first night on the *Brazil.* As she churned her circuitous route into northern latitudes, her hold open to the mounting cold, the death rate climbed to thirty and forty a day. They stripped the bodies, stacked them, and gave the clothing to those who needed it most.

They died of untreated wounds: Doctors worked with no bandages, no medication, no antiseptic.

They died of starvation and dehydration: A quarter of a canteen cup of rice a day was the ration, and what sugar they could steal from the hold below. They were given no water until the third day, and it was black and brackish.

They died of exposure: Some had shorts, a few had ragged shirts. They clung together to share body heat. The weather grew colder, and they begged Wada to close the hatch. He laughed and refused. Snow and sleet fell into the hold.

Chaplains kept morale alive. One shared his scant rations – until he died. Chaplain Nagle nursed the ill – until he too died. Father Cummins led prayers each evening – until, Greeman remembered, "he gave a prayer one night, and the next morning he was dead."

After three weeks of dodging American submarines, the *Brazil Maru* sneaked through wind and high seas to drop anchor in Moji Harbor. It was 29 January 1945 – forty-eight days since they had embarked on their journey through hell.

Japanese medical personnel who boarded to make perfunctory examinations against contagion recoiled horrified from the verminous skeletons; so did those on the docks as the prisoners limped, crawled, and helped each other ashore.

They were stripped on the freezing docks – some died in the process – sprayed with disinfectant, and issued clothing. They were handed captured British shoes without sizing and without socks, then marched through sleeting rain to an open-sided unheated warehouse. Those who could walk carried the weak and wounded.

Jonathan Burns had arrived on an earlier ship. Assigned to the Moji docks, he hunted old friends from the 200th, and when he saw they had no bedding, stole Red Cross blankets for them. Niemon tried to help old friends he found among the 120 taken to Fukuoka en route to Manchuria.

Of the 1,619 who sailed on the *Oryoku*, 450 lived to debark. From the Regiment on that last haunted ship, Karl Schroeder, James Hunter, and Darvin Becker perished from exposure; Joseph Thorpe and Otho Shamblin from dysentery. Here, too, the men of the 200th lost their old friend who had joined Hutch's radio crew, Arden Boellner. Fred Sherman lived a few weeks to die at Fukuoka. So also died Alfonso Melendez, Fred Jordan, William McKenzie, John Beall, Joseph Radosevich, and Clyde Ely. Jack Ellis, Fred Swope, and Howard Craig died aboard ship or immediately thereafter. Frank Thomas nursed, fed, and coaxed friends back to life before he, too, succumbed. So also perished John Gamble.

Of the forty-three men from Old Two Hon'erd who boarded the *Oryoku Maru*, only nineteen were still alive.

Lucy Wilson was scheduled to return to the States in January 1945 – overseas duty for flight nurses was limited to one year – but she begged, and got, a reprieve. As those few prisoners still in the Philippines began to be freed by the returning Americans, she questioned all who might know him: "Where's Dan?" And she kept asking, unbelieving, even when they told her:

"Dead. On the *Oryoku Maru*."

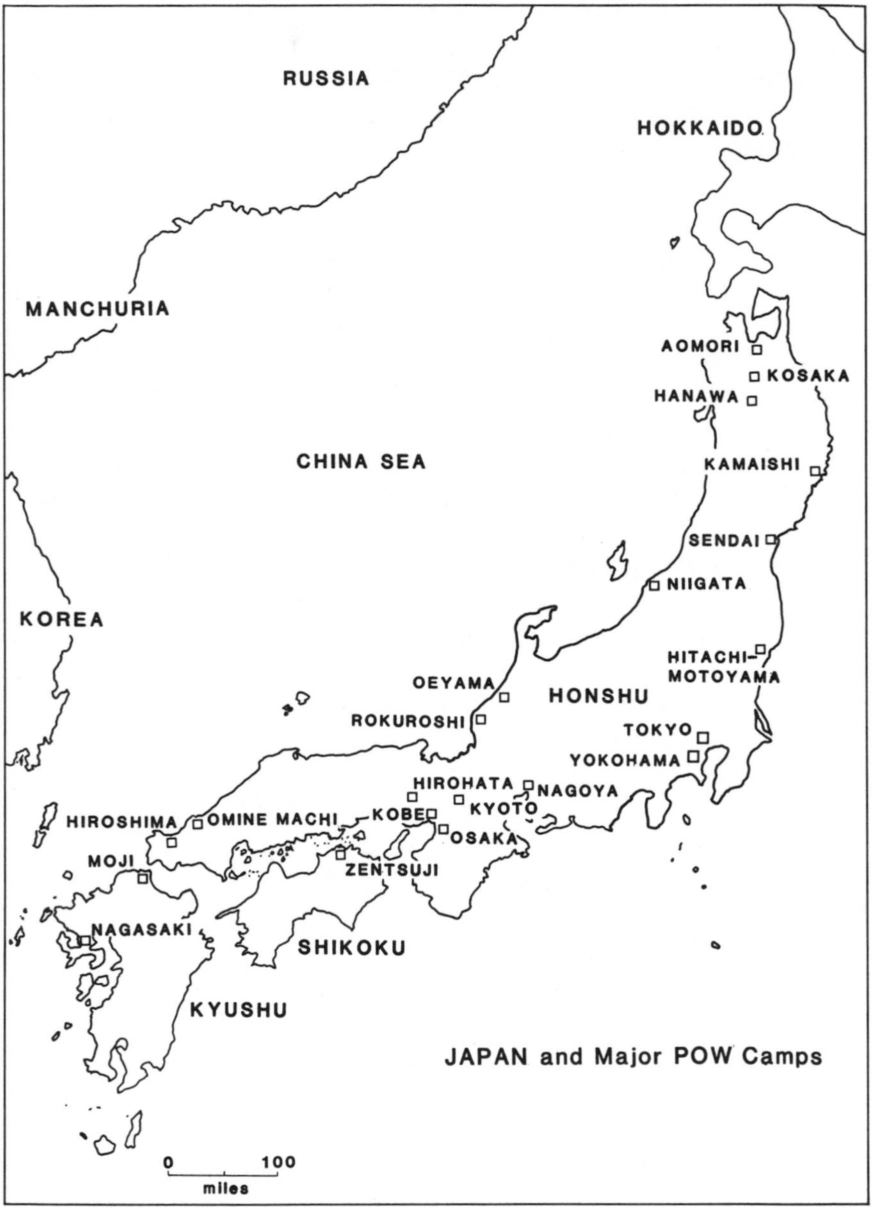
RUSSIA
HOKKAIDO
MANCHURIA
AOMORI
KOSAKA
HANAWA
CHINA SEA
KAMAISHI
SENDAI
NIIGATA
KOREA
HITACHI-
MOTOYAMA
OEYAMA
HONSHU
ROKUROSHI
TOKYO
YOKOHAMA
HIROHATA
NAGOYA
KYOTO
HIROSHIMA
OMINE MACHI
KOBE
OSAKA
MOJI
ZENTSUJI
NAGASAKI
SHIKOKU
KYUSHU
JAPAN and Major POW Camps
0
100
miles

– 24 –

BLOODY BUT UNBOWED

"They'd line us up every morning and make us tip our hats to the Rising Sun. And we'd take off our hats and say, 'Good morning, Mr. Roosevelt!'"
– Sergeant Luther Ragsdale –

Donaldson, stumbling off the *Brazil*, was detained in Moji. "About seventy-five of us were dead within three weeks. They were training Jap corpsmen to give saline injections – you got one and you were dead next morning. I don't know if it was deliberate. After three weeks I could hobble and they took us to Fukuoka 2."

McCahon was with him. "We were in such bad shape, even the Japs realized we had to build a little strength before we could move again." Despite the losses from the last doomed ships, those slated for Korea and Manchuria would still go. McCahon finally located an American doctor. The physician, obviously without combat experience, eyed his patient, who, after Bataan, the Death March, and Philippine prison camps, had just had two ships blown from under him.

"Lieutenant," he said, "you need a bath."

"Yes, you stupid son-of-a-bitch," snapped McCahon. "I know I need a bath. Now get this shrapnel out!"

After several cold wet nights in the warehouse, Aldrich entrained for Tokyo. "In the towns, civilians lined the tracks waving little meatball flags,[1] hurling stones, and spitting at us. Round faces and slant eyes filled the windows of our coach at each stop. Between trains in Tokyo they were issuing us winter clothing when the Nips started screaming and running us to a train. Air-raid sirens were shrilling, and we realized our own people were about to bomb the city.

"So did the engineers, because we got the hell out! Rocking along, we heard the bombs whump behind us over the train's roar, and we grinned. There were Yanks over Tokyo!"

Doolis expected bombs to sever the track. "Sirens and guns blasting – searchlights blazing. We're going ninety miles an hour, and bombs falling all around us. But we didn't get hit, and we went on." Sometime in the night, streaking around a long curve, they saw in the moonlight an entire train, derailed, on its side, and partly burned, black against the pale snow.

Icy air blew through broken windows in the unheated cars, and Argeanas began to cough and shake. By the time they arrived at Kosaka, at the far northern tip of Honshu, pneumonia had set in. Argeanas lived, but many did not.

Amador Lovato marched to Hanawa on snow packed roof high, and found in the unheated barracks, "stoves but no wood. They gave us little thin blankets and a piece of wood that was supposed to be a pillow. We said, 'To hell with that,' and started a fire with them. When they found out, they cut our rations."

Starving Canadians greeted Hank Lovato at Niigata. "They love tea, and I had a package. I'd trade a spoonful for a shirt or trousers, and in two days I was fitted out for winter. They were full of lice, though."

---

[1] One of the more printable terms the men used for the Japanese flag.

* * *

Those from the *Tottori* had fought lice and cold at the Manchurian Tool Company in Mukden since November 1942. "When we hit this country," Alex noted, "it was twenty below zero. We were trucked to an old Chinese military barracks of the century before, half buried for warmth, and full of ghosts. A flue ran the length of the building, and the smoke from the little stove was somehow supposed to keep the temperature up to zero."[2]

Garrett thought "we ate pretty good at the factory till they ran the boss off. Then things changed. The Jap driver who went for food came back by the whorehouse and gave the Chinese whores most all our food."

To stretch their thin diet of soy beans and milo maize, they trapped wild mastiffs – "cannibals by proxy," Sakelares called it. "We'd march to work and back, and see the Chinese dead piled at the edge of the city waiting for the ground to thaw in the spring enough to bury them. Wild dogs would be gnawing on them, and we'd trap them at night to eat."

Pneumonia killed many. Schmitz, who had helped nurse the two hundred left behind at Pusan until half died, continued corpsman duties when the rest were hauled to Mukden. "They got no medicine, and they couldn't eat, and some gave up. I'd kid them, feed them – sometimes just a kind word helped."

When Phillips got pneumonia, "Schmitz looked after me. I was out of it. When I came to, a Jap doctor was leaning against my bunk, asleep. I made a nasty remark, and Schmitz said the guy had brought us medicine from the Jap hospital – which would have been bad for him if he'd been caught. I didn't say any more.

"We lost nearly two hundred men that first winter. We placed our dead in an empty building until the spring thaw."

* * *

---

[2] In the summer of 1943 the prisoners were moved to quarters built specifically for them. Although there was never enough heat, the new complex did have plumbing of sorts, and a reasonably equipped hospital.

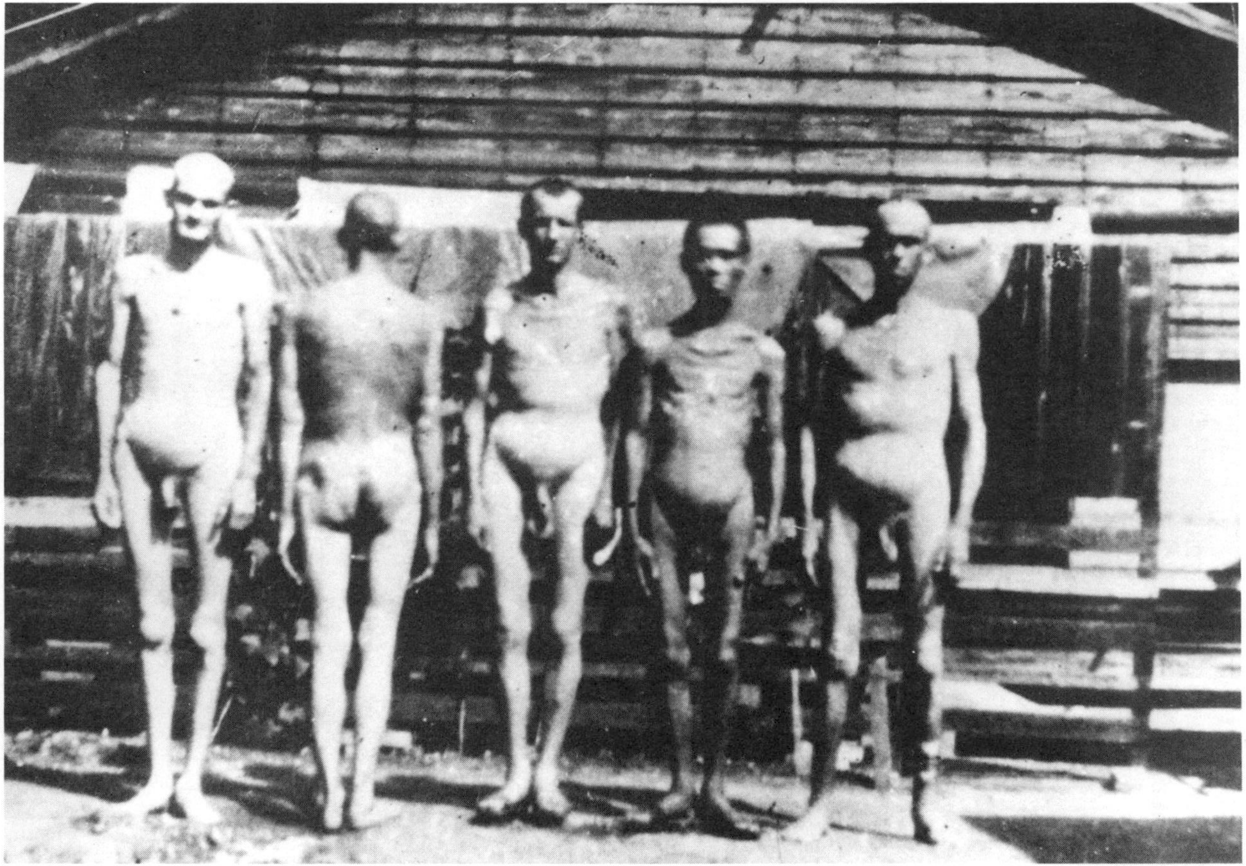

POWs at Fukuoka #3. (Courtesy: Don Harris.)

In November 1944 Peck, with Sage and other senior officers, "went through Mukden at 1:45 a.m. Still going northwest . . . . Very little sleep last four days. When one fell asleep and leaned his head against the window, hat or hair was frozen to the glass." At Chen Chia Tung, Peck found the barracks, "the dirtiest place I ever went into."

A persistent cough, aching teeth, infections, and bitter cold marked Peck's winter. Spring came on high cold winds. "The sky is yellow. They say it is from the Gobi Desert." And on 14 February he wrote nostalgically, "Dearest Eva: Will you be my valentine? *When*?"

To boost production, the Japanese hired the prisoners out to industries. The men stevedored on the waterfronts; they labored in the steel mills and ironworks and shipyards, in factories, mines, and smelters.

On shipbuilding detail at Yokohama, Shillito "didn't see a piece of metal go into that ship that wasn't stamped 'U.S. Steel.'" Chintis was surprised one morning when the *Tottori* – on which he had spent thirty-five days – came in for repairs. "It had been torpedoed – and that crew didn't want to go back out, either. Two days later they were back again with another torpedo."

At Nagoya, Meuli "made shells for bombs and worked on small suicide boats, for use if the Americans landed in Japan." Farmer helped crate the boats – nineteen hundred of them.

At the Yawata Steel Works, Niemon "saw trainload after trainload of shot-down planes come in to be melted down." Mitchell "broke out fire bricks after each pour to reline the molds." Don Harris shoveled clinkers from the furnaces, "hard labor that never stopped. It was hot in summer, and in winter the wind whistled right through you."

At Yodogawa, James "rolled steel drums to be welded. How we have any eyes left I don't know, because they never let us have any protective glasses."

At Kosaka, Aldrich got on a jackhammer crew – he was experienced, he assured them. "I had never seen a jackhammer. But it was a way to keep warm. The honcho told me it was on-the-job training, and when Japan conquered America,

I'd be ahead of everybody else." Johns "did the dirty work. Punched the furnaces with steel rods and busted slag with sledgehammers."

In the copper mines at Hanawa, Amador Lovato "climbed ladders made of sticks tied with bamboos. We carried carbide lamps and the water dripped, and if it hit the flame, it went out and you couldn't see."

The mine Huxtable worked at Hitachi-Motoyama "was 120 years old, and I think it hadn't been retimbered since they dug it. I climbed 754 steps into the mountain. It was hotter than blue blazes down there." Emerging wet in sub-zero weather, many contracted pneumonia.

Cave-ins were frequent. Kedzie "crawled on hands and knees back into the tunnels. You couldn't get a Jap into that mine – the walls were always falling in." After one cave-in, the guards left Bob Aldrich to die. Buddies, at the risk of being buried or severely beaten, stayed behind and dug him out.

At Fukuoka 17, Kindel "held a jackhammer hours on end. We'd crawl through those stinking little shafts with posts on our shoulders to shore up a wall after they'd blasted. If you gave any trouble, they'd beat you."

Surplus officers from other camps were eventually sent to Zentsuji, the 'model' camp, where the Swiss Red Cross was allowed to visit. Boyer arrived early in 1943, to find officers of all Allied nationalities. "They were fairly well fed, and horrified when they saw us, still in shorts and sandals, and skin and bone. As the war began to go against Japan, the Nips cut our rations drastically. Still, it was better than we'd ever had it."

Lingo agreed. "We got a warm community bath once a week. We had a priest and could have Mass. Our library had belonged to Ambassador Grew – we mended books with old tea bags. And we could play our one phonograph on Sunday nights." But their camp was the exception.

"*Shu! Shu!*" The guards rushed into the Yodogawa barracks each morning, bayonets fixed; those who failed to awaken immediately felt their points. Any man not in perfect line for *tenko* was slapped until he fell, kicked until he regained his feet, and often doused with icy water. "You will not sing, whistle, or smile while you work," shrilled the guard. "You will never return to America – you must adapt!"

So began a typical day in all the camps. They washed in cold water, wolfed down their scanty ration of *lugao*, and marched to work.[3]

At Ashio, Huxtable walked through snow too deep for the trucks, "three miles to work, pushed ore carts ten hours, and three miles home." Children mocked them as they passed by pulling down their eyes at the corners to "make like an Occidental."

Life had its lighter moments for men who had learned to savor small things. Gonzales learned to "lean against a timber, shovel, and sleep at the same time." Aldrich looked forward to 'tea' breaks – "no tea, but the water warmed us, and life seemed better." Baldonado escaped the mines when the interpreter – who spoke Spanish but no English – discovered he was bilingual.

Then he learned Baldonado could play a saxophone: He would play the Japanese National Anthem at the commandant's forthcoming party!

"I don't know the Japanese National Anthem."

"I bling you music."

"I don't read music."

"Pray horn and not lead music? You clazy!"

Baldonado learned it by rote, performed successfully, and won the commandant's good will.

They never got warm. "They gave us straw capes, straw hats, straw boots, straw mittens," which quickly disintegrated as Almeraz loaded pig iron on icy docks. Earl Harris "wore shorts until December 22, through several snow storms, because it was not officially winter. When the Red Cross came, they'd issue blankets, and as soon as they left, they'd take them back."

Meuli emerged each night wet from the factory. "We had only one set of clothes, and tennis shoes. We'd try to dry them out at night, but they were still wet in the morning."

---

3 Cf. Myrrl McBride, "From Bataan to Nagasaki: The Personal Narration of an American Soldier," thesis. Sul Ross University, 1948, 168-69. This and other quotations of McBride from thesis and interview.

The men improvised. Smith wore two cement sacks he'd filched. Lingo made a shirt and mittens from a stolen blanket, using thread unraveled from a shelter half.

In Chintis's heatless barracks, "we had to get up many nights and run to keep warm." The walls in Baclawski's "were made of thin boards on studding. The cracks between them were covered with tape, and some hung loose so the wind whistled through. By morning your canteen was solid ice. You never got warm and you never really rested."

At Niigata, Almeraz slept in a tile-roofed barracks, "until a norther hit. In the night we heard the roof creaking under the snow – and then it caved in, and part of it went south. I lay looking at the sky. Some Canadians on the other side got killed."

Trying to keep clean was a challenge. Garrett "used the same razor blade for two years. Sharpened it on a curved piece of beer bottle." In Shillito's camp, "they'd heat a tank once a week for the whole camp to bathe in. But by the time everyone had gone through, it was just mud."

"The Japs wouldn't change water but once a month at Fukuoka 3, for a thousand guys to go through." Don Harris's detail complained. "Hot water from the mill flowed through a concrete enclosure, and our elderly supervisor – he was a civilian and pretty nice – got us some galvanized steel to catch the water. Then the minute we got it working, the Japs ran us out."

Always they were hungry. Baclawski "got a rice ball a day and a cup of seaweed soup. Fish sometimes, and millet or barley with sharp sticks in it that gave you diarrhea. On fish-cleaning detail, if the guards weren't looking, we'd stick a piece of fish tail in our mouth."

Roach "lived mostly on seaweed." Munsey ate fish-head soup. "The eyes floated and there were arguments if one had more than someone else." Bond "counted every bug or worm in your soup to see that you got as many as the next man." Don Harris "washed the maggots out of the fish we got. Once a whale washed ashore, and we ate that till it got so rotten we couldn't stand the smell." When a grain-filled warehouse burned at Tanagawa, the POWs felt lucky to get the burned wheat. Albert Gonzales cooked rice "in a big vat at night, with no light, and sometimes a rat would fall in. That was something extra."

Most of the men received one – some two – Red Cross boxes during their entire stay in Japan or Manchuria. As many as ten men shared one box, and most had been rifled. Later Johns learned, "we were supposed to get one a month, per man. If we had, we could have saved a lot of men. After the war we found warehouse after warehouse stacked to the ceiling with Red Cross packages."

Men were beaten for any reason or none: Foy when he was unable to lift a 270-pound sack of rice, Ojinaga for a small hole in his pants. For being two minutes late for a midnight duty, Munsey was flogged until he passed out. Ream saw a friend beaten to death for writing a satiric poem on the Emperor's birthday.

Gilcrease, extremely ill, neglected to salute a guard. "He clubbed me with his rifle butt, and when I came to, nobody was around and the sirens were screaming. I guess that saved me. I lost hearing in that ear for years, and I'll always have the scar where he fractured my skull."

For yawning in formation, Senter was beaten and kicked in the scrotum. An American officer interceded; but later the guards finished the job. On another occasion he was beaten for blowing his nose on the ground (never having been issued a handkerchief) and kept at attention in the sleet for several hours.

Punishment by exposure was common. Men were made to stand in water until it froze, or to stand at attention holding buckets of water until it was solid. Men were forced to run barefoot in snow, often with feet swollen from beriberi. After the men in Don Harris's barracks complained of cold, "they got us up at midnight every night to do calisthenics, and if we slowed down, they clubbed us."

Although his 'honcho' had sent him, Mendoza was beaten with a saber saw for leaving the mine early. "I opened up and kicked him where it hurt most. A bunch of Japs beat me up and left me laying there with blood all over me, then kneeled me in front of the guardhouse. It was colder than hell, and I was naked, and they beat hell out of me. Then they hung me from the guardhouse rafters from my hands and beat me with a two-by-four. My buddies carried me back to the barracks."

Occasionally the tables turned.

Earl Harris came out of the bath house at Oeyama just as they were changing the guard. "It was colder than hell, and the corporal was marching six Japs down the street. A trench carried waste from the kitchen – and it stank. I saluted, and they did eyes right in response – and goose-stepped into that damned ditch.

"By the time they got out, I was gone!"

Guards varied. Generally the civilian 'pushers,' older and not taught from birth to hate Americans, were more humane than the military guards. When Finley failed to snap to attention quickly enough, guards beat him and made him kneel on a pick handle, his legs weighted with large rocks. "But a garrison Jap took off the rocks and helped me up. He even gave me some raisins they'd stolen from our Red Cross packages."

Caught smuggling food, Chintis was put in solitary confinement, naked and shoeless in February. "The guards slowly and subtly kept moving the brazier fire closer. I was warmer than I'd have been in camp. And they gave me six rice balls – more than I'd had in a month."

Some guards acted friendly to turn informer. At Fukuoka 17 was 'Riverside,' raised in that California city, who disappeared suddenly after the war ended. Another, at Oeyama was Earl Harris's interpreter, "an American-educated sonofabitch. After a time or two of a man holding a rock on his head for twelve hours, we wised up and quit talking around that guy."

A few American officers were considered turncoats. Shillito believed "the guys at Niigata hated Major Fellows more than we hated any of our Jap guards."

Steen did. "If we got a little coal, we'd steal food and cook it at night in the barracks. Fellows would come through kicking it off the stoves, raising hell, throwing men in the guardhouse with no heat.

"Two guys stole a can of salmon. They admitted it. The Americans wanted to handle it, but, by God, Fellows turned 'em over to the Japs. They tied them to a post in the snow. The Canadian died the second night and the American the third. We swore we'd kill the SOB if we ever got the chance."

At Moji 4, when Naval Warrant Officer Dahl overheard Finley promise a sick friend some soybeans, he threatened to turn him in. "He spoke fluent Japanese. He'd send guys to work sick, and some died. One guy worked in the kitchen because he had a shell fragment in his leg. Dahl sent him out and he fell off a plank with a big load and cut an artery. I watched him bleed to death."

Albert Gonzales was one of many who later testified against Naval Lieutenant E. N. Little, mess officer at Fukuoka 17. "He'd turn guys in for little things. One day Nunn was in chow line and Little says, 'What's your name?' He says, 'Nunn, Sir,' and Little says, 'None you shall have,' and didn't let him have any breakfast."

"He hid to eat his food, but you could smell it," Gunter testified. "He sat like a little god on a high stool, with a pegboard, and if you spoke or laughed in chow line, he'd pull your peg and you got no rations.

"One guy that worked in the kitchen scraped some burnt rice to carry to his sick buddy. Little turned him in. They put him in a box – you can't stand up or lay down – and let him starve. We had to march by that box every day, until he died.

"When the war was over, he and his sergeant friend got Jap rifles and barricaded themselves in before the Americans could get to them."[4]

At the other extreme were the many fine officers who could often not only improve conditions for the men, but keep alive their pride as Americans. High among these, Chintis ranked Major L.J. Burchall (Air Commander, RCAF) senior officer at the Yokohama Stadium Camp. "He fought the Japs in his own way. They wanted us to salute their enlisted men, and he said, 'We only salute officers.' So we didn't salute. And we got the hell beat out of us.

4 Alleged collaborations may have simply been faulty judgment, or even a sincere desire to protect the men by avoiding trouble. It was, in any case, hard to prove. Fellows was apparently never formally charged; it was rumored that Dahl later stood court-martial, though the author has found no record; Little was brought to trial, and eventually cleared.

"They wanted us to goose-step, so Burchall said, 'Kick the guy in front of you, and fall down,' which we did, and the Japs said, 'Dumb Americans,' and gave up. We paid the price – but we kept our identity. Our heads were bloody but unbowed."

Shillito admired Dr. Nelson Kaufmann. "He and Burchall worked hand in hand to protect us. Kept us in when we were sick or injured – and we only lost seven men in the two and a half years I was there.

"One morning a Jap medic ordered everybody in sick bay to work, and Burchall said no. That Jap started to slap him, and Burchall decked him. They tried him in Tokyo. Brought him back and kept him in solitary a month. Never gave him any authority again. But he survived. And he never compromised. Never. On anything."

The old foe beriberi still hammered at burning feet, which they tried to ease by sitting at night with feet in buckets of ice water. Pneumonia and diphtheria killed many. American doctors had little to work with, and most of the Japanese physicians were uncaring or sadistic.

When influenza hit Munsey's crew, "the Japs poured powder on our backs and set it on fire, a daily ritual with new areas burned each day, and the previously burned areas reburned." This continued until Dr. Kaufmann put a stop to it.

From Shinagawa Hospital in Tokyo came tales of a Dr. Tokuda who gave bloodstream injections that took ten to twelve agonizing hours to kill the victim; it was not surprising that Gonzo Drake was "scared stiff" to undergo a hernia operation at the hands of a Japanese doctor.

A hypodermic injection eased his apprehensions considerably. "A group of little student nurses were giggling – they'd never seen an American – and when the interpreter said to take off my kimono, I was embarrassed, but too drunk to give a damn. So I thought, 'Buddy, let's give 'em a show,' and I started doing a strip that would've made Gypsy Rose Lee check her hole card.

"I guess the little doctor still saw fear in my eyes. He said, 'Mr. Drake,' in beautiful Oxford English, 'rest your mind. I am a surgeon first and a Japanese second.'"

* * *

Injuries were frequent. When Hernandez and the ore cart he pushed plunged onto rails forty feet below, Senter carried him unconscious to the hospital and left him for dead. Somehow he recovered.

At Moji a plank slipped under Finley. "It tore my leg to the bone, and a steel belt took a chunk of flesh out of my head. I thought I'd lost both eyes. They took me to the warehouse in a cart, and a Jap nurse sewed me up, leg and head, with no anesthesia. I couldn't stand – and they made me walk back to camp."

Albert Gonzales walked upright into a mine shaft one morning, "and by the time we got out we had to crawl. It was settling – you could hear that timber pop. The Japs took off and we stayed and shoveled coal. I figured we'd never make it out. Some did get buried."

When Rhea Tow's jackhammer hit a fissure, "the whole face came down on Nunn and me. Pushed us into some piling, and we were penned there several hours, until some Koreans dug us out."

"Lots of boys lost legs in the mines." Mendoza's was crushed in a cave-in. "It was swollen and full of pus, and the Jap doctor wanted to cut it off. But Captain Hewlett wouldn't let him. He slit it and cleaned it, and in six weeks I was back at the mine. Doc Hewlett saved a lot of guys at Fukuoka 17."

None could save Clyde Ely, who never recovered from his ordeal on the *Brazil Maru*. Don Harris tendered last rites for his old friend. "Major Dorris let Ralph Clark and me take his body on a cart. A chaplain read a service, and some of the old 200th were there to salute. Then we pushed the cart five miles to the crematorium."

They talked.

–"Of home, mostly. Or what happened to some of your buddies."

–"Of food."

–"Of tomorrow, that would be better."

–"Of how we'd help seize the garrison when the Americans came."

They prayed.

Mendoza watched it start "with three or four guys. Then I'd look around and see three or four hundred, and George Craig would start the rosary."

Then Father Duffy came, "skin and bones, so sick he could hardly talk, and he'd say Mass sitting down. He'd say, 'Go borrow' – he didn't say steal – 'borrow some bread,' for Holy Communion. We'd sneak crackers from the Red Cross boxes in the Jap kitchen."

They laughed.

Ragsdale laughed at his captors. "They'd line us up every morning and make us tip our hats to the Rising Sun. And we'd take off our hats and say, 'Good morning, Mr. Roosevelt!'"

Hernandez laughed at punishment. "This Nip was beating us all on the head, and each thump sounded like he hit a cord of wood. And we laughed. Next day we had a contest to see who had the biggest lumps."

Lucas laughed as a guard approached some seated men, "and instead of yelling, '*Kyotski-kedi-nari*,' I yelled, '*Kyotski-bull shit–*' and everybody jumped to attention, '*–nari!*' The guard returned the salute and left, and we all burst into laughter.

"We always had a comeback. The Japs never broke the American spirit."

Russell Hutchison was getting a blood transfusion "when the air-raid sirens went off. The Japs came through clubbing the doctors to get out. I said, 'Doc, stick this damned bottle between my legs and maybe it'll stay warm.' But it pulled the tube off the needle, and the blood went across my eyeballs and in my beard. He crimped the hose and stuck the bottle under me and I lay there in the air raid and all I could see was orange, looking through the blood.

"Two hours later I got my transfusion. I had a violent reaction – there was no way to type blood – but several hours later I started to urinate, for the first time in five weeks. I'd lose two quarts at a time. I got down to – they estimated sixty-eight pounds. I had no control – just kept on and on. Charlie Brown took care of me.

"Finally I said, 'Doc, if you don't stop this, all you're going to send back to Barbara is a little hickey this long, and say, 'There's Russell – he disappeared out of this little thing!'"

It convulsed the ward.

Still, time grew long and life heavy.

Gonzo Drake had one midnight watch. "We were working sixteen hours a day in thin cotton trousers, and slept on slats and scratched all night. Each night they appointed a fire guard. I don't know why, there was no fuel, just a stove as cold as a pawn-broker's heart. We'd been in prison so long. We'd withstood everything they had thrown at us. But sometimes a person's spirit can go so low you'll consider every alternative.

"I sat there and I thought, 'Dear God, what's the use? We're just going to sit here and starve, or be eaten by those damned lice, or beaten to death.' I had a piece of broken glass, and I was looking at my wrists, and seriously considering just – shutting her down.

"And then the door opened, and a little old wizened Japanese guard walked in, and he said, in Japanese, 'What is it?' I just looked at him and shook my head. I couldn't talk.

"He reached in his jacket and pulled out two little sweet potatoes. They were cold and they were shriveled – but they were cooked. He handed me those and patted me on the head, and said, '*Ko-da-mon.*' That means 'child.'

"He walked out and I sat looking at those sweet potatoes. I ate them real slow, so I could savor them. They were the most delicious things I ever in God's life tasted. I looked up and said, 'Lord, I guess you didn't want me to do it.' And from that moment my spirits soared, and they could've cut my head off and I would still have been laughing at those slant-eyed bastards.

"Compassion is where you find it."

– 25 –

NIPPING THE NIPS

"If anybody thinks we aided the Japanese war effort, we didn't. We impeded it wherever we could – we were a nuisance factor."
– Sergeant Nicholas Chintis –

The Japanese officer ordered Ream to demonstrate his facility on a typewriter. "Now is the time," Ream dutifully pecked, "for all good men–" and his eyes twinkled, "–to come to the aid of their country." An old bromide newly charged, and one to which his fellow POWs were mustering wherever they were held; and, though removed from the fields of glory (and promotions), they continued to engage the enemy a thousand ways, from minor ego-denting annoyance to major sabotage.

Finley played mind games. "You had to know how to take a beating. Sometimes when you'd go down they'd kick you. Other times they got madder if you didn't fall. After one guard hit me a couple of times, I figured I'd better hit the ground. I let him knock me down a couple of times. Then he'd had enough."

"They'd try judo – flip us over their shoulders, slap us around. Woody Hutchison was so tall they couldn't reach his neck. So he'd pretend – leap over their shoulder and fall, and put on a real show." Gilcrease kept a straight face.

It was just a matter of out-toughing them mentally, Hutchison shrugged. "I always wanted to be a winner, whether it's pitching pennies or putting your life on the block."

So did his old friend Chintis, against whom he'd played basketball and football in the college circuit back in New Mexico. "I was always competitive, and it became a day-to-day process. I was in the ring with them, biding my time till I could get a punch in. Part of winning was to give them as much trouble as we could, and if anybody thinks we aided the Japanese war effort, we didn't. We impeded it wherever we could – we were a nuisance factor, even when we did some work. Scraping barnacles off ships, cleaning the docks, we'd kick wrenches and stuff into the water. We never could figure why they put up with us."

"They can't get by with this," Aldrich swore. "It wasn't so much 'Yankee Doodle Dandy' stuff as 'Yanks and tanks are coming, and I'm going to be here when they do.' So we'd 'stabilize' them, figure how to con them any way we could."

Finley knew dentists who, when Japanese sought their skills, "got hold of some materials for temporary fillings that, if left in, would rot their teeth out. Our dentists were happy to oblige."

If the enemy hoped to learn anything of value from their prisoners, they were disappointed. "What do you think of your government's foreign policy?" they shot at Shillito in one interrogation. "I told them I didn't even know we had one – and that was probably the only honest answer they got."

When asked if they had ever been gangsters in Chicago, two sergeants said not exactly gangsters, but "they had done some bootlegging." The interpreter ran for a dictionary. And to a loaded inquiry about the kind of ship that had carried him from San Francisco to Manila, a solemn-faced boy drawled,

"A birchbark canoe, the chief means of water transportation in the U.S."[1]

Goofing off gave them rest and slowed Japanese production. Banegas "wore my headband backwards in the mine so I could sit down, maybe take a little nap, and the light pointed at the wall so it looked like I was working. When a Jap came along we'd say 'Air Raid,' and everybody got back to work." The guard who caught him one day broke his jaw. Banegas took his punishment stoically, and promptly resumed the habit.

They stole what beckoned. A bag of fertilizer made of ground bones and fish scraps, packed in Los Angeles and marked "unfit for human consumption" provided a number of meals for McBride, and he stole corn from the stables until "I was ashamed to look an honorable horse in the face." Gulbas, waiting only until the guard turned his honorable back, relieved many a Buddhist shrine of its fruit offerings.

All vied for stevedore details. Johnson stole salt on the docks and traded it to Japanese guards for cigarettes they had themselves stolen. Hernandez always kept his pointed bamboo tube handy to siphon rice into 'loot bags' tied inside his trousers. Don Harris's crew watched a Korean dock worker hide stolen fish behind a pile of bricks, took the fish after he had gone, and watched with innocent faces when he returned for the missing provender.

Stevedoring in Kobe, Rhee's detail smuggled an entire crate of dress shirts into camp. "Everybody had a white silk shirt. But it was dangerous when the Japanese discovered them gone. So we stole a box of potassium manganate and dyed the shirts. That made it safe, because no rust-colored shirts were missing."

Senter's crew "trumped up ways to get rid of a guard, while we'd shortchange the bags of beans in his rail car, until there was just a high stack around the door and nothing behind them."

Shillito, sneaking beans in his mess kit for a buddy starving on coal detail, saw the guards searching the men ahead. "I ducked to the barracks and slipped it to a guy inside who grabbed it and ran – just what the Japs were waiting for. They

---

1 McBride thesis 199-200.

beat us up and clipped half our hair off. Which was ridiculous – we couldn't have cared less. But then we had to stand at attention all night, and every time we moved, they hit us."

Hank Lovato traded beans to men on coal detail. "So they were eating and we were keeping warm at night. We had coal stashed under our blankets, and the Japs were wondering how we kept our stove going. They weren't too bright."

When guards stole grain intended for an ox, and fed it yams (which were plentiful), the animal bloated, and, with a little help from the prisoners, died. Fearing a strange disease, the Japanese ordered it buried. "After dark, several guys slipped out and dug it up. The civilian guards took most of the meat, but some did get back to camp." Munsey ate his share quietly in the night. The evidence was gone by morning.

Lucas had "the best thief in Camp 23. Tolbert would break into Jap warehouses and steal fifty- or hundred-pound bags of rice, ride the empty coal cars into the mines, hide it, and bring it into camp in little bags made of pants legs." When finally caught, he endured a severe beating and three days in a small cage. Next time, he was more cautious.

Phillips stole food at Mukden with a group "organized like a Capone gang. The guys in storage area made a lot of charcoal-gas smoke with a blower and sounded the fire alarm, and while the Japs rushed to it, we raided a boxcar of lard and meat, and ate pretty well for a while. We stashed stuff behind a fake wall we put up in an old building.

"We took the bladders out of some volley balls we got in a Red Cross package, put them under the belly bands we wore, and shot them full of methyl alcohol we stole at the factory. They'd hold about a pint safely. They'd search us when we came into camp, and put their hands right over it, and it felt like tummy. We brought in a bunch."

Rhee, pulling the same trick, filled his too full on one occasion, and it "stuck way out. So at inspection, the fellow in line ahead of me, who had been inspected, stepped back in my line and I stepped into his. He was inspected twice, and the Japs didn't find anything."

Bond nearly got caught with his most prized piece of hot goods, a forbidden pocket knife. "They made me dump everything out of my pockets – and there was that knife. I thought I'd had it. But Japs have one-track minds. That guard looked right at that knife and went on. He'd been told to look for sugar!"

Hamblin broke into a kitchen in the night. When he heard a noise, he hid behind a refrigerator, and discovered a fellow prisoner. As they were eating, another noise made them freeze. They had awakened the night watchman, who began to shout for the military guard. They were trapped. In rushed the guards, brandishing clubs and shouting "*Banzai!*" Both men broke into laughter, gave away their hiding place – and paid the price. But their stomachs were full.

The Americans made the most of every chance. No piece of equipment was safe; no tool was too small, no task too insignificant to scuttle. Ross had little opportunity for sabotage in the steel mill, "but we could slow production – argue, act stupid. We'd stack bricks and 'accidentally' drop one on a Jap's foot. Then we'd get a little break while he chewed us out." Gulbas managed to break every blade he used at the sawmill. McBride dropped equipment from a bridge into the water – once as many as thirty 'oilers' for lubricating bearings in diesel engines. Work stopped while the Japanese checked invoices and made telephone calls, "trying frantically to locate the essential parts."

While tanning leather, Burrola stole oil and glucose. "That served two purposes. We got the soya oil into camp and ate the glucose – it was like sugar candy – and we ruined the leather." Poe became expert at making the tanning solution too strong. "The leather looked all right, but later it would disintegrate like noodles. We'd ruin maybe a thousand hides a day. We sabotaged everything we could. We'd put sulphuric acid in motor bearings, and we'd overload the bearings to burn them out."

A detail poured cement in the factory where Phillips worked. "Machine parts were stacked around the periphery. They would grab a handful, and into the floor they'd go – whole piles of small parts. That milling machine was a loss. They never did assemble it."

Garrett, cleaning lathes, tossed in his share. "We reinforced that concrete with the guts of thosc lathes, and the Japs couldn't replace 'em – they were American made. When the Americans bombed and tore the floor up, it nearly gave us away." Exposed in the gutted foundation lay a vast welter of bolts and gears and hammers and saws. The Japanese were not amused.

Because McBride had acquired some fluency in Japanese, he was asked to translate instructions for operating two captured American field guns. After he did so, the Japanese officer went to the next gun to explain, and McBride unscrewed a plug and drained all the oil from the first gun. "The artillery officer [who apparently had fired the oilless guns, or tried to] was brought into the field hospital as a patient later that day."

When King arrived in Japan, half blind and unfit for hard labor, "they put me on a sewing machine making underwear for the Jap army. I put an extra tuck into each one, where it would cause discomfort." And McCahon, sewing uniforms in Korea, "learned to make a buttonhole that would pass the inspector, and then, about the third time it was buttoned, completely unravel."

It was all part of the wearing-down process, and in many instances they caused real damage to the Japanese war effort. Stevedores and freight handlers sabotaged cargo. In the supply warehouse where he worked, Hank Lovato punched tiny holes in the metal containers destined for Japanese combat troops, so the food inside would spoil before it could arrive.

As Smith loaded gasoline drums on trains, "we loosened the caps and rolled them in the cars cap down, and as the train moved it shook them looser, so by the end of the run, their gas and oil was all leaked out." This was significant, in view of the critical shortage of oil in Japan by then.

"When we loaded rice, we'd throw in a few sacks of sulphur from another loading detail. It heated and expanded with the moisture from the grain, and the force split some of those cars wide open.

"On bomb detail they told us to be careful loading bombs – if the fin got crooked, the bomb wouldn't fall straight. So we'd hit them together when they weren't looking – we bent a lot that way."

Ojinaga, unloading ships, learned useful skills in handling the winches. "We always loaded so the net was lopsided, and as it went over, one guy would pull the cable a little to tip it, so it went to the bottom of the harbor. We dumped one big piece of oil-refinery equipment. The Japs were furious, so the Americans dived for it to calm them down. They got it, but the salt water had ruined it."

Perhaps Ojinaga's finest hour dawned while loading rifles into the hold of a ship bound for combat. No American would die from these rifles, they vowed silently, and began to grin at one another. "Some of the guys went topside to keep watch while we opened every box and took the firing pins out of every rifle – about three hundred – and sealed up the boxes. Then one guy took the pins in a bag and dropped it overboard – right under the eyes of the Japs!"

They obstructed mining operations. "We could push on one side of the rail car," Senter learned, "and make it jump the track. Four or five crews would push their cars onto a bunch of tracks, and the first one out would jump the rail, and they'd pile up. The Japs would scream and yell, and while they were trying to get it back on the track, we'd sit back and rest.

"Later we mixed cement, and we'd dump rail cars of gravel into the hopper and 'forget' to take a shovel out. That took quite a while before they got that stuff out. Scream – man, they'd scream – and we'd just look stupid."

Ojinaga filled his car with rocks, shoveled just enough coal to cover the top, and sent it on its way. Banegas coupled his cars with the hook at an angle, "so it would come loose. We could hear it down the track, like a cyclone, as those cars would come loose and derail. Sometimes it would demolish the whole thing.

"They had electric cables to run the lights and machinery underground, and we'd cut them and throw coal over them and keep on working like nothing had happened. Then the lights would go out and the machinery would stop, and those Japs were like hornets! But they never knew who did it."

Their captors were really angry when Tolbert managed to jam the pumps that pulled the water from the mine at Camp 23. It earned the Americans a three-day holiday.

* * *

They learned small tricks to slow production in smelter, mill, and factory. Meuli "tried to be as dumb as possible, to do everything wrong. They couldn't comprehend how we could be so stupid. They'd yell, 'Dumb *Americanos*,' and we'd nod and agree."

"If we leaned on the jackhammer a certain way," Aldrich learned, "we could break the steel bar that cleaned the mouth of the blast furnace after every pour. Then we'd get to rest while they went for another. It wasn't long before we'd broken every bar they had."

Gulbas applied cold carbon dioxide to heated rifle barrels to crack them. Farmer, crating suicide boats, dropped sand in the engines at every opportunity. James "threw little chunks of steel onto the screw conveyor" at the Yodogawa Steel Mill, "and about halfway through the oven, they'd just tear it to thunder. Then they'd have to cool the ovens several days before they could tear it out and rebrick it. And when we were rolling steel, we'd let our tongs slip and they'd go through and bust the roller." At Yawata, Mitchell "cracked the heads of the stoppers at the bottom, so it poured steel all over the ground. They chewed out the foreman, and we played dumb."

When McBride and his buddy found broken bits in the machine shop at Kobe, they filed and sharpened them, replaced good ones with these, and sold the undamaged ones on the black market. In checking out equipment, they handed the workmen drills slightly larger than called for. "When the machinery was bolted together, the holes were a few thousandth of an inch too large, and the stuff could not stand up long under the strain and vibration." Working on motors, he dabbed "grease-coated hands into emery dust at the grinding wheels and worked it onto the smooth surfaces. The fine dust wasn't noticed, and within a few days motors would be returned for repairs."

Shipyard work offered intriguing opportunities. At the Asano Shipyards, Shillito "knocked down a lot of equipment at the docks. It was American made, and it took American-made parts to repair them. We sabotaged these at every chance, because they couldn't get spare parts. Once it was down, it was down."

When King recovered his eyesight, he was put on shipbuilding detail. "We'd leave out rivets, or put them in loose. And that ship never did run."

"Inspectors checked the rivets, and, if satisfactory, put white paint on them." Munsey filled holes with putty and painted them white, "and no one was wiser. We began to collect all the waste material we could, and when we began to put in the steam pipes, we crammed all that stuff into them. The ship was finally launched, and we learned that our efforts had paid off. The stuffed steam pipes had made the boilers blow up. She was still listing in dry dock when the war was over."

Phillips participated in an elaborate sabotage system in the drafting department of the machine tool factory at Mukden. "These guys had a network of intelligence, from our department down to the machines.

"We'd get a part to draw, with certain measurements, and we'd figure the tolerance. Sometimes the Japs were breathing down our necks in the drafting office, and we'd have to draw them right. So we'd let the machinist know which drawings they were, and he'd screw them up. But if we drew incorrect dimensions, the machinist made them perfect, and they'd still be off. They never did ship a single machine!

"I was transferred to another factory, with a wooden floor that had been swept probably thousands of times with oily sawdust, so the floors were oil soaked. The Japs were deathly afraid of fire.

"Walt Gentry and I, and a Navy fellow named Pinson, were supposed to design a jig for what we figured was a reinforcement on an airplane. It's tough to design in the first place, and even tougher to design it where it looks good and you can do almost all the machining operations on it, but still blow it.

"We spent three months, and it wouldn't work! So that was a failure – or a success, for us. We junked that, and the Jap engineer went crazy, and got us working on another. So there went another three months.

"By that time it was getting cold, and we decided we needed a heater. So we designed one like an electric hot plate, with fire brick and coils of electric wire that would get hot, and we cut a hole in the wooden floor and set it between the floor joists. Even while we were designing it, we began to look at each other and think, if it got hot enough, we could burn the place down! So we didn't insulate it – just a metal box against oily wood. After we installed it, we'd turn the rheostat just so high, and we filed a notch to the point you would turn it without setting the place on fire. Our plan was that the guards would turn it up at night for heat.

"And sure enough, early one morning the whole thing went up! We'd burned down the building with all their gauges and measuring equipment, and a lot of really fine German and American equipment. And the guards got blamed."

In hundreds of ways, from minor annoyance to major destruction, the determined band of prisoners fought the war on their own front. Chintis summed it up:

"We got a lot of beatings out of it. We stuck our necks out, and we got bashed. But we kept our pride, and we kept fighting. We were still in the United States Army. And we were going to win!"

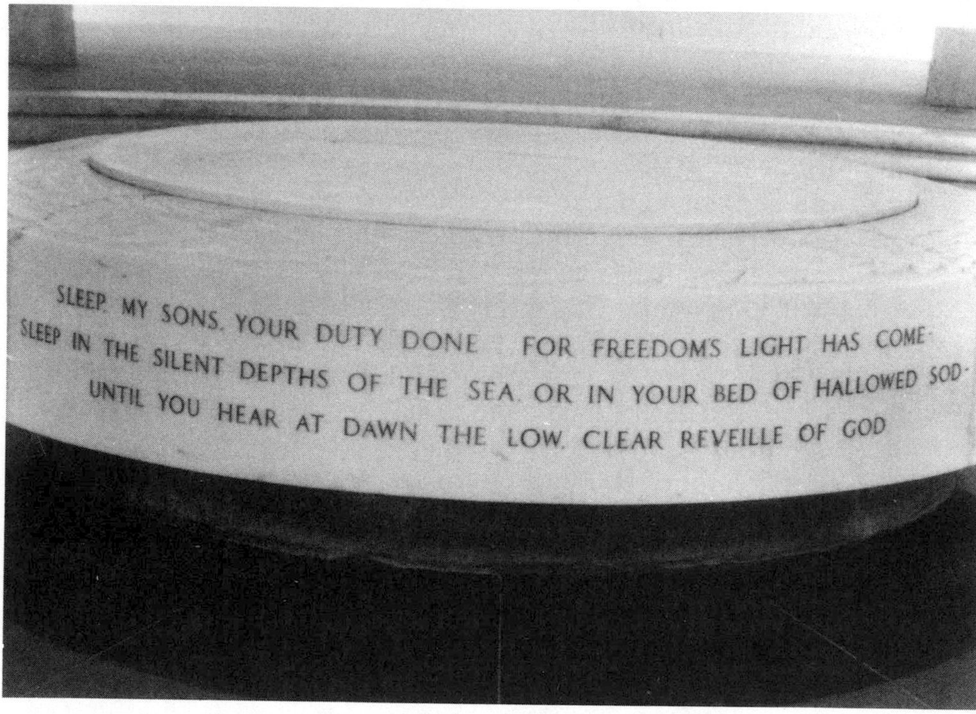

SLEEP MY SONS YOUR DUTY DONE FOR FREEDOM'S LIGHT HAS COME
SLEEP IN THE SILENT DEPTHS OF THE SEA OR IN YOUR BED OF HALLOWED SOD
UNTIL YOU HEAR AT DAWN THE LOW CLEAR REVEILLE OF GOD

Disc at the Pacific War Memorial on Corregidor, dedicated in 1968 to those in the Pacific Theater of World War II who gave their lives for freedom. (Courtesy: Philippine Tourist Bureau.)

BOOK VI

GOD BLESS AMERICA

STATE OF NEW MEXICO
OFFICE OF THE ADJUTANT GENERAL
SANTA FE

GENERAL ORDERS) December 6, 1946
NO. 6)

By authority of Chapter 115, Laws of 1945, an Act entitled "An Act to Provide Recognition to Certain Members of the 200th Coast Artillery, it is hereby ordered that a Ceremony be held in the City of Santa Fe, New Mexico, on Saturday, December 7, 1946, for the purpose of presenting the New Mexico Bataan Medal to personnel assigned to the 200th Coast Artillery (AA) and on duty in the Philippine Islands on December 7, 1941, or to the next of kin of those individuals of that Regiment who now are deceased.

This medal is physical evidence of the love and esteem of the citizens of this State for the valiant men who, as members of the New Mexico National Guard, brought great honor to their State by their bravery, loyalty and devotion to duty.

BY COMMAND OF THE GOVERNOR:

Charles G. Sage

CHARLES G. SAGE
Brigadier General, AUS
The Adjutant General

OFFICIAL:

Charles G. Sage

CHARLES G. SAGE
Brigadier General, AUS
The Adjutant General

– 26 –

YANKS AND TANKS

"The sun was just going down when they broke in to get us. And it was exactly the color of the Japanese sun – that big old round red sun. Only it wasn't rising any more. This sun was setting."
– Private Harold Knighton –

I. The Philippines

On 9 January 1945, after enduring *kamikaze* attacks all the way from Leyte, the first elements of General Walter Krueger's Sixth Army scrambled ashore from Lingayen Gulf on the same beaches from which the wretched survivors of the *Oryoku* had sailed just thirteen days before. MacArthur had returned to Luzon.

It was not too soon for Doyle Decker. From his lonely post he had watched the fires rise from Clark Field when American bombers hit in September; and, as raids increased, he knew it would not be long. "We had a downed American pilot and his gunner for two weeks. They usually tried to make it to the China Sea if they were hit, to where a sub could pick them up. But these couldn't make it – bailed out almost over our headquarters. The Negritos brought them in.

"A few days after the Americans landed, we made our first contact, and got these guys through the Jap lines. But we were still under strict orders to fight only if attacked, so we just went on with our work until the troops reached Angeles. Then – at last – we were united with the Sixth Army."

Unaware of the landings, some five hundred seriously ill Americans and the handful of medical personnel remaining at Cabanatuan watched the occasional high-flying planes they believed were American. They heard the distant drumming of the 'bamboo telegraph' that pulsed through the nights, and saw tense guards grow tenser at the unremitting beat.

Sometimes money, impaled on arrows, winged into the compound from the cogon grass, or messages offering to help the men escape. A premature attempt, warned Colonel Duckworth, would likely get them all killed: Wait a little longer.

Hope grew. So did the belief – based on the threats and the increasing sadism of their edgy guards – that their captors would kill them all before they would allow them to be liberated. MacArthur, too, feared mass retaliations (one had already taken its bloody toll on Palawan) and pressed for a hasty advance and quick liberation.

General Tomoyuki Yamashita, at this point less concerned with a few sick prisoners than his need to hold Route 5 and keep open his supply lines from Manila, was deploying tons of supplies and the bulk of his 275,000 troops for a last-ditch defense in northern Luzon. The POWs watched amazed as their guards marched out of Cabanatuan. They would return, the Japanese warned; the Americans must remain inside the fences or be shot.

Almost immediately the starving men raided the Japanese warehouses of milk, meat, and *camotes*, on which they lived for the next three weeks, unmolested by the Japanese infantry units arriving at the garrison, who largely ignored the American compound.

Meanwhile, the Sixth Army was pushing in three prongs through the northern mountains, across the Central Plain to Clark Field, where they met with savage fighting, and toward Manila. It was a slow and bloody business, through gutted terrain, against a desperate and numerically superior enemy.

On 28 January, warned by guerrilla Captains Robert Lapham and Juan Pajota of the prisoners' danger as the Americans advanced, 120 tough marksmen from the Sixth Army Ranger Battalion and a handful of Alamo Scouts set out to rescue the men at Cabanatuan. Led by Lieutenant Colonel Henry Mucci, they proceeded stealthily from the small town of Guimba to Lapham's headquarters, from which Captain Eduardo Joson's eighty guerrillas guided the long night's march through twenty-five miles of enemy-held jungle. By dawn they reached Pajota's group at Balangkare, coordinated the split-second details, and, with another 250 guerrillas, most armed only with bolos, set out again.

The plan was perilous, but with luck and pluck it could work. The guerrillas would secure the area along the route; they would have carabao carts ready to feed and carry the living skeletons, and they would set up roadblocks on either side of the camp. The Rangers, on a given signal, would open fire to commence the raid.

The Scouts went ahead. Just north of the Pampanga River they reported heavy Japanese troop movements around the camp. Mucci postponed the raid twenty-four hours. Then, before dusk on the thirtieth, they began to cross the river, guerrillas to their assigned areas, Rangers snaking on their bellies through rice stubble and cogon to theirs. Concealed, they waited for dark and the three-quarter moon.

In the medics' quarters inside the camp, Rodriguez closed his diary, walked to the record player someone had 'liberated,' and put on their one scratchy record. "Wai-ait till the sun shines, Nellie . . . . "

In the tailor shop, Villaloboz handed a newly made shirt to a guard and accepted a can of milk in return. "Me and my buddy were getting ready for a good drink . . . . "

Behind the kitchen, West finished butcher detail. "The Jap guard took up our knives and we started back to our barracks . . . . "

Suddenly shots cracked from outside the camp, "and then all hell broke loose." Men hit the ground, believing the long-threatened execution had begun. West saw moon-silvered forms hurling grenades into the guardhouse.

Rodriguez jumped back from the record player. "Yank soldiers rushed in and were shooting the guards, and the Japs let fire a machine gun a couple of yards from where I was standing. The other medics started yelling, 'Ralph, turn off that damned record!'

"The shooting was waist high. Bullets were hitting the mess kits and the wall, and this record was playing, and the guys kept yelling to turn it off. I grabbed the table leg and shook it. I don't know why, but suddenly it was all funny, and I was laughing." The record ended, the arm returned, and it began again. "Wait till the sun shines, Nellie . . . . "

Bullets flew for half an hour before the flare signaled to cease fire and rush the compound. In the sudden quiet, West heard running feet. "I looked, and then I looked again, and thought, 'That's no Jap uniform!' Two guys ran over and said, 'Get to the main gate, PDQ!' – and it was – Americans!

"They hit the tower with bazookas just as we headed out. The Rangers surrounded us and carried those too weak to walk."

The shooting from the tower let up briefly, and Rodriguez, followed by the strains of the waiting Nellie, crawled for the door. "American voices were yelling, 'Get to the main gate!' That was facing the machine gun. I'd get so far and it would fire – and that ditch was small. Then I hit a water pipe. I couldn't go underneath and I was afraid to crawl over.

"Suddenly the machine gun hit the spigot, which hit my head, and I said, 'I'm dead.' Here came a giant, yelling, 'Any Americans around here?' I jumped up and he said, 'Get your ass to the main gate!'

"You could see shadows all over the camp running back and forth. Just as we cleared the gate, a gun exploded from a tank.

It killed a doctor and one soldier."[1] Japanese reinforcement troops had arrived. A contingent of Rangers fought a rear-guard action while the last of the prisoners filed to freedom.

Once across the river, the litter cases were loaded from stretchers onto carabao carts. The rest walked, many, like Villaloboz, barefoot, "through jungle and water and stickers all that night."

Rodriguez, in the last group out, "met opposition down the line, and then we had to cross the river, six feet deep and over my head. I got between Greg Chavez and Foch Tixier – tall guys – and I never touched bottom. Then we ran until we got to the American side. When we got there we couldn't stand. Our bodies just wouldn't hold us up."

At home, though Washington and the media focused on a fast-crumbling Germany, New Mexicans rejoiced. At last – at last – it had begun. The Yanks were returning to free the first of those men who, in valorous defense of Bataan and Corregidor, had lit the torch and rallied a nation.

As the Rangers raced for Cabanatuan, elements of General Robert L. Eichelberger's Eighth Army landed on 29 January on the Zambales coast, proceeded to take Olongapo, and started east. Simultaneously, units from the Sixth marched south to meet the Eighth at Dinalupihan to seal Bataan from enemy withdrawal. It was with these units that Edras Montoya made his first human contact in three years.

Soon after he had watched the bombing of the airstrip, he again mounted his treetop lookout, and, seeing no Japanese, stealthily descended to open country. Spotting an American patrol plane, he waved his arms frantically as the pilot circled; then he followed the direction of the plane.

Bearded, in rags, and without identification, he was uneasy about rejoining his countrymen. But, as they heard his story, suspicion became amazement, and they welcomed him back to the United States Army. "They gave me food and some of their own clothes, and even furnished me a bed and a mosquito net, something I did not have for three years.

[1] Cpl. Roy Sweezy was killed instantly. Capt. James Fisher, the battalion surgeon, died at Balangkare.

"On the front lines, the Americans had lights all over the place. I asked if they were not afraid of being attacked. One said no – they wanted to show the Japs they were ready to meet them. The Americans were having fun."

Montoya was ready to fight. "But the commander said I would be sent home – that we had done our part, and they were taking it from there." Two volunteers mounted machine guns on the back of a Jeep, and, armed with rifles, drove him to Lingayen, where food, a bed, and medical attention awaited him.

He desperately wanted to send a wire to his family, he said, but he had no money. He'd see to that, an officer assured him; as for money – how much did he want? Enough to buy presents for his old Filipino friends, he said, and a three-day pass to deliver them. He got both, and a driver to take him.

Back at Lingayen, he and the wretches just freed from Cabanatuan boarded planes for Leyte, their first leg home. The litter cases were carried on first, and as the rest filed after, someone cried out, and then others, raggedly, from choked throats:

"God Bless America!"

Garcia was not among those freed; two weeks before the raid on Cabanatuan, he had been sent to Bilibid. There, in that great stone wagon wheel, he and other medical personnel tried, without sanitary facilities, to keep wards, kitchens, and latrines relatively clean. They seemed never to rest. On constant call, they helped dysentery-scourged men to the latrines, and, with few rags and no soap, cleaned those who could not make it. Night calls, in the complete black, were major struggles.

Some eight hundred POWs and five hundred civilians within had wasted for months on mildewed rice, sometimes some *camote* vines, and, on good days, a few fish bones. They caught rats from the sewer when they could. In September 1944 a howling typhoon had torn corrugated roofs from some of the buildings and let in driving rains that flooded interiors, in places waist high.

Hope dawned when the first bombs fell on Manila, and grew as the barrage continued. The Yanks were coming – they knew it, but – when? The months stretched long, and the year turned, and men died daily.

"Get to Manila!" MacArthur ordered. "Go around the Nips, bounce off the Nips – but get to Manila!" Not only was speed essential to outmaneuver Yamashita, but alarming reports from his underground sources caused the General to jut his jaw more grimly: The prisoners must be freed – soon.

The over-cautious Krueger plodded. Enemy resistance grew fiercer. Washington ordered MacArthur to release seventy transport ships immediately to be used for more Lend-Lease supplies for Russia, despite his protests that this would jeopardize his entire Philippine campaign.[2] He was further ordered to return the bulk of his naval forces to Admiral Chester Nimitz. Speed became more urgent.

From the north, the 1st Cavalry and 37th Infantry Divisions of the Sixth Army raced each other toward Manila, and the 11th Airborne of the Eighth Army challenged them both from the south. Guerrilla groups, now freed for action, cut Japanese communication wires, blew dams and bridges and ammunition dumps, mined roads, and set up ambushes. The race for Manila was on.

With the bulk of Yamashita's troops in the north, Vice Admiral Denshichi Okochi girded to defend the city with some 30,000 sailors and marines. He would hold Manila or destroy it – and the prisoners and inhabitants therein.

Inside Bilibid, Knighton, almost too weak to move, lay and listened as shells began to fall on the city. "They got nearer, and we could gauge the distance by the time between the blasts and the shells coming over. Then late one afternoon we heard rifle fire, and we knew they were fighting in the streets."

It was 3 February, and advance elements of the 1st Cavalry had hit the outskirts of Manila. Speeding to Santo Tomás,

---

2 Washington apparently believed Russian help against Japan was vital, and MacArthur recorded that his views were neither solicited nor heeded. The supplies thus sent to Russia were, as he later noted, never used against Japan, but were instead used eventually in Korea, against Americans. *Reminiscences*, 244-45.

they freed its civilian internees and fell back to secure their positions. G-2 had not told them of Americans behind the bastions of Bilibid.

From beyond the nearby commotion of massing troops, Knighton heard the crack of approaching rifle fire, the clatter of tanks, and the roar of artillery. Through the high window the sky burned red. The guards grew edgier. "By morning they knew they'd had it, and they loaded up their ducks and pigs and took off. And American flags, that guys had all those years kept hid, began to break out."

Several hours passed. "The fighting got faster and louder," and Knighton felt the strength of hope. The 37th had arrived, learned of Americans in Bilibid, and were prying at the boards of the ancient gates. "There were two walls around the prison, with warehouses in between. About sundown a couple of boys tending the incinerator between the walls heard an awful noise. Suddenly there stood two combat soldiers. They'd seen the fire through a crack and knocked the boards off with their rifle butts.

"'How do we get out of here?' one asked.

"'Get out of here, hell,' they said. 'We been here two years. How do *we* get out of *here*?'

"They found a door and men began to pour in, and everybody was shouting. 'Anybody in here from Little Rock?' 'Anybody from El Paso?' If anyone answered, they'd grab 'em and they were gone!

"The sun was just going down when they broke in to get us. And it was exactly the color of the Japanese sun – that big old round red sun. Only it wasn't rising any more. This sun was setting."

That portion of Bilibid was breached. Early the next morning the larger group from the 37th began to crash the main gates. Garcia "heard somebody digging holes through the walls, and pretty soon they hollered, 'Hey, are you guys Americans?' and they busted the gates and came in."

They faced each other as if from alien planets. For stunned moments the POWs stared, and wondered if these giants in strange uniforms with unfamiliar weapons were indeed the rescuers of which they had dreamed. The troops stared at the filthy, rag-clad bones inside, blinked back tears, and wondered if these were indeed men. Then Americans hailed Americans.

Still penned inside by battle, the now-freed men feasted happily on the K-rations the troops gave them. A soldier Garcia had known at Fort Bliss "went somewhere and brought back bottles of rum. After that – man! Some of us couldn't stand up!"

As the Americans battled block by block, Manila writhed in flame and blast as bombs exploded and the fleeing Japanese torched and detonated its parts, and hideously murdered its inhabitants. By evening flames swept toward Bilibid and the Americans began to evacuate. Through cratered streets and collapsing buildings they filed, through mortar fire and bombs and blood and the roar of artillery, through heat and thick smoke, to an abandoned shoe factory. On the seventh, when it was safe, they returned to Bilibid.

That same day, while the battle still pounded, General MacArthur came to visit. Garcia "had never seen so many stars. A lieutenant gave the General a list of prisoners he wanted court-martialed for stealing food. Well, the General tore up that list and raised hell with the lieutenant. 'These boys have been through enough hell already,' he said, and he told us whatever we wanted on that island we could have. Then he started through the wards."

Knighton was sitting on his bunk, "just down to my weakest point, when someone hollered, 'Attention!' and I pulled up. General MacArthur stepped in and said, 'At ease,' and when he got to my bunk – he looked straight at me.

"'How are you, soldier?' he asked. He kind of slapped me on the shoulder, and – I held together for a second. Then he walked on, and I cried like a baby."

While the battle still roared in Manila, the men from Bilibid were taken to Lingayen Gulf. "They kept us there two or three weeks to fatten us up before they flew us to Leyte, and then kept us there" for what seemed to Garcia, "like ages, and gave us the best food so we wouldn't come back looking like skeletons."[3]

They returned to the States on the USS *Monterrey*. "And there on the ship, in San Francisco Bay" – Garcia didn't recognize him at first – "came Eddie Cantor. He gave us a big show, and girls took telegrams, as many as we wanted, and it was all on him.

"We were in Letterman General Hospital. They gave us a big banquet at the Mark Hopkins, and some of us didn't go back to the hospital. I rented a room for two weeks, and when I went to pay, they wouldn't take any money."

Red Cross personnel met some, with somber news. West had lost his father, and Knighton the grandfather who had reared him. Villaloboz "heard them calling my name, and I was looking for my mother in all those people – strangers, with pictures of their boys, to see if we knew them, to find out if they were coming. Some I knew – and their mothers were there – and you knew they were dead, but you couldn't say nothing about it. And they kept calling my name. It was to tell me my mother had died. Three years before."

On 4 July 1945 MacArthur announced the end of the Philippine campaign. So closed the penultimate curtain of the Pacific drama. One act remained, and it was summed in the terse motto all America echoed:

"On to Tokyo!"

---

3 Then and later with POWs freed from Japan, Korea, and Manchuria, it seems to have been policy to fatten the men before allowing the public to see them. It is also interesting that pictures showing their skeletal condition were suppressed, while only those taken after the food drops and other fattening processes were released, either to spare the families or to prevent public outcries from a people already enraged over the long neglect of the Pacific war in order to 'Get Hitler First.'

II. Japan, Korea, and Manchuria

The boys in the north still waited. With only Japanese propaganda, Chintis "followed the war by where the battles were. They said they were throwing the Yanks back at Leyte. We knew they weren't. As they got closer, we knew we were winning, even though the Japs 'won' every battle."

Shillito "added up the lies about how many ships they'd sunk – there weren't that many ships in the world. Even the Japs knew we could see through this, so they cut off the Nip newspapers – which really made it tough on toilet paper. That's where we missed the news!"

Japanese combat troops grew wary. While repairing the *Tottori*, Chintis noted the crew's reluctance to sail again; and when a *kamikaze* pilot, the son of Ragsdale's honcho, "came home before his final flight, he didn't want to go. He talked to us – he knew a little English. He wasn't sold on this 'dying for the Emperor' business. He was going, but he didn't like it."

The one news item the Japanese rushed to report was the death of Roosevelt. Chintis heard it in the dock yard. "They were gleeful – seemed to think that meant we'd lose the war. I could speak fair Jap, and I pretended I knew who Truman was, and made up all this garbage, and said, 'If you think Roosevelt is bad, just wait'll this guy gets through with you!'"

In Korea, McCahon played Taps for his President, and "thought nothing about it until I got home and read in *Time* how it inflamed the Japs. I may have come close to getting shot that day."

The prisoners on Kyushu first spotted the B-29s in June 1944, when China-based planes hit the Yawata Steel Works. Though raids there and over Tokyo and Nagoya caused negligible damage, the psychological impact was enormous. The Japanese realized that war had reached their homeland, and the POWs knew their long-held faith had substance. Uncle Sam was storming the walls. And the walls were crumbling.

On the night of 9-10 March, 1945, a far more devastating weapon was launched from the Mariannas when 334 Superfortresses swept low over Tokyo, released napalm-filled incendiaries, and destroyed a quarter of the city.[4] The next night they hit Nagoya, and followed with massive raids on Osaka, Kobe, and Yokohama. Conventional raids had proved ineffective. Only the complete destruction of Japanese war production, it became increasingly obvious, could shorten the war and end it without an invasion that would prove far more costly in life.[5]

From his shelter, Munsey saw American planes "bombing the hell out of the industrial area between Tokyo and Yokohama." To watch from the two openings, the prisoners alternated – and sometimes altercated. As a scuffle between an Alabama boy and one from Maine escalated into a fist-flying mini-Civil War, "we began to laugh. Our British friends were even more amused. 'Leave it to the Yanks,' they said, 'to start a fight!'"

Despite their own peril, the Americans cheered as planes dived under low clouds to hit the factories of Osaka. From his barracks, McBride "stood at the windows far into the night" to watch the great city burn into a charred chaos.

At Kobe, Rhee sweated out "a tremendous floating tank with white gas for the Shendo Steel Works," dangerously near his work area, as "our planes came over for a Saint Patrick's Day celebration, so sure of themselves they flew single formation with their running lights on. The next day the factory's steel looked like pretzels – but they had not hit the gas tanks!"

With American control of the Philippines and the China Sea, Japan's supply lines were severed. Beyond, the Burma campaign wound down, and Australian and American troops

---

4 This raid, the most destructive single bombing of the war, cost an estimated 100,000 lives, wounded another 125,000, and left over 1,000,000 homeless, as compared to the A-bombs at Hiroshima, where estimates range from 60,000 to 80,000, and Nagasaki, estimated at between 36,000 and 40,000. The incendiary bombings far exceeded both A-bombs together. A single incendiary raid on 2 August leveled six Japanese cities.

5 Military planners estimated the invasion of Japan would cost over 1,000,000 American lives, to say nothing of Japanese troops and civilians, and almost certainly would guarantee the death of every POW held in Japan, Manchuria, and Korea. In view of the indiscriminate Japanese bombings of civilians as early as 1932 in China, it is ironic that the Japanese government protested these 'inhumane' bombings of their own populace.

hammered at the East Indies. Inside the tightening noose, Japan's perimeter defenses crumbled. Iwo Jima, stepping-stone from the Mariannas, fell on 16 March, and on 21 June, after nearly three months of bloody struggle, Okinawa. Only 350 miles remained to Kyushu – to Japan itself. Finally, with Germany's surrender on 8 May, MacArthur could, at last and realistically, expect ships instead of shoestrings, troops instead of trickles, planes instead of promises.

Fire bombings recommenced in May on Tokyo, Nagoya, Yokohama, and Kobe. "At Yokohama, they started with day raids. The Japs were losing their minds. The big raid hit at night. They came in low and bombed for hours." Shillito saw "a lot of planes hit. We saw men in parachutes burning on the way down. When it was over there wasn't anything left, and we hadn't any water or power."

With others, Chintis "wound up taking care of a lot of Jap civilians brought into our camp. That's Americans – they can be at your jugular vein one minute – but they are compassionate."

With the major centers virtually destroyed, the raids fanned over larger areas, and prisoners throughout Japan took heart as half a hundred cities felt their power. Paul Roessler "had never seen planes that big. The sky was filled, and we heard them dropping their loads in the distance, and it was music."

At Hirohata, Lightfoot saw planes drop mines into the bay. "A guard said they'd missed their target and were duds. Then they'd start to move a ship out, and it would blow up. Some duds!"

Harrington recorded "flight after flight almost directly over us. At night we hear the shrill wail of the sirens. The lights go out and from the distance comes the roar of heavy motors. We hear the explosions in the distance and the windows rattle. Then we smile, for we know Uncle Sam is doing his work well."

The Japanese began to move the POWs from the bombed-out centers to work wherever any now-desperate war production still functioned. American raids followed them. From his barracks on the waterfront at Tsuruga, Hernandez saw "a string of incendiaries hit our camp. Everything was burning and the wind was blowing. My buddy and I started running towards the town, but the fire there was worse. We jumped in a canal and waded back towards camp, with fire on both sides. People were trapped and burning. They burned the whole town."

Only a few metal warehouses at the docks remained. Senter, moved into one of these, was relieving himself at the water's edge when "we heard planes and saw dots on the horizon – carrier-based Grummans, with little wing bombs. They dropped a bomb right in the middle of that warehouse."

Marching through Yokohama, Shillito saw "not a building still standing – only skeletons of one or two, and rubble, waist high, as far as you could see."

Sent to Rokuroshi, Boyer found "no food, and it was too late to plant. We were eating berry roots and drying them for the winter. Once in a while we got bones, and we boiled them until they were soft enough to chew. But we knew there was no way to survive. The snow got five or six feet deep, and the barracks were open, with no heating facilities and no way to winterize them. Still, our morale stayed high, because we saw the B-29s fly over, and we saw the flames and smoke of Fukui."

On Kyushu, Ross "hunkered in a ditch while the Americans hit a fourteen-inch gas line. You think we didn't have fireworks!" Niemon was hospitalized when a five-hundred-pound dud fell. "It lay there several weeks, liable to go off any time. They finally detonated it with a rifle, which made the slate roof cave in – on me!"

The Japanese butcher at Kosaka told Aldrich that "the B-29s – *bi-ni-ji-kus* – were going to bomb Aomori that night. The Americans had radioed them to move out their civilians. Sure enough, that night we heard the explosions and saw the fires. We went wild. We knew it wouldn't be long."

When bombers overflew Niigata, Steen "heard things falling – bombs, we thought – but one didn't explode, and we wondered what in hell was wrong. They were mines, and they really did a job. It got to be a circus."

"They were magnetic," Hank Lovato learned later. "The Japs sent out mine sweepers and combed the bay, didn't find anything, and when the ships came in, these mines rose off the bottom and blew the ships up. Then the Japs would get mad and take it out on us."

It was worth it to Steen, when he saw "ship masts all over that bay. Then one day planes came in low and tore hell out of about thirty ships. They hauled in dead Japs for two hours."

"In late July, some Navy fighters strafed our barracks." After the war, one of the pilots told Shillito, "their target was socked in, and we were a target of opportunity. They really got raked over the coals when they got back to the carrier. They hadn't been told this was a clean target, they weren't to touch it – they were saving Niigata for an atomic bomb!"

Japan prepared for invasion. Tons of food and ammunition lined a network of caves behind the beaches. A militia of some 32 million men and women, augmenting over 2.25 million ground troops, began to arm with everything available, from antique firearms to bows and arrows. They would never surrender. Despite the wreckage of industry, they had by late summer converted over 10,000 aircraft into fighting planes, mostly *kamikaze*, and readied the suicide boats on which Meuli had worked, each containing "four hundred pounds of explosives in the bow, a six-cylinder Chevrolet engine – probably made in the States – and just enough room for one Jap."

The POWs would be the first to die; meanwhile they would be utilized in the remaining war plants. Few had any illusions. Meuli helped dig a cellar, "to protect us from American planes, they said. But they never once put us down there. We concluded it was to put us in and destroy us if the Allies landed."

After incendiaries burned Kindel's barracks, "they set up machine guns to kill us all if they were invaded."

"That kind of took the enthusiasm out of it" for Aldrich at Kosaka, "but it was still exciting to hear our own planes and bombs and know the tide of war had turned."

Boyer watched civilians "sharpening their own spears. They didn't have rifles, but a bamboo spear will kill you as easy as a gun. The orders were to kill us all." They would also prove effective against landing paratroopers.

Warned of a pipeline nearby, Foy was told, "If the Americans land, we'll let the oil out, set it afire, and burn you all to death."

* * *

"A drone will come from out the East," wrote Jack Fleming in Manchuria. "And in that rain of steel and fire/Will come that freedom we desire . . . . " On 8 December 1944 it came, as ninety-one China-based B-29s bombed Mukden. Fletcher thought it "the most beautiful sight I ever saw – diving in, unloading in hard fire, then soaring out of range – a wonderful sight."

"They hit us to the day, to the hour – to the minute almost – that Clark Field was hit three years before," exulted Phillips. "We lay and watched them get a string of factories six miles long – plant after plant, all in a line. Those factories burned for days.

"One B-29 in the first formation drifted a little out of formation and was waggling its wings and bouncing, so we figured something was wrong with the bomb-delivery system. Then it came loose . . . ."

Directly above the cheering men, the bomb plummeted, and, as the men rushed for cover, crashed into their compound. It killed nineteen Americans.

Jack Fleming did not die immediately. He could have survived, a friend told Janie later, had he been in better physical condition. "But he was just a skeleton, shivering from cold, with no blanket. A friend found him one and covered him. When he returned – Jack was dead."

A friend of Burrola's was among the thirty-five injured. "His arm got blown off at the shoulder, and part of his scalp was lifted. The Jap commander told the guys to make recordings to send home begging the President not to bomb any more because we were getting killed. This guy said, 'I've lost an arm, but keep 'em coming! Give 'em hell!' All the boys said that. 'Keep 'em coming! Keep 'em coming!'"

"Japs shipping certain articles out of camp," Peck recorded on 14 April at Chen Chia Tung. "Looks like they expect something to happen up this way and want to get everything south they can." On 11 May he learned through his underground source that Germany had surrendered. The next day: "Something is going on . . . . All trains going north were almost empty this morning. Going south they are piled high with grain.

日本國民に告ぐ

あなたは自分や親兄弟友達の命を助けようとは思ひませんか助けたければこのビラをよく讀んで下さい

數日の内に裏面の都市の内全部若くは若干の都市にある軍事施設を米空軍は爆撃します

この都市には軍事施設や軍需品を製造する工場があります軍部がこの勝目のない戦爭を長引かせる爲に使ふ兵器を米空軍は全部破壊しますけれども爆彈には眼がありませんからどこに落ちるか分りません御承知の様に人道主義のアメリカは罪のない人達を傷つけたくはありませんですから裏に書いてある都市から避難して下さい

アメリカの敵はあなた方ではありませんあなた方を戦爭に引つ張り込んでゐる軍部こそ敵ですアメリカの考へてゐる平和といふのはたゞ軍部の壓迫からあなた方を解放する事ですさうすればもつとよい新日本が出來上るんです

戦爭を止める様な新指導者を樹てて平和を恢復したらどうですか

この裏に書いてある都市でなくても爆撃されるかも知れませんが少くともこの裏に書いてある都市の内必ず全部若くは若干は爆撃します

豫め注意しておきますから裏に書いてある都市から避難して下さい

B-29s showered Japanese cities with leaflets such as these, advising the evacuation of all civilians, prior to massive bombings. (Courtesy: Walter Haut, USAF Ret.)

Yesterday the Japs started to pack things in the warehouse and worked until 2 a.m. . . . . " On 20 May, the POWs entrained for Mukden.

There, Schmitz noted, "they were plowing a big hole, to run us into, we heard, if the Americans started coming, and bulldoze us under. By that we figured it was getting closer."

"Japan is losing the war," a guard told Baclawski at Kosaka. "Our cities are destroyed. The war will end soon."

Evans "could occasionally hear bombing off in the distance. One night there was an almost steady bombardment all night. Some of the Navy guys said it sounded like heavy guns off a cruiser or battleship."[6]

It was. Off Kamaichi, "on 14 July, the American Navy pulled up," about two miles out, Munsey estimated, "and started shelling the steel mill and the town. They managed to close all the railroad tunnels to the outside world. Our barracks were burned and all our belongings. We were taken out to the mountainside."

"Being shelled by those 16-inch guns," Chintis believed, "was the most devastating act of war I ever experienced. Our camp was burned down and the mill was leveled. We were in a state of chaos. We lost about seventy-five men, and we had a lot of burn patients. I took care of sixteen."

Marching to work at Niigata on 27 July, Shillito saw "thousands of leaflets falling all around us. The guards were going crazy trying to keep us from picking them up. Tony King deciphered one." They were copies of the Potsdam Declaration. Japan could surrender unconditionally or be destroyed. The weapon of that destruction, though not named, would be an atomic device, recently – some later said fittingly – perfected high on a New Mexican plateau and successfully tested in a New Mexican desert.

The leaflet King deciphered contained another warning: Evacuate the town immediately, it counseled. The prisoners uneasily wondered why.

---

6 Evans 135.

* * *

Fires from a heavy raid surrounded Hamblin's barracks at Toyama. Climbing to the roof to extinguish sparks, he saw in every direction "fire and confusion. Even the birds were stunned. A pigeon lit near me and I picked him up. Here at last was the retribution that we had often wished," but to Hamblin, "the screams of terror I heard from women and children were no different than I would have heard if this had been an American city." He could not, he confessed, "be glad or feel vengeance."

When bombs hit Maibara on 8 August, Rhee was herded to the hills. "The Japs there kept saying the word *ninchoku.* They were exact and adamant. We didn't know the word. After the raid, I looked in my dictionary. *Ninchoku* meant something electronic. We still didn't know what it was."

The Japanese commandant at Rokuroshi summoned Boyer. "He asked what was this new weapon the Americans had. We decided it must be devastating because he was so wrought up. 'It's so terrible,' he said. 'What kind of weapon is it?' Of course we didn't know, but we went back and told our men, 'We've got something that really blew their minds!' In a few days he called us back and asked again. Whatever it was, we knew something terrible had happened – and it had happened twice."

A guard at Fukuoka blamed McBride for a near-fatal cave in, and beat him "until I suppose I ceased to stir. Perhaps he thought I was dead." When McBride regained consciousness above ground, he heard British prisoners discussing "a huge dark cloud against the sky some thirty miles distant."

What, startled Americans and awed Japanese asked fearfully, was this Great Black Smoke?

– 27 –

"SENSO OWARI"

"And thanks to God, the Rising Sun went down, and the Stars and Stripes went up. Then everybody, sick and crippled, got up off those lousy barracks slats and walked out into the sunshine, and once again we saluted Old Glory."

– Private First Class Marlin E. Sartin –

While McBride lay unconscious on the surface at Fukuoka, Rhea Tow, deep underground, "knew something had happened. Our light went out and our air pressure was dropping. In the main shaft the Japs were gone. We waited for a car, or some word what had happened. Our cap lights were playing out and our air was getting bad, so we started out. We climbed for hours. Topside, we saw smoke and fire from Nagasaki, forty miles away."

* * *

When the Japanese failed to respond to the Potsdam Declaration, Truman made his decision. A mere demonstration, as some advised, would not end the war, he believed, but would imperil all prisoners, and would necessitate an invasion which would cost the lives of over 1,000,000 American troops, countless Japanese, and every POW.

Thc mission would procccd from Tinian as soon aftcr 3 August as weather allowed, to any of four possible targets: Hiroshima, Kokura, Niigata, or Nagasaki. On 4 August, B-29s showered thousands of leaflets on those areas: Evacuate your civilians. Most ignored the warnings.

At 0245 on the morning of 6 August, thc *Enola Gay* lifted from its runway: Destination Hiroshima.

Unloading a coal barge at Oeyama at 0815, James felt the ground shake violently. At Hirohata, Ragsdale saw "smoke across the bay, a terrible black cloud that hung there several days." At Tsuruga, Cisneros watched a mushroom rise, "and debris began to fall on us. Next day the guard said a 'Number One Bomb' blew up a whole city." At Rokuroshi, Foy saw the fire and thought, "My God, the Yanks are landing and the Japs have fired the oil."

Toward morning an eerie fog rolled inland. Stroope felt "a hush over the land, and we knew the guards were afraid of something."

Three days later on southern Kyushu, Kindel "saw a ball of fire across the bay toward Nagasaki, and thought they'd hit an ammunition dump." The ground rolled beneath Tillman "like ocean waves."

Those in the north heard strange tales. "One bomb killed 80,000 people," his honcho told Aldrich. No one believed it. "It killed all the fishes in the bay," a guard told Gilcrease. "We just laughed." When an interpreter described it to Huxtable, "we said he'd had too much *sake*."

That bomb had been intended for Kokura, home of the Yawata Steel Works. Harris heard the circling planes. "But they had firebombed the town, and the fog and smoke were so thick we couldn't even see across the street. So they flew on."

Another alternative was Niigata. A few days after the leaflets fell, "a single plane came over." Steen heard something fall. "There was a huge explosion in the air, like we'd never heard before. Then nothing happened. I've wondered if maybe they did drop one – a dud – and kept it quiet. Because something went off up there." Unlikely – but stranger secrets have been plowed beneath the dumps of history.

In their camps, the prisoners saw fear, despair, and anger among the guards. In Tokyo, the Cabinet stared at doom and debated alternatives.

The barrages resumed. Though Kedzie returned to the mines at Hitachi, "they hadn't any smelter to send the ore to. Then the battleships laid siege, and after that the B-29s, and when the smoke cleared, the city was leveled."

The renewed barrage on Kamaichi seemed to Munsey "even heavier than the first. What was left of the steel mill was now in ruins. We were again moved to another building, as the second one had burned."

"We were a mess – dirty, no food – and that night they issued us white shirts." It meant one of two things, Chintis predicted. "Either the war is over or we're going to die tomorrow."

On 10 August the Imperial Government asked terms. On the twelfth the Allies responded: The Japanese could retain their Emperor, but only subject to the Supreme Allied Commander. While Tokyo debated, a group of fanatic Army officers conspired to seize the Palace, imprison the negotiators, and renew the fighting.

On the fourteenth, a single B-29 snowed leaflets over Tokyo, apprising a startled people of the negotiations; and the Emperor heard the differing opinions of his hastily convened Cabinet. But the final arguments had been delivered at Hiroshima and Nagasaki. The Emperor spoke: His people must suffer no longer. The war must end.

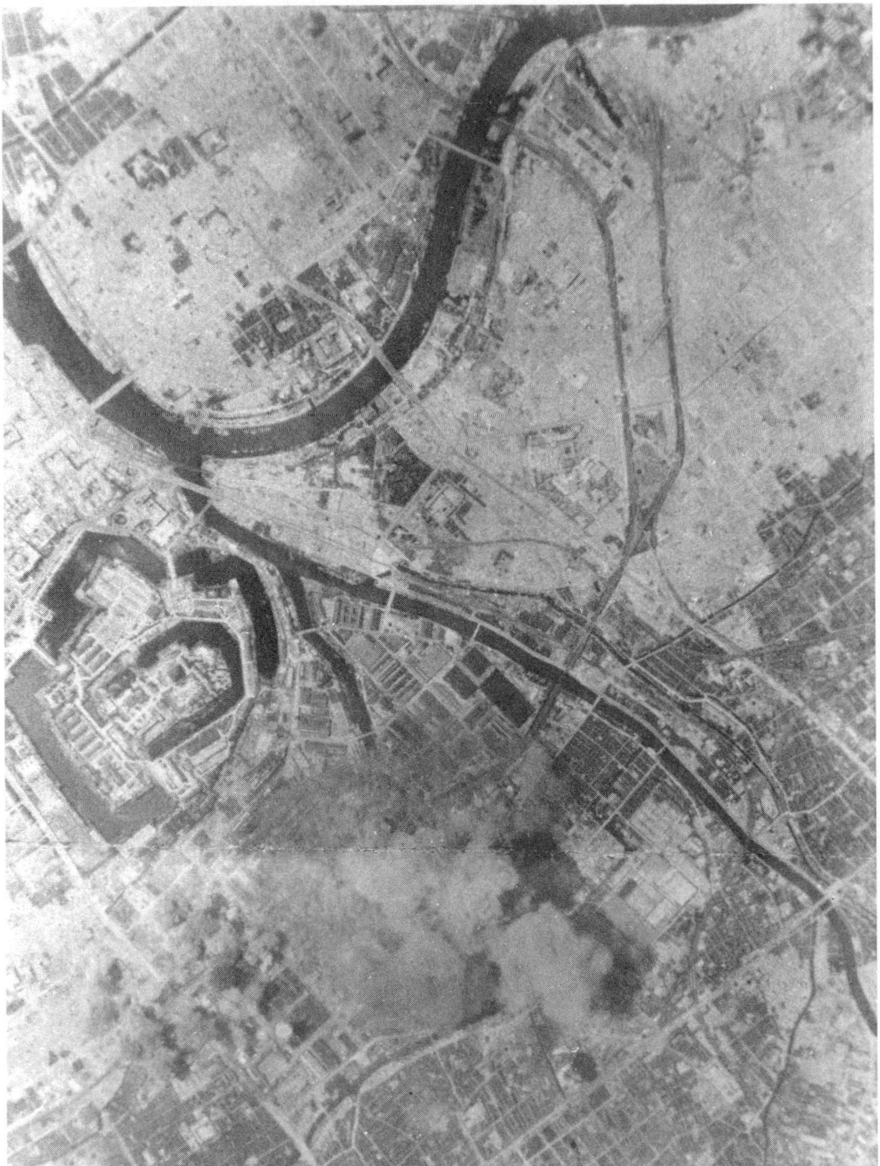

Aerial photograph of Hiroshima burning. (Photo source: Osaka Army ARS. Courtesy: Walter Haut, USAF Ret.)

This decision crushed the revolt.[1] To oppose the Divine Will was unthinkable. That night the Imperial Government transmitted acceptance of Allied terms and announced to his subjects that their Emperor would broadcast an unprecedented message. Never had an Emperor of Japan spoken directly to his people.

What, wondered the stunned nation, would he say?

James was "at the docks when the Emperor broadcast. The Japs all bowed to the loudspeaker. We couldn't understand what he said, but suddenly we didn't have to go back to work." At the steel mill, Don Harris "heard the Emperor say *senso owari* – and we knew what that meant!"[2]

At Rokuroshi, Bond saw senior American officers come from the Japanese commandant's office. "Colonel Miller came into our barracks and said, 'Gentlemen, I've just been informed the war is over!'" There was a long silence, and then Long jumped on a chair. "Well," he hollered, "tell us who won!"

In all the camps, the most notoriously brutal of the guards began to disappear.

Johns "heard the honcho say we didn't have to work for two weeks, and that night they didn't come around to harass us, and nobody was in the guard shack. But they had machine guns outside the perimeter, and we thought they were waiting for us to make a break and then open up."

Gunter "sat in our hut a couple of days, until a guy said, 'I'm going to see if these SOBs will shoot.' He stepped out and nothing happened. Guys started sticking their heads out like rats from a hole, and then began to creep out, till we were all running everywhere. They found rifles stacked at the guardhouse. Some of the guards lived close by – they shot those that was dumb enough to stay around."

At Niigata, Steen "saw them all at attention, and the radio blaring. Then they took us back to camp. Japs were leaving the

---

1 Before the revolt was quelled, the mutineers killed Lieutenant General Takeshi Mori, Commander of the Konoye Division, burned the homes of Prime Minister Kantaro Suzuki and President of the Privy Council Baron Kiichiro Hiranuma, and gained the Palace itself.

2 *Senso owari*: The war is over.

factories and the fields, with shovels and hoes over their shoulders, and all with just blank stares.

"That night they let us have the lights on, and at the guardhouse they started burning papers. After three days we were about to have a riot – hell, we were starving. The war had been over several days, and that damned Fellows knew it, but he was scared to tell us. We'd all sworn to kill him."

Aldrich stood at attention at Kosaka "while the interpreter told us the war was over. We looked at each other. There wasn't a sound. He said he hoped we wouldn't run around the countryside killing and raping women and so on. When he went into the guardhouse, we were still standing dumb. Then suddenly it hit home. We looked at each other and started screaming and yelling. We ripped off our ID patches, and began to sing – 'God Bless America.'"

In Albuquerque, Paul McCahon fought to live long enough to see his son once more. Sapped by war work and long illness, he died the day Tokyo asked for terms. "As did our boys on Bataan, so did 'Mac' give his all for them," wrote Dr. Spensely, and, reflecting the BRO pledge, added, "He did not let them down."[3]

Janie Fleming still monitored her shortwave radio each night. "But – thank God – I wasn't listening the night they broadcast about our nineteen men killed in the Mukden bombing – and read Jack's name. A lady who heard it wrote Jack's mother. His father intercepted the letter. He didn't tell us. I was leaving for work one morning when the Western Union boy handed me the telegram with three black stars. That was the day the world came to an end."

Barbara Hutchison had earlier learned of Russell's death, closed her home, and moved away from the memories. Not until the war was over would she learn he still lived.

Lucy Wilson at last accepted what she had so long refused to believe. "I knew if Dan was alive I would have known it by then. So I said, 'Okay, send me back to the States.' I knew Dan was dead."

---

3 BRO *Bulletin*, No. 5, 8 September 1945.

View from inside prison camp at Mukden, taken with a "liberated" camera, showing Japanese troops filing past to surrender. Factories in the city are evident in the background. (Courtesy: Wallace Phillips.)

* * *

On 8 August Russia declared war on Japan. Armored troops were already racing across the Manchurian border; on the tenth they invaded Korea. Alarmed by the bomb at Hiroshima and fearful he had delayed too long, Stalin meant to assure by conquest what he had gained by guile at Yalta. Soviet troops raced for the spoils.

At Mukden, the Japanese officers grew sullen, and the guards edgy. Sounds of distant firing heralded approaching troops. On the sixteenth, Fletcher saw "a strange plane in the southwest flying out of the sun. As it came over, six men bailed out."

They were an OSS team, one of several 'mercy missions' sent by General A.C. Wedemeyer to prevent the wholesale murder of the POWs before the rescue teams could reach the far areas of Korea and Manchuria.

Stripped and surrounded by an angry squad with bayonets fixed, and forced to kneel, the team, headed by Major James Hennessy, talked fast. The war was over, they insisted. Eventually the confused Japanese escorted them blindfolded to headquarters, and at length to the commandant. Colonel Matsuda contacted Tokyo.

At the leather tannery, Burrola was unaware of the drama in the main camp, "but when they rang the quitting bell early we knew something was up. They were all excited, and they took us back to the main camp."

It was announced next morning.

"WAR OVER!" Peck exulted. "Will be with you soon, dearest."

As MacArthur arranged for the formal surrender, Soviet tanks raced for Mukden, Soviet ships closed in on Dairen and Port Arthur, and Soviet troops seized the Kuriles and south Sakhalin Island. Meanwhile, though technically free, the men at Mukden would remain under Japanese control until liberation troops arrived. "Keep cool," Hennessy advised. "They have the guns."

On the nineteenth, American planes landed with food and medicine. When the Japanese refused to let them unload, they took off and dropped the supplies by parachute.

On the twentieth, the Russians arrived. In his sub-camp, Alex "heard Russian tanks outside, and then bombers from Kunming dropped food. We couldn't assimilate it – eat, vomit, eat, vomit, cry. And they dropped music. First time I ever heard 'Sentimental Journey.' We put speakers on the parade ground and played it over and over.

"Then the Russians hit. We were standing on a building and a Russky fired at the roof. They knocked down the wooden gate with a tank, and a Red stuck his head out and asked, 'Were any of these Japs cruel?' A guy named Pitlak pointed at one standing in a group by the guardhouse, and that Russian opened up his machine gun and chopped all four in half."

Into the main camp rolled the Red troops – "a rag-tag bunch of Siberians," Sakelares called them. Fletcher listened while their general "made a long speech. 'We come to rescue Americanskis,' he says, and wanted us to shoot at the Jap guards. Major General George Parker said we couldn't touch 'em. What he didn't know was there was a lot of 'em 'touched.'"

The ex-POWs swarmed into Mukden when the Soviets declared it an open city for three days. Burrola "put on clothes the Americans had dropped, and took the Jap stuff to town on a wagon, and sold it. We found a warehouse full of beer, and carried a wagonload back to the barracks. Had a great time until the Russians found out. They were not nice."

Sakelares and Skarda "took over a whole brewery until the Reds did the same thing and started shooting at us." At the Mauser factory, Sakelares grabbed a rifle. Phillips was right behind him, "but by the time I got there, the Russians were guarding it too. The OSS commander told us to stay in camp after that before somebody got killed."

Burrola watched the Soviets "strip all the machines out of the factories. They took it out in trainload after trainload – all that big, beautiful American machinery."

Padilla "went AWOL for a week to find out what they were doing. They took out every piece of equipment." Three women in the Soviet Army invited Padilla and his buddies into their

Ernest Montoya at Mukden after liberation with two young Manchu friends. At his left is Soshi, whom the Americans called their "facilitator," because of his help in smuggling food into camp. The Americans made sure Soshi was well cared for after the war. (Courtesy: Wallace Phillips.)

boxcars, "to see how good Americans were at drinking vodka,' they said. Then it got dark and they asked us to stay all night. There was a fight every evening between the Chinese and the Japs, and then the Russians would start firing. So we stayed – for four days. They may have suspected we were spying. Anyhow, they wouldn't let us go. On the fifth day we ran out of vodka and food, and I said I'd go find some – and we took off."

The Russians had come to stay. They turned captured Japanese arms over to the Chinese Communists – despite earlier promises – and became increasingly hostile to Americans. Donaldson awaited evacuation with other critically ill Americans. "They cut the tires on the first American plane in, and we had to wait for more tires to be flown in. The Americans finally got twenty-two of us out, all litter cases."

It was not an isolated act. Poe watched appalled as "those durned Russians cut the tires off of every American plane that sat down." Soon after, they refused to let American planes land.

The Soviets clearly wanted no surveillance, there or elsewhere, particularly by OSS teams. Outside Suchow, they murdered Captain John M. Birch and mutilated his body. In Mukden, as OSS men snapped pictures of gutted factories and glutted trains, the Russians, who had forcibly detained the last Americans, suddenly ordered them out. Hennessy was given twenty-four hours to evacuate.

By October the Russian conquest of Manchuria was complete.

As the news of freedom began to filter into the Japanese camps, men cheered, or wept, or remembered dead comrades and swallowed hard lumps. Senter felt numb. "It was too new – we weren't prepared for it." Woody Hutchison's first thought was "that never again would we go to bed hungry."

When Commander Harold Stassen flew into Niigata to evacuate the seriously ill, the despised Major Fellows enjoined the men to stay inside the compound and left with him. "Stay, hell!" cried the major left in charge. "We won the war. Take those guards' guns and open the gates!"

That was all Shillito needed. "All hell broke loose. The walls started coming down and we headed for town. We never saw a Jap, till we wound up in the red-light district – they hadn't gotten the word. We caroused awhile. We didn't really do anything. About half a dozen guys stayed – I think they were sorry later – and the rest of us went back to camp."

MacArthur placed top priority on locating the camps and sending immediate relief in food, medicine, and clothing until the men could be evacuated. While they waited, the men raided storage areas or scavenged the countryside.

Doolis sent his interpreter for a chicken. "And I took his pistol. That hurt – it was his symbol of authority. And I made him fry my chicken the way I liked it. But – I felt kind of sorry for him, and when I left I gave him back his pistol."

Gulbas butchered the ox that pulled a 'honey wagon' at Nagoya, "and we told the interpreter to get all those yen we hadn't been paid, stuff it into the cart, and not come back."

They began to mark their camps. Those without paint spelled out POW with blankets, grass rugs, or stones. Navy pursuit planes scoured the countryside, some with American flags streaming from their bomb bays, and they dropped notes in cigarette packages. "Just a few more days, boys," read one. "We'll be back," promised another. And at Kosaka: "Japan has just surrendered to Texas!"

The Navy men dropped what food they had, often only K-rations, to suffice until the big drops could come. "Best eating we ever had," swore Pelayo. When a quart of whiskey wrapped in a mattress fell in Meuli's camp, "the medical officer treated it as medicine. We each got one spoonful."

As bombers came over Ashio, Huxtable saw "big sea bags on parachutes come sliding out. The first one hit beyond the fence, tied three guys up in a chute, and drug 'em right out."

At Tsuruga, Senter "and four other radio men took over a Jap radio station, contacted San Francisco, told them we were without food, and gave them our location. In a couple of days we got load after load."

If he had medicine, a doctor at Nagoya pled, he could save some dying men; but the Japanese refused to let them mark the camp. Gulbas suggested Morse code. "We went to the Jap

B-29s over Mukden making one of the many U.S. Air Force food drops to newly freed POWs at war's end. (Courtesy: Wallace Phillips.)

commandant's office, and I said, 'Doc, if he makes one move I'll kill him.' We took his signal equipment up on the guard tower and started flashing SOS to a Navy plane, and he kept circling while I flashed the doctor's list. He dropped a note, 'Medicine under way,' and after a while a B-29 came in and parachuted three big bundles in GI mattresses. That doctor almost cried. They had pills and vitamins – and five quarts of good Stateside whiskey!"

Over Steen's camp "they unloaded food, clothes, medicine, and a picture of the A-bomb at Alamogordo, with a note that said, 'Our ship is cleaned out. The Army takes over tomorrow.'"[4]

When Johns heard the B-29s, he thought, "'This war ain't over yet.' Then one started circling, and the bomb-bay door opened, and we thought, 'That dirty SOB's going to drop it down our pipes.' A note hit in the compound – 'Clear the area, we're dropping food.'"

Falling objects looked to Huxtable like "cans of tomatoes, and the closer they got the bigger they got. They were fifty-five-gallon drums," on red, white, and blue parachutes. The men began to cheer.

Atop his building, Doolis saw a drum hit the end of a barracks. "It went right through, and flattened the whole damn thing. Then it hit the mountainside and exploded. There was peaches and 'K' bars from here to hell. One guy was on the mess-hall roof. It knocked him through holes as it came, and he fell in the soup pot."

Hutchison hid under a bridge as "one hit with an explosion. When the air cleared, I saw it was flour. One barrel was full of candy, and it was soldered, so we got a hammer and chisel, which left a sharp edge, and when I reached in I cut an artery. The blood spewed – but I got my candy bar!"

4 Though the wait seemed long to the anxious men, the operation was remarkable for its speed and engineering. While carrier-based Navy planes scouted, spotted, and flew rescue missions to evacuate the most serious medical cases, Air Corps operational engineers located, amassed, transported to Saipan, and packaged food and medical supplies for the 69,000 prisoners for the estimated 30 days it would take to rescue them, and the 63,000 parachutes needed to drop them. Test flights ascertained load capacities and speed and altitudes for the drops. From 27 August to 20 September, 900 flights dropped 4,470 tons of supplies on 158 camps. MacArthur *Reports*, Vol. 1, Pt. 2, 89-99.

One load hit a bakery, which was immediately drenched with red. "My God," thought Lucas, "they've killed a hundred people." It was fifty-five gallons of ketchup.

Bombs had been bad enough for McCahon, "but to see a fifty-five-gallon drum of fruit salad coming at you – and they turn, and you don't know where they're going to hit – guys were running back and forth. One did hit a fellow. It shattered his leg." Chintis thought it cruelly ironic "to see a man who had starved for four years get killed by a can of peaches."

Steen "filled buckets with soup and juice and pork and beans and fruit – put it in one big pot and stirred it up. We had a fine meal! Later the Air Corps realized those drums were too heavy for the chutes, and they started dropping them in cases strapped together. But they wouldn't stay strapped – it was like a danged air raid."

Shillito grabbed a buddy's arm. "He was blind from beriberi. I just stood there with him. There was no place to go."

Hunger conquered fear. Bond found a friend "laying on his stomach, drinking milk, right off the ground." Chintis found Hershey bars, "scattered all over the hillside. I sat in the middle of them. I'd unwrap one, take a bite, and throw it away. Unwrap another, take a bite – I must have done that to a couple of dozen. And I paid the price that night."

The officers' camp at Rokuroshi still waited. With a 'liberated' Japanese radio, Boyer "picked up broadcasts that the war was over, and to paint POW on our roof for food drops. But we hadn't seen any flyovers, and we had to have food.

"Five officers commandeered a train to Fukui. They'd had a drop, but wouldn't give our men any, until one asked, 'You got any 200th or 515th officers up there?' They said 'Yeah,' and those guys filled blankets full. Our men brought them back, but they said, 'This is just for 200th officers – those damn New Mexicans are still taking care of each other!' Of course we shared. But there it was again – that feeling we had for each other in the old 200th. It was still strong."

Old Glory flew again in every camp.

Lucas, Turner, and Taggert took the colored parachutes to town and told the tailor to make a huge American flag – by morning, they said, even if the whole town worked all night. They got it.

The ceremonies moved the men deeply. James "stood at attention as our flag went up. The tears were big, and they were scalding hot, and they ran down all our cheeks."

Sartin "never forgot those beautiful words, 'Everybody that can walk, come out and salute the American flag!' And thanks to God, the Rising Sun went down, and the Stars and Stripes went up. Then everybody, sick and crippled, got up off those lousy barracks slats and walked out into the sunshine, and once again we saluted Old Glory."

Boyer was one of three officers chosen to raise the new flag at Rokuroshi, "because I had a good pair of britches. I kept them all through the war. I said I'd go naked, but I wouldn't wear my 'victory britches' until we won the war. So I represented the Army. We ran up that homemade flag. We'd had to unravel cloth for thread to sew it with, but it was a great old flag to us. There wasn't a dry eye in the bunch."

Major Dorris from the 200th was senior officer at Fukuoka 3. "[Major Yaichi] Rikitaki, the Jap commander, used to harass Dorris – tell him he was dishonorable and should have committed *hara-kiri*, and never surrendered, and all that stuff." Don Harris relished the day when "Rikitaki surrendered his sword – and Dorris handed it back, and said, 'Now you may commit *hara-kiri*.'"

Rikitaki declined the honor.

Strengthened by food and joy, men grew impatient and many ranged the countryside. Russell Hutchison set out for Camp 23. He rode a baggage car to the end of its run, then walked through the night with an old Japanese guide. At two in the morning he pounded on the gate.

An apprehensive lieutenant appeared. "My God, where did you come from?"

"Don't you know the war is over?"

Only, he said, that the Japanese had gone.

"Do you know Marvin Lucas?"

The lieutenant nodded: Lucas was their American commander.

"*Senso Owari*" – War's End – here snapped with a "liberated" Japanese camera. When Commandant Rikitaki of Fukuoka #3 surrendered his sword to Major Winnifred Dorris of the 200th, Dorris immediately returned it: Having listened endlessly to Rikitaki rant of American cowardice for having chosen surrender to suicide, Dorris here offers him the honor. Rikitaki declined. (Courtesy: Don Harris.)

"Wake him up and tell him to get his butt out here, that the Jap commander's mad!" It was a dirty trick, Hutchison later confessed – but a reunion they never forgot.

Many went in search of American troops. Norval Tow and eight others "stopped a train, kicked the Japs off the first two cars, unhooked the rest, and went to Yokohama."

Armijo gathered parachutes and traded them for *sake*. "Evans Garcia and I got drunk, took over a train, and headed south, where we'd heard there was an American air base. Evans rode with the engineer, and I was back with the chickens and pigs. We got off two days later and crossed the river and walked to the base. God, those guys looked big, and we were so skinny. 'You guys Americans?' they asked, and we said, 'Yeah, Bataan.' They picked us up and squeezed us. Gave us a bath and deloused us, and next day they flew us to Okinawa."

Rhee entrained for Tokyo, "to see the Yanks come in." When an armed *Kempei* tried to stop him, "I grabbed his rifle and pushed him back and went through. We were drunk with victory. In Tokyo, I asked a Jap, 'Where are the Americans?'

"He said, 'In Tokyo? There aren't any!' Christ, we didn't know what to do. Finally we ran into four paratroopers and a reporter who'd come from Yokohama looking for liquor, and we all decided to go to the Imperial Hotel. We stopped a Chrysler limousine with two Navy Japs inside, and said, 'Take us to the Imperial.'

"They said they would like to, but the Admiral was waiting for his car. One of the troops stuck a pistol in the driver's face, and we all piled in.

"The Imperial was filled with reporters. We answered their questions and talked for hours, and they shared their K-rations – which we thought tasted wonderful. At two in the morning, one said, 'Let's get a room,' and he jumped over the desk and got a key. The room was assigned to a Mr. Mishimura, but I wrote him a note. 'We are sorry to cause you discomfort, but your room has been occupied. By us.'"

Ross headed for Yokohama. "Between trains at Moji, we rolled up our shoes in towels for pillows and slept on a cement slab where a building had burned. That night a train came in and a whole Jap army unloaded and bedded down all around us, still carrying their sabers and rifles. We just lay there like we were asleep, until close to dawn we heard a train whistle, and I said, 'I'm getting on if I have to ride the cow catcher.' We almost did – we rode in the tender."

Chintis and two friends hiked over the mountain to a railhead. "We asked for passes to Yokohama and scared the wits out of the man at the depot, wondering who we were and where we came from.

"Several hours out, we pulled on a siding. We were all alone in this car – three of us – and it starts loading up with wounded Jap soldiers. We didn't know what to do – we weren't armed, and we were more or less at their mercy. I offered the captain a cigarette. He just glared.

"At Sendai, a Jap interpreter told us to get off. I said nuts, we were going to Yokohama. He said, 'You're not in very good company. I'll wire ahead for your safety. What are your names?'

"We said, 'Charlie Chaplin, Stan Laurel, and Oliver Hardy.' He took it all down.

"In Yokohama a tough-looking major met us. 'Who is Charlie Chaplin?' I raised my hand. He said, 'Who is Laurel? and Hardy?' They raised theirs. He said, 'Bunch of comedians, aren't you? Well, the colonel doesn't think it's very funny. You were told to stay put, and you're still in the United States Army, whether you realize it or not.'

"The colonel chewed us out for a while, and then he smiled a little. 'I don't know,' he said, 'I guess if I was in your place, waiting around after four years of what you guys went through, I'd probably have jumped camp too.'"

Within a month, recovery teams had gotten all ex-POWs to ports of embarkation. "There'll Be a Hot Time in the Old Town Tonight," blared the Negro band that greeted one group. "What a sensation," Harrington recorded, "to see real Stateside Yankees!"

Few held rancor. Seeing a guard who had lost both legs in a bombing raid, James "loaded him down with food and cigarettes. You know Americans – in the stations, we'd see the little kids that used to spit at us and throw rocks. We'd throw 'em candy and gum. I didn't want to kill any Japs. I just wanted to go home."

While Kedzie was waiting on the pier, "it got dark, and we wanted food. A colonel said the cooks had gone to bed, and we said, 'We don't give a damn, we're hungry.' He left in a huff. Then some men came off the hospital ship drinking beer, and we offered to swap souvenirs for food. A chief petty officer said, 'What'll you take?' We said, 'Four cases of beer and two hundred sandwiches.'" They got them.

On the hospital ships they were deloused. Steen opened his shirt, "and they squirted us with this stuff – really fogged it in there – and the god-durned fleas flew out like butterflies. A couple of hours went by, and I said, 'I'm not being eat on!' It was so calm, you just wanted to lay over and go to sleep."

A shower felt so good to Foy, "they had to run us out." They luxuriated in new clothes. And they ate.

On the destroyer that carried Aldrich from Sendai to Tokyo, "we went through the breakfast line – hot cakes, eggs, bacon, sausage, coffee, milk, toast – and as soon as we'd finish eating, we'd go back through. We ate breakfast all day long."

Baclawski ate twelve eggs. "The fellow next to me ate twenty-one. And Spam – the crew wouldn't eat the stuff, but we just shoveled it down."

And when a Navy nurse asked Harrington what kind of ice cream he wanted, he began to stammer: He had forgotten ice cream came in flavors.

They began to feel detached. When James saw MacArthur approach, "I never even saluted him. He walked right by me, with that corn pipe and about fifteen generals behind him – and I just stood there. I guess he knew I was nuts."

McCahon boarded a hospital ship in Korea. "They didn't know how to handle us. A fellow had malaria chills, and it scared them silly. We said, 'He's okay, just put some blankets on him.' They got rid of us next day and put us on a Liberty Ship."

The long, long journey was nearly done. They must leave their dead behind, and look to life. And yet –

Some wondered if wife or sweetheart still waited, if parents still lived.

Some battled to board the first planes out. More, like Chintis, preferred a slow boat, "to gain some weight and look presentable," or maybe to set their minds to grapple with the new-found freedom.

His father's farewell haunted Ojinaga. "'Don't ever dishonor your country,' he told me. And we were surrendered. It wasn't our choice, but – still, we felt we had failed. I wasn't sure I wanted to go back. I kept remembering those words."

The "Sentimental Journey" had begun. But four years held a lifetime. Each man looked homeward, and felt himself a stranger, and drew closer to his buddies –

They understood.

– 28 –

"O FAIR NEW MEXICO"

"And we jumped off the train and kissed the ground. This – this was – New Mexico!"
– Sergeant Maynard Meuli –

Donaldson was near death when the replacements for the slashed tires reached Mukden. With a blood transfusion at Kunming, he felt the life resurge, enough to survive the flight home to the States. A month later, a larger group entrained at Mukden for Port Arthur, and there boarded a transport for Okinawa.

Sakelares thought he'd never make it home. "First the Russians wouldn't let us out; then the worst typhoon they'd ever had struck; and then we hit a mine. We were a hundred miles from nowhere and sinking, in waves like mountains."

Phillips "heard it slam the forward magazine, wash out and back in, and hit the engine room. Our power was gone and we

Going Home: Phillips snapped this picture shortly after a mine hit the transport he, Fletcher, Sakelares, and Calvin Buckner were aboard. The gush of water marks the resultant hole in the forward magazine. (Courtesy: Wallace Phillips.)

were bobbing like a cork. A cruiser alongside laid oil on the waves and radioed a seagoing tug. There was no panic. Just disgust. 'Wouldn't you know,' one guy said, 'on our way home – and we hit a mine.'"

Fletcher "sat out there a long time, thinking we were goners, and settling fast, till here come a tug." Close by, Sakelares heard a radioed command to abandon ship, "but our Captain refused, and we laid in the storm a couple of days, until that tug towed us into Buckner Bay. We'd barely climbed out when the ship sank."

Those freed in Japan were funneled through Yokohama and the battle-gutted Okinawa – muddy, blackened, with areas of uncleared land mines, and rows of new-made crosses. Rhee "crawled through caves where they'd burned the Japs out. And later they told us – those caves still held snipers!"

In a Red Cross tent, an older man approached Phillips and Calvin Buckner, "finds out we're POWs, and says he'd round up a couple of vehicles next day and show us some new aircraft. He had no insignia, and we figured he was a gunnery sergeant.

"Next morning four flights of Hellcats came over so low the mess tents started flapping. There in a Jeep sits our friend, with insignia on today – a Marine Corps general! We started to salute, and he says, 'None of that crap.' He couldn't get any vehicles, so he brought the air show to us. They were good – flying under phone wires – having a ball.

"'And you know,' the general said, 'half of 'em don't even shave every day!'"

The sight of women unnerved many. Armijo saw his first WAACs and "wondered what had happened to the Army." Phillips and Buckner sat in a Red Cross shack, "awed by the hostess. We hadn't seen an American girl for four years. We just sat and listened to her talk. It was beautiful."

Beautiful, Aldrich agreed, but terrifying. "Nurses would bring us coffee, and ask if we wanted anything – and we were too tongue-tied even to answer." On a hospital ship, Doolis stood in his shorts, "with my arms and legs all skinny, and my stomach sticking out from all that sudden food, and I said to the nurse, 'This is a hell of a way to meet the first friendly white woman I've seen in four years!'"

* * *

Going home.

Next stop, Luzon. They crammed into whatever could fly, many onto wooden benches rigged in bomb bays. When the door jarred loose on a plane alongside Steen's, those in the bay fell to their deaths. "They didn't have their chutes on. Hell, we didn't either – we were in the tail, playing with the machine guns – pretending we were shooting Japs."

Some flew through typhoons. Rhee, in an "old DC-3 that was jumping like a folk dancer," clung to his seat. Those with Kedzie "had Mae Wests, but no cartridges to inflate them." A few planes went down.

Sailing was slower, though less hazardous, and it had its compensations. Norval Tow boarded a transport "a *kamikaze* had knocked the bridge off of. It was crippled, and it was slow, but they fed us – anything we wanted, anytime!" What did they want most? Ice cream! They ate gallons.

Reunions were jubilant, and tearful. Shock pierced their joy when, seeking old comrades, they found so few returned. Romero spied Tony Reyna and Jimmy-K Lujan, from his pueblo, called out their Indian names, "and then we are all crying like a baby."[1]

At the 29th Replacement Depot, staging area for the last leg home, the New Mexicans sought each other out and held a grand reunion. The Regiment was back together – what remained of it. Processing and interrogation caused problems for some. Sakelares found a friend crying, "because he couldn't prove who he was – the Japs had taken our dog tags – and we had to wait for fingerprinting."

The seriously ill were evacuated quickly. The rest stood by – "to fatten us up," Boyer was told, "before anyone in the States

[1] A number of theories try to explain the disproportionately high percentage of American Indian deaths in prison camps, ranging from an alleged genetic intolerance for the rice diet to a proposed psychological inability to adjust to the loss of freedom. Perhaps the most compelling answer is one given the author by a pueblo-born survivor: "We speak English and Spanish okay. But when a man is very low he needs to talk in the language of his soul. They send us all different places, you know. My people died of loneliness."

saw us." But the sudden food took its toll. Many, like Banegas, "gained weight so fast my face hurt when I touched it, and my legs puffed up so it hurt to walk."

Given money and the run of the island, most headed for Manila, bombed, blackened, but bustling – "a sprawling ghost city of tents," Harrington found it. Those debarking from the USS *Noble* were warned against the liquor, "most of which is wood alcohol," and advised that "venereal disease is rampant."

"MacArthur ordered the MPs to leave us alone unless we were stealing, raping, or killing," and in their new freedom, Don Harris saw "guys wander off and miss their boats. They didn't care, though – they'd get another." Burrola "wouldn't go home. I was with my old buddies, and we were having too much fun."

At a Red Cross dance, Bond laughed at Suttman, "in really bad shape from beriberi. But he danced, and for once, never stepped on his partners' toes – he couldn't lift his feet that high!"

There were tensions. Ross arrived "just before the big race riot. You could feel it in the air. In the cabarets there'd be the blacks lined up on one side and the whites on the other, all glaring. A sailor told us, 'Don't go to the latrine alone – go with your buddies, with your rifle loaded.' We had no side arms, so we bought daggers and hid 'em under our shirts. My wife said, 'Of all things to bring home!'"

If some delayed leaving, thousands more, like James, chafed at the docks. "I pestered that sergeant, and heard 'Sentimental Journey' a million times, I guess. I was the last Carlsbad man to get home, except for one that missed several ships because he was in Manila drunk."

Farmer was surprised to hear his name called to "stand by for Air Alert! They said I was allowed fifty-five pounds of baggage. I didn't have fifty-five pounds of baggage, and I didn't know what it was all about." Neither did Greeman; but they soon learned they were among eighty heroes of Bataan, chosen from all ranks and services to form a ceremonial detail to represent their comrades. It was fitting that fourteen were New Mexicans.

Dignitaries met them at Hickam Field, to begin five days of festivities in Honolulu; and on 25 September they flew over the

Golden Gate, circled San Francisco, and landed at Hamilton Field. Greeman walked across the tarmac – on American soil – and into the arms of his wife. After a ticker-tape parade through cheering crowds and a banquet at the Saint Francis, they finally headed for Letterman General Hospital and a badly needed rest.

Farmer's best buddy, Bob Mitchell, came home in "the sorriest Liberty Ship in the fleet. Smokingest thing they had, never been in dry dock, and completely wore out." Niemon's ship "backed into a tug, busted the rudder, and we limped across the Pacific." So did Lovato's, after two boilers blew up their second night out. Aldrich was twenty-five days at sea, "and enjoyed every one of them." Most did. They must sip freedom in small swallows. Their minds, like their stomachs, must learn to handle the heady stuff.

The ships' galleys were kept open continuously. Bond discovered a case of canned milk in the wardroom, "and we forgot the coffee. The mess orderly couldn't believe we could drink that much milk." A sailor told Don Harris "that we were averaging five cans a day each, and we ate gallons of ice cream. When I was liberated, I weighed eighty pounds. I doubled it going home."

Going home.

Old fears began to lift, and a sort of euphoria buoyed them along the voyage. Then they were no longer sailing "from," but "to." To what? they began to ask. To parents no longer living? To wives no longer waiting – and who, they shrugged, could blame them?

America! Those topside saw the faint blue line of land before the loudspeaker blared. Then from below the men began to stream. Yelling, laughing, some crying, they crowded the rails. "Home alive in '45!"

The blue haze began to solidify, and the land took form. "And then," as Aldrich's ship approached, "the talk fell off. Everyone got very quiet, and you saw a lot of tears. Then some damned sailor said, 'What do you know – Honolulu!' and broke the spell. Some guys took after him, but not far – they didn't want to miss the sight.

"And finally, that afternoon, like it was floating above the mist, we looked up and saw that great, beautiful arch – the Golden Gate!"

A stevedore strike in San Francisco caused a few ships to be diverted to Seattle. Huxtable was disgusted – his family was waiting in California. Niemon's friends from Seattle were delighted, "until they made us stay aboard all night. So they jumped overboard. The MPs chased them – but there was no way they could get those guys back on board."

Most docked in San Francisco. As Banegas passed under the Golden Gate, we broke out some booze we'd been saving, just for that moment." Roessler had been up since one o'clock in the morning, "to see the harbor lights." Crowds lined the great bridge to see the ships bring in the boys, and bands greeted them at the docks. They played songs new to the men, among them a popular air called "Don't Fence Me In." Few of the ex-POWs were amused.

Families thronged at the docks. Peck wondered if he had "that [same] vacant, lost look as I made my way down seeking Mrs. Peck, if the sight of one lone figure in the crowd transfigured me the way a glimpse of Helen did to Bill [Reardon]. For that one figure, the wife of a returning man, was symbolic of all we had missed . . . . "

Chintis had not told his wife when or where he would arrive. "I'd seen those reunions along the way, first in Manila, where a few had wives. They were crying, we were crying, everybody was crying. Same thing in Hawaii. And I swore I wasn't going to have an emotional display.

"But she found out I was at Letterman. Somebody said, 'Your wife's on her way over,' and I ran to the reading room. I watched her come up the sidewalk and into the room – now here's a girl I haven't seen in four years – and I put a paper over my face. I just didn't want to have it there. She looked around and went out.

"I slipped out, and I came up behind her, and I tapped her on the shoulder, and said, 'Looking for somebody?'"

It was a new and strange America to which they returned. New customs, innovations, and slang bewildered them, and even the once familiar seemed new. They must reacquaint themselves with their country, and with friends and families who could never understand. There was more to bridge than time.

"America had made great strides," Munsey found, "and I had not participated. I was not sure I could cope. The nurses thought they really had a bunch of nuts on their hands. Money meant nothing. One guy saw a lady looking at a diamond watch in a jewelry store, bought it for her, and walked off. Another bought an old car, and a cow, which he tied behind the car, drove to town, walked off, and left the whole thing.

"I was not that flakey, but I had some real concerns. When I left, *The Grapes of Wrath* had been barred from the college library; now *Forever Amber* made *The Grapes of Wrath* look like a fairy tale. The first song I heard was Spike Jones burping his way through 'Tea for Two,' [and wondered] if I was returning a real misfit."[2]

So did Aldrich. "We couldn't sleep on beds – we weren't used to it. After hospital bed check, we'd all jump out and lie on the floor." When trains roared by near Phillips's ward, "we'd hit the floor, and then feel stupid, but the nurses said they'd seen a lot of that."

Roessler found "everything different. When we held chairs for the hostesses at the USO, we were told, 'We don't do that anymore.' And when they talked about ration stamps, we didn't know what they meant."

Lovato resented the German POWs. "Those damn guys were fat and well dressed, and had nice barracks – clean sheets and everything. Hell, women even came and got them for dates!"

Hospital personnel took Kedzie's clothes. "Then when we asked to go to town, they didn't have our uniforms. We scrounged some clothes, took a cab to town, and bought uniforms, then got some liquor, joined a locker club for five dollars, and didn't go back to the hospital for three days."

When a doctor refused Don Harris a pass to town, "we put that guy in a shower, clothes and all, and went anyhow." So did

2 Quotations from Munsey's unpublished memoir have been condensed and their order somewhat transposed.

Schmitz – in his pajamas. "We caught a cab to a bar, and told a curious policeman we were just off the ship. He said, 'Have some drinks, and when you're ready to go back, I'll take you.'"

After initial processing, the men were sent to military hospitals nearest their homes. Most of the New Mexicans went to Bruns General in Santa Fe. On hospital trains they clacked and clattered across the desert to the purple mountains and the big blue skies of home. West was "never so glad in my life to see those wide open spaces." After the green Philippines, "it looked pretty brown" to Aldrich, "but it looked like home. Through Arizona we began losing men. Every time the train stopped, guys got off, and wouldn't get back on. They were back – not in New Mexico, but back to the desert. Another train would eventually pick them up."

Bond gazed at the endless sand as they neared their windy state. "Here came Wad Hall, and he said, 'Come on, we're about to cross the line. In five minutes we'll be in New Mexico! Bet?' I called him and we took off to the observation platform.

"'We're here!' he yelled, and suddenly the damnedest gust of wind hit, and my campaign hat went sailing across the prairie. I said, 'You win – we're in New Mexico!'

"In Gallup, Wad gave a big fat Navajo woman twenty dollars to get him a bottle of whiskey. She took off, and that was the last we saw of her. Or the money."

"They let us off the train for five minutes. And we jumped off, and kissed the ground." Meuli's voice still broke, forty years after, recalling the moment. "This – this was – New Mexico!"

From Gallup they rolled toward Albuquerque, where families clustered at the depot. Though Jack would not come back, Janie Fleming was there to meet his friends. "Jack Bradley got off the train and fell into his mother's arms, and I saw a man from my husband's camp greet his wife. Those were the days that were tough. Then they got back on the train, and we drove on to Santa Fe to meet them there."

Return was in the nature of sacrament. Public welcomes along the way gave outward and visible signs; the inward grace was private. It came to Phillips between Albuquerque and

Lamy Junction, where buses were to meet them for the last short ride to Santa Fe. "It was night, and warm, and the windows were open. There were dim lights on the train. Then it started to rain, and with it came the smell of sagebrush – and there was not a dry eye.

"We knew then we were home."

Janie Fleming waited for friends in the Santa Fe bus station, with families who crowded the large waiting room. It was almost midnight when the bus arrived. As each soldier stepped off, a microphone blared his name.

As a Spanish name was called, Janie saw the boy's mother step forward, a tiny frail *doña*, wrapped in a *rebozo*, black over her white hair. The boy saw his mother and fell on his knees, said a prayer of thanks for his delivery, and another for those – a brother perhaps – who would never come.

Still on his knees, he crossed the room and buried his face in his mother's *rebozo*: New Mexico enfolded her own, the living and the dead.

More families waited at Bruns. As the men arrived, armed with money and furloughs, hearts pounding with strange emotions – joy, hope, disbelief, and some fear – they passed into the large 'rec' room, and into the arms they had dreamed of for so long.

The great moment held also heartbreak. Ross saw "some sad faces – like Tommy McGee, who came home without his brother. Bill died just a month before the end." A friend of Burrola's "found out his wife had divorced him. He was pretty low." Aldrich spotted his father immediately, then looked around and asked, "Where's Mom?" His father's stricken face answered the question. Neither son had received his letters.

Some had not told their families they were coming. Hoping to surprise his mother, Don Harris caught a bus. "At Las Cruces we went into a cleaners to get our clothes pressed and look decent before we got to Silver City. The lady knew we were ex-POWs, and said, 'Take 'em off,' and we started undressing right there. We weren't used to civilization. She shooed us into a room, pressed our clothes, and didn't even charge us."

Before he boarded a bus to see his fiancée, Fletcher called the high school where she taught. Miss Bivens could not talk, he was told. "I'm on long distance," he pled. "Why can't she?"

"Because," snapped the operator, "the schoolhouse is on fire!"

Roessler had only to call a cab to go home, then had it let him off at Guadalupe Church, to walk the last ten blocks and savor Santa Fe. He, too, learned he had lost his father.

Munsey, "not sure I was all there," dreaded meeting his parents, and "when we got home, the house was full of friends and relatives. I was not ready for them; I just wanted to get reacquainted with my family."

Then began the long process of adjusting. They must face mothers whose boys did not return. Greeman found Deming "too depressing. They lost so many men – a family would ask about a son who didn't come back, or a wife why her husband died – and we'd all grown up together. It was hard."

Some found their wives had remarried, or sweethearts had given up. Many had waited; the wedding business accelerated. Armijo saw his baby daughter – now four years old – for the first time. Communities gave banquets for their returning heroes, who weren't sure they were ready yet for banquets.

A large number made the pilgrimage to the holy *Santuario* at Chimayo, to seek, in the miraculous healing mud, cures for their wounds, or to give thanks for their return. Mendoza drove his mother to the shrine of the Virgin of Guadalupe in Mexico to fulfill a pledge she had made.

Nerves were on edge. People didn't understand. Many gave up trying to communicate, and refused to talk about their ordeal. Hank Lovato found it "traumatic getting home. I couldn't sleep on a bed. I just wandered around, night after night, or slept on the floor." All had nightmares. Don Harris had recurring dreams of bombs coming at him. Sakelares relived horrors – one of seeing a friend die for humming "God Bless America."

Some began to drink. While on furlough, Gunter "went to work to keep from staying drunk all the time. You'd go into a cafe or bar, and somebody'd pick up the tab. So I started driving a taxi – slowed me down a little."

"We were shot physically," Woody Hutchison believed, "and mentally. In our own little world, in prison camp, we made out all right, but when it came time to face relatives, to come back to civilian life, it was very difficult. We'd lost our confidence. Walking down the sidewalk I saw my reflection in a window, and it nearly scared me to death."

The doctors gave them ten years to live and said they could never beget children. Both prognoses would prove false, but they accepted them at the time, and vowed to enjoy life as long as they had it. Even that, they knew, would take time.

As their leaves expired, they returned to Bruns, to readjust together. Janie Fleming found them "like men in a dream." But the men of Old Two Hon'erd still looked after each other.

(They continued to do so. Through the years, Leo Padilla always kept San Miguel beer in his Albuquerque bar for Bob Aldrich. "Why let that Anglo in?" his Hispanic clientele grumbled. "He's my brother," shot back Padilla. "Lay a hand on him and I'll slug you." But that was later.)

Garcia felt at home at Bruns with his buddies. "Everybody had a fifth of hooch. You could lift up any pillow on any bed, take a drink, and put it back." Santa Fe – small, offbeat, and sympathetic – was an ideal place to recover. "We asked the head nurse if we could date the nurses, and she said, 'As long as I don't know it.' Once we were in La Fonda[3] with nurses, and she came in, did an about face, and took off. She didn't want to give anybody any trouble. That's how everybody was in Santa Fe.

"One day we decided to go fishing. We knew all the state cops. One was visiting a brother and left the keys in his car. So we stole it and went to Pecos. I'd blow the siren when cars got in our way. We finally called in and said, 'Martinez, we're using one of your cars.' 'The hell you are,' he said. Then he said, 'Oh hell. Okay. But for God's sake, don't wreck it.' In a few days we drove it to police headquarters and they took us back to the hospital. We could get by with anything in Santa Fe."

---

[3] Historic inn, and social hub of Santa Fe.

* * *

Lucy Wilson was in Washington trying to sort out her life when a letter came from her mother. Out fell a cablegram – from Manila, with love from Dan. She raced for the phone. "Mama, where did this come from?"

"I don't know, but two dozen roses just arrived!" Lucy caught the next plane to Big Sandy, Texas. More roses were waiting; so was Dan, at Bruns Hospital.

"I called my chief nurse and said, 'Sankie, what am I going to do? He's changed, and I've changed, and I can't marry him. But I can't tell him on the phone.'

"She said, 'Lucy, go and see him,' and she went with me to Santa Fe. They had long dark wards in Bruns, and Dan was coming in one end and I was in the other, and I knew if I didn't tell him that minute, I wouldn't have the nerve. So I said, there in front of everybody, 'Dan, I can't marry you!'"

For the next few days she vacillated and returned home still undecided. But the stubbornness that had brought Dan Jopling home propelled him to Big Sandy that weekend. Three days later they headed back for Santa Fe, man and wife.

New Mexico's sons were home, and every community welcomed them. Leaves expired, they returned to Bruns, and Santa Fe staged the largest, and the official, homecoming for its proud 200th. They named 13 November 'Bataan Day.' A special edition of the *Santa Fe New Mexican* rejoiced in their return. Businesses closed in the bunting-draped, flag-festooned old town, and Santa Feans turned out in colorful fiesta dress. Many men cut short their furloughs to be with the Regiment on this day of celebration.

Bands, floats, and marchers – one group of girls carried gold stars for those who had fallen – passed before the heroes on their reviewing stand in the plaza, and in the afternoon, Las Vegas and Santa Fe high schools staged a football game in their honor. Only five years before – but five eternal years – many of those now feted had played on those same teams. Cocktails, a banquet, and a ball at the Elks Club ended a day of nostalgic, tear-misted joy.

* * *

It was not all rejoicing. They had begun the day with prayer, and it was that solemnity they deepest felt and longest remembered. Archbishop Byrne himself celebrated High Mass for the entire Regiment. Historic old Saint Francis Cathedral overflowed as the tragically reduced Regiment prayed for those comrades, and families for those sons, who would never return.

Together they intoned the responses, but separately and privately they whispered the words that had sustained them – their prayer, their battle cry, their defiance of death, their buoy of hope, and their pledge of faith:

"God Bless America."

He already had, in these sons He had given her.

INSIGNIA, LINEAGE, AND HONORS
HERALDIC ITEMS

Coat of Arms: 200th Coast Artillery (AA)

Shield: An Avanyu sable. The Avanyu, three arms embowed conjoined at the shoulders, each ending in a triangular head bearing five points.

Crest: On a wreath of the colors or sable, a coiled rattlesnake.

Motto: *Pro Civitate et Patria.* (For State and Country.)

Symbolism: The Avanyu was a sacred emblem of the ancient Cliff Dwellers of New Mexico, and is still regarded by the Pueblo Indians as the giver of water, the guardian of springs and streams, and therefore the preserver of life, and hence a symbol of prosperity and happiness. It symbolizes victory, and the motion and energy of life, and their epiphanies, the 'whirling sun' and 'lightning in air,' suggestive of the firepower and defense mission of the unit.

The serpent (represented on the State Seal) symbolizes wisdom. Found in damp places, snakes are perceived as guardians of water, and hence of life. The rattlesnake in America represents freedom, and the diamondback is a native of New Mexico.

Coat of Arms: 515th Coast Artillery (AA)

Devise: A flaming sword behind a gold stylized Philippine Sun bearing a red annulet issuing dual parallel rays per saltire, all within two gold sea lions at each side facing out and in reverse to one another, looped tails conjoining with the ends of three horizontal wavy blue bars, and paws grasping a red scroll arced across the top and bearing the inscription "Guardian of the Flame."

Symbolism: The sea lions derive from the Arms of Luzon, where the Regiment served in World War II. The three wavy blue bars symbolize the three Presidential Unit Citations awarded for Manila, Bataan, and defense of the Philippines. The Philippine Sun signifies the Philippine Presidential Unit Citation. The annulet and rays per saltire represent the sun, or Zia symbol, on the State flag of New Mexico.

LINEAGE AND HONORS

LINEAGE:

Organized 1 September 1880 of companies in the New Mexico Volunteer Militia as 1st Regiment and expanded 18 February 1882 to form 1st and 2d Regiments with headquarters at Socorro and Albuquerque, respectively. Both regiments expanded 25 April 1883, 1st Regiment to form 1st Regiment and 2d Cavalry Battalion; 2d Regiment to form 2d Regiment and 1st Cavalry Battalion.

1st Cavalry Battalion reorganized and redesignated 14 September 1883 as 3d Battalion, 1st Regiment of Cavalry; concurrrently 2d Cavalry Battalion reorganized and redesignated as 1st Regiment of Cavalry (less 3d Battalion) to comprise 12 troops. Reorganized 10 November 1885 as 1st Regiment of Cavalry (less 3d Battalion, which was expanded, reorganized, and redesignated as 2d Regiment of Cavalry). Concurrently 2d Regiment redesignated as 1st Regiment of Infantry, with headquarters at Santa Fe (moved to Albuquerque 15 August 1886).

1st Regiment of Infantry and elements of 2d Regiment of Cavalry consolidated 24 December 1890 and redesignated 1st Regiment of Infantry.

1st Regiment of Cavalry disbanded 29 December 1893 and its remaining troops attached to 1st Regiment of Infantry.

The New Mexico Volunteer Militia reorganized 12 September 1896 as 1st Battalion of Cavalry, comprising 5 troops, with headquarters at Santa Fe. Redesignated the New Mexico National Guard 17 March 1897. Redesignated 1897 the 1st Squadron of Cavalry.

Remaining in State service, and volunteering as individuals, the 1st Squadron of Cavalry reorganized to form the 2d Squadron (Troops E, F, G, and H), 1st United States Volunteer Cavalry, also known as the 'Rough Riders.' Mustered into Federal service 6-7 May 1898 at Santa Fe. Mustered out 15 September 1898 at Montauk Point, New York, to continue in State service as the 1st Squadron of Cavalry. Reduced in 1902 to a single troop (Troop A, Las Vegas) and attached to the 1st Regiment of Infantry 5 February 1908. In 1908 the 1st Regiment of Infantry consolidated with Troop A, to be designated as the 1st Regiment of Infantry.

Mustered in Federal service 16 July 1916 at Albuquerque for service on the Mexican border. Mustered out at Columbus, New Mexico, 5 April 1917. Recalled into Federal service 21 April 1917; mustered out 11 June 1917 at Albuquerque.

Regiment broken up 19-24 October and elements reorganized and redesignated as elements of 115th Train Headquarters and Military Police, and the 143d and 144th Machine Gun Battalions, elements of the 40th Division. Military Police section of 115th Train Headquarters and Military Police reorganized and redesignated 27 October 1918 as the 40th Military Police Company, an element of the 40th Division; concurrently the 115th Train Headquarters and Military Police reorganized and redesignated as the 115th Train Headquarters. 115th Train Headquarters demobilized 25 April 1919 at Camp Kearny, California. 143d and 144th Machine Gun Battalion demobilized at Camp Grant, Illinois. 115th Train Headquarters, 40th Military Police Company demobilized 2 May 1919 at Camp Kearny, California.

The former 1st Regiment of Infantry reconstituted in New Mexico National Guard 16 July as a separate squadron of Cavalry, Troop A (Albuquerque) and Troop B (Carlsbad). Federally recognized 26-28 July 1920. Expanded, reorganized, and redesignated as 1st Cavalry 3 December 1920. Redesignated 2 May 1922 as the 111th Cavalry. Headquarters federally recognized 4 May 1924 at Santa Fe. Assigned to 23d Cavalry Division 5 November 1923. Relieved from assignment 15 March 1929.

The 111th Cavalry converted and redesignated 26 April 1940 as 207th Coast Artillery. Redesignated 1 July 1940 as 200th Coast Artillery (Antiaircraft). Inducted into Federal service 6 January 1941 at home stations. Reconstructed 21 March 1942 from all elements of the 200th Coast Artillery (AA), 515th Coast Artillery (AA), and Battery A, 2d Coast Artillery (Philippine Army) and designated Groupment "A" (AA). Reorganized 7 April 1942 (less Battery A, 2d Coast Artillery, Philippine Army) and redesignated Provisional Coast Artillery Brigade (AA).

Were surrendered 9 April 1942 to Japanese *14th Army* in Philippine Islands. Formally inactivated 2 April 1946 at Fort Mills, Philippine Islands.

Although this account ends with the formal inactivation of 'Old Two Hon'erd,' the lineage continues to the present 200th Air Defense Artillery, NMNG.

ANNEX

Constituted July 1923 in the Organized Reserves as the 515th Coast Artillery. Organized November 1924 with headquarters at Topeka, Kansas.

Withdrawn from Organized Reserves 19 December 1941 and allotted (less equipment and personnel) to Regular Army Forces in the Far East; concurrently activated at Manila, Philippine Islands, with personnel of the 200th Coast Artillery (AA), New Mexico National Guard.

All elements of the 515th and 200th Coast Artilleries (AA), plus Battery A, 2d Coast Artillery (Philippine Army), consolidated and reorganized 21 March 1942, and designated Groupment "A" (AA). Reorganized 7 April 1942 (less Battery A, 2d Coast Artillery, Philippine Army) and redesignated the Provisional Coast Artillery Brigade (AA).

Were surrendered 9 April 1942 to the Japanese *14th Army* in the Philippine Islands. Formally inactivated 2 April 1946.

CAMPAIGN PARTICIPATION CREDIT

Indian Wars
- New Mexico 1881
- New Mexico 1882

War with Spain
- Santiago

World War I
- Streamer without inscription

World War II
- Philippine Islands

DECORATIONS

Presidential Unit Citation (Army), Streamer embroidered CLARK FIELD (200th Coast Artillery cited; WD GO 14, 1942)

Presidential Unit Citation (Army), Streamer embroidered MANILA 1941 (515th Coast Artillery cited; WD GO 14, 1942)

Presidential Unit Citation (Army), Streamer embroidered BATAAN (200th and 515th Coast Artillery cited; WD GO 14, 1942)

Presidential Unit Citation (Army), Streamer embroidered DEFENSE OF THE PHILIPPINES (Military and Naval forces of the United States engaged in the defense of the Philippines cited; WD GO 22, 1942, as amended by DA GO 46, 1948)

Philippine Presidential Unit Citation, Streamer embroidered 7 December 1941 to 10 May 1942 (200th and 515th Coast Artillery cited; DA GO 47, 1950)

Officers - 200th & 515th Coast Artilleries (AA)

In the absence of official rosters, this list was compiled from those of General Sage and Colonel Peck. Because they were prepared from memory while in prison camps, they may not be entirely accurate. Any names appearing in both the foregoing and following lists represent those men who were promoted to officer rank after March 1942.

Allen, 2Lt Joe L.
Anderson, 1Lt V.O.
Ashby, Capt Jack G.
Bailey, 1Lt Glenn E.
Bayne, Capt Alvin L.
Beall, Capt James F.
Becker, 2Lt Darwin C.
Beyers, Capt Melvin O.
Blueher, 1Lt William G.
Bond, Capt Dow G.
Boyer, Capt Jack K.
Bradley, 1Lt Jack W.
Brown, Capt Charles M.
Brown, 1Lt George R.
Bryant, Capt O.C.
Burson, Capt Curtis E.
Cain, LtCol Memory H.
Candiello, 2Lt Samuel A.
Chaney, 2Lt James W.
Colvard, Lt Col George T.
Compton, Capt Robert J.
Cox, 2Lt Tom C.
Craft, 1Lt Dean H.
Craig, 1Lt Howard G.
Curtis, 2Lt Austin J.
Darling, 1Lt Gerald L.
Davis, 2Lt Dwayne A.
Donaldson, Capt James W.
Dorris, Maj Winnifred O.
Ellis, 1Lt Jack L.
Ely, Capt Clyde E., Jr.
Farley, Capt John W.
Fields, Capt Albert K.
Forni, 2Lt Frank A.
Foy, 2Lt Thomas P., Jr.
Gamble, 2Lt John D.
George, Capt Anthony R.
Gonzales, Capt Reynaldo F.
Greeman, Capt Gerald B.
Grimmer, Capt Frank C.
Hartford, 2Lt Oliver
Hazlewood, Maj James H.
Henfling, Capt George W.
Howden, Capt Frederick B.
Hunter, 1Lt James E.
Hutchison, Capt Russell J.
Irish, 1Lt Clayton E.
Jeffus, Capt Hobart P.
Jopling, 1Lt Daniel W.
Jordan, Capt Fred H.
Junker, 2Lt Edward J.
Kells, 2Lt David E.
Kemp, Capt Eddie T.
Kennaman, 2Lt Jack R.
Lambert, 2Lt Thomas M.
Lee, 2Lt Gordan A.
Limpert, 2Lt Dan C.
Lingo, 1Lt Edward F.
Long, Capt Julian O.
Lucas, Capt Marvin H.
Luikhart, Lt Col John C.
Lutich, 2Lt Louis P.
McCahon, 1Lt James H.
McCartney, 1Lt Dan A.
McCollum, Maj Virgil O.
McKenzie, 1Lt William J.
McMinn, Capt James M.
Meek, 1Lt Douglas L.
Melendez, Capt Alfonso M.
Millard, 1Lt Melvin K.
Miller, Maj. Henry M.
Montoya, 1Lt Antonio A.
Oden, 2Lt J.A., Jr.
Parker, Capt Ted E.
Peck, Col Harry M.
Radosevich, 2Lt Joseph R.
Randolph, 2Lt William P.
Reardon, Maj William B.
Remondini, 1Lt Robert J.
Richards, 2Lt James F.
Riley, Maj Richard M.
Rogers, 2Lt J.
Rogers, 2Lt Lloyd D.
Sadler, Capt James E.
Safford, 2Lt Charles V.
Sage, BGen Charles Gurdon
Sawyer, Capt Tom J.
Schroeder, Capt Karl W.
Schuetz, Capt William C.
Schurtz, Maj Paul W.
Shamblin, Capt Otho L.
Sherman, Capt Frederick S.
Shimp, Capt Neil B.
Skarda, Capt Cash T.
Skiles, 1Lt Leonard W.
Smith, Capt Burney H.
Stiles, 2Lt LeMoyne B.
Stump, Capt Claude W.
Suttman, 2Lt Al T.
Taggert, Capt Thomas R.

Thomas, 2Lt Frank C.
Thorpe, 1Lt Joseph D.
Thwaits, Capt James R.
Thwaits, 2Lt Pryor
Tucker, 2Lt Lee C.
Turner, Capt Frank M.
Turner, Maj John W.
Van Cleve, 2Lt Lawrence C.
Vinette, Capt Dallas P.
Walker, 1Lt Allen B.
Wheeler, 2Lt Alvin F.
Witten, LtCol Oliver B.

200th Coast Artillery Roster - Enlisted Men*

Headquarters Battery

Almeraz, Pvt Frederico S.
Apple, M/S Nelson W.
Aranda, Pvt Sixto O.
Atkins, S/S Thomas E.
Baclawski, M/S Arthur M.
Bell, PFC Robert N.
Brewer, Cpl Fred M.
Brooks, Cpl Bernard E.
Brown, PFC Joseph T.
Bruce, Pvt William L.
Burhans, Pvt Earl V.
Burns, PFC Jonathan P.
Burrell, M/S Thomas C.
Burruss, Pvt Eugene
Byrne, S/S Lawrence H.
Chairas, Pvt Francisco H.
Chavez, Pvt José S.
Chesser, PFC Norman J.
Cisneros, PFC Tomás G.
Curry, PFC Kleo I.
Darling, Cpl George E.
Diaz, Pvt Pablo A.
Erwin, 1/S Jack G.
Estrada, Pvt Roberto W.
Flohrs, Sgt Duane H.
Ford, Cpl Virgle L.
Gallegos, Pvt Antonio J.
Garcia, Pvt Ramón S.
Garrett, Pvt Alvin W.
Graves, Pvt Willis P.
Gulbas, Pvt Irving
Gutierrez, Cpl Joe B.
Haynes, Sgt Glenn R.
Hill, Pvt Donald E.
Howe, PFC Wallace A.
Huxtable, T/S James T.
Johns, PFC Robert G.
Kros, Pvt Donald R.
Lansford, Pvt Jack L.
Lewis, M/S Brooks B.
Lewis, Sgt Jack S.
Lindsay, Cpl Y.C.
Long, Pvt Carl M.
Malak, Pvt Stephen L.
McCan, Cpl Clarence M.
McCubbin, PFC Buell
McDermott, Pvt Carlos T.
Mendoza, PFC Louis O.
Meuli, M/S Maynard C.
Montoya, Sgt Carlos R.
Pacheco, PFC Alberto D.
Patterson, Pvt Rufus A.
Peña, Pvt Juan B.
Poe, Sgt Alfred
Prosser, PFC Barney E.
Roessler, Pvt Norbert R.
Sacson, Pvt Gunnar E.
Sakelares, Sgt Angelo H.
Schwartz, Cpl Jim E.
Thompson, PFC Fred D.
Waldron, PFC Ralph
Warner, S/S Glenn O.
Weaver, T/S Lonnie M.
Weisdorfer, Pvt Lawrence A.
Welsh, PFC Thomas W.
Whelchel, M/S Warren W.
Williams, Pvt Joe M.
Wolf, PFC Sidney R.
Wolfe, PFC Clinton V.
Wyckoff, S/S Earl F.
Zimmerman, S/S Willard F.
Zumwalt, PFC Fred W.

Medical Corps

Barela, Sgt Pat F.
Campbell, S/S Roger D.
Chavez, PFC Horace
Chavez, Pvt Ralph P.
Chavez, PFC Tony P.
Davis, Pvt Gus L.
Day, PFC Henry W.
Garcia, PFC Abel
Garcia, PFC Robert
Garcia, PFC Salvador J.
Griego, PFC Sipriano
Hasso, Pvt Charles E.
Higgins, Cpl Howard
McCarty, Pvt John A.
Morris, Cpl Michael A.
Murphy, PFC John J.
Orosco, S/S Arnold A.
Padilla, PFC Jake P.
Palasota, Pvt Sam M.
Schubert, T/S Charles A.
Storts, Pvt Arthur L.
Tixier, PFC Foch F.
Ulrich, Pvt Ernest H.

Band

Baca, PFC Ernest
Baldwin, PFC Robert D.
Burrell, Sgt Donald W.
Case, PFC Clair L.
Chamberlin, PFC Jack B.
Clark, PFC Donald
Clark, Cpl Russell
Domenicali, PFC Pete
Franchini, PFC Frank
Gabaldon, PFC Frank A.
Heinsohn, PFC Wilber W.
Hobbs, PFC Roy D.
Horabin, PFC William S.
Jezek, PFC Joe E.
King, Cpl George F.
Norris, Sgt William M.
Palmer, T/S Thomas M.
Patton, S/S Newton J.
Pyatt, PFC Earl E.
Ramirez, PFC Cipriano B.
Ramirez, PFC Salvador H.
Rouse, Sgt Titus W.
St. Clair, Pvt John W.
Tafoya, PFC Herman O.
Warth, PFC Henry K.
Wells, PFC William J.

Headquarters - 1st Battalion

Armstrong, Pvt Auben E.
Bailey, PFC Jollie
Barka, Pvt Thomas
Bell, Pvt Leonard R.
Boyd, PFC Grady
Burnett, 1/S James A.
Campbell, PFC Bob A.
Campbell, S/S Kenneth A.
Carrillo, PFC Manuel
Cast, Pvt Elzie L.
Castillo, Pvt Filimon C.
Chavez, Pvt Clovis G.
Chavez, Pvt Joe D.
Cockrell, Pvt Clifton
Dotson, Cpl Alonzo
Duncan, PFC Charles L.
Dunsworth, S/S Robert J.
Duran, Pvt Delfido L.
Eagle, Pvt Eldwin J.
Ewing, PFC Richard D.
Francis, Sgt J.B.
Gallegos, PFC Miguel E.
Gallegos, Pvt Reynaldo D.
Garcia, Pvt Manuel T.
Gilcrease, Cpl Arthur H.
Gilman, PFC Harold C.
Gipp, Pvt John H.
Guye, S/S Earl W.
Harrington, Sgt Neal J.
Harrison, PFC Arthur J.
Harvey, PFC Charles D.
Hein, Pvt Edward H.
Hern, PFC Ed M.
Holyak, Pvt John
Huerta, Cpl Raul
Jarnagin, Pvt Willie C.
Leiker, Sgt William J.
Lovato, PFC Frank N.
Lujan, Pvt Leopoldo
Miller, S/S Frederick C.
Orrill, Sgt Robert K.
Owen, Pvt Paul M.
Pacheco, Pvt Pedro
Patton, Cpl John P.
Paulson, Pvt Lloyd G.
Perehinczuk, PFC Chester J.
Pitman, Pvt Leo
Rogers, Cpl Willis L.
Sarracino, PFC Frank B.
Schiffner, Sgt James F.
Stephens, PFC Sidney O.
Stever, Pvt Archie D.
Tenorio, Pvt Pedro
Updike, PFC Richard H., Jr.
Vlasak, Pvt Charlie J.

Headquarters - 2nd Battalion

Adair, Pvt Don C.
Aldrich, Cpl Jack H.
Aldrich, Sgt Robert L.
Althaus, Pvt Rubin M.
Begley, PFC Samuel C.
Berlanga, Pvt Martin
Bishop, PFC Frank S.
Bowman, Sgt Thomas C.
Chalk, Pvt Junior A.
Cherne, Pvt Clem J.
Cummings, Pvt Warner W.
Dosher, PFC William J.
Gallegos, Pvt Nick L.
Greathouse, Cpl Doyle R.
Hatch, Pvt Claude A.
Hill, PFC J.T.
Hoyl, PFC John B.
Hutton, PFC Roy J.
Ireton, PFC Carl V.
Johnson, S/S Olin W.
Keeton, Pvt Leland L.
Kieyoomia, Pvt Joe L.

200 - Headquarters - 2nd Bat. cont.

LeVelle, Cpl Edward G.
Lee, Pvt Cleovis M.
Lee, Cpl Roy
Lee, Pvt Walter L.
Lightfoot, PFC Jefferson O.
Lucero, Cpl Robert
Luna, Pvt Candido
McMillan, PFC George P.
Manasse, S/S Solly P.
Miller, PFC Douglas W.
Montano, Pvt Gabriel B.
Morris, Pvt Gordin L.
Morrison, S/S Lester A.
Novinski, Pvt Clement J.
Prehm, Pvt Ernest D.
Prince, Sgt Sam A.
Rhee, PFC Heinz L.
Rogers, PFC Harry A.
Saiz, Pvt Santiago S.
Smith, 1/S J.M.
Taylor, Pvt McKean D.
Tixier, Cpl Wendelin F.
Tonelli, Cpl Mario G.
Valdez, Pvt Eloy
Weeks, PFC Orie B.
Whitmer, Pvt Harold L.
Wisdom, S/S William W.

Battery A

Antonio, Pvt Sam J.
Archuleta, Pvt Manuel R.
Armijo, S/S Reynold P.
Atencio, PFC Santa Cruz
Baca, PFC Alfred
Baldonado, PFC José M.
Baldonado, Sgt Juan T.
Bandoni, Cpl Joseph J.
Banegas, Pvt Lorenzo Y.
Barela, Pvt Julio T.
Barreras, Cpl Eliseo M.
Beaudoen, Pvt Charles R.
Bohn, Pvt Thomas P.
Borchert, Pvt Freeman F.
Botello, Pvt Pete
Breustedt, Pvt Charles W.
Cady, Pvt Harris Y.
Calkins, Sgt Llewellyn I.
Carr, PFC Leslie J.
Carson, Pvt Lupe B.
Cata, Pvt José I.
Chaffin, 1/S Roy M.
Chapa, Pvt David N.
Chavez, Pvt Beltrán
Chavez, Pvt Berto
Chavez, Sgt Ernest A.
Cheama, Pvt Ernest H.
Clements, PFC W.T.
Cordova, Pvt Edward
Cordova, Pvt Hilario
Cordova, PFC Richard L.
Cortez, Pvt Guadalupe F.
Crabtree, Pvt Glenn L.
Daugherty, PFC Benny J.
DeVenzio, Sgt Orlando J.
Deemer, PFC Carl E.
Drake, PFC Aaron C.
DuBois, Pvt Robert E.
Duran, S/S David J.
Duran, Pvt Joe I.
Duran, Cpl Michael R.
Eresh, PFC Peter J.
Evans, Cpl Robert L.
Ferrari, PFC Domenic
Fleming, PFC Leslie G.
Foster, Pvt Henry B.
Foster, PFC Lee A.
Frame, Sgt Kenneth C.
Fredieu, Pvt Louis
Fulton, Pvt Leonard P.
Gaitan, Pvt Manuel O.
Gannon, S/S Harold J.
Garcia, Pvt Enriques
Garcia, Cpl Raymond J.
Gray, S/S Justin G.
Greer, Pvt Edward C.
Griffin, Pvt Iulus A.
Guenther, PFC William C.
Gutierrez, Pvt Eleito
Harris, PFC Carl S.
Haws, Pvt Claude B.
Hays, Cpl Joseph
Holton, Pvt George T.
House, Pvt Jess C.
Howell, PFC Clayton F.
Hudgens, PFC Sidney R.
Hutchins, PFC Rowland H.
Jackson, Pvt Elvin E.
Jones, Pvt Everett M.
Jones, Cpl James J.
Kasero, Pvt Antonio
Kindel, PFC Merle A.
Klocker, PFC George M.
Knight, Cpl William L.
Kranc, Pvt Norbert J.
Lawson, Pvt Dave B.
Lente, Pvt Seferino
Looney, Pvt Virgel L.
Lovato, S/S Henry A.
Lovato, Pvt Rosenaldo
Lowe, Pvt Harold S.
Lucero, Pvt Natividad J.
MacIntosh, Pvt Daniel F.
McKenzie, Pvt James D.
McLaughlin, Sgt Egbert B.
McWilliams, PFC Dale M.

200 - Bat. A cont.

Maldonado, Pvt Polo V.
Malnati, PFC Lloyd G.
Mann, PFC Oscar C.
Marquez, PFC Manuel O.
Martin, Pvt Frank G.
Martinez, Pvt Eduardo
Martinez, Pvt Emilio M.
Martinez, Pvt Tony A.
Martinez, Pvt Trinidad G.
Mascarenas, Pvt José E.T.
Masser, Pvt Edmund J.
Millenbaugh, S/S Paul D.
Miller, PFC Roy E.
Mitchell, Pvt Harwell H.
Montoya, PFC Tony B.
Morris, Pvt Jimmie
Mucha, Pvt Frank J.
Muller, T/S Gottlob C.
Nance, Pvt Hugh B.
Nieto, PFC Frank C.
O'Rourke, Sgt Vincent C.
Oldham, PFC Adrain E.
Ortiz, Pvt Benny G.
Ortiz, Pvt Cruz
Padilla, Sgt Orville F.
Palmbach, PFC Myron A.
Parchman, Cpl William E.
Payne, PFC Grayford C.
Perez, Pvt Alfonso
Pickens, PFC James V.
Prettner, S/S Richard C.
Pruette, Sgt Jack N.
Pruss, Pvt Harry J.
Quintana, Pvt José L.
Roberts, PFC Wayne D.
Rodriguez, Pvt Juan J.
Rodriguez, Pvt Luís
Romero, Sgt Frank S.
Romero, PFC Joe S.
Romero, Cpl Louis G.
Ruebush, S/S Elbert L.
Saavedra, Sgt Fidel L.
Salcido, Pvt Henry
Sanchez, Pvt Alfredo F.
Sanchez, Pvt Victor F.
Sandoval, Pvt Eduardo A.
Sandoval, Pvt Filadelfio
Savoie, PFC David C.
Serna, PFC Placido P.
Sharp, Pvt Alvin W.
Silva, Pvt Joe R.
Sisneros, Pvt Felipe G.
Smith, T/S Timothy H.
Smith, Pvt William D.
Spiker, PFC Virgil J.
Starkey, PFC Walter A.
Steen, PFC Harry E.
Taylor, PFC William R.
Tellez, Pvt David O.
Towner, PFC Joseph E.
Trujillo, Pvt Jesús P.
Urioste, Pvt Joe
Vaughn, PFC Eugene C.
Vigil, Pvt Eliseo G.
Vogt, Pvt Herman H.
Walsh, PFC Paul A.
Whitley, Pvt Calvin E.
Whittaker, Cpl Carl C.
Wilcoxson, Sgt John J.
Williams, PFC Ben F.
Willie, Pvt Wilson E.
Wilson, PFC Robert A.
Witt, Cpl Robert E.
Wysong, Cpl Jeff A.
Zender, PFC Richard L.

Battery B

Analla, Pvt Santiago S.
Anaya, Pvt Ramón S.
Archuleta, Pvt Amadeo
Armijo, Pvt Pete M.
Armijo, PFC Salvador J.
Baca, Pvt Juan E.
Bain, Pvt Charles V.
Bangs, Pvt William L.
Barela, Pvt Antonio J.
Bergquist, Cpl Francis E.
Blattman, Cpl Robert M.
Bloomfield, Cpl Don C.
Bollen, Cpl George H.
Borunda, PFC David G.
Borunda, Pvt Robert
Brown, PFC James R.
Brown, Pvt Marvin L.
Brown, PFC Norman C.
Calanchi, Pvt Louis B.
Campbell, Pvt Coyle A.
Cardenas, PFC Marcos S.
Carriere, Pvt Joe M.
Cassias, Sgt Joe T.
Clark, Cpl William B.
Cole, Pvt Olen
Cordova, Pvt Julian Z., Jr.
Dawes, Sgt Homer R.
Diaz, Pvt Louis A.
Erbacher, Cpl John M.
Evans, Pvt William R.
Fleming, PFC Claude
Fleming, Sgt John W.
Franklin, PFC Ben, Jr.
Gachupin, Pvt Gregorio

200th - Bat. B cont.

Garcia, PFC Benny C.
Garcia, Pvt Leonides L.
Griffing, PFC John W.
Hamilton, PFC John
Hammond, Sgt Fred J.
Hawley, PFC William L.
Hayes, Pvt Albert
Heard, Cpl James B.
Herbert, Pvt Irwin H.
Holland, 1/S William C.
Holt, Pvt Lawrence L.
Hutchison, Cpl Woodrow M.
Jaramillo, Pvt Tranquilino
Jones, Cpl Alton R.
King, PFC Warnar A.
Kuretich, PFC Tony A.
Lerma, Pvt Juan S.
Lewis, Cpl Ralph C.
Lopez, Pvt Lorenzo
Lucero, Pvt José L.
Lucero, PFC Nano C.
McCombs, PFC Earn L.
McCormick, Pvt James C.
McCreary, PFC Paul E.
McDaniel, PFC Delbert R.
McKnight, Pvt Arlan
McVey, PFC Urban F.
Mendenhall, Pvt Jake H.
Miller, PFC Robert F.
Montoya, S/S Manuel L.
Montoya, PFC Orlando R.
Morris, Pvt Burl M.
Oberton, PFC John
Oliver, Pvt E.C.
Ortiz, Pvt Billie
Overmier, S/S William C.
Padilla, PFC Leo J.
Page, Sgt Candido L.
Palumbo, Cpl Paul
Parker, PFC William R.
Perea, Pvt Tom
Plemmons, PFC Carl K.
Ream, PFC Glenn G.
Redd, Pvt Talmadge W.
Roberts, Pvt A.J.
Rohrabaugh, S/S Thomas C.
Romero, Pvt Benito A.
Romero, Pvt Claudio
Romero, Pvt Frank
Ruiz, Pvt Joel R.
Sanchez, Cpl Charles F.
Sanchez, Pvt Valentíne
Sartin, PFC Marlin E.
Sattem, PFC Eldred
Savedra, Pvt Teodoro
Schultz, PFC Albert F.
Sedillo, Sgt Johnnie J.
Selva, PFC Caesar J.
Sims, Pvt James D.
Smith, Pvt Claude O.
Smith, PFC Herbert H.
Sora, Pvt Pragedis M.
Spensley, PFC Homer V.
Suarez, Pvt Manuel N.
Triplett, Sgt Preston E.
Vanover, PFC Elmer L.
Verhagen, Pvt Elmer H.
Vidaurri, Pvt Manuel, Jr.
Vigil, Pvt Modesto J.
Viitanen, PFC Arnold E.
Villa, Pvt Raymond
Villarreal, Pvt Elias
Wall, Pvt Lester L.

Battery C

Alderete, Pvt Ramón S.
Allred, PFC William M.
Apodaca, Cpl Ramón
Armijo, Cpl Ernesto J.
Armijo, 1/S Manuel A.
Baker, S/S Marvin L.
Blazevich, Pvt John
Boyles, PFC John T.
Bright, PFC William L.
Celusniak, PFC Louis B.
Chacon, Cpl Amadeo
Chavez, Pvt Adolfo, Jr.
Coleman, Sgt William R.
Contreras, Pvt Francisco
Contreras, PFC Juan
Copeland, Pvt Sid
Cree, PFC George W.
Duke, Sgt Lewis E.
Duran, Pvt Barney A.
Duran, Pvt Robert
Gannon, Pvt Charles F.
Garcia, Sgt Cruz
Garcia, PFC Tomás
Gateley, Pvt William E.
Gater, PFC Hubert B.
Gebhard, PFC Roy B.
Gloria, Pvt Andrés E.
Gonzales, Cpl Rubel
Greenberg, Pvt Hyman
Gutierrez, PFC Jesús B.
Gutierrez, PFC John F.
Hagedorn, PFC William J.
Hamblin, PFC Orland K.
Hatton, PFC Everette C.
Herrera, PFC George S.
Hill, Pvt Alfred C.
Hoskins, Pvt Earl C.
Howard, PFC George W.

200th - Bat. C cont.

Hubbell, Pvt Harold
Iskra, PFC Charles
Jackson, Cpl Robert C., Jr.
James, PFC Vernie L.
Jim, Pvt Glenn
Kiesov, Sgt Walter C.
Lawrence, Pvt Wayne O.
Leyba, Pvt Macedonio B.
Leyba, Pvt Ramón B.
Lopez, Cpl Genaro B.
Lopez, Pvt Nicolas
Love, Cpl Johnny E.
Love, Cpl William E.
Lucero, PFC Alphonso M.
McAndrew, PFC Harold J.
McCants, PFC Herbert W.
McCombs, Pvt Leonard R.
McGee, PFC William D.
Merritt, Pvt Thomas A.
Milligan, Pvt Chesley
Morgan, Pvt Jacob C., Jr.
Muñoz, Pvt Manuel M.
Nunn, Cpl David M.
Ojinaga, Pvt Vicente R.
Oliver, Pvt Enoch C.
Owen, PFC Roy E.
Phillips, Sgt Connie D.
Pyetzki, Cpl Merrill H.
Reyes, Pvt Eusebio
Reyna, PFC Antonio
Riley, Pvt Glendon S.
Rivera, Cpl Gavino
Roberts, PFC James S.
Robinson, S/S James A., Jr.
Rodriguez, Pvt Basilio L.
Roessler, S/S Paul A.
Romero, PFC Eugenio M.
Sanchez, Pvt Alfonso M.
Sanchez, Pvt Cristobal D.
Sanchez, Pvt Frank
Sanchez, Sgt Pete
Sanchez, PFC Teofilo M.
Savedra, Pvt Elías
Simoni PFC Tony P.
Slaughter, Pvt Lonnie T.
Smith, PFC Albert D.
Stephens, PFC Edgar J.
Sweat, Pvt Albert F.
Tafoya, Pvt Eddie A.
Tafoya, Pvt Gabriel
Teague, Sgt Rufus D.
Thomson, Pvt Francis R.
Tovar, PFC Alex E.
Trujillo, PFC Manuel
Turrieta, Pvt Carlos T.
Unger, Pvt Robert S.
Urioste, Pvt John
Van Beuning, Cpl John G.
Van Buskirk, PFC Francis H.
Veal, Cpl Richard A.
Vigil, Pvt Vicente P.
Villaloboz, Pvt Macario
Vivian, Pvt Sam
Waldman, Pvt Arthur
West, PFC Robert L.
White, Pvt William B.
Wiest, Pvt John H.
Williams, Cpl Robert L.
Woolworth, PFC Jesse
Yates, Cpl Otis

Battery D

Archuleta, Pvt Markie R.
Argeanas, Cpl James
Barker, Sgt Truman M.
Barreras, Pvt Joe
Barron, Pvt Ernest C.
Birner, Cpl Ernest M.
Bowra, PFC William G.
Boyd, Pvt James C.
Brewer, Sgt Clinton R.
Burrola, Pvt Reginald
Burrola, Sgt William M.
Bush, PFC Denzel O.
Byars, PFC Marlett E.
Chavez, Pvt David
Chavez, PFC Louis
Chavez, Pvt Oziel
Chavez, Pvt Raymond
Cimerone, Pvt Lorenzo P.
Cornell, S/S Walter P.
Crawford, PFC Robert C.
Crowder, Pvt Henry F.
Dallago, PFC Valentíne R.
Diaz, PFC Porfirio, Jr.
Diaz, PFC Solomon L.
Duke, Pvt George B.
Duncan, Pvt Ralph E.
Edmonds, PFC Homer L.
Espinosa, Cpl Damian
Etter, Jr., Cpl David R.
Evans, PFC Donald D.
Fragua, PFC Pablo
Galindo, Cpl Anthony Q.
Garcia, Pvt Abedon
Garcia, Pvt Uvaldo
Garduño, PFC Adolfo C.
Gates, Cpl Leonard D.
Gomez, PFC Fernando, Jr.
Gonzales, Pvt Anatolio
Gonzales, Pvt Eliseo R.
Gonzales, PFC John J.
Gray, S/S Everitt W.
Grijalba, Pvt Manuel F.

200th - Battery D cont.

Gunter, Pvt James C.
Gutierrez, Pvt Pablo P.
Hamilton, Cpl Johnny
Hardy, PFC Richard J.
Hernandez, Pvt José G.
Hernandez, PFC Lorenzo
Herrera, Pvt Eusebio
Keilholz, PFC Ervin
Lovato, Pvt Juan S.
Lucero, PFC Celso H.
Lyons, Pvt Howard F.
McBride, Pvt Myrrl W.
McGee, PFC John T.
Madrid, Pvt Catalino
Madril, Pvt Susano
Martinez, Pvt Antonio
Martinez, Pvt Benjamin E.
Martinez, Pvt Domingo B.
Martinez, Pvt Rosenaldo
Menini, Cpl Carlo A.
Meyer, PFC Vernon L.
Montoya, Pvt Andrés A.
Nickerson, Pvt José B.
Nunn, Sgt Charles R.
Oja, Pvt Onnie A.
Osborne, PFC Benjamin L.
Paiz, Pvt Juan
Parks, PFC Wyman L.
Perea, Pvt Ignacio G.
Perez, Pvt Aniseto
Phillips, Cpl Harold V.
Pribble, Sgt Foy E.
Quintana, Pvt Carmel
Ramirez, PFC Dagoberto S.
Ratcliffe, S/S Thomas W.
Ray, PFC Clarence
Regalado, PFC Tony
Regaldo, Pvt Cruz
Roberts, Sgt Lester L.
Robertson, Pvt James A.
Romero, Pvt Dave E.
Ruiz, Cpl Espeedie G.
Sagash, PFC Charles D.
Salazar, Pvt Faustin
Sanchez, Pvt Joe L.
Santillanes, Pvt Valentíne S.
Scanlon, PFC Raymond G.
Schneider, Pvt Hilbert I.
Schoolcraft, Pvt Aldon L.
Schovanec, PFC Joe
Schuette, Pvt Walter F.
Sena, Pvt Sam
Shaw, PFC Carl
Shaw, PFC Harley L.
Sheriff, Pvt Marvin R.
Smith, Pvt Averill H.
Stemler, PFC Joseph A.
Tafoya, Pvt Martin J.
Tammony, 1/S Edward F.
Tecumseh, PFC Julius H.
Ticken, Pvt Herbert J.
Torres, Pvt Trinidad H.
Villanueva, Pvt Joe R.
Wallace, Cpl Frederick J.
Wasson, PFC Wayne N.
Welch, Sgt Robert J.
Williams, PFC Mervin J.
Wisneski, PFC Johnnie
Zamora, Pvt Zaragosa C.

Battery E

Abel, Pvt Johnnie L.
Andreoli, PFC Guido
Beal, PFC Bryon C.
Begay, Pvt Keats
Begaye, Pvt John Y.
Boese, Pvt Abram R.
Box, PFC Minter
Bryant, S/S T.B.
Burton, Cpl George W.
Chavez, PFC Laudente
Chrisco, PFC Howard T.
Clay, PFC Reece L.
Cochran, Cpl Rochell
Dibble, Pvt Lloyd M.
Drake, Cpl Henry A.
Ferrell, Pvt John P.
Fought, PFC Leon Z.
Garcia, Pvt Ben T.
Glentzer, PFC Paul C.
Gribble, PFC Sam H.
Hernandez, Pvt George V.
Hobbs, Pvt Homer B., Jr.
Houston, PFC Walter W.
Huchton, Pvt Robert D.
Jackson, PFC Wendell R.
James, Pvt Toney
Jauriqui, Pvt José G.
Johnston, PFC Buren D.
Jones, Sgt Melvin E.
Jordan, PFC Alvin A.
Kelly, Cpl Marshall E.
Knighton, PFC Harold A.
Krolikoski, PFC Stanley J.
Lopez, Pvt David
Lunasee, Pvt Edgar
McLendon, PFC William E.
Madrid, Pvt Ambrosio
Mauldin, Sgt Cecil E.
May, Cpl John W.
Medina, Pvt Eutimio
Medina, Pvt Miguel
Mestas, Pvt Julian A.

200th - Battery E cont.

Mondello, Pvt Luke
Monk, Cpl Glendell L.
Montes, Pvt Alejandro G.
Moore, PFC William J.
Munsey, Cpl Cone J.
Nez, Pvt Sam
Noffsker, Sgt W.A.
Nuñez, Pvt Inocencio
Oliver, Pvt Robert K.
Peña, Pvt Primitivo N.
Pepper, PFC Kemp C.
Perry, PFC Delbert W.
Pilling, PFC William D.
Ramos, Pvt Lalo
Reynolds, Cpl Floyd C.
Reynolds, Pvt Harmon A.
Reynolds, Sgt John E.
Riley, Sgt Prentice G.
Roach, PFC Lee C.
Robinson, PFC Leonard L.
Rodgers, Cpl Wayne C.
Roe, Pvt Marion
Ruckman, Sgt Oscar A.
Ruckman, 1/S Oswald C.
Sandoval, PFC Bertram O.
Sherwood, PFC Virgil E.
Shields, Cpl John S.
Smith, Pvt Samuel J.
Stirman, Cpl Earl R.
Stone, PFC Clyde
Suazo, Pvt Thomas D.
Ticer, Cpl Neal C.
Tidwell, PFC Durrell A.
Tillman, Pvt Willie L.
Torres, Pvt George S.
Torrez, Pvt Joe T.
Trujillo, Pvt John B.
Uzzel, PFC Cecil C.
Vigil, Pvt Abelino
West, PFC John D.
Wiggins, Sgt Christopher A.
Williams, Sgt Harry O.

Battery F

Adams, PFC Don H.
Ammons, Cpl N.J.
Austin, PFC Thomas U.
Baca, Pvt Eligio
Ballou, Cpl William G.
Barberia, Sgt John C.
Beasley, Sgt Leon D.
Berger, PFC Steve
Biri, Pvt Henry F.
Bohannon, PFC Carl E.
Bounds, PFC George W.
Branning, Pvt Adam
Brewster, Pvt Burl A.
Brown, PFC Mavis S.
Brunt, PFC Loyal B.
Buckner, Sgt Calvin C.
Burkeholder, Cpl Eugene P.
Buse, S/S Sam P.
Byard, PFC Robert A.
Cardin, Pvt Thomas G.
Castleberry, PFC Roy C.
Charmelo, Pvt Albert C.
Chavez, Pvt Ben T.
Choate, Pvt Bruce N.
Conner, PFC John A.
Cox, Cpl Donald H.
Cox, Pvt Oscar A.
Crabb, Pvt Jessie W.
Cullum, Cpl Franklin R.
Dansby, Sgt Donald M.
Davis, Sgt Kenneth E.
Dunlap, PFC Robert L.
Fevurly, PFC Lester E.
Foster, PFC Carl C.
Fugate, Cpl Henry C.
Garner, PFC Lee S.
Gore, PFC Oliver A.
Grange, PFC John V.
Guerra, Pvt Carmen, Jr.
Hamrick, Pvt Eugene E.
Herrera, Pvt Lorenzo R.
Hightower, PFC Charley C.
Hill, PFC Elmer
Hillard, PFC Guy W.
Hood, Pvt Henry A.
James, Sgt Charlie F.
Johnson, Cpl Howard W.
Keller, PFC Rollie H.
Kemp, Cpl Newton F.
LaRue, Cpl Virgil
Lane, Pvt Kenneth L.
Loman, Cpl Louis E.
Long, Pvt Martin S.
Loya, Pvt José M.
Malone, Sgt Richard R.
Malone, PFC Robert M.
Martinez, Pvt Joe F.
Mash, PFC Jessie F.
Montaño, Pvt Joe S.
Morris, PFC Jeff W.
Nesbitt, Cpl Mason H.
O'Brien, Cpl Wayne H.
Paddock, Sgt Thomas E.
Papadeas, Sgt Constantine L.
Parson, PFC James O.
Peterson, Pvt Albert L.
Petruzela, PFC Alexander F.
Phillips, PFC Wallace R.
Philpott, PFC Chester A.
Pruiett, Pvt Gayle M.

200th - Battery F cont.

Rachall, Pvt Adrain
Richardson, PFC William B.
Ridgeway, PFC James N.
Ruehalski, Sgt Anthony J.
Rupe, Sgt Jackson J.
Sanchez, PFC Frank J.
Sanchez, Pvt Moses
Schlick, Cpl Emory C.
Simeroth, PFC Joseph B.
Stabrylla, PFC John P.
Strain, Cpl James L.
Suarez, Pvt José C.
Syrinek, Pvt Frank
Tafoya, PFC Gilberto G.
Terry, Cpl Roy T.
Thompson, PFC James R.
Tice, PFC Alton W.
Tidwell, Pvt Bryan M.
Tidwell, PFC George C.
Trujillo, Pvt Dionicio
Utter, Pvt Walter D.
Valencia, Cpl Bernard G.
Vidal, Pvt Ben
Ward, 1/S Floyd E.
White, PFC Allen J.
Whitted, Cpl Jess J.
Wilkerson, Pvt Edward L.
Williamson, PFC Thurman B.
Witherspoon, Sgt Phil
Wright, PFC Sammie
Yahnozha, PFC Homer
Young, PFC Robert E.

Battery G

Alex, Sgt Stephan H.
Allen, Sgt James P.
Anderson, PFC Harold M.
Archuleta, Pvt Telesforo V.
Arledge, Pvt Garrett M.
Atencio, Pvt Arquin G.
Barnes, Pvt William M.
Brink, Pvt Alfred E.
Burchfield, PFC Waldon L.
Bustamante, Pvt Nestor
Canales, Pvt Fidel
Carpenter, Cpl Robert E.
Casaus, Pvt Juan, Jr.
Catlett, Cpl Dick W.
Cavanaugh, Pvt Bernard
Cisneros, Pvt Ramón B.
Clark, PFC Charles T.
Clark, PFC Louis L.
Coffindaffer, PFC Rexell B.
Colburn, PFC Quentin D.
Cook, Cpl Thalis R.
Covert, Sgt Delbert O.
Danielson, Cpl Dorance J.
Duncan, PFC Joseph J.
Ellegood, Pvt Gilbert H.
Enriquez, Cpl Alfredo
Espalin, PFC Damacio, Jr.
Franco, Pvt Porfirio G., Jr.
Fuentes, Pvt Bruno G.
Gallegos, Pvt Adolfo
Gallegos, PFC José B.
Garcia, Pvt Clemente
Garza, PFC Plutarco
Gomez, Pvt Virgilio
Gonzales, Pvt Agustin
Gonzales, Pvt Frankie D.
Griego, Pvt José I.
Guillen, Pvt Othon Q.
Gurulé, Cpl Bedelio F.
Hamilton, Pvt Joyl H.
Harris, Sgt Donald C.
Harsh, Cpl Melvin C.
Haws, Pvt Alfred A.
Hernandez, Pvt Arturo
Hernandez, Sgt Cipriano M.
Hodges, Cpl Thomas O.
Hollingsworth, Sgt Wellington E.
Hooten, Pvt William R.
Huerta, Pvt Trino C.
Hulbert, Sgt Melvin F.
James, Cpl John A.
Levin, Pvt Solomon D.
Levrier, Pvt Alfredo N.
Luther, Cpl Robert N.
McCool, PFC Parker
Mahler, PFC Wayne L.
Manuelito, Pvt Joe C.
Martinez, Pvt George
Martinez, PFC Jeremias G.
Martinez, PFC Luciano
Mata, Pvt Antonio U.
Mitchell, Sgt Robert E.
Montoya, Pvt Edras S.
Moore, Cpl Ralph E.
Osowski, Cpl John E.
Percy, Pvt Ralph M.
Pintarelli, PFC Robert P.
Pitsor, PFC Richard G.
Pomillo, Cpl Anthony
Ponce, PFC Julian
Ramirez, Pvt Cenobio
Salars, S/S William E.
Salaz, Pvt Luciano G.
Saputo, Pvt Vincent
Scally, 1/S Henry F.
Schmitz, Cpl Eugene W.
Simoni, Sgt Fred S.
Snyder, Cpl Eugene F.
Starnes, Pvt Fred C.
Taylor, PFC Charles E.

200th - Battery G cont.

Taylor, PFC William M.
Uhl, Cpl Dean E.
Van Winkle, Sgt Ernest E.
Vandagriff, Cpl Thurman I.
Wagner, Pvt Emil K.
Ward, Pvt John C.
Winter, PFC William J.
Worthen, Sgt Elmer L.
Youngblood, Sgt Vernon A.

Battery H

Besher, Pvt Floyd R.
Boggs, Sgt Robert K.
Brinkerhoff, PFC Walter W.
Brown, PFC Ocie E.
Burch, PFC Ray
Burrola, Sgt Joseph M.
Butler, PFC Irvin R.
Cardenas, Pvt Eloy P.
Carrillo, Pvt Joe E.
Casaus, Pvt Max M.
Cates, PFC Marvin F.
Charlie, Pvt Thomas
Concha, Pvt Fernando
Cordova, Pvt Filadelfio
Cordova, Pvt José
Cox, PFC Alfred R.
Davenport, Pvt Rubin H.D.
Decker, Pvt Doyle V.
Del Frate, PFC Armando
Fincke, Sgt Herbert C.
Fletcher, Pvt Pinex
Fowler, Cpl Dwight H., Jr.
Garcia, Pvt Ernesto N.
Garcia, Pvt Manuel J.
Gonzales, Pvt Maclovio A.
Gonzales, PFC Telesfor
Graves, Pvt Warren D.
Hallett, Pvt Ben S.
Harris, Sgt Earl R.
Herring, PFC Louis R.
Jones, Sgt James B.
Kairunas, Pvt Joseph J.
Kathman, Cpl Clemens A.
Kierer, Pvt Peter
King, PFC David L.
Lemke, PFC John A.
Lerner, Pvt Morris L.
Leslie, Pvt Ben F.
Lucero, Pvt Gustavo R.
Lucero, Pvt Jerry
Lujan, S/S Jimmie
Lujan, Sgt Jimmie K.
Lujan, Pvt Joe I.
Maestas, Pvt José G.
Mares, Pvt George
Mares, PFC Raymond V.
Martin, Pvt Harry
Martin, Pvt Leonard B.
Martinez, Antonio B.
Martinez, Pvt Juan J.
Martinez, Pvt Luciano S.
Mascarenas, Pvt José L.
Medina, PFC Joe A.
Medina, PFC Robert
Miera, Pvt Moises
Montgomery, PFC Alton L.
Montoya, Cpl Ben
Montoya, PFC Horacio H.
Montoya, PFC Onofre
Montoya, PFC Teodoro J.
Moore, PFC Robert J.
Nickolas, Pvt John
Padilla, Pvt Jake J.
Palmer, Cpl Arthur C.
Priest, Pvt Lowell
Ragsdale, Cpl Luther E.
Reid, Pvt Melvin L.
Rivera, PFC Phillip F.
Roberts, Pvt Keyton F.
Roberts, PFC James S.
Romero, PFC Richard G.
Romero, Pvt Santana S.
Rowland, Cpl Albert
Salaiz, Pvt Reynaldo L.
Salas, Pvt Felix M.
Sandoval, Pvt Ambrocio J.
Santistevan, PFC Gustavo R.
Santistevan, Sgt Thomas
Sarracino, Pvt Santiago
Schellstede, Pvt Leslie J.
Scruggs, Pvt Hollis
Segura, Cpl Joe A.
Shelton, PFC General Lee
Sisneros, Pvt José G.
Steagall, Cpl Irwin U.
Suttles, PFC Ernest O.
Swaim, PFC Richard B.
Tafoya, Sgt Miguel N.
Thomas, PFC Charles B.
Treider, Pvt Melvin O.
Trujillo, PFC Charles A.
Trujillo, Cpl Martin E.
Trujillo, Sgt Paul
Valdez, Pvt Belarmino J.
Vandagriff, Pvt Arthur C.
Vickrey, 1/S John M.
Vigil, Pvt Conrado G.
Willoughby, Cpl Jacob N.
Zimmer, Cpl George E.

515th Coast Artillery Roster - Enlisted Men

Headquarters Battery

Adkins, PFC Jessie W.
Brooks, M/S Delbert H.
Burrus, Sgt Charles M.
Cain, M/S James R.
Chavez, PFC Miguel N.
Clark, Sgt Ralph F.
Finley, M/S Jesse L.
Frere, Pvt Richard E.
Gardner, PFC Lee J.
Hamilton, M/S James M.
Hutto, S/S Calvin R.
Jones, T/S George M.
Jones, S/S Wilson W.
Keeler, S/S John A.
Lockhard, Cpl Edwin S.
Martin, 1/S Adrian R.
Miller, M/S James S.
Moseley, S/S John J.
Pelayo, PFC Lee R.
Robbins, PFC Arthur W.
Rodgers, S/S Robert L.
Roehm, Pvt Robert R.
Sanchez, Pvt Alfonso B.
Thomas, PFC Ted T.
Villarreal, Pvt Virginio P.
Waldrop, PFC Melvin T.
Waltmon, Sgt Melvin C.
Welsh, Cpl Melvin F.

Medical Corps

Archibeque, Pvt Esperidion
Chaires, Pvt Miguel H.
Chavez, Sgt David A.
Chavez, S/S Edward E.
Chis Chilly, Pvt Levi
Cochran, Pvt William R., Jr.
Crowson, Pvt Oscar J.
Garcia, PFC José S.
Herr, Pvt Clifford E.
Huling, Pvt Orall L.
Rodriguez, PFC Ralph, Jr.
Stevens, T/S Orlando
Sullivan, Cpl Murray M.

Headquarters - 1st Battalion

Ashcraft, S/S J.W.
Beck, PFC Garrison V.
Blauer, PFC Robert L.
Boyd, Cpl Harmon E.
Brown, 1/S Earl R.
Johns, Sgt Robert L.
Kilwy, Cpl Milton
Millard, Sgt Cleophas
Montgomery, PFC Lee R., Jr.
Rubio, Cpl David J.
Sandoval, PFC Larry R.
Smith, S/S Clarke G.
Smith, Cpl Mark A.
Thomas, PFC Billy J.
Villaseñor, PFC Gregorio M.

Headquarters - 2nd Battalion

Chalk, PFC Dean R.
Drummond, 1/S Orville E.
Goll, Pvt Kermit L.
Jones, S/S Morgan T.
Kedzie, Cpl Donald H.
Kiely, Sgt Bud J.
Lopez, Cpl Eliseo
Nieto, PFC Joe G.
Parker, Pvt Albert L.
Rockwell, Sgt Reuben
Rutledge, Pvt Robert H.
Taylor, Pvt Jeptha P.
Walker, PFC DeForrest B.
Wilkerson, Sgt Vincent W.
Williams, S/S James R.

Battery A

Abraham, Cpl Ned L.
Archuleta, Pvt Fred E.
Armour, Sgt Jesse J.
Baca, Pvt Ignacio
Barela, PFC Herman P.
Bull, Cpl Malcolm T.
Chato, PFC Melvin
Chavez, Sgt Ernest J.
DeHerrera, PFC Vlademar A.
Driggars, Pvt George L.
Dunagan, Cpl Damon W.
Fails, PFC Alvin H.
Flowers, S/S John R.
Genovese, PFC John A.

515th Battery A cont.

Gilliland, Sgt Hubert F.
Godfrey, PFC Robert R.
Heck, PFC Marion W.
Henry, PFC Boyd N.
Histia, PFC David S.
Hood, PFC Johnnie D.
Hughes, PFC Eugene L.
Johnson, PFC Floyd J.
Klinekole, Cpl Bruce
Leyba, Cpl Max
Lopez, PFC Albino
Lopez, Pvt Gregorio
Maldonado, PFC Miramon
Manuelito, PFC Leo A.
Meyer, Sgt William H.
Miller, PFC Laddie
Montoya, Cpl Ernest
Moses, PFC John B.
Mott, PFC Eugene
Nateswa, PFC Paul R.
Noffke, PFC William G.
Nunn, PFC Thomas H.
Olguin, PFC Faustino
Ozimkiewicz, PFC Stanley F.
Pacheco, PFC Benjamin
Panno, PFC Andrew J.
Phebus, S/S William W.
Phelps, Cpl William A.
Plubell, PFC Leroy G.
Porras, PFC Emilio T.
Quintana, PFC Patricio J.
Ray, PFC Reuben E.
Roybal, Cpl Carlos F.
Salazar, PFC Sam D.
Senter, S/S Albert C.
Smith, S/S George L.
Stine, Sgt John P.
Tanner, PFC Brooks L.
Trujillo, PFC Edwin E.
Vigil, PFC Tito M.
Watson, 1/S Alvin F.
Williams, Sgt Charles N.

Battery B

Aguilar, Pvt Manuel A.
Anderson, PFC Maxwell G.
Austin, Cpl John H.
Baca, Sgt Raymond F.
Barker, Pvt Haymond L.
Barnes, PFC Bulen
Barnes, Pvt Lellon
Blythe, PFC Howard O.
Booth, Cpl Charles R.
Bowman, Sgt Wesley S.
Brantley, Cpl Clarence D.
Chavez, Pvt Lazaro A.
Chavira, Cpl Joe B.
Coggeshall, Sgt Charles A.
Cohen, PFC Solomon
Cordova, PFC Adolfo, Jr.
Coriz, PFC Domingo
Donnelly, Cpl Francis E.
Doolis, PFC Demetri L.
Finley, S/S Jack L.
Funk, Cpl Virgil F.
Garcia, Pvt Francisco
Garcia, Pvt Manuel
Garde, Cpl Arthur C.
Gavord, PFC Charles B.
Gobble, Pvt Henry A.
Huston, Cpl George H.
Johnson, Pvt John L.
Kenney, Sgt Raymond L.
Landon, 1/S Edwin S.
Light, Pvt Wayne E.
Long, PFC Thomas V.
Lueras, Cpl Ernest G.
McCarty, Pvt Charles N., Jr.
McKinley, Pvt Chee
Maes, Pvt Robert J.
Mann, PFC Arthur O.
Martinez, PFC Belarmino
Milligan, PFC Sam
Muñiz, Pvt Ignacio
Norton, S/S John W.
Ortiz, Pvt Frank
Osuna, Pvt Santiago Mc.
Parada, Sgt Nick V.
Peterson, Pvt Dennis J.
Powell, PFC George R.
Quintana, Pvt Martin, Jr.
Romero, Sgt Joe F.
Roper, Sgt Ollin A.
Rorie, Cpl William E.
Salazar, Pvt Manuel
Sanchez, Cpl Joe
Sanchez, Pvt Napoleon T.
Sandell, Sgt Jessie D.
Sass, Cpl Martin E.
Sedillo, Pvt Ralph
Slade, Pvt James R.
Sokol, Pvt Mike
Tellez, Pvt Enrique G.
Tenorio, Cpl Don G.
Thompson, PFC Leonard R.
Tindol, Cpl George I.
Trask, Cpl Richard A.
Vasquez, Pvt Maximiano
Virgil, Pvt Trinidad M.
Watson, Cpl Don
Wilkerson, Pvt Buster
Young, Cpl James R.
Zaruba, Pvt Jerry C.

Battery C

Agens, Cpl Royal E.
Baca, Pvt Pablo
Beger, Pvt Wilbur J.
Bell, Cpl Francis E.
Bickford, Cpl Harlan C.
Blea, Sgt Juan
Bolton, Pvt Shelley L.
Bradley, Pvt J.L.
Brown, S/S Bill W.
Cable, Cpl Dwight R.
Campbell, Cpl Aubrey L.
Carrillo, Sgt Abie A.
Chavez, Pvt Ray S.
Cheney, Cpl Charles E.
Craig, Cpl George M.
Daly, 1/S Richard J.
Fajardo, Pvt José D.
Garcia, Pvt Valentín M.
Guerrera, Pvt Paul C.
Gurulé, Pvt Juan F.
Harman, Sgt Lloyd R.
Harrison, Pvt Ferrill E.
Hernandez, Cpl Adolfo S.
Latham, Sgt Henry P.
Lopez, Pvt Samuel
Lucero, Cpl Joe T.
Lucero, Pvt José G.
Lujan, Cpl Errett L.
Maness, Sgt Lloyd L.
Mares, Pvt James G.
Martinez, PFC Manuel
Martinez, Cpl Theodore G.
Miller, Pvt Charleston J.
Milliken, PFC George J.
Moulton, Pvt James C.
Mueller, PFC Adolph F.
Niemon, Cpl Wayne W.
Odell, Pvt James G.
Olmstead, Sgt Barnes
Ortega, Cpl Pete
Padilla, PFC Jesús A.
Paiz, Pvt Benito A.
Parker, PFC Edgar B.
Pasurka, Sgt Carl A.
Pearce, PFC Milton A.
Pounds, Pvt Chester O.
Quintana, PFC Aurelio
Quintana, Cpl Pat A.
Radcliff, Pvt Clarence W.
Rael, Pvt Marcos R.
Ramos, Pvt Andrés G.
Ramos, Pvt Juan, Jr.
Reeves, Pvt Lloyd H.
Rhodes, Pvt Woodrow W.
Romero, Pvt Santiago
Ross, PFC William C.
Ruiz, Cpl Eloy
Saiz, Pvt Reynaldo
Sedillo, Pvt Adan N.
Sena, Pvt Louis
Silva, Cpl Jesús M.
Sims, Sgt Charles H., Jr.
Smith, PFC Arthur B.
Snyder, PFC Vernon A.
Strus, Pvt Walter P.
Swope, S/S Fred H.
Taves, PFC Harold R.
Tobar, Pvt Antonio J.
Trujillo, PFC Ralph J.
Tucker, PFC Raymond T.
Wallace, Cpl Virgil V.
Williams, PFC Elzie C.
Wright, Sgt Durward H.

Battery D

Aimes, Cpl Virgil L.
Amy, Sgt Robert N.
Apodaca, PFC Balta M.
Arceneaux, PFC Frank S.
Archuleta, PFC Benerito A.
Armijo, Cpl Carlos A.
Baker, Pvt Charlie W.
Barron, Pvt Charley R.
Bolf, PFC Tony
Calderon, Cpl Arthur J.
Chavez, Cpl Juan M.
Constant, Sgt John V.
Cooksey, Cpl Buford F.
Davis, Sgt Robert Clee
Diaz, Pvt Joseph G.
Duran, Cpl Frank A.
Edwards, Pvt Darrell C.
Fierro, Pvt Miguel S.
Flores, PFC Ruben
Franklin, Pvt David H.
Gallegos, Pvt Moises R.
Garcia, Pvt Cleofas
Garcia, Pvt Pedro
Garduño, Cpl Espiridion A.
Garley, PFC Silverio
Gonzales, PFC Carlos G.
Graham, Pvt Eddie
Hise, Cpl Harold C.
Hnidak, Cpl John S.
Hunt, S/S Thomas E.
Jones, Pvt Frank G., Jr.
Landavazo, PFC Ephren J.
Light, Pvt Jake W.
Longoria, Pvt José A.
Lopez, Pvt Luis
Lugibihl, Cpl Myron R., Jr.

Mirabal, Pvt Lorenzo
Moore, Pvt Henry I.
Mora, PFC Trine
Otero, Pvt Ernest Z.
Parra, Cpl Simon R.
Pecarich, Sgt Frank H.
Pence, PFC Raymond K.
Pruehsner, Cpl Orville A.
Reyes, Pvt James B.
Reyes, Pvt Tommy B.
Rodarte, Pvt Jerome G.
Rollie, Sgt Edward L.
Romero, PFC Amado
Sabbota, Cpl Isadore
Sanchez, Cpl Adelardo I.
Sanchez, Cpl Gregorio M.
Sanchez, Pvt Joe M.
Silva, Cpl Agapito G.
Singer, Pvt Joseph
Sisneros, PFC Anselmo, Jr.
Smith, Pvt Henry L.C.
Stober, Sgt Carl A.
Tafoya, Pvt José M.
Terrazas, Sgt Nick
Thomas, PFC Wayne R.
Valdez, Pvt José I.
Vertz, Cpl Edward J., Jr.
Vigil, Pvt Antonio J.
Walker, Sgt Dale W.
Whiteman, Sgt Rufus E.
Wilson, S/S Frank E.
Wyper, 1/S Menzies, Jr.
Ybaben, PFC Erminio L.

Battery F

Antosiak, PFC Alexander J.
Armour, Cpl LaFaye
Bacak, PFC John J.
Bailey, Cpl Marvin
Bain, PFC Francis G.
Barrera, Pvt Gregorio
Bianco, Pvt Frank
Brink, Sgt Ralph S.
Brown, Pvt Ocia J.
Bunch, Sgt William P.
Cater, Pvt Jack A.
Chapman, Pvt Raymond
Chavez, PFC Cipriano
Clanton, Cpl Arnold R.
Cruz, PFC José C.
Davis, Sgt Gene R.
Donati, Sgt John P.
Espinosa, Pvt Luís G.
Farmer, Cpl Glen
Galdikas, Pvt John F.
Gomez, PFC Juan
Gonzales, Pvt Albert M.
Haney, Cpl Russell L.
Hernandez, Pvt Edubigen E.
Hernandez, Pvt Simon R.
Hnulik, Sgt Richard A.
Holcomb, Pvt Jesse C.
House, Cpl Roy J.
Hunter, Cpl James P.
Johnson, Cpl Walter R.
Kish, Cpl Steven
Knight, Cpl Robert J.
Kolocek, Pvt Walter
Lara, Pvt Porfirio
Leber, Sgt Frederick W.
Loggins, Cpl Larry A.
Mitchell, Sgt Charles E.
Montoya, Pvt Pedro A.
Moore, Sgt George G.
Morris, PFC Everette M.
Morton, Sgt Roy M.
Omtvedt, PFC Clifford M.
Peña, Pvt Dionicio R.
Pope, Cpl Edward K.
Prada, Pvt Julian, Jr.
Pulice, PFC Michael
Quintana, Pvt Herman S.
Robinson, Sgt George W.
Rodriguez, Cpl Gerardo
Romero, Pvt John C.
Romero, Pvt Manuel A.
Sanchez, Cpl Lawrence M.
Sanders, Pvt Astor N.
Santos, Pvt Jesús
Serrano, Pvt Ernesto O.
Smith, 1/S Joe D.
Springer, Pvt Boyce
Stephens, Pvt Robert E.
Tafoya, PFC Marcelo
Torres, Pvt Miguel R.
Trujillo, Pvt Juan A.
Ulibarri, Pvt Manuel
Vela, Pvt Fidel
Warren, PFC Roderick E.
Westbrook, PFC Joe
Wharton, Pvt Clarence A.
Wolfenbarger, Cpl Leonard L.
Womack, Sgt Paul F.
Yonan, Pvt Frank L.

Battery G

Alderete, PFC Feliciano R.
Brown, PFC Douglas F.
Burke, Cpl Richard P.
Bussell, Cpl Rhodun M.
Byers, Sgt Lloyd R.
Chavez, PFC Asier
Chintis, Cpl Nicholas
Coffey, PFC Kenneth
DeLuna, Pvt Juan S.
Delgado, Pvt Ignacio A.
Duncan, Sgt Baylor
Dzierlatka, Pvt Stanley J.
Escalante, Cpl Abel R.
Gale, 1/S Arvil L.
Garcia, Pvt Fidel
Gentry, Sgt Walter J.
Goforth, PFC Joseph K.
Gomez, Pvt Clyde D.
Hall, Sgt Wallace A.
Henderson, Cpl Luther A.
Herrera, Pvt Nestor
Howell, Sgt Burl C.
Huddleston, Cpl LeRoy
Hunt, PFC Richard B.
Hunter, Cpl Ellis M.
Hynes, PFC George J.
Jensen, PFC Billy E.
Johns, Sgt David
Jones, Cpl Curtis C.
Jones, Pvt Gerald L.
Kelly, Cpl Harry
Long, PFC Edgar V.
Lovato, Pvt Amador B.
Lucero, Pvt Santiago
Lunsford, PFC Buford L.
McGraw, PFC August
Maddux, Sgt Aubrey L.
Martinez, Sgt Louis F.
Martinez, Pvt Marcos
Mayes, Cpl James A.
Melvin, PFC Aaron B.
Mitchell, Cpl William J.
Noche, Cpl Fausto
Olson, Cpl Raymond H.
Otero, Pvt Trinidad F.
Peña, Pvt Laurencio
Peralta, Pvt Mike S.
Polansky, Pvt Louis B.
Quintana, Pvt Antonio
Rodriguez, Pvt Albert
Romero, Pvt Aristotel S.
Romero, Pvt Emilio E.
Ruiz, Cpl Sirenio C.
Salazar, Pvt Leonardo M.
Sanchez, Pvt Juan J.
Savage, PFC Lee L.
Shillito, Sgt Winston H.
Sidney, Pvt David
Silva, Pvt Vincent
Skweres, Pvt Stanley
Sprunk, Sgt Jack D.
Stevens, PFC Dorris
Swagart, Pvt Rex R.
Tafoya, Pvt Jesús M.
Tafoya, Pvt Martin A.
Torres, Sgt Bensis
Tow, Sgt Rhea F.
Tsosie, Pvt Neal S.
Turrieta, Pvt Vicente
Upchurch, Sgt Walter J., Jr.
Vallo, Pvt Peter D.
Wallace, PFC Ira D.

Battery H

Alderete, Pvt Manuel
Beck, Cpl Edgar R.
Beck, PFC James W.
Bell, PFC Chunkie F.
Burchell, Sgt Etcyl E.
Clark, Pvt Charles E.
Clayton, Pvt Kermit
Coca, PFC Joe L.
Corona, Pvt Ramon Z.
Cotten, PFC John C.
Domroehs, Cpl Edward H.
Dorrance, Pvt Arthur A.
Fay, Pvt Burnise L.
Fogerson, Sgt Jack D.
Frere, Pvt Richard E.
Fuentes, Pvt John M.
Garcia, Pvt Evangelisto R.
Garde, Pvt Pascual
Gardner, Pvt Herschel R.
Ginnings, Cpl Vernon V.
Goddard, Pvt John R.
Graef, 1/S Calvin R.
Grooms, Pvt Hershel A.
Hall, Sgt Milus L.
Healy, Pvt Thomas G.
Herring, Pvt Lester D.
Jones, Pvt Carl W.
Kanally, PFC Billy B.
Kelsey, Sgt Gustav
Lauscher, Pvt Howard A.
LeRoux, Sgt Luís G.
Lee, PFC Tom
Lorenz, Cpl Delbert M.
Lucero, PFC Lupe
McLeod, PFC Joseph E.
Manzanares, Pvt Benjamin
Mares, Sgt Charles M.
Mathews, Cpl Alexander H.

515th - Battery H cont.

Mitchell, Sgt Robert D.
Moss, Cpl John D.
Munson, Sgt Lloyd W.
Murrell, PFC Loye E.
Neville, Sgt John W.
Nolan, Sgt William A.
Oldenettel, Pvt Arnold H.W.
Oles, Sgt Charles W.
Oliphant, Cpl James L.
Ortega, Pvt Gene
Parrish, Pvt Jack A.
Pope, Pvt James F.
Ramirez, Pvt Juan
Richmond, PFC Ohmer O.
Rivera, Pvt Adolfo E.
Rogers, Sgt Joel L.
Rolstad, Cpl Herbert J.
Romero, Pvt José M.
Sanchez, PFC Stephen J.
Sandoval, Cpl Arthur
Scott, Sgt Chester R.
Sherman, PFC Herbert
Sills, Pvt Robert B.
Silverstein, Cpl Louis A.
Smith, Pvt Austin J.
Stine, Cpl Lyle C.
Taylor, Pvt Luís
Tow, Cpl Norval E.
Trujillo, PFC Armando E.
Trujillo, PFC Reynaldo
Wall, Pvt John H.
Whitlock, PFC Louis H.
Will, Pvt Grover L.
Wynn, Cpl Lloyd P.

* The enlisted rosters for the 200th and 515th Coast Artillery CA (AA) and the following list were compiled from a pre-departure roster make at Ft. Bliss in August 1942, the Ft. Stotsenberg roster in October 1941, and the final payroll roster of March 1942. This information is as accurate and complete as the author was able to determine. For specific information on these individuals, see ...*It Tolled for New Mexico* by Eva Jane Matson, Yucca Tree Press, 1992.

* * *

The following men of the 200th and 515th were, as nearly as the author can ascertain, killed in action (KIA) or transferred to other units (T) between 9 December 1941 and 9 April 1942, or were wounded and evacuated (E) on 1 January 1942. Absent or conflicting data, however, make total accuracy almost impossible. Where uncertainty exists, no designation appears.

Almeraz, Manuel G. (KIA)
Aragon, Felix
Armijo, Matias A. (?)
Aycock, Charles M.
Azzarele, Charles J.
Baca, Thomas G.
Bacak, John J.
Beckman, Harold C.
Beserra, Julio T.
Beyers, Melvin O. (E)
Black, Billie M. (KIA)
Caldikas, John F.
Casaus, Sotero
Cordova, Adonaiz N. (?)
Curtis, Austin J.
Delgado, Magdaleno S. (KIA)
Diaz, Pedro A. (KIA)
Dwyer, Edmund J. (KIA)
England, James R.
Ferguson, William G., Jr.
Franco, Lorenzo M. (?)
Gallegos, Gregorio B.
Garcia, Frank M. (E)
Garcia, Nicholas A. (E)
Garcia, Reuben E. (KIA)
Garner, John E.
Grafton, Clifford L. (KIA)
Gregory, Howard S.
Gross, Clifford F.
Guest, Patrick F. (KIA)
Guker, Reginald F.
Hayter, Tony F.
Hedstrom, Harold E.
Herring, Herman A.
Hervatin, George V.
Hoddy, William A. (T or R)
Hodgson, Charlie H.
Hopkins, James A.
Hoskins, Calvin R.
James, Benjamin L.
Jaramillo, Terecino (KIA)
Kraemer, August M.
Leber, Frederick (KIA)
Lewis, Lloyd T.
Lyall, Lawrence L.
McGarrigle, James D.
Manzanares, Elías
Martinez, Louis

Martinez, Tony
Micheli, Arthur A. (KIA)
Moore, Raymond D.
Moseley, Juan F.
Nicholson, Chester (T)
Northcutt, Milton M.
Pasquale, Joseph L. (T)
Polansky, Louis B. (KIA)
Sanders, Douglas (KIA)
Scales, Eugene V.
Schmid, Roy W. (KIA)
Sena, José A.
Seymour, Clinton C. (T)
Smith, Edward G.
Smith, Ellward G.
Smith, James G.
Smith, Samuel J.
Stillwell, Joseph
Summers, Roy H., Jr. (KIA)
Tapia, Juan F.
Trejo, Felipe N. (KIA)
Turbett, Alva (KIA)
Verdugo, Raphael H.
Weidler, Henry
Wright, Lonnie Q.
Zarate, Israel G.

PRIMARY SOURCES

I. Interviews and/or letters from each of the following.

NAME	GRADE	BATTERY	UNIT
ALDRICH, Jack H.	CPL	HQ/2nd Bn	200th
ALDRICH, Robert L.	SGT	HQ/2nd Bn	200th
ALEX, Stephan H.	SGT	G	200th
ALMERAZ, Frederico S.	PVT	HQ	200th
ARGEANAS, James	CPL	D	200th
ARMIJO, Manuel A. 'Army Joe'	F/SGT	C	200th
BACLAWSKI, Arthur M.	M/SGT	HQ	200th
BAILEY, Jollie	PFC	HQ 1st Bn	200th
BALDONADO, José M. 'Pepe'	PFC	A	200th
BANEGAS, Lorenzo Y.	PVT	A	200th
BOND, Dow G.	CAPT	G	515th
BOYER, Jack K.	CAPT	D	515th
BRADLEY, Jack W.	1/LT	D	515th
BREWER, Fred M.	CPL	HQ	200th
BUCKNER, Calvin C.	SGT	F	200th
BURCHFIELD, Walden L. 'Jack'	PFC	G	200th
BURNS, Jonathan P.	PFC	HQ	200th
BURROLA, William M.	SGT	D	200th
CHANEY, James	2/LT	G & F	200th
CHAVEZ, Juan M. 'Bob'	CPL	D	515th
CHINTIS, Nicholas 'Nick'	CPL	G	515th
CISNEROS, Tomás G.	PFC	HQ	200th
CUMMINS, Ferron E.	T/SGT		34th Pur Sqdn
DECKER, Doyle V.	PVT	H	200th
DONALDSON, James W.	1/LT	G	515th
DOOLIS, Demetri L.	PFC	B	515th
DRAKE, Aaron C. 'Gonzo'	PFC	A	200th
EVANS, William R.	PVT	B	200th
FARMER, Glen	CPL	F	515th
FARQUHAR, Roger B.			6th Army
FINLEY, Jack L.	S/SGT	B	515th
FLECK, Roger L.			111th Cav.
FLETCHER, Penix	PVT	H	200th
FOY, Thomas P.	2/LT	F	200th
GALE, Arvil L.	F/SGT	G	515th
GARCIA, Salvador J. 'Baja'	PFC	MED	200th
GARRETT, Alvin W. 'Ike'	PVT	HQ	200th
GILCREASE, Arthur H.	CPL	HQ/1st Bn	200th
GONZALES, Albert M.	PVT	F	515th
GONZALES, Rubel	CPL	C	200th
GRAEF, Calvin R.	F/SGT	H	515th
GREEMAN, Gerald B.	CAPT	C	200th
GULBAS, Irving	PVT	HQ	200th

GUNTER, James C.	PVT	D	200th
GURULÉ, Bedelio F. 'Bill'	CPL	G	200th
GUYTON, Benson	LT/COL		60thCAC AA
HARRINGTON, Neal J.	SGT	HQ/1st Bn	200th
HARRIS, Donald C.	SGT	G	200th
HARRIS, Earl R.	SGT	H	200th
HAYNES, Glenn R.	SGT	HQ	200th
HERNANDEZ, Adolfo S.	CPL	C	515th
HEIMAN, Herschel G.	SGT		59thCAC AA
HUTCHISON, Russell J.	1/LT	H	515th
HUTCHISON, Woodrow M.	CPL	B	200th
HUXTABLE, James T.	T/SGT	HQ	200th
JAMES, Charles F.	SGT	F	200th
JOHNS, David	SGT	G	515th
JOHNSON, John L.	PVT		515th
JOPLING, Daniel W.	1/LT		515th
JOPLING, Lucy Wilson	1/LT		Army Nurse Corps
KEDZIE, Donald H.	CPL	HQ/2nd Bn	515th
KINDEL, Merle A.	PFC	A	200th
KING, George F. 'Tony'	CPL	Band	200th
KNIGHTON, Harold A.	PFC	E	200th
LIGHTFOOT, Jefferson O.	PFC	HQ/2nd Bn	200th
LINGO, Edward F.	1/LT	B	515th
LOVATO, Amador B.	PVT	G	515th
LOVATO, Henry A.	S/SGT	A	200th
LUCAS, Marvin L.	CAPT	A	515th
McBRIDE, Myrrl W.	PVT	F	200th
McCAHON, James H.	1/LT	Band & HQ	200th
McCORMICK, James C.	PVT	B	200th
McDERMOTT, Carlos T.	PVT	HQ	200th
McMINN, Mrs. James			
MABINI, Fernando			Phil Scouts
MENDOZA, Louis O.	PFC	HQ	200th
MEULI, Janie Fleming			
MEULI, Maynard C.	M/SGT	HQ	200th
MITCHELL, Robert D.	SGT	H	515th
MONTOYA, Edras S.	PVT	G	200th
MUNSEY, Cone J.	CPL	E	200th
NIEMON, Wayne W.	CPL	C	515th
OJINAGA, Vicente R.	PVT	C	200th
OVERMIER, William C.	S/SGT	B	200th
PADILLA, Orville F.	SGT	A	200th
PELAYO, Lee	PFC	HQ	515th
PEÑA, Primitivo N.	PVT	E	200th
PHILLIPS, Wallace R. 'Dub'	PFC	F	200th
POE, Alfred	SGT	HQ	200th
PULICE, Michael 'Mike'	PFC	F	515th
RAGSDALE, Luther E.	CPL	H	200th
READ, Louis B. 'Lou'			31st Inf
REAM, Glenn G.	PFC	B	200th
RHEE, Heinz L.	PFC	HQ/2nd Bn	200th

ROACH, Lee C.	PFC	E	200th
RODRIGUEZ, Ralph, Jr.	PFC	MED	515th
ROESSLER, Paul A. 'Rocky'	S/SGT	C	200th
ROMERO, Santana S.	PVT	H	200th
ROSS, William C. 'Charley'	PFC	C	515th
SAKELARES, Angelo H. 'Sak'	SGT	HQ	200th
SARTIN, Marlin E.	PFC	B	200th
SCHMITZ, Eugene W.	CPL	G	200th
SENTER, Albert C.	S/SGT	A	515th
SHILLITO, Winston H.	SGT	G	515th
SKARDA, Cash T.	CAPT	H	515th
SMITH, Arthur B.	PFC	C	515th
STEEN, Harry E.	PFC	A	200th
STILES, LeMoyne B.	2/LT	A	515th
STROOPE, Winfred			USAAC
TILLMAN, Willie L.	PVT	E	200th
TOW, Norval E.	CPL	H	515th
TOW, Rhea F.	SGT	G	515th
TRASK, Richard A.	CPL	B	515th
VILLALOBOZ, Macario 'Max'	PVT	C	200th
VILLASEÑOR, Gregorio M.	PFC	HQ/1st Bn	515th
WEST, John D.	PFC	E	200th
WILLIAMS, Robert L. 'Gladiola'	CPL	C	200th

II. Unpublished Diaries, Depositions, Theses, Papers, and Memoirs.

Alex, Stephan H., Unfinished manuscript.
Baldonado, José M., Diary.
Bond, Dow G., Diary.
Brown, Charles M., "The Oryoku Maru Story." August 1982.
Cain, Memory H., Testimony given before War Crimes Tribunal.
Cummins, Ferron., Memoir.
Gamble, John., Diary.
Hamblin, Orland K., Memoir.
Harrington, Neal J., Diary.
Kaelin, Charles R., "Tribute: To the Cabanatuan Dance Band and the Cabanatuan Art Players 'Lousy!'"
Kaufman, J.L., Cmndr. Philippine Sea Frontier, to Chief of Naval Ops., Report. 25 Jan 1945.
McBride, Myrrl W., "From Bataan to Nagasaki: The Personal Narrative of an American Soldier." Unpublished thesis for Master's Degree, Sul Ross State Teachers' College, Alpine, TX. August 1948.
McMinn, James., Testimony given before War Crimes Tribunal, 18 Sept. 1946.
Montoya, Edras., Unpublished manuscript.
Munsey, Cone J., Memoir.
Peck, Harry M., Report of Operations and Personnel, 515th Coast Artillery (AA).
Sage, Charles G., Report of Operations, Annex IX, USAFFE-USFIP Report of Operations.
Schmitz, Eugene W., Letters.
Stiles, LeMoyne B., Diary.

SELECTED BIBLIOGRAPHY

Abraham, Abie. *Ghost of Bataan Speaks*. New York: Vantage Press, 1971.

Adams, Clarence. "ADA Guardsmen Train at Bliss." *Air Defense Magazine*, Oct-Dec 1978.

American Ex-POW National Medical Research Committee. *The Japanese Story*. Stan Sommers, pub. 1980.

Arthur, Anthony. *Deliverance at Los Baños*. New York: St. Martin's Press, 1985.

Ashton, Paul. *Bataan Diary*. Privately published, 1984.

Beard, Charles A. *President Roosevelt and the Coming of the War*. New Haven: Yale University Press, 1948.

Belote, James H. & William M. *Corregidor: The Saga of a Fortress*. New York: Harper & Row, 1967.

Benedict, Ruth. *The Chrysanthemum and the Sword*. Boston: Houghton Mifflin, 1946.

Brackman, Arnold C. *The Other Nuremburg: The Untold Story of the Tokyo War Crimes Trials*. New York: Quill. William Morrow, 1987.

Brereton, Lewis H. *The Brereton Diaries: The War in the Air in the Pacific, Middle East and Europe 3 October, 1941-8 May, 1945*. New York: William Morrow, 1946.

Brougher, William E. *The Long Dark Road*. Privately published, 1946.

__________. *South to Bataan, North to Mukden: The Prison Diary of Brigadier General W. E. Brougher*. Athens, Georgia: University of Georgia Press, 1971.

Brown, Charles T. *Bilibid Prison: The Devil's Cauldron, a Fragment from that Mosaic*. San Antonio, Texas: Naylor Co., 1957.

Byas, Hugh. *Government by Assassination*. New York: Alfred A. Knopf, 1942.

Case, Blair. "Clark Field: Air Defense Debacle in the Philippines." *Air Defense Magazine*. Jan-Mar 1982.

Chunn, Calvin E., ed. *Of Rice and Men: The Story of Americans Under the Rising Sun*. Los Angeles: Veterans' Pub. Co., 1946.

Churchill, Winston S. *The Second World War*. Vol. III, *The Grand Alliance*; Vol. IV, *The Hinge of Fate*; Vol V, *Closing the Ring*; Vol. VI, *Triumph and Tragedy*. Boston: Houghton Mifflin, 1950, 1951, 1953.

Coleman, John S., Jr. *Bataan and Beyond: Memories of an American P.O.W.* College Station, Texas: Texas A&M Press, 1978.

Conroy, Robert. *The Battle of Bataan: American's Greatest Defeat*. New York: The MacMillan Co., 1969.

Craig, William. *The Fall of Japan*. New York: The Dial Press, 1967.

Craigie, Sir Robert. *Behind the Japanese Mask*. London: Hutchinson, 1945.

Dull, Paul S. & Michael T. Unemura. *The Tokyo Trials: A Functional Index to the Proceedings of the International Military Tribunal for the Far East*. Ann Arbor: University of Michigan Press, 1957.

Dunn, Benjamin. *The Bamboo Express*. Chicago: Adams Press, 1979.

Dyess, William E. *The Dyess Story: The Eye-Witness Account of the Death March from Bataan and the Narrative of Experiences in Japan*. New York: C. P. Putnam's Sons, 1944.

Eichelberger, Robert L. with Milton Mackaye. *Our Jungle Road to Tokyo*. New York: Viking Press, 1950.

Evans, William R. *Kora!* Rogue River, Oregon: Atwood Publishing Co., 1986.

Falk, Stanley L. *Bataan: The March of Death.* New York: W. W. Norton, 1962.
Feis, Herbert. *The Road to Pearl Harbor.* Princeton, New Jersey: Princeton University Press, 1950.
Feuer, A. B., ed. *Bilibid Diary: The Secret Notebooks of Commander Thomas Hayes, POW, the Philippines, 1942-1945.* Hampden, Connecticut: Archon Books, 1987.
Ford, Corey. *Donovan of O.S.S.* Boston: Little Brown, 1970.
Grew, Joseph C. *Ten Years in Japan: A Contemporary Record Drawn from the Diaries and Private and Official Papers of Joseph C. Grew, United States Ambassador to Japan, 1932-1942.* New York: Simon & Schuster, 1944.
__________. *The Turbulent Era: A Diplomatic Record of Forty Years, 1905-1945..* Boston: Riverside Press, 1952.
Gurulé, Bill F. *Fleeting Shadows and Faint Echoes of Las Huertas.* New York: Carlton Press, 1987.
Hamilton, James M. *Rainbow Over the Philippines.* Chicago: Adams Press, 1974.
Hibbs, Ralph Emerson. *Tell MacArthur to Wait.* New York: Carlton Press, 1988.
Hoito, Edoin. *The Night Tokyo Burned: The Incendiary Campaign Against Japan, March-August 1945.* New York: St. Martin's Press, 1987.
Hoyt, Edwin P. *Japan's War: The Great Pacific Conflict, 1853-1952.* New York: McGraw-Hill, 1986.
Hull, Cordell. *Memoirs of Cordell Hull.* New York: MacMillan, 1948.
Hunt, Frazier. *MacArthur and the War Against Japan.* New York: Scribner, 1944.
Hunt, Ray C. & Bernard Norlinger. *Behind Japanese Lines: An American Guerrilla in the Philippines.* Lexington, Kentucky: University Press of Kentucky, 1986.
Ind, Allison. *Bataan: The Judgment Seat: The Saga of the Philippine Command, United States Army Air Force, May 1941 to May 1942.* New York: MacMillan Co., 1944.
James, D. Clayton. *The Years of MacArthur.* 3 Vols. Boston: Houghton Mifflin, 1970-1985.
Johnson, Forrest B. *Hour of Redemption: The Ranger Raid on Cabanatuan.* New York: Manor Books, 1978.
Jolly, John Pershing. *History, National Guard of New Mexico.* n.p. 1964.
Keith, Billy, *Days of Anguish, Days of Hope.* Garden City, New York: Doubleday, 1972.
Kerr, E. Bartlett. *Surrender and Survival: The Experience of American POWs in the Pacific 1941-1945.* New York: William Morrow, 1985.
Knox, Donald. *Death March: The Survivors of Bataan.* New York: Harcourt Brace Jovanovich, 1981.
Krueger, Walter. *From Down Under to Nippon: The Story of the Sixth Army in World War II.* Washington, D.C.: Combat Forces Press, 1953.
Lawton, Manny. *Some Survived: An Epic of Japanese Activity During World War II.* Chapel Hill, North Carolina: Algonquin Press, 1984.
Layton, Edwin T., et al., *And I Was There.* New York: William Morrow, 1985.
Leahy, William D. *I Was There: The Personal Story of the Chief of Staff to Presidents Roosevelt and Truman, Based on His Notes and Diaries Made at the Time.* New York: Whittlesey House, 1950.
MacArthur, Douglas. *Reminiscences.* New York: McGraw-Hill, 1964.

Mallonee, Richard C. *The Naked Flagpole.* San Rafael, California: Presidio Press, 1980.
Manchester, William. *American Caesar: Douglas MacArthur.* Boston: Little-Brown, 1978.
McCoy, Melvin H. & Steve Mellnik as told to Wellborn Kelley. *Ten Escape from Tojo.* New York: Farrar & Rinehart, 1944.
McGee, John H. *Rice and Salt: A History of the Defense and Occupation of Mindanao During World War II.* San Antonio, Texas: Naylor Co., 1962.
Mellnik, Stephen M. *Philippine Diary, 1939-1945.* New York: Van Nostrand Reinhold, 1969.
Miller, Ernest B. *Bataan Uncensored.* Long Prairie, Minnesota: Hart Publications, 1949.
Morison, Samuel Eliot. *The Rising Sun in the Pacific, 1931-April 1942.* Vol. III, *History of the United States Naval Operations in World War II.* Boston: Little Brown, 1948.
_________. *The Two-Ocean War: A Short History of the United States Navy in the Second World War.* Boston: Atlantic Monthly Press, Little Brown, 1963.
Morris, Eric. *Corregidor: The End of the Line.* New York: Stein & Day, 1981.
Olsen, John E. *O'Donnell: Andersonville of the Pacific: Extermination Camp of American Hostages in the Philippines.* Privately Printed, 1985.
Parker, T. C. "The Epic of Corregidor-Bataan." *U.S. Naval Proceedings*, Jan. 1943.
Peck, Harry M., Brig. Gen., NMNG 1908-1948: Entries in personal journal maintained as POW and reported in *Albuquerque Journal*, 30 October 1945 through 8 June 1946.
Phillips, Claire "High Pockets," & Myron B. Goldsmith. *Manila Espionage.* Portland, Oregon: Binfords & Mort, 1947.
Quezon, Manuel. *The Good Fight.* New York: Appleton, 1946.
Quinn, Michael A. *Love Letters to Mike.* New York: Vantage Press, 1977.
Reischauer, Edwin O. *The United States and Japan.* Cambridge, Massachusetts: Harvard University Press, 1957.
Romolo, Carlos P. *I Saw the Fall of the Philippines.* Garden City, New York: Doubleday, Doran, 1943.
Schultz, Duane. *Hero of Bataan: The Story of General Jonathan M. Wainwright.* New York: St. Martin's Press, 1981.
Stewart, Sidney. *Give Us This Day.* New York: W. W.Norton, 1957.
Sulzberger, C.L. *World War II.* New York: American Heritage Press, 1985.
Tansill, Charles Callan. *Back Door to War.* Chicago: Regnery, 1952.
Taylor, Vince. *Cabanatuan: Japanese Death Camp: A Survivor's Story.* Waco, Texas: Texian Press, 1985.
Toland, John. *But Not in Shame: The Six Months After Pearl Harbor.* New York: Random House, 1961.
_________. *The Rising Sun: The Decline and Fall of the Japanese Empire, 1936-1945.* New York: Random House, 1970.
Vance, John R. *Doomed Garrison: The Philippines: A POW Story.* Ashland, Oregon: Cascade House, 1974.
Volckmann, R. W. *We Remained: Three Years Behind the Enemy Lines in the Philippines.* New York: W. W. Norton, 1954.
Wainwright, Jonathan. *General Wainwright's Story: The Account of Four Years of Humiliating Defeat, Surrender, and Captivity.* ed. Robert Considine. Garden City, New York: Doubleday, Doran, 1946.

Weinstein, Alfred A. *Barbed Wire Surgeon.* New York: MacMillan Co., 1947.
Willoughby, Charles A. *The Guerrilla Resistance Movement in the Philippines, 1941-1945.* Vantage Press, 1972.
Wolfert, Ira. *American Guerrilla in the Philippines.* New York: Simon & Schuster, 1945.
Wright, John M., Jr. *Captured on Corregidor: Diary of an American P.O.W. in World War II.* Jefferson, North Carolina: McFarland & Co., 1988.

Official Histories, Papers, and Documents

Hunter, Kenneth E. *The War Against Japan.* Washington, D.C.: Office of Chief of Military History, Department of the Army, 1952.
Kaufman, J. L., Commander Philippine Sea Frontier, to Chief of Naval Ops., *Report.* January 1945.
MacArthur, Douglas. *Reports of General MacArthur.* 5 Vols. in 4 Pts. Prepared by his General Staff. Charles A. Willoughby, ed. Department of the Army. Washington, D.C.: GPO, 1966.
Matloff, Maurice, and Edwin Snell. *Strategic Planning for Coalition Warfare: 1941-1942.* U.S. Army in World War II. Washington, D.C.: GPO, 1953.
Morton, Louis. *The Fall of the Philippines.* U.S. Army in World War II. Department of the Army, Office of the Chief of Military History. Washington D.C.: GPO, 1953.
__________. "Germany First: The Basic Concept of Allied Strategy in World War II." *Command Decisions.* Kent Roberts Greenfield, ed. Office of the Chief of Military History, Dept. of the Army. New York: Harcourt Brace, 1959.
__________. *Strategy and Command: The First Two Years.* U.S. Army in World War II. Washington, D.C.: GPO, 1962.
Sage, Charles G. *Report of Operations.* Annex IX, USAFFE-USFIP.
Smith, Robert R. *Triumph in the Philippines.* U.S. Army in World War II. Washington, D.C.: GPO, 1963.
United States Congress. Joint Committee on the Investigation of the Pearl Harbor Attack. *Hearings.* 79th Cong. 1st & 2d Sess. 39 Vols. Washington, D.C.: GPO, 1946.
United States Congress. Senate. Committee on the Judiciary, Internal Security Subcommittee. *Institute of Pacific Relations Hearings.* 82d Cong. 1st Sess, 15 Pts. Washington, D.C.: GPO, 1952.
United States Dep. of State. *Papers Relating to the Foreign Relations of the United States.* Washington: U.S. GPO, 1943.
United States Dept. of State. *Peace and War: United States Foreign Policy 1931-1941.* Washington: U.D. GPO, 1943.
United States Dept. of War. "World War II Honor List of Dead and Missing: State of New Mexico." Prepared by the Adjutant General for the War Dept. Bureau of Public Relations. Washington: June 1946.
Watson, Mark Skinner. *Prewar Plans and Preparations.* United States Army in World War II. Office of the Chief of Staff. Washington: U.S. GPO, 1950.

INDEX